FINANCIAL TIMES

MASTERING INVESTMENT

Your Single-Source Guide to Becoming a Master of Investment

Executive editor **James Pickford**

FT Prentice Hall
FINANCIAL TIMES

London New York San Francisco Toronto Sydney Tokyo Singapore
Hong Kong Cape Town Madrid Paris Milan Munich Amsterdam

PEARSON EDUCATION LIMITED

Head Office:
Edinburgh Gate
Harlow CM20 2JE
Tel: +44 (0)1279 623623
Fax: +44 (0)1279 431059

London Office:
128 Long Acre
London WC2E 9AN
Tel: +44 (0)20 7447 2000
Fax: +44 (0)20 7447 2170

Website: www.financialminds.com

First published in Great Britain in 2002

© Compilation: Pearson Education 2002

Note: Licences have been granted by individual authors/organizations for articles throughout this publication. Please refer to the respective articles for copyright notice.

ISBN: 0 273 65926 X

British Library Cataloguing in Publication Data
A CIP catalogue record for this book can be obtained from the British Library.

All rights reserved; no part of this publication may be reproduced, stored in a retrieval system, or transmitted in any form or by any means, electronic, mechanical, photocopying, recording, or otherwise without either the prior written permission of the Publishers or a licence permitting restricted copying in the United Kingdom issued by the Copyright Licensing Agency Ltd, 90 Tottenham Court Road, London W1P 0LP. This book may not be lent, resold, hired out or otherwise disposed of by way of trade in any form of binding or cover other than that in which it is published, without the prior consent of the Publishers.

10 9 8 7 6 5 4 3 2 1

Typeset by Land & Unwin, Northamptonshire
Printed and bound in Great Britain by Ashford Colour Press, Hampshire

The Publishers' policy is to use paper manufactured from sustainable forests.

Contents

Introduction, *James Pickford* — vi

1 Principles — 1

Introduction to Part 1 — 3
The heart of the matter, *Peter Bernstein* — 4
How to build a share index, *Paul Marsh* — 9
Seeking out investment value in styles, *Elroy Dimson* and *Stefan Nagel* — 17
Markets and the business cycle, *Jeremy Siegel* — 24
Poor returns that disguise a bonus for investors, *Roger Edelen* — 30
Principles of bond portfolio management, *Stephen Schaefer* — 36
Corporate bonds and other debt instruments, *Stephen Schaefer* — 42
The use and abuse of derivatives, *Christopher Culp* — 46
The past and future for real estate, *Richard Georgi* — 52

2 Valuation and returns — 57

Introduction to Part 2 — 59
A model weighting game in estimating expected returns, *L'uboš Pástor* — 60
Insights from portfolio theory, *Raman Uppal* — 67
Valuing old and new companies, *Oren Fürst* and *Nahum Melumad* — 75
Valuing companies: simulations, options and partnerships, *Oren Fürst* and *Nahum Melumad* — 83
Intangibles: not seen but must be heard, *Chris Higson* — 89

3 Trading and prices — 97

Introduction to Part 3 — 99
The past, present and future of trading stocks, *Lawrence Glosten* and *Charles Jones* — 100
The role of equity trade costs in investment results, *Donald Keim* and *Ananth Madhavan* — 107
Equity loans: how to sell what you do not own, *Christopher Geczy*, *David Musto* and *Adam Reed* — 113
Consolidated limit order book: future perfect or future shock? *Kenneth Kavajecz* — 118

4 Asset allocation — 125

Introduction to Part 4 — 127
How to mix assets to match needs, *Suresh Sundaresan* — 128
Asset allocation and the importance of active investment strategies, *Craig MacKinlay* — 135
The equity premium puzzle, *Rajnish Mehra* — 141
Working hard for better returns, *John Heaton* and *Deborah Lucas* — 147
Investing with death in mind, *Charles Kindleberger* — 153
Stocks and bonds in the portfolio lifecycle, *Steven Davis* and *Rajnish Mehra* — 157

5 Global investment — 163

Introduction to Part 5 — 165
The logic that lies behind overseas diversification, *Robert Hodrick* — 166
Taking stock with foreign exchange, *Robert Aliber* — 173
An open and shut case for portfolio diversification, *Ian Cooper* — 179
Room for improvement in protecting investors, *David Beim* — 186

6 Hedge funds — 193

Introduction to Part 6 — 195
Optimizing returns in a risk-conscious world, *Kaveh Alamouti* — 196
Getting an edge from flexibility, *Majed Muhtaseb* — 201
Creative funds that have come into their own, *Vikas Agarwal* and *Narayan Naik* — 207

7 Risk — 215

Introduction to Part 7 — 217
A formal approach in a risky business, *Christopher Culp* — 218
The varying nature of volatile forces, *Menachem Brenner* — 224
Too much being left to chance by personal investors, *Greg Elmiger* — 231
A model approach to using technology, *Terry Marsh* and *Paul Pfleiderer* — 237

8 Investment psychology — 243

Introduction to Part 8 — 245
Investors seek lessons in thinking, *Nicholas Barberis* — 246
In search of money for nothing, *Francisco Gomes* — 252
The perils for investors of human nature, *Simon Gervais* and *Terrance Odean* — 257
The curious case of Palm and 3Com, *Owen Lamont* — 261
The art and craft of reading the market, *Bruce Kamich* — 267

9 Governance — 273

Introduction to Part 9 — 275
Seeking value from changes in Europe, *Rory Knight* and *Deborah Pretty* — 276
Disclosure: inside information for all, *Ewen Cameron Watt* — 281
The bottom line to a social conscience, *Geoffrey Heal* — 287

10 Early-stage investing — 295

Introduction to Part 10 — 297
Business as usual after boom and bust, *Amar Bhidé* — 298
Investing in private equity, *Andrew Metrick* — 305
Reading the signs from first-day returns, *Kent Womack* — 313

11 Regulation — 321

Introduction to Part 11 — 323
Regulation and asset management, *Julian Franks*, *Colin Mayer* and *Luis Correia da Silva* — 324
Why managers hold on to risk, *Charles Himmelberg* and *Glenn Hubbard* — 331
Ways of taking care of tax, *Terry Shevlin* — 337
The coming of the single financial regulator, *Howard Davies* — 344

Subject index — 349
Name index — 356
Organization index — 358

Introduction

Mastering Investment is the *Financial Times*'s essential guide to the principles and practice of investment. It represents the fruits of a partnership between the FT newspaper and the world's leading academic authorities on the subject. The series first appeared in international editions of the newspaper in ten weekly instalments from May 2001, and covered all aspects of this complex and subtle activity, from financial markets, investment strategies and valuation to portfolio management and global investing.

Mastering Investment has arrived at a timely moment. In the 1990s, investment in certain sectors – technology and internet firms, the media and telecommunications markets – drove stock values to unprecedented heights and gave rise to the cult of the dot-com company, most often realized in highly over-subscribed IPOs and heavy investment in companies with little or no financial record. US investors enjoyed the longest bull market in history and many market commentators foretold the end of the business cycle.

Such predictions were unfounded. Spring 2000 saw the beginnings of a global economic downturn that continues at the time of writing. The technology, media and telecoms sectors suffered greatly in the slowdown, yet old-economy sectors also found themselves under pressure.

At such a time, *Mastering Investment* represents a return to sanity by reminding readers of the basic principles of good investing. The book is divided into 11 parts, corresponding to core topics in the discipline: principles; valuation and returns; trading and prices; asset allocation; global investment; hedge funds; risk; investment psychology; governance; early-stage investing; regulation. Some of these are concerned with explaining how the world's financial centres trade using different financial instruments and examine current issues in the mechanics of market transactions; others cover more focused issues, such as hedge funds, flotation and ethical investment. Throughout the book authors have used real-life examples to illustrate their arguments and take an international approach to topics where appropriate.

Mastering Investment is not written for complete beginners in the field. It is concerned with professional investment, and therefore from time to time authors assume some knowledge of fundamental concepts, such as bid-ask spreads or the yield curve. However, readers will find different styles and levels of writing, some technical, others narrative or historical. In a world where shareholder value becomes ever more important, corporate managers as well as financial specialists will find much to attract and inform them.

The bulk of articles have been written by leading academics from four business schools: Chicago Graduate School of Business, London Business School, Columbia Business School and the Wharton School of the University of

Pennsylvania. These schools, renowned for their investment expertise, have given generously of their time and effort and richly deserve thanks for making the project possible. We have also drawn on the expertise of practitioners in the field, such as Peter Bernstein, Howard Davies and Kaveh Alamouti. Together they have produced an invaluable survey of the subject, marshalling fundamental principles, investment practice and cutting-edge thinking.

James Pickford, Executive Editor, FT Mastering

Principles 1

Contents

The heart of the matter 4
Peter Bernstein, New York consultancy

An incisive article which singles out the themes of uncertainty, risk and fallibility of the human psyche, and cautions against reliance on previous data for future decision-making.

How to build a share index 9
Paul Marsh, London Business School

The movements of financial indices are important and are used to monitor the performance of investment professionals and to create index funds.

Seeking out investment value in styles 17
Elroy Dimson, London Business School
Stefan Nagel, London Business School

Investments come in many shapes and sizes. This article introduces the concept of style investing.

Markets and the business cycle 24
Jeremy Siegel, University of Pennsylvania

For investors who think they can predict the state of the economy, the potential rewards are enormous. Yet our hisorical record for economic forecasting is decidedly poor.

Poor returns that disguise a bonus for investors 30
Roger Edelen, University of Pennsylvania

It is becoming conventional wisdom that the performance of mutual funds is disappointing compared with a passive benchmark index. So why have investors poured $7,000bn into them in the US alone?

Principles of bond portfolio management 36
Stephen Schaefer, London Business School

This article describes bonds and their relationship with equity investment.

Corporate bonds and other debt instruments 42
Stephen Schaefer, London Business School

Using derivatives alongside bonds, managers can now use their expertise in bonds to create portfolios that behave like equity portfolios.

The use and abuse of derivatives 46
Christopher Culp, University of Chicago Graduate School of Business

A discussion of bond portfolio management shows how returns from different government bonds are highly correlated.

The past and future for real estate 52
Richard Georgi, Soros Real Estate Investors

This article surveys property markets around the world and describes the dynamics of their economic cycle.

Introduction to Part 1

Mastering Investment opens with a discussion of the central characteristic of investment activity: the quest to predict a hidden future. All the paraphernalia of the financial world – stocks, bonds, derivatives, indices, funds – are the different mechanisms by which investors can profit from accurate predictions. In this part authors discuss some of the major types of security, the construction of indices and the importance of the business cycle.

The heart of the matter

Uncertainty creates the opportunity that is fundamental to markets and must be embraced by investors. **Peter Bernstein** provides some food for thought.

Peter L. Bernstein is president of a New York consultancy that publishes a newsletter for institutional investors. He wrote *Against the Gods: The Remarkable Story of Risk*.

What is at the essence of good investment? The short answer is you pays your money and you takes your choice. As the articles in this book reveal, investors are confronted with a dizzying array of instruments, strategies, goals and controls, a drumbeat of advice and counsel from experts, and a deluge of statistics. Worse, most of these seem to have short half-lives: yesterday's answer often turns out to be tomorrow's wrong number. Inflation looms or subsides, growth waxes and wanes, policies shift, instruments appear, markets evolve, returns spreads break precedents, and fresh information floods in.

And yet beneath all this lies the essence of investment: the hidden future. If we held the key to that mystery, we would have no need for the elaborate investment paraphernalia that confronts us and we could dispense with experts and their mountains of statistics. One instrument and strategy would suffice. But the key to the secret is denied us. Fleeting shadows are all we can discern.

Those who believe they can distinguish between light and shadow back there are fooling themselves. Surprise in investing is inescapable, not an incidental anomaly. If the road ahead were always clear, we would readily adjust to what we see and tomorrow's price would always equal today's. But capital markets are continuously assailed by the unexpected. How else can we explain volatility? Just the experience of the past three decades is sufficient to prove the point.

The hidden future

Nevertheless, uncertainty is friend as well as enemy. Only with uncertainty is there opportunity. If we knew the whole future, returns would be baked in the cake and decision-making would be a lost art.

Investors devote too little time considering what they can glean from the distinction between a hypothetical future we know for certain and the real world of uncertainty we face each day. What would happen if we were empowered to remove uncertainty from tomorrow? Even though no one has ever been to that hypothetical world, we can discover a clear and simple answer to this question, drawn from the real world itself.

In their calmer moments, investors recognize their inability to know what the future holds. In moments of extreme panic or enthusiasm, however, they become remarkably bold in their predictions: they act as though uncertainty has vanished and the outcome is beyond doubt. Reality is abruptly transformed into that hypothetical future where the outcome is known. These are rare occasions, but they are also unforgettable: major tops and bottoms in markets are defined by this switch from doubt to certainty.

The switch is precisely why these are major tops and bottoms: at such moments, convictions about the future are so strong that no force is left to extend the current price trend further in the direction from which it has come. The cake is baked, just as in the hypothetical world where the future is truly known. If, in the real world, the future evolves as anticipated, asset prices will go nowhere at best. But if expectations are exaggerated by panic or euphoria, asset prices will go into reverse. If expectations are wrong, betting against the majority will pay off in a big way.

Consider the long-term bond market in the autumn of 1981, when year-on-year inflation in the US had already passed its peak of close to 15 per cent and was on the verge of dropping into single digits. This time is especially vivid for me, because I came close to being thrown out of a meeting for recommending to a charitable foundation that they sell all their US Treasury bills, then yielding about 10 per cent, to dive into the long-term Treasury market where yields were 14 per cent. The investment committee I was confronting included the president of a bank whose primary business was investment management, a senior partner of one of the big Wall Street houses, and a managing partner of a famous consulting firm, to say nothing of a group of timorous creatures from outside business and finance. Judging from his red complexion, the bank president appeared to be on the verge of apoplexy.

My argument, however, was simple and did not depend on a forecast, even though I could hardly believe the US would succumb to double-digit inflation for another 30 years. With yields at 14 per cent, there was little to lose even if the frightened men had sufficient foresight to know for certain that inflation was a long way from coming under control. If they were wrong, however, there was a killing to be had. And a killing indeed it was. The yield on Treasury bills fell by 600 basis points over the next year and kept on going downwards.

It is naive to believe that majority opinions are always wrong. On the other hand, the outcomes when such opinions are right may be entirely different from what may happen when the majority is wrong. There is where opportunity lies.

The business of risk

At the same time, however, the enemy is often ourselves: uncertainty means our decisions can turn out to be wrong. The goal of investment has always been wealth creation, but the process of investment must involve managing uncertainty, or cushioning the impact of surprise. Nothing else explains the variety of instruments and strategies, and the endless thirst for information that confront us.

Some investors face the challenges of uncertainty by exercising direct control over the outcome of their decisions – they give up liquidity by owning the majority share of their businesses. But the great mass of investors are minority and passive participants, powerless to influence the fate of the enterprises on which they choose to depend. This is a role no rational person would accept without a valid exit strategy. Hence, these investors manage uncertainty by accumulating paper assets with ready markets where they can expect their decisions to be reversible.

This choice in favour of marketable securities opens two paths to increased wealth. The first is the cash flow that would accrue to any owner or lender. The second path is unique to this form of investment: minority investors in marketable assets must pin their hopes on the prices other investors will pay for these assets, or on the willingness and ability of debtors to live up to their contracts to repay principal. Cash flows plus the resources – and whims – of others comprise the total payoff from these investment choices. Both components of total return are outside the control of the investor. So is the future value of money. Investment is risky.

In the old days, investors came to grips with uncertainty by applying a mass of foolishness, rules of thumb, narrow mindsets and mythology. Stocks, by and large, were for the adventurous or for investors who limited their equity exposures to a small percentage of their total wealth. Risk management for other investors meant settling primarily for cash flows from debt instruments, eschewing the exquisite risks of depending on others to set the value of their assets.

Until the mid-1950s at least, legal trusts in the US were limited in what they could hold in equities, while so-called "prudent man rules" kept many trustees on the defensive until well into the 1980s. After all, during the near-150 years between the end of the Napoleonic wars and the onset of the second world war, inflation was only a wartime phenomenon, making the purchasing power from high-grade bond yields about as close to certainty as anything could be, in dramatic contrast to the volatility of stock returns.

The harrowing years of the Great Depression and the terrifying inflation shocks of the 1960s and 1970s provided investors with hard lessons about how little they knew about what the future held for either stocks or bonds. At the same time, however, these experiences inspired academics to build a powerful set of theories to explain the nature of investment and the behaviour of financial markets. Even with the limitations of theory, we have come a long way since those not-so-good old days in understanding the management of the risks and opportunities of uncertainty, even if we have little progress to show in foretelling the future or calming market volatility.

In the process, we have learned a great deal about managing portfolios and analyzing risk/return trade-offs, about the fundamental distinction between portfolios and individual holdings, about diversification, about evaluating the consequences of loss, about the principles of security selection and the attractions of hedging, and about what makes security markets (that is, investor behaviour) tick. Nevertheless, until future cash flows and selling prices are baked in the cake – which is never – uncertainty will remain the core around which each of these tools is arrayed.

It is interesting to observe, however, that a key element of financial theory – the efficient market – bears a strong resemblance to the hypothetical state where the future is known rather than uncertain. The theory of market efficiency postulates that our highly competitive capital markets are thronged by countless sophisticated investors armed with masses of information and elaborate techniques of analysis. Consequently, no single investor can know more than the market as a whole about what is happening and what is going to happen. The information constantly being incorporated into asset prices therefore always reflects the best possible interpretation of everything known.

In our hypothetical world of certainty, information incorporated into asset prices is always complete and correct. What, then, is the difference between the ideal and reality? In the world where everything is known, there is no such thing as new information. In the real world, information incorporated into asset prices is complete and correct only for the moment: new information, as yet unknown, is always just around the corner. In both worlds, trying to outguess the market is risky. In one world, however, the cake is baked; in the other, it is always being cooked.

In the long run

The impossibility of prying loose from uncertainty can lead investors to try to escape the inevitable difficulties of decision-making by assuming the problem away. One path leads to excuses for procrastination, while the other leads to resignation. Neither path is a wise option.

I have fond memories of a fellow trustee, a high officer in a well-known bank, who always proposed postponing action "until the uncertainty diminishes". No argument could persuade him to mend his ways. Yet he erred on three levels. First, his recommendation was based on the dubious assumption that the current status of the portfolio was optimal, even for a level of uncertainty he found most uncomfortable. Second, he assumed the sheer fact of uncertainty was not already fully reflected in asset prices, as it so clearly was in the autumn of 1981. Finally, he perceived uncertainty to be a variable rather than a constant.

Although the first two assumptions were at least open to debate, the perception of uncertainty as a variable is no minor matter. In meetings with this colleague, I always recalled an advertisement in *The Wall Street Journal* from my earliest days in investment management. The advertisement pictured a group of men pondering a chart on the wall. The quotation under the picture read: "It is always a difficult time to invest." The words have stuck in my memory ever since.

If we never know the future, we never know the future! When we think we know, we are setting ourselves up for trouble. Trend is not destiny: we are no more able to extend smooth lines into the future than a sailor can observe what lies ahead in choppy seas. The safest management system is to view uncertainty as a constant rather than a variable.

Procrastination, however, is far less troublesome than resignation. The most perilous element in this whole affair is the belief that somehow, somewhere, time will itself eliminate uncertainty while investment returns remain inviolate – to succeed, in other words, without really trying. The long run is the most popular candidate for this appetizing role. Yet how can we justify blind faith in an uncertain future to provide what we expect and hope? The very long run of the past, out of which such dreams are composed, is a collection of short runs, each of which was unique because it was the consequence of the events that preceded it.

Singular sequences, splattered with surprises, constitute a dubious database for projecting future events. None of these short runs is likely to replay in the future in recognizable garb, unless we can replay the events that preceded it, which can occur only if we can replay the events preceding that episode, and so on back to the beginning.

History furnishes us with lessons about market behaviour, but it is dangerous to estimate expected returns over the long run by extrapolating elements of the long-run past that cannot be reproduced. Furthermore, while no one would dispute J.P. Morgan's maxim that capital markets will fluctuate, there is no predestined mean to which markets must recover. A difference of even one or two percentage points of return over 20 or 30 years compounds into wildly disparate levels of terminal wealth.

We are stuck with uncertainty. Mastery of investment begins and ends with that, perhaps the only fact in the whole matter. If, then, the future provides no safety nets and no auto-pilots, even the wisest, best informed and toughest will be wrong from time to time. Successful investors are those who have an eye to survival for when disappointments arrive. Some will aim in that direction by taking big risks to sock away jumbo returns from once-in-a-lifetime opportunities. If experience is any guide, all but a few of those intrepid players will disappear in time, even after the rare occasions when they win big.

It is best to know the rules of the game, eloquently set forth by French poet Paul Valéry: "Once destiny was an honest game of cards which followed certain conventions, with a limited number of cards and values. Now the player realizes in amazement that the hand of his future contains cards never seen before and that the rules of the game are modified by each play."

Investment is unlike many other fields of endeavour: because uncertainty is lodged in its heart, most of the victories are to the tortoises, not the hares.

Copyright © Peter Bernstein 2002

Further reading

Bernstein, P.L. (1993) *Capital Ideas: The Improbable Origins of Modern Wall Street*, New York: Free Press.

Bogle, J.C. (1999) *Common Sense on Mutual Funds: New Imperatives for the Intelligent Investor*, New York: John Wiley.

Ellis, C.D. (1998) *Winning the Loser's Game: Timeless Strategies for Successful Investing*, New York: McGraw-Hill.

Malkiel, B.G. (2000) *A Random Walk Down Wall Street*, New York: W.W. Norton.

How to build a share index

Stock market indices may not be a matter of life and death, but they are vital as investment benchmarks. **Paul Marsh** explains how they are constructed.

Paul Marsh is Esmee Fairbairn Professor of Finance at London Business School. He has designed several indices and worked with Elroy Dimson on the FTSE 100.

Can a stock market index number really matter so much? Clearly not, but to investors, it can seem so. Market indices are the benchmarks we use to monitor markets and judge performance. We love them, we hate them, but we cannot live without them. Here we review the role of indices and give guidelines for index construction. We describe how indices are used in performance measurement, index funds and measuring long-run returns.

We need indices

It would be hard to discuss investments without indices. We could not answer even such basic questions as "How's the market doing today?", "How did technology stocks perform last year?" or "Have shares beaten bonds over the long run?"

Indices have many purposes. First, they are used to monitor and measure market movements, whether in real time, daily or over decades. A good index will tell us how much richer or poorer investors have become. Second, equity and bond indices are economic barometers, while equity indices are leading indicators. Monitoring markets and comparing movements with data such as wages, profits and inflation helps us to understand economic conditions and prospects. Third, indices provide essential benchmarks in fund management. A managed fund can communicate its objectives and target universe by stating which index or indices serve as the standard against which its performance should be judged. Fourth, indices underpin products such as index funds, exchange-traded funds, and options and futures on indices. These index-related products form a several trillion-pound business and are used widely in investment, hedging and risk management.

Finally, indices support research (for example, as benchmarks for evaluating trading rules, technical analysis systems and analysts' forecasts), risk measurement and management, and asset allocation and international diversification decisions.

Coverage

Indices are all-pervasive, with more than 4,000 in operation. Equity market indices, such as the Dow, Nikkei, Dax and FTSE 100, tend to be the best known. But indices are also important for other assets such as government and corporate bonds, commodities, currency baskets and retail prices.

As well as market indices, there are numerous sub-indices. For equities, these cover sectors, size bands, investment styles and even ethical and religious dimensions; for bond indices they span maturities and credit risk categories. There are international indices that aggregate country indices into regions (such as Asia), currency zones (such as the euro), market types (such as emerging markets) and worldwide indices. While this article focuses on equity indices, the principles apply to all types of index.

Averaging

Index construction is straightforward in principle, involving a process of averaging and weighting. Indices start at a base date when they are assigned an initial value, such as 100 or 1000. Later values depend on the weighted average return on the constituents.

Consider an index with base value 1000 and three constituents, shares A, B and C, which at the base date all had market values of £1bn. By the next day, assume the share prices had changed by +20%, +8% and –10%. The average return was (20 + 8 – 10)/3 = 6% and hence the index value will be 1000 · 1.06 = 1060. The guiding principle is that the percentage change in the index (6%) should represent the change in value of the market. The market in our example contains three stocks, worth £3bn initially, and £1.2 + £1.08 + £0.9bn = £3.18bn on the next day. The percentage change in value is (£3.18bn/£3.00bn) – 1 = 6%, so our index value of 1060 is verified.

This example uses arithmetic averaging, that is, we totalled the three returns and divided by three. This is the correct method used by most indices. Some early indices used geometric averaging and this survives in indices such as the US Value Line Geometric Index and the FT Thirty Share Index. The geometric average of n returns is the nth root of the product of (one plus) the percentage returns, minus one. In our example, the geometric average return is: [3 (1.2 · 1.08 · 0.9)] – 1 = 5.26%.

This gives an index value of 1052.6 rather than the correct figure of 1060. The geometric average is always less than the arithmetic average, so investors can always beat a geometric index by buying and holding its constituents. One needs to be aware of this when looking at longer-term returns based on geometric indices.

Weighting

For indices to reflect changes in market value, they must be based on weighted-average returns, where the weights reflect each stock's value. Assume that companies A, B and C are no longer equal in size but start with market capitalizations of £1bn, £2bn and £3bn. The value of our three-share market is £6bn. The weighted average return over the next day is: $(1 \cdot 20\% + 2 \cdot 8\% + 3 \cdot -10\%)/6 = 1\%$.

Hence the index value is 1010. Again, we can check that this corresponds to the change in market value. Initially, the market was worth £6bn. The next day, it was worth £1.2bn + £2.16bn + £2.7bn = £6.06bn. The percentage change was (£6.06bn/£6.00bn) – 1 = 1%, so 1010 is correct.

Some early indices used equal, rather than market capitalization, weighting. Such indices will give an unbiased estimate of the true market return only if large and small stocks perform in line, which is seldom the case. Other indices, including the Dow Jones Industrial Average (DJIA) and Nikkei 225, use share price weighting, so that higher price (rather than capitalization) stocks receive greater weight. Although such indices are adjusted for stock splits, splits still lead to lower index weightings, and vice versa for consolidations. Price weighting has no economic rationale and is hard to justify or interpret.

Some complications

While index construction is simple in principle, there are many complications in practice. Share returns can be hard to compute for companies undergoing complex events and restructuring. International indices need to adjust for currency movements and exclude stocks that are unavailable to, or too illiquid for, foreign investors. Even capitalization weighting has become controversial and many now argue for free-float weighting.

Many European stocks have large government or family holdings and many Japanese stocks have sizeable cross-holdings. Advocates of free float argue that if, say, 75 per cent of a stock is government-held, its index weighting should be 25 per cent. This reflects the "investable" weight or "free-floating" shares that public investors could hold. The concern is that if such stocks had 100 per cent weightings, this might stimulate demand, especially from index trackers, which could distort the market.

There is a distinction between cross-holdings and non-public holdings. Cross-holdings should be excluded to avoid double counting. The extreme case is closed-end investment companies, which consist solely of cross-holdings. Index providers recognize this by publishing variants of their indices without investment companies. But cross-holdings can also be prevalent for companies other than investment trusts, especially in Japan. Morgan Stanley Capital International (MSCI) estimates the average free float is just 65 per cent in Japan, versus 94 per cent in the US and 92 per cent in the UK, with much of this difference arising from cross-holdings.

Arguments are less clear cut for non-publicly held shares. If an index is to approximate closely the "market portfolio" of financial theory, it should include, not exclude, the non-traded portion of a company's equity. There are also debates about how free float is defined. For example, why exclude family-held shares, which could be traded, but include shares held by index funds? Despite these caveats, major index providers, such as FTSE International, MSCI and Dow Jones Stoxx, are all switching to free float.

Other principles

There are three other principles of index design. First, an index should provide the widest, most representative coverage of its target segment. Interestingly, the best-known indices fail this test. The Dow Jones, for example, covers just 30 US blue chips. It survives through history and affection. It began in 1884 and was the first published index, then with 11 constituents. Charles Dow had neither computer nor calculator, hence his limited coverage. Today, 30 stocks is far too few.

Figure 1 shows the performance of four US indices over the year to the end of March 2001. All fell, but by different amounts. The DJIA, with its limited coverage and blue-chip focus, fell 10 per cent. The more broadly based but still large-cap-oriented Standard & Poors 500 fell 23 per cent. In contrast, the Nasdaq, with its technology focus, fell a massive 60 per cent. The best measure of the US market is provided by the comprehensive Wilshire 5,000, which, despite its name, covers more than 7,000 stocks. This fell by 26 per cent. The choice of index matters and it is ironic that the broadest and best index is the least known.

Total returns and dividends

Second, indices should measure total return. Investment returns comprise income plus capital gains or losses. Ignoring either leads to serious bias when measuring long-term returns. Yet many early equity indices measured just capital gains, ignoring dividends. Conversely, but equally seriously, early bond indices often recorded just yields, ignoring price movements. While short-run equity performance is driven by capital appreciation, long-term returns are driven by reinvested income.

FIGURE 1   Four US indices: year to end-March, 2001

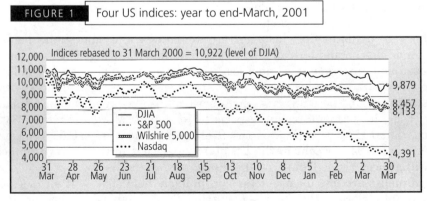

Source: Dimson, Marsh and Staunton (ABN AMRO/LBS), 2001

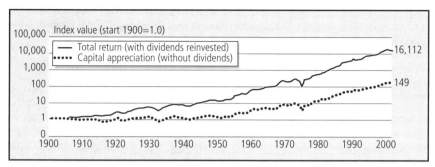

FIGURE 2 UK equity returns with/without reinvested dividends

Source: Dimson, Marsh and Staunton (ABN AMRO/LBS), 2001

Figure 2 shows this. It gives the cumulative capital gain and total return over the past 101 years on the ABN AMRO/LBS UK Equity Index. The sum of £1 invested in 1899 would have grown to £149 by 2001 if dividends had been spent or squandered. In contrast, with dividends reinvested, £1 would have grown by 108 times as much to £16,112. Clearly, unless indices incorporate reinvested dividends and so measure total return, they will be of little value for measuring long-term performance.

Trackability

Third, good indices must correspond to an investment strategy that could be set up in advance and followed in real life. Apart from dealing costs and taxes, an index tracker fund should be able to replicate index performance. This rules out geometric indices or those using price averaging, since these are not replicable. But there can also be other problems, relating to over-frequent rebalancing, and bias in back histories.

If indices are rebalanced too often, this can lead to bias and excessive turnover. In 1984, the Vancouver Stock Exchange had to announce there was a cumulative error in its index of more than 100 per cent. This was caused by bid-offer bias, a technical problem arising from over-frequent rebalancing. More recently, a different rebalancing problem occurred with the FTSE SmallCap Index.

All small-cap indices need periodic rebalancing so that they continue to track smaller companies. Over-frequent rebalancing, however, is costly for tracker funds, as small-caps have high dealing costs. Given this trade-off, most small-cap indices rebalance annually. The FTSE SmallCap not only rebalances annually but also experiences constituent changes whenever there is a promotion to, or demotion from, the FTSE 350 (the largest 350 stocks). During 2000, there were so many promotions and demotions that an index fund seeking to track these changes would have led to turnover of 128 per cent, even ignoring the annual rebalancing. This is very high even compared with actively managed funds.

High turnover plus the impact of numerous constituent changes made the

SmallCap hard to beat and three out of four small-cap fund managers failed even to match it (see Dimson and Marsh, 2001). In contrast, about half of these funds beat the more broadly based Hoare Govett Small Company Index, which is rebalanced yearly. This is what one would expect with a well-designed benchmark.

Avoiding bias

When a new index goes live, it is common practice to provide investors with a back history of performance. When indices are constructed retrospectively, it is crucial to ensure they do not use hindsight. Serious biases arise if constituents are tilted towards stocks that subsequently survived or grew large, or towards sectors that later became important.

When the UK's FTSE 100 Index was launched in 1984, a British newspaper published a six-year back history. This was constructed from the 100 largest stocks at the launch date of the index, rather than starting with the 100 that had been largest six years before. Clearly, six years earlier, investors did not know which stocks would subsequently perform best and grow largest. This led to back-history returns being erroneously overstated by 5 per cent a year.

A similar problem arose with the pre-1955 back history for the Equity-Gilt studies, which for over 40 years (from De Zoete and Gorton, 1955, to Barclays Capital, 1999) were regarded as the authoritative source of long-run UK returns. Research by Dimson, Marsh and Staunton (2000) using the more broadly based ABN AMRO/LBS UK Equity Index from 1900 to 2000 found that, because of survivorship and success bias, the returns before 1955 in the Equity-Gilt studies were considerably overstated. The study has been revised by Barclays Capital (2000), although its early coverage remains limited.

Performance measurement

Indices are widely used as benchmarks in performance measurement. For a general UK equity fund, for example, the FTSE All-Share Index provides a suitable naive benchmark. We say "naive" because an investor with no stock-selection skills could match the FTSE All-Share simply by holding its constituents and running a tracker fund.

When measuring performance, we are therefore seeking evidence of the fund beating its benchmark by at least the incremental management fees charged. If not, the fund manager has added no value.

Performance measurement is naturally more complex than this and three caveats are needed. First, comparing fund performance with indices is slightly unfair, because indices incur no dealing or other costs. Some transaction and administrative costs are involved in running even an index tracker, although for large market tracker funds, such costs should be low. Second, performance measurement should embrace risk as well as return and there are many ways of adjusting for risk (see a standard textbook, such as Alexander, Sharpe and Bailey, 2001). The important question that risk adjustment addresses is whether the fund manager took on a higher or lower level of risk than the benchmark index and whether this can explain any apparent out- or underperformance.

Third, performance should be judged only over long periods. This is because markets are volatile and luck plays a major role. Skilful managers can experience runs of poor performance, while a monkey picking stocks from a hat would have successful years, and even good multi-year runs. Research shows that few equity fund managers can expect to outperform by more than 1 per cent a year after fees and costs. With this level of skill, it takes at least 25 years to confidently tell luck from judgement.

Index funds

A second major use of indices is to underpin a wide range of financial products, the most important of which are index funds. These portfolios track an index. They are passively managed, that is, no views are taken about which stocks are over- or undervalued and transactions are limited to those needed to keep the portfolio in line with index changes.

Index funds first appeared in the US in 1971 following academic studies that found active fund managers had mostly failed to beat market indices by enough to cover their expenses. Index funds also offered maximum diversification at a low cost. Dealing costs were low because there were few transactions, while management fees were minimized since portfolios could be managed mostly by computers.

Over the past 30 years, index funds have become enormously successful, with trillions of pounds invested worldwide. Their subsequent growth has been fuelled by further research continuing to cast doubt on the value of active management. Today, about 30 per cent of US funds and 10–20 per cent of UK funds are directly indexed. A far larger proportion of fund managers (perhaps a majority) surreptitiously track their benchmark index, or match closely index weightings. These are known as "closet indexers" or "index huggers". Whatever the merits of this, indices have clearly had a huge influence on investment management practices.

Measuring the risk premium

Indices also allow us to measure long-run rates of return and the reward investors have received from investing in equities rather than risk-free investments. This reward for risk is known as the equity risk premium and is measured as the difference between returns on equities and those on either government bills or bonds. The equity risk premium is extremely important. It is central to projecting investment returns, calculating the cost of capital, valuing companies and shares, appraising projects within companies and determining fair rates of return for regulated utilities. All these applications require an estimate of the prospective risk premium, whereas, by definition, the only premium we can measure is the historical premium.

Figure 3 shows the historical risk premium for 15 countries relative to both bonds and bills. Relative to bills, the annualized premium is 4.7 per cent for

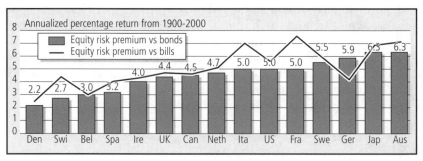

FIGURE 3 Annualized equity risk premiums relative to bonds and bills

Source: Dimson, Marsh and Staunton (ABN AMRO/LBS), 2001

the UK, 5.6 per cent for the US and 5.1 per cent averaged across all 15 countries. Relative to bonds, the premiums are slightly lower: 4.4 per cent for the UK, 5.0 per cent for the US and 4.7 per cent for the 15-country average.

Over the 20th century, equity investors enjoyed a substantial risk premium, and over the past 50 years it was higher still. Are these figures a good guide to the future? No one knows, but the study from which these estimates were taken concluded that the premium will be lower over the next 100 years. We can be certain of only one thing. If in 100 years' time we wish to check this prediction, to do so we will continue to be reliant on high-quality, well-constructed indices.

Copyright © Paul Marsh 2002

Further reading

Alexander, G.J., Sharpe, W.F. and Bailey, J.V. (2001) *Fundamentals of Investments*, 3rd edn, New Jersey: Prentice-Hall.
Barclays Capital (1999) and (2000) *Equity-Gilt Study 1999* and *Equity-Gilt Study 2000*, London: Barclays Capital.
De Zoete and Gorton (1955) *Equities and Fixed Interest Investment*, London.
Dimson, E. and Marsh, P. (2001) "Index rebalancing and the technology bubble", *Journal of Asset Management*, 3(1), 1–10.
Dimson, E., Marsh, P. and Staunton, M. (2000) *The Millennium Book: A Century of Investment Returns* and (2001) *Millennium Book II: 101 Years of Investment Returns*, London: ABN AMRO/London Business School.

Seeking out
investment value in styles

Classifying investments provides a way of assessing share portfolios and measuring the performance of investment managers and even the economy. **Elroy Dimson** and **Stefan Nagel** explain.

Elroy Dimson is a professor of finance at London Business School.

Stefan Nagel is a doctoral student at London Business School.

A glance at the unit trust section of the *Financial Times* or the mutual funds section in the *Wall Street Journal* reveals that fund management companies tend to label products using a few common categories. Funds will frequently carry attributes such as small-cap, growth, value and international. Similarly, money managers tend to present themselves to institutional clients as, for example, an aggressive growth, a large-cap or a technology manager. Categorizations of this kind usually imply that a fund or a manager invests in a distinct group of stocks that share some characteristics. In recent years the term "investment style" has become popular to describe this phenomenon.

In spite of the recent emergence of the term, style investing is by no means novel. For example, the value style, which refers to investing in companies that trade at low ratios of share price to measures of their fundamental value, can be traced back at least to the 1930s. However, only in recent years has the notion of investment styles become pervasive. Styles have become essential in developing, analyzing and evaluating investment strategies. The style perspective may also provide an insight into the forces underlying price movements.

Table 1 describes some important styles based on UK equity market segments. This list is by no means exhaustive. Furthermore, there are additional styles when an international perspective is taken. For example, emerging markets themes or the recently popularized eurozone investment strategies may also have style status. Various combinations are possible. There may be small-cap growth, European-value and others.

TABLE 1 — Important UK domestic categories

Value	Stocks that trade at low multiples of price to measures of fundamental value. Ratios used to define value strategies include the dividend yield, the price-to-earnings ratio and the ratio of price to book value per share. Such stocks tend to feature relatively low expected earnings growth. In recent years value stocks have concentrated in established, stable industries such as manufacturing, utilities and foods.
Growth	Companies with strong growth expectations. These commonly trade at prices that are high relative to current earnings, dividends or book values.
Momentum	Stocks that have performed very well recently. Usually focuses on periods up to one year. The assumption is that recent good performance will continue. This style has become increasingly popular.
Contrarian	In contrast to the momentum strategy, these stocks have performed badly. However, contrarian strategies commonly look at performance over several years, whereas momentum strategies usually focus on the past year.
Small-cap	Companies with small market capitalizations. The Hoare Govett Smaller Companies Index, for example, targets the bottom tenth of the UK market by aggregate market value.
Micro-cap	Stocks with extremely small market capitalizations. The ABN AMRO/LBS MicroCap Index, for example, covers UK companies that represent the bottom one per cent by aggregate market value.
Large-cap	The biggest companies, also known as blue chips. Whereas small-cap and micro-cap investors hope for relatively good performance from small companies, large-cap investors prefer safety.

Why classify?

There seems to be no compelling reason why a fund might, for example, restrict itself to growth stocks only. So why classify stocks into styles? At a basic level, styles may arise from a human desire for classification. Each day, stock market investors face an enormous flow of information and a diverse set of investment opportunities. Classifying assets may help investors to ease their burden in processing information and provide structure. Indeed, much of the variability in stock returns can be traced to variability of the asset classes to which a particular stock belongs. For example, when a small company shows a high return, this often coincides with strong returns for other small companies.

The role of investment consultants may also contribute to the importance of investment styles. Investment consultants are hired to assess managers' skills on behalf of their clients. In measuring a manager's performance, the consultant often wants to assess skill in selecting stocks relative to the performance of the style a manager follows. As a result style-based performance measurement and style-based benchmarks have become common.

How themes emerge

There seems to be some rationale for categorizing stocks into styles. However, how do these styles arise? Why do investors perceive some asset characteristics to be of such importance that a style emerges? An important factor in defining a style is the degree of co-movement of prices within a group of securities. In some cases the reason for the classification is obvious. This is true, for example, for styles defined by geographical location. Domestic stocks will move more with each other than with stocks traded abroad. Similarly, stocks within a particular industry tend to move more with each other than with stocks in other industries. An interesting example is the effect of the single currency on styles in the euro area. Many observers argue that the single currency will foster the co-movement of economic fundamentals across countries. As a result, a shift seems to have occurred, away from country styles towards pan-European industry styles.

Perhaps the most powerful contribution to the emergence of a style, however, comes from historical performance. In 1934, Benjamin Graham and David Dodd documented the superior performance of strategies that invested in high dividend yield stocks in the US. This gave rise to the value style (although it may not have been called a style then). The superior performance of the "nifty-fifty" group of US blue-chip stocks, including IBM, Kodak and Xerox, in the early 1970s may have marked the emergence of the growth style. The popularity of this style was powerfully reinforced by the spectacular performance of growth stocks in the 1990s. In a similar vein, strong performance over several years gave rise to the new economy and TMT (technology-media-telecommunications) styles at the end of the 1990s.

In some cases, academic research contributed to the birth of a style. In 1981 a study by academic Rolf Banz at the University of Chicago showed that small-cap stocks had outperformed large-cap stocks in the US by a margin that could not be explained by conventional measures of risk. This led to the creation of Dimensional Fund Advisors, an investment company set up by Chicago graduates to capitalize on this finding. Its small-cap fund was the most successful launch in financial history. It sparked the creation of other small-cap funds and indices in the US, UK and other countries. A style was born. Similarly influential have been studies by Eugene Fama and Kenneth French in 1993, who documented a strong premium for value stocks, and Narasimhan Jegadeesh and Sheridan Titman in 1993, who reported high historical returns to momentum strategies.

Many style indices have been created to track style-based market segments. Style index mutual funds have emerged that give investors an alternative to actively managed funds, but without restricting their choices solely to tracking of market-wide indices.

Historical record

The historical return record is an important aspect of any style. Some investors may use this to guide portfolio decisions. Long-term return histories can be informative about the riskiness of, and prospective returns from,

FIGURE 1 Cumulative performance of small-cap and micro-cap styles in the UK

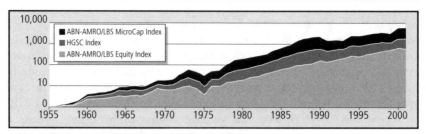

Source: Dimson, Marsh and Staunton (2002)

FIGURE 2 Cumulative performance of value and growth styles in the UK

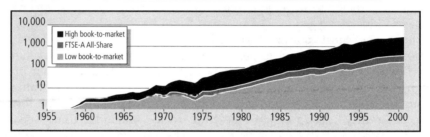

Source: Authors' calculations and FTSE-A. Series start in July 1955. For description of data see Dimson, Nagal and Quigley (2001)

FIGURE 3 Annualized returns on various style 1956–2000

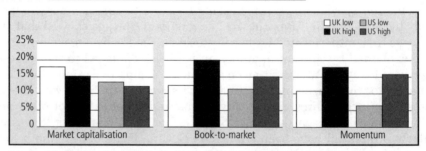

Sources: Dimson, Marsh and Staunton (2002), Center for Research in Security Prices, Compustat, Kenneth French and authors' calculations. For description of the data see Dimson, Nagal and Quigley (2001), and Fama and French (1993)

investing in a particular style. More recent history also provides a basis for assessing the stock selection skill of investors or managers known to have focused on a particular style. Finally, style returns can also be useful for analyzing the macroeconomy. Return differentials between small and large companies, for example, may contain information on the state of the economy.

Figure 1 shows the record on small-cap and micro-cap versus large-cap investing. This graph is based on investing £1 at the beginning of July 1955 in either a large-cap, small-cap or micro-cap portfolio. It highlights performance differences between large and smaller companies in the UK.

Figure 2 focuses on value versus growth. The value and growth portfolios depicted are based on the ratio of book value of equity to market value of equity. Value stocks are those with a high book-to-market ratio and growth stocks those with a low book-to-market ratio. This graph shows that value investing has paid off extremely well. An investment of £1 in July 1955 would have grown to £2,990 by the end of 2000. In contrast, the low book-to-market portfolio would stand at £172. The performance of the market-wide FTSE All-Share Index is somewhat closer to growth than to value. This reflects the fact that in the UK small companies on average had high rather than low book-to-market ratios.

Figure 3 looks at average style returns in the UK and US. These are computed as annualized returns, that is, geometric averages. This figure confirms earlier observations. Looking at the UK figures first, stocks with low market capitalizations outperformed those with high capitalizations. The spread is about 3 per cent. High book-to-market UK stocks have produced returns that are more than 7 per cent higher than those from a growth portfolio. Figure 3 also provides information on the performance of a momentum strategy. A strategy that bought stocks that did well over a period of six months before portfolio formation would have yielded much higher returns than a strategy that bought stocks with poor recent performance. The difference is about 7 per cent in the UK before commissions and other trading costs.

These patterns are not unique to the UK. Figure 3 also gives the US record. With respect to market capitalization there appears to be a small size premium in the US. However, there is an important difference between the US and UK that can make a simple comparison like this misleading. In the UK the small-cap portfolio is tilted towards value stocks, magnifying the reward to smaller companies. In the US, the small-cap portfolio is tilted towards growth stocks, which have underperformed historically, and this dampens the US size premium. If one were to do a more sophisticated analysis, considering book-to-market as well as market capitalization, a size premium would emerge. The second set of bars confirms that low book-to-market stocks in the US have underperformed compared with their high book-to-market counterparts, as they did in the UK. The momentum effect is similar to the UK.

These substantial differences highlight the role of style exposure in determining investment performance. In effect, returns to an investor may be more dependent on the portfolio style than on any skill in picking individual stocks.

Rotation

People who seek to diversify may wish to invest in a multi-style portfolio. Others who anticipate outperformance of a particular style, for example based on the historical performance record, might concentrate their investments. Active managers, whose specialization is in some segment of the market, will also emphasize a specific style. A third possibility is to rotate styles and change the weight placed on a particular theme over time.

Style rotation is based on the idea that returns on particular styles may be predictable. This means that a model for forecasting style returns is needed to implement style rotation strategies. In the past decade a wide array of variables has been suggested for forecasting style returns. These include macroeconomic variables, recent style performance, measures of the spread in valuation ratios between styles and measures of investor sentiment. Armed with a model that has sufficient forecasting power, an investor may then be able to enhance portfolio performance by changing exposure to certain styles over time.

There are some reasons why one might be able, to some extent, to forecast style returns. For example, at least a part of the return differential in average returns between value and growth stocks appears to reflect differences in risk. Therefore, in times when investors demand high premia for bearing risk (for example when the economy is doing badly), future spreads between value and growth should tend be high. On the other hand, if investor sentiment plays a role in determining style returns, a prolonged history of superior performance of a certain style could indicate sentiment-driven overvaluation, which would imply relatively low future returns on this style.

However, to be a viable investment approach, style rotation strategies need to earn the transaction costs they incur. Rotation requires considerably higher portfolio turnover than simple buy-and-hold strategies. Therefore, the question arises whether the predictability of style returns is high enough for rotation to be profitable after transaction costs. Empirical evidence is not encouraging. A study by Mario Levis and Manolis Liodakis in 1999 found that potential profits from style rotation between small and large or value and growth stocks were lost in transaction costs.

Performance

Nobel laureate William Sharpe has pioneered the application of style-based analysis of portfolio management problems. In an article in 1992 he observed that usually around 90 per cent of the variation in return on mutual funds can be explained by these funds' exposure to a few asset classes, such as bonds, bills, large-cap and small-cap stocks, value and growth stocks, and some others. In other words, to a large extent an investor could have replicated the performance of these funds by investing passively in a mixture of these asset classes or styles.

This raises two questions. First, if most of the funds' performance can be replicated by investing in passive portfolios, one may be tempted to invest in the passive portfolios right away, without hiring a more expensive active manager. Second, if we are interested in an active manager's skill in picking stocks, we may want to measure performance relative to a passive benchmark that replicates the style exposure of his portfolio. This would help determine how much the manager contributed to performance. For unit trusts it has been common to compare managers with a peer group that follows a similar style. With style analysis this is becoming common practice for evaluating other portfolio managers, too. It is possible to estimate how much style exposure has contributed to a manager's performance and how much is due to skill in selecting individual stocks. Style-based performance evaluation has become widespread, with investment consultants providing detailed performance attribution services to clients.

Style analysis works well for managers whose style exposure is relatively constant. However, for managers who choose a style rotation approach, the methodology is not as successful. Such style rotators will insist that their skill lies in selecting the right style at the right time.

Conclusion

Are styles a passing fad or will they continue to be important in investment management? Currency union within Europe has accelerated the trend for analyzing industries on a pan-European basis, and for some sectors, such as pharmaceuticals, oils and financials, a global perspective is needed. The relative performance of value and growth stocks appears to be increasingly aligned across countries, as shown by recent fluctuations of technology stocks. These developments suggest that co-movements of groups of stocks and the impact of investment styles have become permanent features of markets.

Copyright © Elroy Dimson and Stefan Nagel 2002

Further reading

Banz, R. (1981) "The relation between return and market value of common stocks", *Journal of Financial Economics*, 9, 3–18.

Dimson, E., Marsh, P. and Staunton, M. (2002) *Triumph of the Optimists: 101 Years of Global Investment Returns*, NJ: Princeton University Press.

Dimson, E., Nagel, S. and Quigley, G. (2001) "Value versus growth in the UK 1955–2000", working paper, London Business School (http://www.london.edu/faculty/edimson).

Fama, E.F. and French, K.R. (1993) "Common risk factors in the returns on stocks and bonds", *Journal of Financial Economics*, 25, 23–49.

Jegadeesh, N. and Titman, S. (1993) "Returns to buying winners and selling losers: implications for stock market efficiency", *Journal of Finance*, 48, 65–91.

Levis, M. and Liodakis, M. (1999) "The profitability of style rotation strategies in the UK", *Journal of Portfolio Management*, Fall, 1–14.

Sharpe, W.F. (1992) "Asset allocation: management style and performance measurement", *Journal of Portfolio Management*, Winter, 7–19.

Markets and the business cycle

The gains to be had by predicting the economic cycle are enormous. The problem is that economists cannot get their forecasts right, says **Jeremy Siegel**.

Jeremy Siegel is Russell E. Palmer Professor of Finance at the Wharton School of the University of Pennsylvania.

Markets and the economy often are not synchronized, so it comes as no surprise that many investors dismiss economic forecasts when planning their market strategies. The substance of Paul Samuelson's quote from *Newsweek* in 1966 remains true more than 30 years later: "The stock market has predicted nine out of the last five recessions!"

Yet investors should not dismiss the business cycle too quickly when choosing a portfolio. The stock market still responds powerfully to changes in economic activity. Although there are many "false alarms", akin to 1987, when the market collapse was not followed by a recession, stocks almost always fall before a recession and rally rigorously at or even before signs of an impending recovery. If you can predict the business cycle, you can beat a simple buy-and-hold strategy for equity investments.

But this is not easy. To make money by predicting the business cycle, you must be able to identify peaks and troughs of economic activity before they occur, a skill very few, if any, economists possess. Business-cycle forecasting is popular not because it is successful – most of the time it is not – but because the potential gains from successfully calling business booms and busts are so large. But before we do this, it is important to look at who calls the business cycle.

Marking the cycle

In the US, business cycles are dated by the National Bureau of Economic Research (NBER), a private organization founded in 1920. In its early years, the bureau's staff compiled comprehensive chronological records of changes in economic conditions in many industrialized countries. In other countries, recession may not be declared in such a formal manner. In the UK, for example, investors might look to the Bank of England, the UK Treasury or the Confederation of British Industry for indications of a recession.

It is commonly assumed that a recession occurs when real gross domestic product (GDP), the most inclusive measure of economic output, declines for two consecutive quarters. But this is not necessarily so. Although this is a reasonable rule of thumb, it is not used by the NBER. For example, the 1981 recession occurred when there was only a single disastrous quarterly decline in GDP followed by a flat quarter. The bureau looks at many other indicators, including real personal income and sales, employment and industrial production to date peaks and troughs of the business cycle.

Between 1802 and 1997, there were 41 US recessions, averaging nearly 18 months, while expansions averaged almost 38 months. This means that, over 195 years, a third of the time has been spent in recession. However, since the second world war there have been nine recessions, averaging 10 months, while the expansions have averaged 50 months. So in the post-war period, the economy has been in a recession only a sixth of the time.

Turning points

Almost without exception, the stock market turns down before recessions and rises before recoveries. In fact, of the 41 US recessions, 38, or 93 per cent, have been preceded (or accompanied) by declines of 8 per cent or more in the total stock returns index. The three that were not were the 1829–30 recession, the recession that followed economic adjustment immediately after the second world war, and the 1953 recession, where stock declines fell just shy of the 8 per cent criterion.

Table 1 summarizes return behaviour for the nine US recessions since the second world war. You can see that the stock return index peaked anywhere from zero to 13 months before the beginning of a recession. The recessions that began in January 1980 and July 1990 are among the few where the stock market gave no advance warning of the downturn. During the post-war period, if you wait until the stock returns index has declined by 8 per cent before signalling a business-cycle peak, then the stock market leads the business cycle by an average of only 1.3 months. This signal ranges from a lead of 10 months in the 1970 recession to a lag of three months in the 1990–91 recession. In all but two of the post-war recessions, an 8 per cent decline in the returns index led the business-cycle peak by less than one month, giving little advance warning of an impending recession.

As the Samuelson quote indicates, the stock market is prone to false alarms and these have increased since the second world war. Excluding the war years, there have been 12 episodes since 1802 when the cumulative returns index for stocks fell by 8 per cent but the drop was not then followed by a recession within the next 12 months. In the 19th century this happened five times and in the 20th century seven times. Every occasion in the past century occurred after the second world war.

The 1987 decline of 29 per cent, from August to November, is the largest

TABLE 1 — Recessions and stock returns

Recession	Peak of stock index 1	Trough of business cycle 2	Lead time between peaks 3	% decline in stock index from (1) to (2) 4	Months between 8% stock index decline and (2) 5	Maximum 12-month % decline in stock index 6
1948–49	May 1948	Nov 1948	6	−8.74	0	−8.19
1953–54	Dec 1952	Jul 1953	7	−3.91	no decline	−7.18
1957–58	Jul 1957	Aug 1957	1	−5.05	−1	−13.90
1960–61	Dec 1959	Apr 1960	4	−8.28	0	−8.20
1970	Nov 1968	Dec 1969	13	−12.19	10	−25.50
1973–75	Dec 1972	Nov 1973	11	−16.20	7	−40.10
1980	Jan 1980	Jan 1980	0	−0.00	−2	−8.90
1981–82	Nov 1980	Jul 1981	8	−4.08	−1	−14.20
1990–91	Jul 1990	Jul 1990	0	0.00	−3	−13.92
		Average	5.6	−6.49	1.3	−15.56
		Std. dev.	4.4	5.10	4.4	10.17

decline in the nearly two-century history of US stock returns data after which the economy did not fall into a recession. Table 2 compares the trough in the stock return index and the trough in the NBER business cycle. The average lead time between a market upturn and an economic recovery has been 5.1 months and the range has been narrow. This compares to an average 5.6-month lead time between the peak in the market and the peak in the business cycle, with a much greater variability in these figures. As we shall see, stock returns rise more in a recession in anticipation of a recovery than they fall before an economic downturn.

Timing the cycle

Table 3 displays the excess returns to investors who can time their investment strategy in relation to the peaks and troughs in economic activity. Since stocks fall before a recession, investors want to switch out of stocks and into Treasury bills, returning to stocks when prospects for recovery look good. Excess returns are calculated by assuming that investors who lead the business cycle switch out of stocks and into bills before the peak of business expansions and switch back before the trough of recessions. In contrast, investors who lag the business cycle switch out of stocks and into bills after the cycle peak and back into stocks after the cycle trough. The excess returns are measured relative to a buy-and-hold stock strategy of the same risk as the timing strategies employed previously.

In the post-war period, the excess return is minimal over a buy-and-hold strategy if investors switch into bills at the peak and into stocks at the trough of the business cycle. In fact, investors switching into bills just one month

TABLE 2 — Expansions and stock returns

Recession	Trough of stock index 1	Trough of business cycle 2	Lead time between troughs 3	% rise in stock index from (1) and (2) 4	Months between 8% stock index rise and (2) 5
1948–49	May 1949	Oct 1948	5	15.59	3
1953–54	Aug 1953	May 1954	9	29.13	5
1957–58	Dec 1957	Apr 1958	4	10.27	1
1960–61	Oct 1960	Feb 1961	4	21.25	2
1970	Jun 1970	Nov 1970	5	21.86	3
1973–75	Sep 1974	Mar 1975	6	35.60	5
1980	Mar 1980	Jul 1980	4	22.60	2
1981–82	Jul 1982	Nov 1982	4	33.13	3
1990–91	Oct 1990	Mar 1991	5	25.28	3
		Average	5.1	23.86	3
		Std. dev.	1.73	8.59	1.41
2001–01	Apr 2001	Sep 2001?	?	14.78	?

TABLE 3 — Percentage excess returns around business cycle turning points

		Lead			Peak	Lag			
		4 month	3 month	2 month	1 month	1 month	2 month	3 month	4 month
Lead	4 month	**4.8**	4.0	4.2	4.1	3.3	2.7	2.1	2.2	1.9
	3 month	4.0	**3.3**	3.5	3.3	2.6	1.9	1.4	1.5	1.3
	2 month	3.3	2.6	**2.8**	2.6	1.9	1.2	0.7	0.8	0.7
	1 month	2.5	1.8	2.0	**1.8**	1.1	0.5	0.0	0.1	0.0
Trough		1.9	1.2	1.4	1.2	**0.5**	−0.2	−0.7	−0.6	−0.7
	1 month	1.5	0.8	1.0	0.8	0.1	**−0.6**	−1.1	−1.0	−1.1
Lag	2 month	0.9	0.2	0.4	0.2	−0.5	−1.1	**−1.7**	−1.6	−1.7
	3 month	0.5	−0.2	0.0	−0.2	−0.9	−1.5	−2.1	**−2.0**	−2.1
	4 month	0.3	−0.4	−0.2	−0.3	−1.1	−1.7	−2.2	−2.1	**−2.2**

after the business cycle peak and back into stocks just one month after the business cycle trough would have lost 0.6 per cent a year compared with the buy-and-hold strategy.

Interestingly, it is more important to forecast troughs than peaks. An investor who buys stocks before the trough of the cycle gains more than an investor who sells stocks an equal number of months before the business-cycle peak. The maximum excess return of 4.8 per cent per year is obtained by investing in bills four months before the business-cycle peak and in stocks four months before the business-cycle trough. The strategy of switching between bills and stocks gains almost 30 basis points (30/100 of a percentage point) in average annual return for each week during the four-month period in which investors can predict the business-cycle turning point.

Extra returns from forecasting the cycle are impressive. An increase of 1.8 per cent a year in returns, achieved by predicting the business-cycle peak and trough only one month before it occurs, will increase your wealth by 60 per cent more than any buy-and-hold strategy over 30 years. If you can predict the market four months in advance, the annual increase of 4.8 per cent in returns will more than triple your wealth over the same time compared with a buy-and-hold strategy.

Can the cycle be predicted?

Billions of dollars are spent trying to forecast the business cycle. As we have just seen, it is not surprising that Wall Street employs so many economists desperately trying to predict the next recession or upturn since doing so dramatically increases returns. But the record of predicting exact cycle turning points is poor.

For more than 15 years, Robert J. Eggert has been summarizing the forecasts of a noted panel of economic and business experts. These forecasts are compiled each month in *Blue Chip Economic Indicators*. In July 1979, the publication indicated that a strong majority of forecasters believed a recession had started – forecasting negative gross national product (GNP) growth in the second, third and fourth quarters of 1979. However, the NBER declared that the peak of the business cycle did not occur until January 1980 and that the economy expanded throughout 1979. By the middle of the next year, the forecasters were convinced a recession had begun. But as late as June 1980 they believed the recession had started in February or March and would last a year, a month longer than the average recession. This prediction was reaffirmed in August, when forecasters indicated the US economy was halfway through the recession. In fact, the recession had ended the month before, in July, and the 1980 recession turned out to be the shortest since the war.

Forecasters' ability to predict the 1981–82 recession, when unemployment reached a post-war high of 10.8 per cent, was no better. The headline of the July 1981 *Blue Chip Economic Indicators* read: "Economic exuberance envisioned for 1982." Instead, 1982 was a disaster. By November 1981 forecasters realized the economy had faltered and optimism turned to pessimism. Most thought the economy had entered a recession (which it had done four months earlier), nearly 70 per cent thought it would end by the first quarter of 1982 (which it did not, instead tying the record for the longest post-war recession, ending in November) and 90 per cent thought it would be mild, like the 1971 recession. Wrong again. In April 1985, with expansion well under way, forecasters were asked how long the economy would be in an expansion. The average response was 49 months, which would put the peak at December 1986, more than three years before the cycle actually ended. Even the most optimistic forecasters picked spring 1988 as the latest date for the next recession to begin.

Following the stock crash of October 1987, forecasters reduced their GNP growth estimates of 1988 over 1987 from 2.8 per cent to 1.9 per cent, the largest drop in the 11-year history of the survey. Instead, economic growth in 1988 was nearly 4 per cent, as the economy failed to respond to the stock market collapse.

Conclusion

Going into 2001, the US was enjoying its longest economic expansion in history. Yet signs of a slowdown were unmistakable and there were strong indications that the economy was in, or soon would be in, a recession. The bull market topped out at the end of March 2000 and by April 2001 the S&P 500 index had fallen almost 27 per cent, exceeding the average 12-month declines before post-war recessions. Since the April low, the index has rallied significantly as investors predict that the economic slowdown will end soon. Using the historical average, the market says the bottom of the economic slowdown will be five months after the low, in September. Only time will tell if the market again can predict the end of recession.

Stock values are based on corporate earnings and the business cycle is a prime determinant of these earnings. The gains of being able to predict turning points in the economic cycle are enormous. Yet doing so with any precision has eluded economists. And in spite of the growing body of economic statistics, predictions are not getting much better.

The worst course an investor can take is to follow the prevailing sentiment about economic activity. This will lead to buying at high prices when times are good and everyone is optimistic, and selling at the low when recession nears its trough and pessimism prevails.

Lessons to investors are clear. Beating the stock market by analyzing real economic activity requires a degree of prescience that forecasters do not yet have. Turning points are rarely identified until several months after the peak or trough has been reached. By then, it is too late to act.

Copyright © Jeremy Siegel 2002

This article is adapted from the article "Does it pay stock investors to forecast the business cycle?" in *Journal of Portfolio Management*, Fall 1991, 18, 27–34 and Chapter 12 of *Stocks for the Long Run*, 2nd edn, McGraw-Hill. (1998) The material benefited significantly from discussions with Professor Paul Samuelson.

Poor returns that disguise a bonus for investors

Most studies suggest funds perform badly relative to a passive benchmark, yet they are still very popular. **Roger Edelen** examines the reasons why mutual funds are big business.

Roger M. Edelen is an assistant professor of finance at the Wharton School of the University of Pennsylvania.

Last year, a third of stock holdings by US households were in the form of open-end mutual funds, up from 11 per cent in 1990. In total, open-end US funds now manage almost $7,000bn. What accounts for their success?

When it comes to the services that open-end mutual funds provide, it is not hard to get the impression that enhanced returns are the primary consideration. The subject dominates promotional material, performance rating agencies and academic research. Paradoxically, the conclusion from studies is that the fund industry is not enhancing investment returns relative to a passive benchmark. Indeed, most studies show that the typical mutual fund offers a return (after expenses) of 1 per cent a year lower than a passive benchmark return – a significant reduction. Given this evidence, it is difficult to believe that an enhanced investment return is indeed the primary service behind the growth of mutual funds.

One possibility is that mutual fund "services" are a deceit cooked up by expensive marketing campaigns. This explanation seems inadequate. In which other industry do consumers toss about $7,000bn on the strength of a good story linked to vacuous services? Are mutual funds unique in their ability to dupe the consumer? Moreover, one does not have to look far to find credible, albeit mundane, explanations for their popularity.

Mutual funds offer a diversified position in just about any asset class you might want to target, with as much cheap liquidity as you could ask for, so the cost of making an investment or withdrawing capital is very low. Little is heard about diversification and liquidity benefits from the funds themselves, or from ratings agencies, because these features are generic. By law, funds are diversified and free liquidity is ubiquitous. Still, a highly liquid position in a diversified portfolio targeted to a specific investment objective is clearly a boon.

Consider the alternative – cobbling together an investment portfolio on one's own. The administrative costs of building a typical fund portfolio of 80 or so stocks from a specific investment objective or asset class would be onerous for any investor. One must identify the relevant securities, choose among them and execute the trades. Moreover, these costs must be borne each time the investor seeks to alter the investment focus, say, from small-cap aggressive stocks to high-grade corporate bonds. Shifting in and out of asset classes at any frequency short of a few years would be prohibitively costly to administer without mutual funds. With mutual funds, administering a complete overhaul of the portfolio is a relatively trivial task.

Administrative costs are just the beginning. There is also the matter of explicit transaction costs. For the large investor these might be as low as 0.25 per cent of assets each time the portfolio is refocused. For small investors they are substantially larger. Indeed, for those investing less than, say, a few hundred thousand dollars, transaction costs would amount to at least 2 or 3 per cent. These costs make liquidity in a diversified, directly held portfolio impossible for most investors and costly and onerous even for the wealthy. In this light, it is not hard to imagine that the success of mutual funds can be attributed to the liquidity service they provide. Even if fund managers offer no return enhancement, the typical investor is vastly better off using mutual funds.

Are the demands for liquidity in a diversified portfolio really so large that the liquidity advantage of mutual funds provides a serious economic benefit? Consider the numbers. In 2000, US investors purchased more than $1,600bn of shares in US-domiciled funds and redeemed $1,300bn. The explicit trading costs that these fund shareholders would have borne had this "trading" involved portfolios of directly held securities would have been in the region of $10bn, using a conservative estimate of transaction costs of 0.5 per cent.

Administrative costs are difficult to quantify, but a quick calculation is instructive. Assuming a typical transaction of $20,000, this suggests that around 100m transactions took place in 1999. Executed without the benefit of mutual funds, each transaction would involve selecting a targeted diversified portfolio of directly held securities, executing 80 purchase trades and 80 sale trades, and updating book-keeping and tax records. Even if these tasks could be executed at a rate of two hours per transaction, which seems optimistic, we are talking some 80,000 man-years of effort at 50 hours a week. The implied administrative savings offered by mutual funds would be $4bn, assuming an average annual salary of $50,000.

Thus there seem to be 14bn reasons a year for investors to flock to mutual funds, irrespective of whether they offer enhanced returns.

The downside

A typical mutual fund enjoys substantial economies of scale over individual investors in both the administrative and transaction costs of maintaining a liquid, diversified position. But offering a liquidity service that amounts to trillions of dollars a year does entail costs for funds. Indeed, the academic studies that draw negative conclusions about the returns offered by mutual funds may be painting a misleading picture. After all, each study assumes that fund managers incur zero costs in providing liquidity.

The correct benchmark for assessing fund managers' return-enhancement services is one that removes the cost of liquidity. This can be done in two steps: first, by identifying the relation between liquidity services and fund returns; second, by determining the realized level of liquidity services provided, that is, the fund's actual redemptions and subscriptions activity. Multiplying the level of liquidity service provided by the erosion in performance that the service causes then gives the right benchmark for evaluating returns.

A 1999 study of 165 randomly sampled funds done in this way by the author found that the average return offered to investors over five years was about the same as that from a passive benchmark less the funds' average expense ratio. In other words, fund management appeared to offer no return enhancement. This result is similar to other studies. Funds consistently underperform by an amount that roughly matches expenses.

The study went on to evaluate the return-enhancement service offered by funds after considering liquidity demands. The typical liquidity demand was substantial. The median fund had annual inflows of about 38 per cent of assets under management and outflows of 34 per cent of assets. Variation was substantial. At some funds, typical flow is less than 10 per cent of assets, while at others it is upwards of 100 per cent. Likewise, the same fund can experience flow in some months that is 5–10 times as large as that in other months.

These significant variations provide a way to detect the costs that fund managers face in fulfilling their liquidity service. In particular, there should be a relatively large degradation of return performance when liquidity demands are large and relatively good return performance when demands are slight. To detect this pattern, liquidity demands must be substantial. However, the numbers indicate that this is likely to be the case.

Performance issues

There are many ways to measure return performance. The most common approach is the market-adjusted return or "alpha" measure, which picks up stock-selection skills and market-timing measures. The service of providing liquidity to investors, that is, fund redemptions and subscriptions ("flow"), can degrade performance on both dimensions.

Alpha performance

All stocks tend to move with broad indices, such as the Standard & Poor's 500 or the FTSE 100. This reflects the fact that stocks operate within the same economy. When combined into a portfolio this tendency is more concentrated because idiosyncratic factors tend to cancel one another out. Alpha performance measures seek to strip out broad market movements when judging a fund's return. That is, the fund manager is not given credit or blame for economy-wide forces acting on a portfolio.

There can be many alpha measures, depending on the indices and factors used to strip out common tendencies in stock returns. It has become common to use a three-index approach: a broad market index, an index relating to small-cap stocks, and an index relating to growth stocks. The idea, then, is that the fund manager must have selected the right stocks at the right time if the portfolio exhibits positive returns (that is, "alpha") after taking out broad-market and sector returns.

Providing liquidity can degrade a fund's alpha because it forces the fund manager to trade in and out of specific stock positions when there is no other reason to trade. In some cases, the counterparty to such a trade may also be "uninformed" so the trade is neutral for both sides (no degradation of alpha). But there are surely cases in which the counterparty is motivated by private knowledge. By definition, when an informed party trades against an uninformed party, the former wins. That is, the informed trader gets positive alpha at the expense of the uninformed party. So, liquidity-motivated trading comes out even on some trades and loses on others. On average, providing liquidity for investors degrades alpha performance.

Market-timing performance

Most funds target a fully invested position, meaning they strive to keep all capital invested in the markets. However, if the fund manager had a correct notion that the market was likely to do poorly in the near future, the fund's return would be enhanced by building up a large temporary cash position. Likewise, when the manager correctly anticipates strong market returns, the fund's overall return is enhanced by investing all available funds and perhaps more through leverage.

This is called market-timing performance. Successful market timing is indicated by a positive correlation between the fund's stock position and the market return (or a negative correlation between the fund's cash position and market return).

Providing liquidity tends to degrade a fund's market-timing performance if fund flows are associated with market returns and the fund manager does not immediately offset shifts in cash with stock trades. Intuition suggests there could be a relation between aggregate cash flows into equity funds and market returns. Evidence supports such a relation. That being the case, a fund experiencing cash inflows will find itself less than fully invested when a market rises. Likewise, a fund experiencing redemptions will find its cash position depleted (that is, relatively heavily in the market) just when the market pulls back.

Performance and liquidity

The key to an alpha performance effect is that investors' liquidity demands force the fund manager to trade. This author's 1999 study finds a strong link between investors' liquidity demands and the fund's trading activity. In particular, servicing investors' liquidity accounts for yearly trading volume equal to 50–60 per cent of fund assets, or about a quarter of the average fund's total trading activity. This substantial volume of "forced" trading from servicing investors' liquidity needs plausibly hinders the fund's alpha performance. To test this, the study related the fund's alpha measure of performance, month by month, to the fund's realized volume of redemptions and subscriptions. There is strong evidence of a damaging effect. In particular, each additional dollar of liquidity-motivated trading that the fund manager has to undertake seems to elicit a decline in alpha of about 1.5 cents.

When all liquidity-motivated trades are taken into account, the average accumulated annual effect on alpha performance is about 1.6 per cent of fund assets. To benchmark fund managers' return enhancement services in a fair way, the appropriate benchmark should be a passive portfolio return less a 1.6 per cent charge for liquidity services provided. Weighed against this adjusted benchmark, the average fund studied scored an alpha of about zero, after expenses. Thus, the typical fund manager's stock picks appear to enhance returns sufficiently to cover the expense ratio charged against the fund.

The study also examined the market-timing performance of funds and found, perversely, that managers tend to time the market negatively. Again, this result is consistent with other studies. Might it also be attributed to the provision of a liquidity service?

The key to understanding this performance effect is that investors' liquidity demands put the fund in an ill-timed cash position. It is possible to test for adverse influences from investor cash flows by simply adding a control for flow to the market-timing relation. That is, one can separate out (a) the relation between market returns and the fund's cash position that is concurrent with realized cash flows from (b) the relation that results from a manager's actions. In assessing the return enhancement service provided by the fund, consider only the second component of decomposed market-timing performance. The result is that all of the perverse, negative market-timing evidence found in the sample is directly attributed to realized investor cash flows. Indeed, fund managers turn out to have some skill, albeit weak, in market timing.

Conclusion

Funds perform a variety of services. While return enhancement is the most glamorous, often-cited service, others are at least as important. In particular, mutual funds offer a liquid position in a diversified portfolio targeting a specific asset class or sector. For most investors, this greatly improves their investment opportunities. In particular, positions can be acquired and liquidated with minimal costs.

There have been countless academic studies of the return enhancement service of funds. Most conclude that the fund industry does not enhance returns, but almost all do so under the faulty assumption that the liquidity service of funds has no bearing on returns. Unfortunately, this is not the case. Liquidity is costly for everyone, funds included. This helps explain the seemingly paradoxical result that investors have flocked to mutual funds in spite of the abysmal performance record that academics have ascribed to the industry. When faced with the costs of liquidity in a portfolio of directly held investments, investors seeking both liquidity and enhanced returns see the "poor" net performance of mutual funds as nothing but a boon.

Copyright © Roger Edelen 2002

Further reading

Edelen, R. (1999) "Investor flows and the assessed performance of open-end mutual funds", *Journal of Financial Economics*, 53: 439–66.

Edelen, R. and Warner, J. (2001) "Aggregate price effects of institutional trading: a study of mutual fund flow and market returns", *Journal of Financial Economics*, 59: 195–220.

Ferson, W. and Warther, V. (1996) "Evaluating fund performance in a dynamic market", *Financial Analysts Journal*, 52 (6): 20–8.

Warther, V. (1995) "Aggregate mutual fund flows and security returns", *Journal of Financial Economics*, 39: 209–35.

Principles of bond portfolio management

Stephen M. Schaefer is Tokai Bank Professor of Finance at London Business School.

In this article, **Stephen Schaefer** discusses the differences between bonds and equities and shows how investors select and manage portfolios.

This article describes a framework for managing bond portfolios. The central idea is that, in many markets, risks of investing in bonds can be expressed in terms of exposure of a portfolio to a relatively small number of factors. Portfolio managers must decide on the level of exposure to each factor and choose bonds or other instruments that will give the required level of exposure in a cost-effective way.

In the seven largest industrial democracies, institutional investors manage around $27,000bn in assets, of which more than half is held in bonds and loans. Bonds come in a bewildering variety – more than 1,800 different country/type categories – but the field divides broadly into government and non-government issues. In the latter group, bonds issued by corporations form the most important segment, but there are other non-governmental sectors. In the US, for example, mortgage-backed bonds constitute just under 20 per cent of the market compared with 25 per cent for corporate bonds.

The task of managing this vast pool of assets has attracted rather less attention than that of managing equity portfolios. While the two roles have similarities, there are important differences, mainly involving the characteristics of bond and equity returns rather than a difference in principle.

Compared with returns on equities, bond returns (at least for bonds with a relatively low level of default risk) tend to be much more highly correlated with one another. This means diversification is less important than for equity markets; there it is difficult to focus a portfolio on assets the manager regards as offering the best value without changing significantly the risk characteristics. As the portfolio becomes more concentrated, less of the potentially diversifiable risk is actually eliminated. Because bond returns tend to be more highly correlated with each other it is easier to concentrate a portfolio on "best-value" assets without at the same time taking on diversifiable risk. In bond portfolios, therefore, diversification is less important than in equity portfolios and deciding which assets to hold and not to hold is relatively more important.

In most bond markets, the rate of return over a short period, such as a week or a month, on individual bonds and portfolios can be represented in terms of the asset's exposure to a small number of factors and the "unexpected" portion of the change in each factor (that is, the difference between the value that actually occurs and the value expected). This is represented in Equation 1.

EQUATION 1

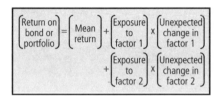

For example, in the market for government bonds, prices are typically well explained by the yield curve. Changes in the curve can be modelled in terms of changes in one or two "factors", such as, say, the 10-year rate and the spread between a long rate and a short rate. Additional factors account for fluctuations in the difference in yield between corporate and government bonds ("yield spread"). In the mortgage-backed market, other factors are needed to capture fluctuations in the rate of prepayment.

In Equation 1, the "mean return" gives the average rate of return the portfolio will earn. The remaining terms together give the amount by which the actual rate of return on the portfolio will deviate from its average value. So these terms describe the risks to which the portfolio is exposed.

The average return comes from two sources. First, as discussed later, exposure to factors driving returns may generate a risk premium, that is, an average rate of return greater than the short-term riskless interest rate ("cash"). The second source is asset selection: the ability of a manager to pick assets that offer "good value" in the sense that they have high expected returns relative to the risks they attract. Because bonds tend to be highly correlated they can be substituted for one another relatively easily and managers who are able to identify good-value bonds can focus on these without greatly increasing risk.

Substitutability between bonds is shown in Table 1. It gives the correlation between monthly returns on eight benchmark UK gilts of various maturities between 1 and 20 years from December 1987 to February 1998. First, the table shows the high degree of correlation between bonds of maturities of 10 years and over: these have a correlation of 0.95 or higher. Second, the rightmost column shows the correlation between individual bonds and the return on a portfolio equally weighted over the eight bonds.

Notice that the correlation between the portfolio and bonds with a maturity greater than five years is, again, very high (0.94 and above). A correlation of

TABLE 1	Correlation between monthly returns on UK gilts								
	Maturity of bond								*Equally weighted portfolio*
	1-year	2-year	3-year	5-year	7-year	10-year	15-year	20-year	
1-year	1								0.70
2-year	0.93	1							0.84
3-year	0.87	0.97	1						0.91
5-year	0.79	0.92	0.97	1					0.97
7-year	0.72	0.86	0.93	0.98	1				0.99
10-year	0.62	0.77	0.85	0.93	0.97	1			0.99
15-year	0.52	0.68	0.77	0.87	0.93	0.98	1		0.96
20-year	0.44	0.62	0.71	0.82	0.89	0.95	0.99	1	0.94

unity would mean that an investor could achieve returns equal to those on the portfolio by investing in a combination of a single bond and cash. In government bond markets, a portfolio containing two or three bonds will generally allow an investor to replicate closely the return characteristics of most investment portfolios.

This degree of substitutability between assets is characteristic of government bond markets and quite different from the high levels of asset-specific or idiosyncratic risk that is typical of equities. Other bond markets, in particular the corporate market, are somewhere in between.

Government bonds

As suggested earlier, the high correlation between the returns on government bonds of different maturities can be represented in terms of their common dependence on a small number of factors. A variety of methods can be used to identify these factors, but in most cases an intermediate-term rate, such as the yield on a 10-year bond, and the "spread" between a short-term rate and a long-term rate works well.

These factors explain a large part – typically more than 90 per cent – of the variability of the yield curve and, hence, of bond returns. A well-known study of the US Treasury market by Bob Litterman of Goldman Sachs and José Scheinkman of the University of Chicago showed that a three-factor model of the yield curve explained between 94 per cent and 99 per cent of daily returns on US Treasury bonds. The third factor in this and most other studies typically accounts for only 1 or 2 per cent of the total.

The first factor, which behaves more or less like an intermediate-term rate, produces a roughly parallel shift in the whole curve. The second factor changes the shape, flattening or steepening the curve (see Figure 1). The actual shift in the curve on any day, or over a week, is the result of a combination of shifts in

FIGURE 1 — Effects on yield curve

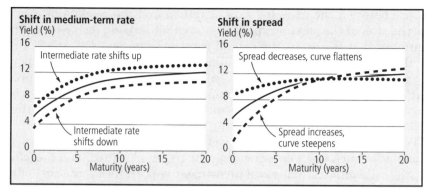

Source: Author's calculations

both the level and the slope. If we define the factors in this way, the correlation between them is usually small. Changes in the overall level of rates (the effect of shifts in the intermediate rate) are generally unrelated to changes in the slope (the result of shifts in the spread).

The sensitivity of a bond's price to a shift in factors is called the bond's exposure. It is a generalization of a risk measure called "duration".

Choosing exposures

In Equation 1, changes in factors are outside the manager's control. However, a manager can choose the extent to which a portfolio is exposed to these factors. What are the consequences of this choice?

Risk

First, the factor exposures determine that part of the overall risk of the portfolio that derives from the risk of the factors. In most cases, again where default risk is not significant, this will account for most of the risk. In the case of government bonds, if we use the intermediate rate and the spread as underlying factors, the volatility of the portfolio return can be worked out from a portfolio's exposure to these factors, the volatilities of the factors themselves, and correlation between the factors.

For many managers, the relevant measure of risk is not the volatility of the total rate of return but the volatility of the "tracking error". This error is the difference in the rates of return on the portfolio held by the manager and on a benchmark portfolio (usually prescribed by the pension fund or other investor that hires the manager – the "plan sponsor"). Here the calculation is almost the same except that, instead of using the actual exposure of the portfolio to each factor, the difference between the actual exposure and the exposure of the benchmark is used. A portfolio where the exposures of actual and benchmark portfolios are the same has negligible tracking error if the factors account for the majority of the return variability.

Portfolio risk premiums

In most theories on pricing risky assets, the risk premium on an asset (the difference between the expected rate of return and the riskless interest rate) equals the sum of the asset's exposure to each underlying factor times the risk premium on that factor. In the capital asset pricing model (CAPM), the only factor that has a non-zero risk premium is the return on the market portfolio. The exposure of an individual asset is called beta. The risk premium predicted by CAPM is beta times the risk premium on the market portfolio. In arbitrage pricing theory (or extended versions of CAPM), there may be more than one factor but the form of the relation is the same.

Calculations such as this are widely used in corporate finance and investment for such tasks as estimating the required return (and therefore the appropriate discount rate) for real investment opportunities, the cost of capital for regulated utilities, and the expected return on investment portfolios with particular risk characteristics. In the case of government bonds, if we use the intermediate-term rate and the spread as underlying factors, the risk premium on a bond or a portfolio can be written as Equation 2.

EQUATION 2

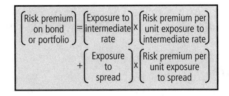

In theory, choosing exposure to the intermediate rate (the "level" of rates) and to the spread fixes the risk premium on a portfolio. The question, however, is: what are the risk premiums associated with exposure to the level of interest rates and to the spread?

A common argument is that long-term bonds, which have more exposure to fluctuations in rates, are riskier than short-term bonds. Therefore, the risk premium on long-term bonds should be positive and, since long-term bonds have more exposure to intermediate rates, the risk premium per unit of exposure to intermediate rates should also be positive. However, this argument has weaknesses. First, it ignores the supply side. If the expected return on long-term bonds is higher, borrowers will pay more if they finance with long-term bonds. If this were the case, why would borrowers not use shorter-term bonds? Second, it is a mistake to assume long-term bonds are riskier for everyone. Pension funds and life insurance funds, for example, with long-term liabilities, have a natural demand for long-term bonds. This tends to push up their price and reduce expected return.

Evidence in favour of a positive risk premium on long-term bonds is mixed. Using data for 1900 to 2000, academics Elroy Dimson, Paul Marsh and Mike Staunton of London Business School have estimated the risk premium on long-term government bonds as 1.0 per cent a year in the UK and 0.7 per cent in the US. However, even with 100 years of data these estimates are not clearly statistically distinguishable from zero. The UK risk premium is around 0.76 standard errors above zero and the US premium is 0.88 standard errors above zero; both figures are substantially below accepted levels of significance. My calculations on UK gilt returns from December 1987 to February 1998 confirm these results for exposure to the long rate and also fail to find a significant risk premium associated with the spread.

Predictability

The analysis so far states that a portfolio's exposure to underlying risk factors largely determines its risk. Also, because risk premia associated with the intermediate rate and the spread are difficult to distinguish from zero, the exposure has apparently little effect on its long-run expected return. In contrast, the risk premium associated with exposure to the equity market has been strongly positive (around 7–8 per cent in the UK and the US over the past century). This means that, in the long run, investors holding equities can expect to outperform an investment in short-term riskless instruments. However, in the absence of a strong positive risk premium on long-term bonds, investors in bonds cannot necessarily expect to outperform cash even in the long run.

Outside the long run, however, factor risk premiums may vary predictably. Here, Equation 1 has different implications. For example, Antti Ilmanen of Salomon Brothers has found the spread between five-year and three-month rates has a correlation of just over 0.2 with excess return (the difference between actual rate of return earned and the riskless interest rate) on bonds over the following month.

Other effects include the level of real yields and the ratio of a weighted average of past stock market wealth to the current stock market level. Thus, even though long-run risk premiums on bonds may be close to zero, the risk premium over the next month, say, may be predictably positive or negative depending on the slope of the term structure and recent performance of the market.

Copyright © Stephen Schaefer 2002

Further reading

Ilmanen, A. (1995) *Forecasting US Bond Returns?*, Salomon Brothers, August.
Ilmanen, A. (1996) "Does duration extension enhance long-term expected returns?", *Journal of Fixed Income*, September.
Litterman, R. and Scheinkman, J. (1991) "Common factors affecting bond returns", *Journal of Fixed Income*, June.

Corporate bonds and other debt instruments

Stephen M. Schaefer is Tokai Bank Professor of Finance at London Business School.

In the last article, **Stephen Schaefer** explained how bonds are selected and managed. Here he examines the subject of corporate bonds.

The price of nearly all types of debt depends on the underlying yield curve, that is, the relation between yields on government bonds and maturity. The yield curve itself depends on such factors as the intermediate rate and the spread (the difference between long- and short-term rates). For government debt these factors account for virtually all variability of returns, but once we consider other categories, such as corporate debt, additional factors become important.

The most obvious difference between corporate debt and government debt is the risk of default: in other words, the possibility that the equity holders will give up their control rights over the company, exercise their right to limited liability and default on the debt. Clearly, the likelihood that equity holders will do this is linked to the value of the assets of the company. If the assets are worth more than the shareholders owe the lenders, it makes sense to pay off the debt and retain ownership of the company. Only when the assets of the company are worth less than the amount owed is default in the interests of the equity holders.

Because the likelihood of default goes up with a fall in the value of the company's assets, there is a positive relation between the value of corporate debt and the value of corporate assets. Table 1 shows the results of regressing an index of (a) high-grade corporate bonds and (b) high-yield (low-grade) corporate bonds against (i) returns on the Standard & Poor's 500 and (ii) returns on an index of government bonds. The S&P is included as an index of the value of corporate assets on which corporate debt depends for repayment.

The results accord with intuition. Both the high- and low-grade bonds have a statistically significant relation with the return on the S&P but the sensitivity for the low-grade bonds is more than four times higher. For these bonds, a 1 per cent fall in the S&P results in an 18 basis point (0.18 per cent) fall in the value of the bonds.

| TABLE 1 | Sensitivity of returns on corporate debt to returns on the S&P index returns on an index of long-term government bonds |

		S&P	Government bonds	R2
High-grade corporate bonds	Coefficient	0.042	1.01	0.93
	t-statistic	4.20	36.5	
High-yield corporate bonds	Coefficient	0.182	0.24	0.25
	t-statistic	4.90	2.34	

Source: Data from Merrill Lynch. April 1992 to March 1999, monthly

The nature of limited liability means holders of corporate debt have effectively sold an option to the shareholders (the option to default). This has a number of important implications. First, it means that those variables that are important in pricing options – particularly volatility – are likely to be important in pricing corporate debt. Indeed, Pierre Collin-Dufresne and research colleagues have shown the credit spread (the difference in yield between corporate and otherwise similar government bonds) increased, as expected, with increases in the implied volatility of options on the S&P. Duen-Li Kao has shown credit spreads on US corporate debt had a correlation of 0.5–0.6 with the volatility of the yield on 10-year government bonds. One interpretation of the latter result is that a rise in interest rate volatility increases volatility of the present value of the company's debt and therefore the chance that this value may exceed the asset value and trigger default.

Option pricing

The second implication, and one that has interesting ramifications for investment managers, is that the conventional method of pricing options, the Black-Scholes model, can also be used to price corporate debt. This approach gives the "fair value" or "intrinsic value" of the debt relative to the price of default-free government debt and the value of the company's assets that collateralize the debt.

So far, though, this exercise does not seem to work very well. When analyzed in this way, typical corporate debt prices are too low. In other words, they are lower than the cost of a portfolio designed to mimic the behaviour of the corporate debt, consisting of riskless debt and equity in the company issuing debt.

According to academics Jing-zhi Huang and Ming Huang, the gap between theory and practice is relatively wide. Instead of using data on individual bonds, Huang and Huang use data on credit and default rates for credit-rating categories (AAA, AA and so on). They then calculate the theoretical credit spread using an option-pricing based model. The exercise is designed to produce a default rate equal to that estimated by the rating agencies. For the AA category, for example, the model produced a credit spread of around 10 basis points while the average in the market was over 90 basis points.

> **Box 1 Enhanced equity index funds: how bond experts compete in the equity market**
>
> There are a number of institutional portfolios and mutual funds in which the fund investments are in bond-related assets (for example, mortgage-backed securities) but where the fund characteristics are those of an equity fund. These funds, run by fixed-income managers, compete in the market for equity funds. A common product is a portfolio designed to produce a return equal to that on the S&P 500 plus a premium. This is an example of a so-called "enhanced" index fund.
>
> The strategy used in these cases has two parts. The first is the selection of the portfolio of bond assets. This part uses the manager's expertise since it is here that a manager may add value by selecting assets that represent "good value". This portfolio is exposed to the factors that drive this particular bond market, for example, yield curve factors, credit factors and mortgage factors.
>
> The second step is therefore to use derivatives to eliminate, that is, hedge, as much of this risk as possible. In an ideal case the returns on the portfolio at this stage would be similar to cash plus the premium that results from the manager's expertise in selecting assets.
>
> Having eliminated exposure to the unwanted bond-related risk factors, the third step is now to add exposure to the equity market. This would typically be achieved using a swap in which the manager would pay the short-term interest rate to receive the return on the S&P 500 index. (The same result could also be achieved by buying futures contracts on the S&P.) The net result is a portfolio that will behave like the S&P 500 equity index but where the outperformance, if any, derives from the manager's investment in bonds, not equities.

The reason the model produced such a small spread is this. Ignoring for a moment the effects of risk premia on pricing and assuming that in the event of a default the bond-holder would receive nothing (an overly conservative assumption), the yield spread on a bond will be approximately equal to the probability of default per year.

In the study by Huang and Huang, the parameters were chosen so the probability of default on a 10-year AA bond corresponded to the rating agency estimate of 0.1 per cent a year. So it is no surprise that the yield spread produced by the model also turns out to be around 0.1 per cent or 10 basis points. Since this is different from the 90 basis point average spread actually observed, we must conclude that the market either thinks that default is much more likely than the rating agencies or, more probably, requires a reward for some feature of the return on corporate bonds other than default risk.

The jury is still out on what this missing factor might be. However, evidence suggests it is not connected with the issuing company itself but is systematic across corporate issues. One possibility is that it is a reward (in the form of a price discount) for the generally low levels of liquidity in the corporate bond market. If this is the case then investment managers for whom liquidity is less important than the average may regard the corporate bond sector as good value.

Risk management

In the last article you will have seen that the factor risk exposure of a portfolio provides a means of calculating its risk. In fact, it is also a useful framework for managing risk. For a portfolio of government bonds, the exposure to the intermediate rate and the spread may be changed in a number of ways. The most obvious is by buying and selling the bonds themselves. On occasions, however, he may wish to separate the determination of the factor exposure of the portfolio from the choice of assets. For example, he may wish to have a large exposure to a particular long-term bond because it may seem good value, while at the same time having only a moderate exposure to shifts in the level of rates. This could be achieved by combining a long position in the "good-value" long-term bond with a short position in another "fair-value" or "expensive" bond. A much more practical method is to use derivatives, for example, by selling bond futures contracts.

The possibility of using derivatives to separate the factors to which a portfolio may be exposed, and to separate risk factors from the particular choice of assets, has potentially important consequences for managing bond portfolios and even for the pattern of competition in investment management. We have just alluded to one implication, namely, the possibility of using derivatives to separate the decision to hold a particular bond, for example, a long-term bond, from the risk exposures it would usually carry.

Conclusion

Other implications, however, may be more far reaching. If we consider the range of assets that may be included in a bond portfolio – for example, government bonds, corporate bonds, mortgage-backed securities and so on – a particular manager may have expertise in some of these areas but not all. In such cases it may make sense for the investor, such as a pension fund, to ask the manager to hold only those classes of assets in which he has expertise. The investor is then able to combine these portfolios and to use derivatives to produce the overall pattern of risk exposures that makes sense for the fund but which may be quite unrelated to the exposures taken on by each manager. From time to time the manager may do this himself in order to produce a fund that has the exposures on one market, such as the equity market, while his expertise lies elsewhere, say, in the corporate bond market or in mortgages.

In the past, competition between portfolio managers was compartmentalized to a large extent by the asset categories in which their expertise lay: an equity expert produced portfolio returns that looked like equities; a bond manager produced bond returns. But we recognize an "equity portfolio" in terms of its exposure to equity risk factors and, using derivatives, these can be added to portfolios that are actually invested in bonds. At the same time, further derivatives can eliminate exposure to the bond-related risk factors. Such strategies, already in use by some companies, provide a mechanism to break down the barriers that previously limited competition between managers to those managing similar categories of assets.

Copyright © Stephen Schaefer 2002

The use and abuse of derivatives

Futures and options have been unfairly blamed for some high-profile financial disasters, but this should not hinder their growing use, says **Christopher Culp**.

Dr Christopher L. Culp is an adjunct associate professor of finance at the University of Chicago Graduate School of Business and managing director of CP Risk Management LLC in Chicago.

In spite of their popularity, derivatives are regarded by many as unfathomable and dangerous financial instruments that have caused several high-profile multi-million-pound losses in the past decade. They are gaining acceptance in some circles while being derided in others. Which view is correct? Are derivatives complex, exotic back doors to leveraged gambling, or are they indispensable in reducing costs, managing risks and fine-tuning investment?

This article looks at the role of derivatives in investment management. It covers what they are, how they are traded, and their uses – and abuses – in investment management.

Basic types

Most people use derivatives. If you tell a car rental company you will bring the car back with a full tank of petrol rather than taking a car with a full tank, you are evaluating a derivatives position. If you ask for part of your pay tied to performance, you are asking to be paid with derivatives. Giving customers 30 days to pay is akin to giving them a derivatives-like option of not paying at all.

Most financial instruments can be viewed as combinations of the basic types of derivatives – forwards and options. As early as the 12th century, fairs in England and France provided opportunities for merchants to contract for the purchase or sale of a specified amount and quality of a commodity on a specified date at a price fixed on the day of the negotiation. A simple "forward contract" may be negotiated in March to buy 5,000 bushels of wheat in June for a fixed price, say £3/bu. If the market price is £3.05/bu. in June, the purchaser – or "long" – makes a profit of £0.05/bu. or £250. The wheat that the long has bought for the pre-contracted £15,000 now has a market value of £15,250.

Contracts can also be entered to sell, where a seller "shorts" the asset. Indeed, any forward contract has both a "long" and a "short". Forwards, like all derivatives, are bilateral contracts – unique agreements between counterparties. For every buyer/long, there must be a seller/short.

Forwards can be used to buy and sell numerous "underlying assets", including physical commodities as well as financial assets such as foreign exchange or bonds. In addition, forward contracts may be cash-settled, where at maturity a cash flow is exchanged in lieu of an asset. The amount of the cash flow is based on the value of a reference rate or index (for example, the London interbank offered rate or the FTSE 100).

Many financial instruments can be viewed as combinations of derivatives-like forwards. A common example is a "swap", an agreement between two parties to exchange an asset or cash flow. A typical swap involves exchanging a fixed cash flow for an asset or cash flow whose value varies over time. Such a swap is equivalent to a portfolio of forward contracts that are bundled as a single instrument. In an equity swap, for example, a company may agree to pay every six months for two years the cash equivalent of 1,000 shares of company Aristotle in return for the cash equivalent of 1,000 shares of company Plato. No stock changes hands, but the value of the contract is determined by the difference in the prices per share of the two companies on each of the swap's reset dates. The same result could be accomplished by going long on four forward contracts of 1,000 shares in company Plato stock and short four forward contracts on 1,000 shares of company Aristotle's equity, with the maturity dates of the four forwards being after 6, 12, 18 and 24 months.

The second basic type of derivatives contract, an "option", gives holders the right, but not the obligation, to buy or sell an asset on or before a set date. A "call" option gives holders the right to buy and a "put" option gives the right to sell. When a call or put option is sold, the seller/writer must honour the purchaser's right to buy or sell if the purchaser "exercises" that right. Whereas forwards create unlimited liability, purchased options are limited-liability assets that act as a price insurance. In exchange for honouring such potentially unlimited liability exercises, option writers collect premiums from option purchasers.

Like forwards, options can be based on a variety of assets, reference rates or indexes. The most common types of options are either European or American. The former allows holders to buy or sell only on the option's expiration date, whereas the latter can be exercised by the buyer at any time on or before the option's expiration. Options that allow exercise on one of a few specific dates before expiration are dubbed "Bermuda options" because they lie between the two.

Like forwards, options can be combined with other products to yield new financial instruments sold as a package. A convertible bond, for example, is equivalent to a debt instrument plus an equity option or warrant. A series of call options on interest rates when maturity-matched and combined with a floating-rate loan, to take another example, is equivalent to a capped floating-rate loan.

Apart from mixing and matching forwards and options to create products, numerous contracts can be viewed as derivatives. Option-like contracts include performance-based pay packages, the option to make part or full payment on a credit card, the option to delay a capital expenditure decision, the option to switch inputs or outputs in a production process, and so on. Indeed, corporate securities can be viewed as option contracts – debt as a short put and equity as a long call, both written on the assets of the company, with a striking price equal to the face value of that debt.

Exchange trading

Negotiating forward and option derivatives is done using fax, telephones and the internet. A typical swap dealer is an intermediary who enters into virtually any transaction, generally on either side (long or short) of the contract. Dealers thus transact with end-users, as well as providing customized transaction services for their customers. A bank dealer, for example, may provide services to derivatives customers going well beyond derivatives dealing into cash management, custodial services, asset management and classical commercial banking.

That many derivatives are negotiated in a relatively opaque and highly decentralized dealer market is not surprising. This is the price for being able to customize fully the terms of a financial instrument – to know that what you get in terms of features and price may well not resemble what your competitor gets. At the same time, not everyone values customization, opacity and relationship management with a swap dealer. Some companies simply want to get a derivatives deal done cheaply and as quickly as possible and, provided the counterparty performs on the deal, are willing to transact with almost anyone. For such companies, exchange-traded derivatives provide an alternative to off-exchange forwards, swaps and options.

The most popular exchange-traded derivatives, futures contracts, are economically equivalent to forward contracts with a few important exceptions. First, exchange-traded derivatives are standardized in many aspects, such as maturity date, settlement method, underlying asset type and quality, and delivery location. Off-exchange derivatives, by contrast, may be fully customized, provided the two parties agree on terms.

Exchange-traded derivatives are usually cleared centrally. This means a trader on a futures exchange need not worry about the credit risk of the trader on the other side of the transaction – unlike the forward or swap participant, whose contract value depends on counterparty performance. Immediately after a futures trade, the clearing house for the exchange interposes itself as counterparty to both traders. The exchange and clearing house may be the same organization, as in the case of the Chicago Mercantile Exchange or Chicago Board of Trade, but this need not be so. Transactions on the London International Financial Futures Exchange (LIFFE), for example, are cleared by the London Clearing House. Indeed, the trend has been towards separate "listing" and "clearing".

An implication of standardized futures is that they can be "offset" before maturity. If company Melville agrees with company Conrad to go long on three-month gold futures but does not actually want the gold, Melville can go back into the market before final delivery and enter into an offsetting short. The company need not revisit Conrad because the original deal has been legally transformed into an agreement of company Melville to buy gold in three months from the clearing house. Because both transactions are with the clearing house, Melville has taken itself out of the market, with only the price difference to be paid or collected.

The offset system, together with standardization of exchange-traded derivatives, makes these derivatives markets highly liquid and deep, and hence often cheaper than their off-exchange cousins. Off-exchange derivatives, by contrast, can only be "unwound" before maturity if the original counterparty consents. This can be time-consuming and expensive.

Another distinction between futures and forwards/swaps is the use of margin, a type of performance bond that must be posted by traders to help mitigate losses incurred by the clearing house in the event of a default. If a trader is unable or unwilling to honour contractual obligations, he forfeits this performance bond. In addition, at least daily, the values of all open futures and exchange-traded options positions are marked to current market prices. Net winners may withdraw their profits, which are financed by deposits of additional margin made by losers. These daily payments and collections are called "variation margin", the effect of which is the de facto renegotiation of futures contracts each day to current market prices.

A final important distinction between off- and on-exchange derivatives is their regulation. For mainly historical reasons, exchange-traded derivatives in most countries are subject to heavier regulation. Such rules cover issues ranging from fraud and manipulation to cumbersome procedures for getting regulators' approval to list a new product. Exchanges listing derivatives can claim the benefit of "public regulation" (as opposed to the self-regulation of off-exchange markets), but only at the cost of delayed innovation and compliance.

Traders once faced a reasonably clear trade-off in considering whether to use off-exchange forwards and swaps or exchange-traded futures. If you wanted the credit risk protection of a central counterparty relying on a system of margin and daily resettlement, you went to the futures market. You perhaps also went to the futures market for transparent pricing, depth, significant liquidity and ease of unwinding or offsetting your position. But in getting these benefits, you sacrificed the ability to customize a deal. Over the years, the distinctions between off-exchange forwards and exchange-traded futures have narrowed. Today, exchange-traded derivatives can be customized, making them more like off-exchange derivatives. Off-exchange derivatives, in turn, are often subject to collateral requirements and governed by performance guarantees that provide credit risk protection similar to that once offered only by exchanges.

In addition, new insurance products called "Alternative Risk Transfer" resemble off-exchange derivatives. The formerly separate worlds of exchanges and off-exchange bilateral contracts have begun to merge into a single global capital market, but how can investment managers use this integrated capital market?

Investment

Given the derivatives-related losses in the mid-1990s at Barings, Procter & Gamble, Metallgesellschaft and Long-Term Capital Management, should use of derivatives by investment managers be cause for worry? The answer depends, of course, on how they are used. In the case of Barings, rogue trader Nick Leeson used them to run a fraudulent off-the-books operation. Had he stuck to futures, Barings would still be around. Similarly, Procter & Gamble used derivatives to bet on interest rates. When the bet turned out wrong, the company lost out. But derivatives did not cause the loss; swaps were just used to place the bet.

In fact, asset managers who avoid derivatives are likely to be subject to greater criticism than if they use them. Take the example of a pension plan that chooses to hold 60 per cent stocks and 40 per cent bonds for a year. If the market rallies in the first two quarters, the fund will find itself over-invested based on its original holdings. The firm can sell stocks, but this can be expensive. Alternatively, the firm can short stock index futures or equity index swaps, so reducing exposure to equities "synthetically" – but at much lower cost than if the stocks themselves had to be sold. Such "synthetic asset allocation" is especially prudent if the market is expected to reverse, which would necessitate a second rebalancing.

Derivatives can also be used to fine-tune investments. Many institutional investors cannot short stocks and cannot use unlimited-liability instruments such as equity swaps. By using option contracts such as "rainbow" or "spread" options, however, an investment manager can bet on the relative performance of several stocks or stock baskets for a price while locking in a maximum loss of the option premium paid. A spread option on the Nasdaq return relative to the FTSE 100, for example, invests on the performance of Nasdaq stocks against UK blue chips, but because it is an option, the manager cannot lose more than the premium paid for the position.

Consider a mutual fund with 30 per cent of its assets allocated in equities listed in markets outside its home country and currency. If the fund considers its managers' expertise to be stock selection, the fund may prefer not to avoid the exchange rate risk that international equities can create. Derivatives provide an easy solution in which the fund buys foreign stocks, "hedges" the exchange rate risk using forwards or futures and options, and ends up with an investment whose performance is a function of the equity price moves of foreign stocks as if they were denominated in the home currency of the fund.

To take a more recent example, what if a pension plan or mutual fund wants to diversify into a new asset class altogether, such as catastrophic insurance or bank debt used to fund mergers and acquisitions? Indeed, the performance of such asset classes as investments can be attractive on a return-to-risk basis, especially when they are part of a bigger, globally diversified portfolio. Without derivatives, it is difficult for funds to access these asset classes. But with the use of innovative credit derivatives such as total return swaps, investing in bank debt becomes possible. Derivatives-like ART products offered by the insurance industry have also helped promote new asset classes, particularly in catastrophic insurance.

Derivatives and risk

Derivatives can be abused, but so can other instruments. Risk management ensures that the risks taken are those to which investors want to be, and think they are, exposed. If derivatives are used by a hedge fund to exploit potential misevaluations arising from corporate actions and the fund loses money, this is not a risk management failure, provided investors knew about the investment. But if those same derivatives lost investors money because they were structured or managed improperly, risk management would have helped avoid the loss.

Asset managers should avoid risk management strategies that are biased against derivatives. Derivatives can replicate cash flows on many traditional financial instruments and, in turn, instruments such as stocks and bonds are themselves types of derivatives. So a risk policy specific to financial instruments is unlikely to be of much help. It is best to focus on a policy in which risk itself is controlled, regardless of whether risk is created by using derivatives or simply by, say, using reverse repurchase agreements and repurchase agreements to lever up a classical securities portfolio.

Derivatives can reduce costs of asset allocation rebalancing with limited liability instruments and avoid risks by hedging. Responsible use of derivatives is a reason to cheer, not shrink in horror.

Copyright © Christopher Culp 2002

Further reading

Culp, C.L. (2001) *The Risk Management Process: Business Strategy and Tactics*, New York: John Wiley.
Hull, J.C. (2000) *Options, Futures, and Other Derivatives*, Upper Saddle River, NJ: Prentice-Hall.
Jarrow, R. and Turnbull, S. (1999) *Derivative Securities*, New York: South-Western Publishing.
Smithson, C.W. (1998) *Managing Financial Risk*, New York: McGraw-Hill.

The past and future for real estate

Property may be seen as boring by some, but with $4,000bn in global assets, it is an investment market that deserves closer attention, says **Richard Georgi**.

Richard Georgi is managing partner of Soros Real Estate Investors, a global private equity property investment fund affiliated with the Soros Group.

Property, or real estate, is generally considered a "boring" asset class involving buildings, such as homes and offices. In fact, it includes diverse assets ranging from industrial parks and distribution centres to health clubs, resorts and pubs. The definition covers not only bricks-and-mortar but also private property operating companies that manage or service property as well as public investment vehicles, private property debt and public property debt securities. The value of the global commercial property market amounts to an estimated $4,000bn, making it the largest asset class.

The pricing model for property is a combination of the cash flow, or "rent", it is capable of generating and the "multiple" of cash flow investors are willing to pay for it. Given that the appropriate multiple is derived from the underlying cash flow's security of income and potential for growth, the rent tends to drive the multiple. Rent can be secured in the form of a simple lease agreement or as a percentage of the revenues or profits of the operating business using the space; some hotels and large retail shopping centres, for example, operate in this way.

Given that rents are derived from the capacity of the market to use space, the analysis of values boils down to a study of supply and demand. Because demand can change quickly but supply takes years to build, the market is never stable and tends to be cyclical. In addition, property is complicated by the fact that it is an inherently local business. Although the value of property is affected by global macroeconomic trends and capital market events, property is by definition a fixed asset and therefore subject to local lease structures, tax codes, regulations, legal rights and customs. These factors, along with the size of the market and the unique nature of each asset, create a large and inefficient marketplace.

This can create great opportunities for the well informed or disastrous results for the less experienced. To be successful, therefore, the market demands that investors understand the property cycle and see how value is created. Likewise, in conceiving a strategy, investors must be able to respond to changing fundamental conditions and anticipate opportunities in what is now a global market.

Why invest?

Despite the challenges of investing in property, this form of investment can create tremendous wealth by generating consistently attractive returns. In the past 14 years other asset classes have generated greater returns on average, yet property has outperformed shares and bonds in certain periods, including the adverse market conditions of 2000, while suffering far fewer setbacks. In an article in 2001, Robert Bellinger and Judy Lemkin discussed property as a component of investment portfolios and offered a comparison of asset classes: since 1934, shares and bonds have each generated negative returns 25 per cent of the time, while property has had negative returns only 5 per cent of the time.

The same study provided an analysis of Sharpe ratios, a means of comparing different investments defined as "a measure of excess return generated by additional risk taken". This reveals that private equity property investments have generated risk-adjusted returns that are nearly 10 times those of the Standard & Poor's 500 and 25 times those of bonds.

Property can also play a crucial diversifying role. It gives a strong current cash flow, a low correlation with other assets such as shares and bonds, and an inverse relationship with inflation. An April 2001 study by Real Estate & Portfolio Research demonstrated that property, on average, generates a 7.9 per cent return (75 per cent of its overall return) via current cash flow, compared with an income return of 1.1 per cent for shares.

The value drivers also differ from those of shares and bonds. The same study highlighted that property enjoys a low return correlation with other asset classes (0.38 with shares and 0.31 with bonds). Finally, because property values rise with inflation, property appreciates in a rising-rate environment that adversely affects the values of shares and bonds.

Timing

The property market generally ebbs and flows with changes in economic demand and supply. As discussed, property derives its value from its cash flows and the multiple of cash flow assigned to it. Cash flow growth results from increases in rent brought about by a combination of rising demand and limited supply in any particular market. While demand for space can change quickly – sometimes overnight – the supply process is constrained by funding, permitting, planning and commercial processes. As a result, supply takes longer to match demand, sometimes up to five years or more depending on the market. Consequently, property occupancy markets are often unbalanced.

Globalization and advances in information technology are changing the way people work, shop and live. This has caused the principle of "location, location, location" to become less important than "timing, timing, timing". When macroeconomic conditions are adverse and property markets are falling, business and investors may witness bankruptcies, foreclosures and distressed asset sales. As fundamental conditions improve, the market eventually stabilizes and, with renewed economic demand and limited supply, rents begin to rise again. As rents rise, yields fall in anticipation of growth and property values increase even more dramatically.

When rents reach a level that is high enough to justify new development, additional supply is added to the market and eventually rental growth slows. This is usually followed by consolidation and, more recently, equity and debt securitization, which allows the broader market to participate indirectly in the asset class. Unfortunately, stability rarely lasts long because all too often additional supply is still under construction when the economy falters, creating excess space in an environment where demand is falling.

Where to invest

Let us consider market opportunities in the three primary money centres: the US, western Europe and Japan. The US economy has slowed after years of robust growth driven largely by consumption (negative savings and full employment) and investment (a bull market and the advent of new technologies), neither of which has proved sustainable. In 2001, the Federal Reserve aggressively lowered interest rates to head off a recession, yet there remains much uncertainty about the near-term future.

The extended bull market has made US property markets relatively crowded and overcapitalized at a time when the economic slowdown will lead to softening rents and growing vacancies. Figure 1 shows the historical cycle

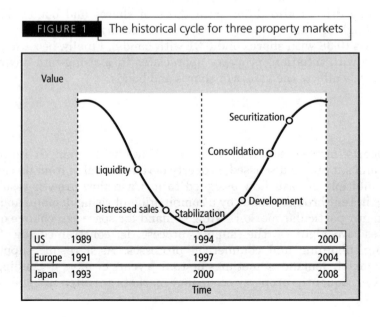

FIGURE 1 The historical cycle for three property markets

for the three property markets and indicates that the US is at or near its peak. There is limited opportunity in today's US property market and a dramatic slowdown in the speed of transactions in 2001 suggests there are now more sellers than buyers.

By contrast, the outlook is positive for Europe. Since the mid-1990s, Europe has benefited from cyclical recovery, increasing structural reforms and a sustained period of military security. It is adapting to global competition with regulatory changes, increasingly open markets and an acceptance of shareholder value. While not unaffected by a US slowdown, monetary union, a positive trade balance, regulatory reform and new technologies suggest that Europe is heading for a period of moderate growth, low inflation, improved productivity and increased consumption. Europe's property market will therefore benefit from continued economic demand. Combined with high barriers to new supply, rents are likely to continue growing. At the same time, pressure on governments to privatize assets should continue to generate investment opportunities.

Japan, the world's second largest economy, has suffered from a decade of economic stagnation, exacerbated by structural weaknesses and government involvement in commercial and industrial affairs. Japan's economic malaise is an extreme case of a common international phenomenon. In the past two decades many industrialized countries have experienced economic bubbles characterized by excess money supply, asset values, bank loans and production. The remedy is typically a recession. Lack of leadership and poor policy decisions in Japan have prolonged this.

When an economy is changing, property markets tend to change with it. Since Japan's companies and wealthy individuals have invested heavily in property, property markets should be at the centre of the country's restructuring plans. For many distressed, highly geared companies, property has therefore become a non-core business that can be sold relatively quickly to improve their financial health. Investors should see a massive sale of attractive assets at distressed prices. Economic growth will in turn increase the value of these assets, marking a structural recovery.

In short, as an economy goes up, property values follow. Similarly, as one market slows down, another opens up. Investing early in the cycle entails more risk but higher returns. From this simple analysis, investors should consider selling or refinancing in the US, investing in Europe and examining distressed sales in Japan.

Changing skills

Historically, high-return property investing has involved good financial timing. Investors traditionally made profits by identifying, pricing and underwriting undervalued assets. The important skills for this approach were quantitative analysis, financial engineering and property-specific skills that could be exploited after the investment had been made.

Recently, as property markets have become more global, investors have begun to use a strategic investment approach that targets businesses that service, develop or occupy buildings. Property is at once a local and a global business. This makes investing in foreign markets challenging. Given the local nature of property-specific skills and the difficulty of investing from abroad, investors are forming partnerships with local operators.

Although traditional assets and quantitative analysis are the foundation of good property investing, the strategic property investor will use macroeconomic analysis, incentive-based operating structures and long-term business plans to create value. For instance, a single hotel asset might be a profitable investment, but a well-managed hotel business involving several assets is likely to generate more value. An example is the French extended-stay hotel chain Citadines. Created by the merger of two portfolios, Citadines successfully sold its resort properties, rebranded its city-centre assets, brought in sophisticated yield management systems and launched a pan-European expansion programme. Today it is by far Europe's largest and most successful extended-stay hotel business.

Similarly, offices can be fruitful as stand-alone investments, but when investors also take on facilities management and outsourcing, returns are likely to multiply. Mapeley and Trillium, two UK property outsourcing companies, are good examples of market leaders in a rapidly growing industry. They control or have under contract the management of about 100m square feet, all of which they acquired between 1998 and 2001.

Strategic property investing emphasizes good timing, scalable business planning and strong leadership. Good timing means investing where economic, demographic, social, technological or political changes create a favourable environment. Scalable investments are those in which the business can grow through acquisitions, mergers or development. Strong leadership refers to the need for talented local managers with industry expertise to identify and exploit competitive advantages.

To achieve the best results, the interests of all parties must be aligned. As the definition and geographic scope of property expands, economic analysis, strategy and managerial skills become as important as location and physical attributes.

Property is a complex global asset class that plays a strong role in a balanced investment portfolio. As investors demand more sophisticated business plans and target more complex investments around the globe, property will generate returns that are consistently competitive with other asset classes. Perhaps property will then shake off its image as the least "interesting" asset class.

Copyright © Richard Georgi 2002

Further reading

Bellinger, R.B. and Lemkin, J.K. (2001) "The case for property in an investment portfolio", Lend Lease.

Real Estate & Portfolio Research (2001) "Why real estate? An investment rationale for institutional investors", *Real Estate/Portfolio Strategist*, 5, 4 April.

Valuation and returns 2

Contents

A model weighting game in estimating expected returns 60

L'uboš Pástor, University of Chicago Graduate School of Business

The estimation of expected returns is vital for money managers and corporate finance professionals. This article sets out some common approaches from asset pricing theory and assesses their effectiveness.

Insights from portfolio theory 67

Raman Uppal, London Business School

This article charts the history of investment theory, identifying its most important contributors and explaining its fundamental concepts.

Valuing old and new companies 75

Oren Fürst, Columbia Business School and **Nahum Melumad**, Columbia Business School

Valuation is one of the biggest challenges investors face. However, different models of valuation abound and none is perfect. Here, the most common techniques and their pitfalls are discussed.

Valuing companies: simulations, options and partnerships 83

Oren Fürst, Columbia Business School and **Nahum Melumad**, Columbia Business School

Financial tools called simulations can help investors assess the variability of important factors needed to gauge a company's worth.

Intangibles: not seen but must be heard 89

Chris Higson, London Business School

Intangible assets such as brands are not recorded in the balance sheet, yet their effect on a company's share price can be formidable.

Introduction to Part 2

Valuation is a central skill for the serious investor – it enables future returns to be estimated and different assets to be compared with each other. In this part writers discuss the methods of valuation available to investors and highlight any adjustments that need to be made for particular classes of asset. Other parts examine the equity premium and ask whether it is reasonable to assume that stocks will continue to give a more attractive return than bonds in future.

A model weighting game
in estimating expected returns

L'uboš Pástor is an assistant professor of finance at the University of Chicago Graduate School of Business.

In spite of their importance, there is no absolute agreement on how expected returns should be estimated. **L'uboš Pástor** examines the options and finds judgement plays a part.

Overstating the importance of expected returns in investments is difficult. For money managers, expected returns on assets are important inputs to portfolio decisions. For corporate managers, the expected return on their company's stock is central to the company's cost of capital and thereby affects which projects the company decides to undertake.

Expected return estimates also affect consumers. Charges set by utility companies are set to ensure the utility earns a "fair rate of return", defined by regulators as the utility's cost of capital. Our energy bills partly depend on how regulators estimate expected returns on utility stocks.

Unfortunately, expected returns are elusive as well as important. Finance professionals differ on how they should be estimated. This article compares the relative merits of common approaches to this challenging task and argues that the best estimates are produced by combining theory with historical returns data and judgement.

Looking to history

"I know of no way of judging the future but by the past," said American revolutionary Patrick Henry. One simple estimator of an asset's expected return is a sample average of its historical returns. Unless we suspect that expected return changes in a non-trivial way over time, the sample average return is an unbiased estimator of expected future return – that is, it is not systematically higher or lower than the true expected value. The unbiased nature of this method is its main advantage.

However, getting things right on average is not the only objective. You might have overheard a joke about three econometricians who went hunting and came across a deer. The first one fired a shot and missed by 10 metres to the left. The second one missed by 10 metres to the right. Instead of firing, the third one shouted in triumph: "We got it!"

The main disadvantage of the sample average is its imprecision. Suppose we want to estimate expected return on the stock of General Motors (GM), traded on the New York Stock Exchange. Using monthly returns from January 1991 to December 2000, the sample average return on GM is 14 per cent a year. The standard error, the usual statistical measure of imprecision, is huge: 10 per cent a year. With 95 per cent confidence, the true expected return is within two standard errors of the sample average, or between –6 per cent and 34 per cent a year. We want to be more confident than that!

Would the precision increase if we used weekly instead of monthly data? No. Although higher-frequency data helps in estimating variances and covariances of returns, it does not help in estimating expected returns. Intuitively, what matters for expected return are the beginning and ending prices over a given period, not what happens in between. The only way to get a more precise average is to collect more data. For example, if we use GM returns back to December 1925, the historical average is 15.5 per cent and the 95 per cent confidence interval narrows to between 8.7 per cent and 22.3 per cent. However, the gap is still too wide. Moreover, GM today is very different from 70 years ago, so the estimate could be contaminated by old data. In general, as we add older data, we gain precision at the expense of introducing potential bias. Striking a balance is difficult and needs sound judgement.

Despite its drawbacks, the long-run average return is a popular estimator for expected returns on aggregate market indices. Unfortunately, we have no theory for what the expected market return should be. Luckily, for individual stocks and most portfolios, we can rely on estimates produced by theoretical asset pricing models. Those estimates tend to be substantially more precise than sample averages.

Theory is good

Finance theory says riskier assets must offer higher expected returns and asset pricing models quantify this. The capital asset pricing model says a stock is riskier the more closely its price moves with prices in the market as a whole. The appropriate measure of risk is therefore the degree of a stock's co-movement with the market, which is summarized by a measure called beta (B). Expected return, E(r), on a given stock is linearly related to the stock's beta. Specifically, the expected stock return in excess of the risk-free rate rf ("expected excess return") can be expressed using:

$$E(r) - rf = B \cdot E(rm - rf)$$

The constant of proportionality, E(rm – rf), is the expected excess return on the market as a whole. It is often called the equity premium.

The value we choose for the risk-free rate rf depends on our objectives. To forecast expected stock returns over the next month, the appropriate risk-free rate is the yield to maturity on a Treasury bill that matures in one month. If we want to estimate a company's cost of capital to value the company's future cash flows, the risk-free rate should be derived from a longer-term Treasury bond. The bond's duration should be close to the duration of the company's cash flows. Very long-term bonds should be avoided, because their yields might also reflect premiums for risks such as inflation.

Does the above equation solve all our problems? Not quite. The elements on the right side, beta and the equity premium, need to be estimated. Beta is typically estimated by regressing monthly stock returns on market returns over the most recent 5–10 years. For example, the estimate of GM's beta using its monthly data from January 1996 to December 2000 is 1.11.

How much data should we use to estimate beta? The trade-off is similar to that involved for sample averages: the further we go back in time, the higher the statistical precision of the estimate, but the bigger the possibility of introducing bias from old data.

Unlike sample averages, however, here it often pays to use more frequent data. For example, whereas the 95 per cent confidence interval for GM's beta based on the monthly data is 0.65 to 1.57, this interval based on weekly data is tighter, 0.69 to 1.08. GM's beta estimated using weekly data is 0.88.

However, going from monthly to weekly data is recommended only for the most liquid and volatile stocks. For other stocks, some week-to-week price changes are simply movements between the bid and ask prices around the true price, which introduces additional error. Also, it may take time for market-wide news to affect the prices of illiquid stocks, which biases the usual beta estimates downward. Conveniently, betas of illiquid stocks can be estimated using an alternative approach developed by economists Myron Scholes and Joseph Williams.

It is clear from the GM example that estimates of beta contain a fair amount of noise. A useful way of reducing that noise is to "shrink" the usual estimates to a reasonable value, such as 1. This is reasonable because the average beta across all stocks is 1, by construction. The "shrinkage" estimate of beta is the weighted average of the usual sample estimate and of the shrinkage target. For example, the "adjusted" betas reported by Merrill Lynch put a 2/3 weight on the sample estimate and a 1/3 weight on the value of 1. The adjusted beta for GM is therefore:

$$(2/3) \cdot 0.88 + (1/3) \cdot 1 = 0.92$$

Shrinkage betas can be justified as "Bayesian" estimators, named after the 18th-century English mathematician Thomas Bayes. They reflect not only data but also prior knowledge or judgement. Bayesian estimators have solid axiomatic foundations in statistics and decision theory, unlike many other estimators used by statisticians.

Before seeing data on GM, we know it is a stock, so a good prior guess for GM's beta is 1. Also, we know more about the company; for example, we know which industry it operates in. Since the average beta among carmakers is about 1.2, a reasonable prior guess for GM's beta is 1.2.

How much weight we put on the guess and how much on the estimate depends on the precision of the sample estimate and on the strength of our prior beliefs. Those beliefs can be based for example on the dispersion of betas among carmakers: the stronger the concentration around 1.2, the more weight we put on the prior guess. With equal weights on the prior guess and the weekly sample estimate, GM's industry-adjusted beta is:

$$(1/2) \cdot 0.88 + (1/2) \cdot 1.2 = 1.04$$

Unfortunately, the CAPM says nothing about expected market return and estimating the equity premium is more difficult than estimating betas. More frequent data do not help and there is no obvious prior guess. The most common approach is to average a long series of excess market returns, which leads to equity premium estimates of 5–9 per cent a year, depending on the sample period.

A 2001 equity premium study by Robert Stambaugh and the author puts the current premium in the US at 4.8 per cent a year. This estimate comes from a model in which the premium changes over the past 165 years. Combining this estimate with GM's industry-adjusted beta and a 6 per cent risk-free rate, the CAPM estimates GM's annual expected return (its cost of equity capital) at 6 per cent plus (1.04 · 4.8 per cent), which comes out at 11 per cent.

Imperfect models

The CAPM is just a model, not a perfect description of reality. Indeed, many academic studies reject its validity because some stock return patterns seem inconsistent with the model. Does this mean we should throw the model away and rely only on model-free estimators, such as the sample average return? No! Every model is "wrong", almost by definition, because it makes simplifying assumptions about our complex world. But even a model that is not exact can be useful.

It is again helpful to adopt a Bayesian perspective and combine what the data tell us with our best prior guess. While the data speak to us about expected return through the sample average return (14 per cent a year for GM), our prior guess can be based on finance theory such as the CAPM (11 per cent a year for GM). The resulting estimate is a weighted average of the two numbers. The weights depend on how strongly we believe in the model and on how well the model compares with the data.

This Bayesian approach is developed in another study by Robert Stambaugh and the author (1999). The study finds that even if we have only modest confidence in a pricing model such as the CAPM, our cost of capital estimates should be heavily weighted towards the model. Average stock returns are noisy, so they should receive small weights. In other words, theory is more powerful than data when estimating expected stock returns.

To make the water muddier, the CAPM is not the only theoretical model of expected returns. Competition comes from multi-factor models, in which expected return depends on the stock's betas with respect to more factors than just the market. The factors can be either macroeconomic variables (for example, a five-factor model developed by Nai-fu Chen, Richard Roll and Stephen Ross) or portfolios formed based on companies' characteristics (for example, a three-factor model of Eugene Fama and Ken French) or even return series constructed using statistical techniques such as factor analysis.

Opinions vary on which model is best and the jury is still out. Meanwhile, what are we to do? A sensible solution is to construct a weighted average of expected return estimates from all models that we are willing to consider, including the "no-theory" model that produces the sample average estimate. Each estimate should be weighted by the probability that its parent model is correct.

Where do we get these probabilities? It helps to be aware of the relevant research, but in the end this is a matter of judgement. The author believes that, despite its weaknesses, the CAPM has the strongest theoretical foundation and should receive the largest weight. Other models should be weighted according to their theoretical support and empirical success.

Uncertainty

Although pricing models generally produce expected return estimates that are significantly more precise than sample averages, uncertainty remains. Research by Fama and French shows standard errors of more than 3 per cent a year are typical for estimates of industry costs of equity based on common pricing models. Where does the uncertainty come from? Is it more important that we do not know the true beta, the exact value of the equity premium, or that we do not know the right model?

Interestingly, not knowing which model is right turns out to be less important on average than not knowing the parameters within each model. That is one conclusion from the author's 1999 study. We should therefore spend less time searching for the right model and more time trying to improve estimates within each model. In addition, uncertainty about the premium is bigger than uncertainty about betas, which makes the intangible equity premium the biggest source of uncertainty in the companies' cost of capital estimates.

As popular as they are, asset pricing models are not the only option for estimating the cost of capital. Another approach that is often used for regulated utilities in the US is based on the Gordon growth model, described by M.J. Gordon in 1962. This gives the cost of equity as equal to the sum of the current dividend yield and the long-term dividend growth rate. This approach is generally favoured less by academics, for several reasons. It makes the strong assumption that dividends will grow for ever at the same rate. Besides, there is no theory to help us estimate the dividend growth rate, which is unfortunate because the cost of equity estimate is very sensitive to that rate. This approach therefore strongly reflects opinions about a company's prospects.

A moving target

There is an emerging consensus in academia that expected returns vary over time. For example, expected stock returns seem to be related to the business cycle – they tend to be higher in recessions and lower in expansions.

Among the variables that have been found useful in explaining the time-variation in expected stock market returns are the aggregate dividend-price ratio (D/P) and earnings-price ratio (E/P). Low values of these ratios have historically predicted low returns. In other words, when prices are high relative to the fundamentals, future returns are on average low, especially at longer horizons such as 10 years ahead.

The predictive power of the D/P and E/P ratios was reinforced in 2000 when the Standard & Poor's 500 index lost 10 per cent of its value while the ratios were at their historical lows. However, these predictors worked poorly in the 1990s, when low D/P and E/P peacefully co-existed with high stock market returns.

"If you torture the data long enough, Nature will confess," said the Nobel prize-winning economist Ronald Coase. If you search enough variables, you will find a variable that appears to predict returns. However, this apparent predictability exists by chance and such "data-mined" variables will not work in the future. An interesting example of data mining was provided in an article by Peter Coy (1997), who quoted David Leinweber, managing director of First Quadrant, a money-management company. Leinweber "sifted through a United Nations CD-Rom and discovered that historically, the best predictor of the S&P 500 was butter production in Bangladesh". Good luck if you try to make money on this – you'll need it.

Fortunately, economists have come up with reasons for D/P and E/P having predictive power. Difficult questions remain, though. Is the predictive relation linear? What is the best way to estimate the unknown parameters of this relation? What other predictors should we include?

If it is hard to estimate expected returns when they are constant, it is even harder when they change with time. There is no simple recipe for estimating expected returns. Since data are noisy and no theory is flawless, judgement enters the process at several points. There is nothing wrong with that. After all, economic theories themselves ultimately reflect our judgement about how the world behaves.

Given the importance of expected returns and the huge uncertainty associated with them, the finance profession clearly needs to invest more in their estimation. Such an investment will undoubtedly provide a high expected return. But please don't ask me for an exact number.

Copyright © Ľuboš Pástor 2002

Further reading

Chen, N., Roll, R. and Ross, S. (1986) "Economic forces and the stock market", *Journal of Business*, 59, 383–403.

Coy, P. (1997) "He who mines data may strike fool's gold", *Business Week*, 16 June.

Fama, E.F. and French, K.R. (1997) "Industry costs of equity", *Journal of Financial Economics*, 43, 153–93.

Pástor, L. and Stambaugh, R.F. (1999) "Costs of equity capital and model mispricing", *Journal of Finance*, 54, 67–121.

Pástor, L. and Stambaugh, R.F. (2001) "The equity premium and structural breaks", *Journal of Finance*, August.

Scholes, M. and Williams, J. (1977) "Estimating betas from nonsynchronous data", *Journal of Financial Economics*, 5, 309–27.

Insights from portfolio theory

Potential investors face several fundamental questions in building an optimal mix of stocks. **Raman Uppal** outlines the theories available to answer them.

Raman Uppal is an associate professor of finance at London Business School.

This article addresses some of the fundamental questions facing investors. How should they evaluate stocks? Should evaluation be based only on expected return or also on the riskiness of the stock? How is the risk of a particular stock or a portfolio of stocks measured? How can a portfolio be designed that is optimal over a particular period of investment, that is, one that gives the best trade-off between risk and expected return? How is this portfolio different from one that is optimal when there are several trading opportunities over the investment horizon? In answering these questions, some of the main insights of portfolio theory are explained and their relation to managing investments described.

Return and risk

It has long been recognized that most investors dislike risk, yet until 1952 the connection between the risk and return of individual stocks had not been studied seriously, and the relation between the risk and return of a portfolio had not been considered at all. Economist John Maynard Keynes, an astute individual by any standards, viewed the best investment strategy as one where you put all your money in the few stocks about which you felt favourably, without any regard to diversification. Thus, if you were favourably disposed towards rail companies, your entire portfolio should be invested in their stock.

In 1952, however, academic Harry Markowitz published an article on this subject that was to win him a Nobel prize. He said it was not enough to look at the expected return from a particular stock. Instead, an investor should also consider the risk of this stock. Moreover, by investing in more than one stock, an investor could

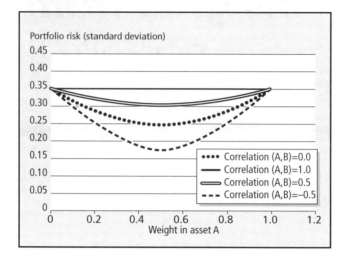

FIGURE 1 — Gains from diversifying across two risky assets

reap the benefits of diversification that lead to a reduction in the riskiness of the portfolio. Gains from diversification come from the fact that the returns on different stocks do not move in the same way all the time (unless they are all from the same industry or sector). In academic parlance, as long as the correlation of the stocks is not 1, diversification will reduce risk.

Figure 1 shows the effect of diversification in reducing the risk of a portfolio consisting of two stocks with the same standard deviation (in this case, 35 per cent or 0.35) but with different degrees of correlation. The risk of the portfolio is shown as a function of investment in the first asset. When the proportion of total wealth that is invested in asset A is zero, the portfolio volatility is the same as the volatility of asset B, which is 35 per cent. However, as investment in asset A is increased, the volatility of the portfolio drops, until a minimum is attained when equal amounts are invested in both assets. In short, the volatility of the portfolio return is less than the volatility of returns from each individual asset. The size of the gain from diversification depends on how low the correlation is between the assets: the less they co-vary with each other, the more risk is reduced.

The important insight here is that the risk for individual asset returns has two components. The first is systematic risk, which is the market risk and cannot be diversified. Second, there are non-systematic risks, which are specific to individual assets that get diversified away as one increases the number of assets in the portfolio, as shown in Figure 2. For a well-diversified portfolio, the volatility of each asset contributes little to portfolio risk and it is the correlation between assets that determines portfolio risk. Consequently, it is better for investors to hold diversified portfolios.

Now that we understand the gains from diversifying, the question arises of how to identify the best level of diversification, or the optimally diversified portfolio. Markowitz defined a portfolio as efficient if it maximized the expected return for a given level of risk. The set of all efficient portfolios is referred to as the Markowitz frontier. Figure 3 shows the portfolio frontier for

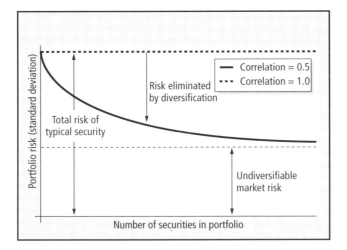

FIGURE 2 Diversifying away unsystematic risk

just two stocks, IBM and Merck, with monthly returns and correlations given by Table 1.

Any portfolio which lies on the upper part of the curve representing the frontier is efficient – it gives the maximum expected return for a given level of risk. Further, Figure 4 plots the efficient frontier for different hypothetical values of correlation between IBM and Merck. It shows that as correlation between stocks falls from the maximum of +1 towards the minimum of –1, the upper part of the frontier curve moves in a north-westerly direction. Investors prefer this, because risk decreases and expected return increases in this direction.

TABLE 1 Mean return and correlation (%)

	IBM	Merck
Mean return	1.49	1.00
Correlation of IBM with ...	100.00	39.68
Correlation of Merck with ...	39.68	100.00

The portfolio frontier of risky assets can be found by solving a non-linear optimization problem. Depending on how much risk an investor is willing to bear, a portfolio should be chosen on the efficient frontier with the appropriate level of risk. The main limitation of this approach to identifying the optimal portfolio is that we need to know the correlations between all risky assets, and for each investor (or for each level of risk) we have to solve a new optimization problem.

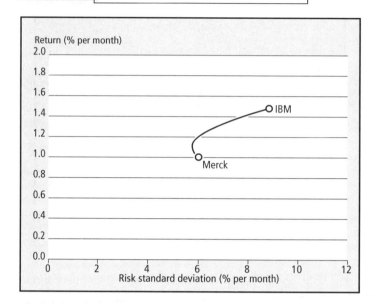

FIGURE 3 — Portfolio frontier with two risky assets

Tobin and CAPM

Academic and Nobel prize winner James Tobin resolved this limitation in 1958. He showed that if investors could invest in a risk-free asset in addition to risky stocks, the frontier portfolios are combinations of a risk-free asset (such as a bank account) and a portfolio of only risky assets. The efficient frontier in this case is a straight line. And, as shown in Figure 5, every investor would like to choose a portfolio on the line going through the tangency portfolio, T, rather than through another point, say q, because the portfolios on the line-segment through T offer more return for the same risk than portfolios on the line through q.

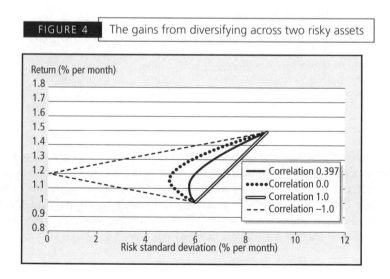

FIGURE 4 — The gains from diversifying across two risky assets

| FIGURE 5 | Efficient portfolios with a risk-free asset and many risky assets |

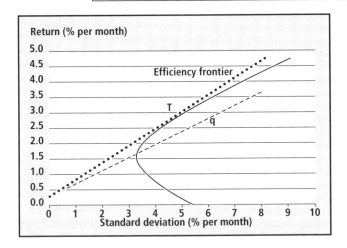

Consequently, every investor's portfolio can be constructed by investing in only two portfolios: the riskless asset and the portfolio T, consisting only of risky assets. Because the only portfolio of risky assets that is held by any investor is T, it implies that all investors hold risky assets in the same proportion – the proportion being that of the tangency portfolio. Thanks to the insight of Tobin, we have to identify only a single portfolio of risky assets, portfolio T.

The crucial question, then, is how to identify the constituents of portfolio T. First, we know that in equilibrium demand must equal supply. Second, the supply of all risky assets is the market portfolio, that is, when we consider the aggregate of all assets in the market, we get exactly the market portfolio. From these observations, it follows that the tangency portfolio demanded by investors is equal to aggregate supply of all risky assets, the market portfolio, denoted as M in Figure 6. The credit for this insight, and the implications for

| FIGURE 6 | The capital asset pricing model (CAPM) |

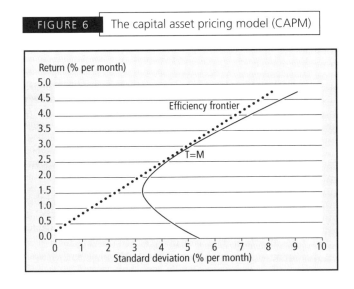

INSIGHTS FROM PORTFOLIO THEORY

stock returns, goes to William Sharpe, John Lintner, Jan Mossin and Jack Treynor.

In addition to identifying the tangency portfolio as the market portfolio, they also demonstrated the following point. The excess return on a risky asset, over and above the return on a riskless asset, must be equal to the beta of the asset times the risk premium on the market portfolio. (The beta of an asset is a measure of its co-movement with the market portfolio, relative to the total variability of the return on the market portfolio.) The result is often called the capital asset pricing model and provides the basis for measuring the expected returns for any company that is publicly quoted. Their analysis gives the following insights:

- The market portfolio is an efficient portfolio that lies on the Markowitz frontier; that is, the market portfolio must offer the highest possible expected return given the level of risk from holding this portfolio.
- Any combination of the market portfolio and the risk-free asset is a frontier portfolio.
- In equilibrium, the only portfolio of risky assets that investors hold is the market portfolio, since this is equal to the tangency portfolio.
- Since everybody holds the market portfolio, the risk of an individual asset is characterized by its correlation with respect to the market.
- The part of the risk that is correlated with the market portfolio, the systematic risk, cannot be diversified away; thus investors need to be compensated for bearing systematic risk.
- The part of an asset's risk that is not correlated with the market portfolio, the unsystematic risk, can be diversified away by holding a frontier portfolio; thus, bearing unsystematic risk need not be rewarded, and therefore, an asset's unsystematic risk does not affect its risk premium.
- In equilibrium, the tangency portfolio is the same as the market portfolio. Thus, investing in a riskless asset and the market portfolio is an efficient portfolio strategy.

Dynamic portfolio

The above story is about finding a portfolio that is optimal over a single investment period. However, the riskless rate as well as the expected return and riskiness of stocks change over time; thus, the efficiency frontier will change over time. Consequently, investors will want to trade and revise their portfolio in response to changes in investment opportunities. How should investors choose an initial portfolio so it is optimal not just over one period but over the investor's entire investment horizon? In academic terms, how can one determine a portfolio that is dynamically optimal?

This problem was solved by academic Robert Merton, again a Nobel prize winner, in two articles published in 1971 and 1973. He showed how it was possible to extend the CAPM to settings involving many different factors and over different periods of time. His main insight was that the portfolio chosen at the initial date must not only lie on the efficient frontier but must also provide the best hedge against future changes in the set of investment opportunities.

Conclusion

We can summarize the main results of modern portfolio theory as follows:

- Diversification reduces risk.
- Variances of individual assets contribute little to portfolio risk.
- Correlations between assets determine the risk of a portfolio.
- Investors hold frontier portfolios; a large asset base improves the portfolio frontier.
- With a risk-free asset, frontier portfolios are linear combinations of the risk-free asset and tangency portfolio.
- In equilibrium, the tangency portfolio equals the market portfolio.

Over several different investment periods, the optimal portfolio has two components: one that is optimal for a single-period investor and lies on the efficient frontier, and the second that provides the best hedge against future changes in the efficiency frontier.

To keep this article short and simple, several issues relevant to portfolio optimization have not been discussed. Most important of these is how to estimate the expected return and correlations upon which the entire optimization exercise relies, and how to account for the fact that one can estimate the risk and return only with a certain amount of error. Other issues relate to market frictions. For instance, how can one account for transactions costs and taxes when choosing the optimal portfolio? These questions are the focus of research.

The insights from modern portfolio theory underlie the investment strategies of individuals and financial institutions. The gains from diversification motivate investors and mutual funds to hold a broad range of equities rather than just a few stocks. Index funds, which track the market portfolio, are designed to make it convenient for investors to invest in a large number of equities. The understanding that it is the systematic rather than the unsystematic risk of a security that matters, and that systematic risk is measured by the correlation of the security with the market, leads to the beta measure. This is widely used to determine the return a stock must offer investors. Finally, the extension of the portfolio model to account for investment over more than one trading horizon is now being used to design dynamic portfolio strategies.

Copyright © Raman Uppal 2002

Further reading

Bernstein, P.L. (1993) *Capital Ideas: The Improbable Origins of Modern Wall Street*, New York: Free Press.

Markowitz, H.M. (1952) "Portfolio selection", *Journal of Finance*, 7, 1, 77–91.

Merton, R.C. (1971) "Optimum consumption and portfolio rules in a continuous-time model", *Journal of Economic Theory*, 3, December.

Merton, R.C. (1973) "An intertemporal capital asset pricing model", *Econometrica*, 41, September.

Sharpe, W.F. (1964) "Capital asset prices: A theory of market equilibrium under conditions of risk", *Journal of Finance*, 19, 425–42.

Tobin, J. (1958) "Liquidity preference as behavior toward risk", *Review of Economic Studies*, February, 67, 65–86.

Valuing old
and new companies

There are many ways of valuing businesses. **Oren Fürst** and **Nahum Melumad** assess them and show how to adapt them for technology companies.

Oren Fürst is the co-director of the Technology Valuation Executive Program at Columbia Business School and Managing Director of Strategic Models LLC.

Nahum Melumad is the James L. Dohr Professor of Accounting, co-director of the Technology Valuation Executive Program and chairman of the accounting division at Columbia Business School.

Legendary investor Warren Buffett told shareholders of Berkshire Hathaway that his method of valuing assets is based on the saying "a bird in the hand is worth two in the bush". As Buffett suggests: "To flesh out this principle, you must answer only three questions. How certain are you that there are indeed birds in the bush? When will they emerge and how many will there be? What is the risk-free interest rate? ... If you can answer these three questions, you will know the maximum value of the bush and the maximum number of the birds you now possess that should be offered for it. And, of course, don't literally think birds. Think dollars."

The "bird in the bush" theorem does indeed identify an underlying theme in valuation. In applying this piece of wisdom, however, investors face a variety of models and methods, used by different investors for different types of companies. In this and the next article, while some economic principles and valuation models are applicable to all companies, the relevance of certain characteristics in these models differs significantly for various types of companies. In this article we focus on the general valuation framework.

Some investors, such as Buffett himself, shy away from attempting to value companies that do not have a long track record or that operate in industries the investors do not feel comfortable in evaluating. While investors are strongly advised not to invest in companies they do not feel able to evaluate themselves (even with the help of professionals), lack of past performance or uncertainty about the future should not by themselves deter investments. The tools we discuss allow you to judge for yourself whether the risks of an investment are offset by the potential rewards.

Components of valuation

Any valuation has to include a thorough analysis of a company's business model. Such an analysis should lead to an understanding of the interactions among the components of the business model. These include the direct and indirect effect (through interactions) of such factors as technology, the pricing model, the management team, the company's intellectual property and its production and service costs.

The authors' framework for such an analysis is called the 8-Factor Business Model Analysis™. It focuses on the ability of a company to maximize its value by combining the components of its business model, thereby optimizing its competitive position, and its ability to retain a high level of profitability or attractiveness to strategic buyers. Only after such an analysis can a valuation take place. Further, understanding a company's lifecycle has a dramatic effect, in particular when valuing technology companies. As we shall see, it allows investors to forecast net cash flows, estimate their value and judge the relative importance of the various options to which companies have access.

Multiple-based methods

One of the most common methods of valuing companies is the multiples method. This identifies a set of companies that are comparable on various dimensions, such as area of operation, maturity and size. It looks at the set of appropriate variables for comparison and then compares the ratios of market valuation to these variables. The ratios are then applied to the parameter values of a specified company.

Historically, the most commonly cited ratio is the earnings multiple (P/E),

FIGURE 1   8-Factor Business Model Analysis™ diagram

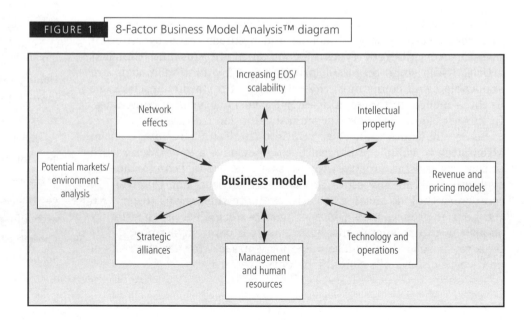

expressed as the market price per share divided by the earnings per share (price/earnings or P/E). Recently, other multiples have become popular, such as the revenue multiple, possibly as a result of lack of meaningful earnings.

It is important to understand that valuation based on multiples is meaningless if the variables used for comparison do not reflect the ability of a company to create value for its shareholders. Analysis based on multiples typically relies on the peer group's current results and forecasts made by market participants (such as equity research analysts). In market sectors that have little history, selecting appropriate parameters is difficult and market participants tend to change their perspectives on such multiples. As a result, many investors use parameters that seem to explain the market valuation of other companies in the sector, sometimes disregarding their economic link to future profitability.

In most cases, therefore, we do not prescribe multiples as a central mechanism for valuation. Regardless of the explanatory power of a multiple for pricing at a specific time, unless the multiples are logically and economically related to future profitability of the company or to the way potential buyers of a company value it, they are meaningless. History shows that periods of incorrect valuation can last for a long time and lead to opportunistic behaviour by companies. For example, in many industries, companies are valued by future revenue multiples (for example, in the construction industry). That may give companies incentives to sign money-losing contracts before trying to raise capital, even at the expense of future profits.

When looking for companies to provide a comparison, the selection process is crucial. Leading companies in an industry may receive a premium in the marketplace, reflecting the premium pricing they can charge or the increased profitability (due to economies of scale) they may achieve. In addition, the financial leverage and equity risk differences (associated with factors such as the companies' cost structure) could explain differences in multiples. Similarly, multiples should be used carefully when comparing companies in different environments. For example, during the wave of listing of internet service providers and privatized telecommunications companies, many analysts' reports compared companies from different countries based on their market value per subscriber across countries. This did not always take full account of differences in growth rates, costs of providing services and the ability to price services across countries.

In most cases multiples should be based directly on profitability. This can be measured as the ratio of enterprise value (that is, the market value of equity plus debt) to EBIT (earnings before interest and income taxes) and price to earnings per share; or operations, such as price to sales, whether these ratios are based on current or forecast values. Others may need to be used, typically where the industries concerned have not shown meaningful reported profitability because of their early stage of development. Investment can adversely affect reported profitability, as well as a lack of meaningful revenue (in which case measures based on revenue are also meaningless).

However, investors should be wary of measures that do not refer to the cost of obtaining future profitability, for example, ratios based on simple EBITDA (earnings before interest, income taxes, depreciation and amortization).

Multiples that incorporate the cost of the capital and the required capital expenditures are useful in this context (see below). Such adjusted mechanisms, which are based on current and forward-looking adjusted income measures, are applicable in most situations involving publicly traded and private companies. However, these measures are not always adequate by themselves in very early-stage industries, where revenue is scarce, and should be used with other tools.

Supplementary information on financial stability and the prospects of a company can be derived from balance sheet multiples, such as enterprise value to total assets or equity market value to equity (market to book ratio). These ratios are highly relevant in mature industries. However, in growth industries relying on intellectual property, they may distort analysis unless the asset base (or equity) is adjusted for the pitfalls of some accounting rules. For example, the value of intangible assets (which may have been written off) may make these ratios seem out of context.

Forecasted earnings-based methods

Perhaps the most common valuation technique is the free cash flows method. The starting point is based on forecasting the company's free cash flows available for shareholders (or to all its capital providers). These include earnings, adjusted for expenses and income that are not in cash (for example depreciation) and adjusted for required investments and changes in working capital. The series of forecast free cash flows is then brought to current values by discounting it using the company's cost of equity (or overall cost of capital).

A conceptually equivalent method is based on forecasting the company's excess earnings (essentially, net income after charging for the cost of capital used to achieve it). Similar to the free cash flow method, the series of forecast excess earnings is then brought to current values by discounting it using the company's cost of equity. Here, investors use the intuition that a company is creating wealth only if it provides earnings that reward capital providers for the risks they take. The method, the origins of which can be traced back a century, is becoming widely used in academia, as well as in business circles, and appears, in different forms, under such names as Economic Value Added (EVA), Super Profits and Abnormal Earnings.

We have developed our own version of the method, the adjusted residual income (ARI) model. The method works well in most situations and can help in particular with technology-related companies, as well as with other companies that have significant components of intangible assets. It incorporates available information reported by the company and market participants, as well as the characteristics of companies in their early years of development. The amount of income, after a charge for the cost of capital, reflects the net value created for shareholders during the period (if the measurement is based on adjusted income available to shareholders) or the value created for all capital providers (when the measure is based on adjusted operating income).

The starting point for this calculation is adjusted net income. The adjustments are mainly related to items that were included in the financial reports (or excluded) in a manner inconsistent with their underlying economics. For companies that rely on intellectual property, one of the main components is the adjustment for research and development investment. Under current accounting rules, this item is typically charged in the year incurred. Because R&D greatly affects future profitability, it should be treated for valuation purposes as an asset whose value depreciates with time, based on analysis of the company and the characteristics of its industry. Investors should therefore determine the expected life of these assets by measuring the effectiveness (in short, productivity and profitability changes) of R&D in that industry or similar industries. In many industries, R&D assets tend to have a life of three to five years. Naturally, the process affects income figures, as well as the balance sheet.

Over the long run, any capitalization and depreciation scheme should yield the same valuation, provided long-term assumptions are properly adjusted. However, most analysis, and in particular multiple and ratio analysis, is focused on the first few years of forecasts. For these years, in which the company may experience rapid growth, the impact of capitalization could be enormous.

To illustrate, consider a company in which R&D assets have a life of five years. Assume the company's starting revenue is £1,000, revenue grows at 20 per cent a year, the gross profit margin is 30 per cent and R&D investments are 15 per cent of sales. Ignore taxes and other expenses. The company is funded fully by equity with an initial value of £5,000.

The equity for any period is the sum of the previous year's equity and this year's net earnings (assuming no dividends are paid and no new capital is issued). Figure 2 compares the ratios of net income to equity, called return on equity (RoE), and the adjusted RoE, which incorporates the revised mechanism of capitalizing R&D. The R&D charge is the amortized R&D asset less the capitalized R&D for any year. In the early years, the net R&D charge has a large effect on net income (the numerator in the RoE ratio), while the R&D asset (part of the denominator in the ratio) has a higher impact in the later years. As a result, the adjusted RoE is significantly higher than RoE in

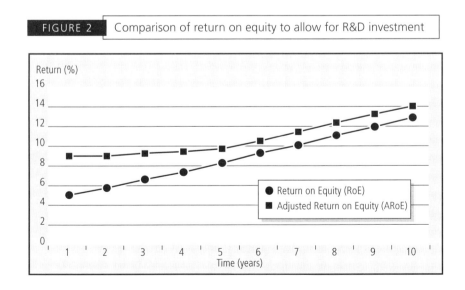

FIGURE 2 Comparison of return on equity to allow for R&D investment

the early years. However, as the company matures, the difference reduces as the net R&D gets closer to zero (that is, the amortization of the R&D asset becomes similar to the capitalization of the year's R&D). Naturally, this pattern depends on parameters such as the growth rate and R&D intensity (typically measured by industry ratios such as R&D to revenue or R&D to other expenses).

The next step in deriving the ARI is to charge for the use of capital, based on the company's cost of equity multiplied by the adjusted equity (or the weighted cost of capital, if the measures are based on net operating income and, correspondingly, the total adjusted asset base). This measure gives a series of forecasts that can be discounted to current values. The sum is then added to the current equity (or total asset) base, to yield the valuation. The adjusted residual income measure can also be used for several analyses, for example, by comparing the ratios of market value to adjusted residual income, or adjusted capital, as in the above example.

Is ARI different from methods involving free cash flows? Not conceptually. Both approaches come from the same formula that states that a company's value equals the sum of its discounted expected dividends and should yield the same results. However, in practice, there will often be differences in the results of these models. These have to do with the implementation effects of the models: the information required for estimation, the forecasting period chosen, and the company's managerial discretion over the forecasted items.

Forecasting period

A full valuation model would require a forecast made of every income flow and balance sheet item in perpetuity. Clearly this is impractical, so the valuation process is split into two components. The first component reflects the value of the company over the forecasting period. For that period, we derive the stream of annual residual income, or free cash flows, based on detailed forecasting of revenue and expense items, as well as the balance sheet items. The second component is analyzed by assuming some permanent (or decaying) growth rate of the forecast item (that is, residual income or free cash flow) in the last detailed forecast year and capitalizing this item. Alternatively, an expected multiple is assumed for the main estimated parameter.

For example, a P/E multiple may be applied to the forecast net income at that period. This would be based on the anticipated prevailing multiple at that point for similar companies, taking account of the company's expected ability to grow and maintain its competitive position over the long term. Note that while it is normal to have positive growth rates for other forecast parameters such as earnings, after the proper adjustments are made for the accounting numbers, it is rare to find companies that can retain an ability to obtain positive residual earnings for long periods of time. Therefore, investors should take care when determining growth rates beyond the forecasting horizon.

Naturally, the more value beyond that detailed forecasting period, the more the forecast is subject to estimation error. However, as the raw data for this second component (the terminal value) rely on detailed analysis of earlier periods, the longer and more accurate are the forecasts in these periods, the better the estimate will be for the second component and therefore the entire valuation.

The discount rate

To bring the series of free cash flows (or residual income) to current value, we need to determine the proper interest rate for discounting them. This cost is the rate of return investors require for investment in a project with similar risk characteristics. That should be the cost of equity (if we forecast the series of streams for equity holders) or the weighted average cost of capital (if we forecast the series for entire capital providers).

There are many ways of estimating the cost of equity. However, it is typically derived using a combination of methods, taking account of the stage of development of the company, the industry in which it operates and the stage of development of the industry. Perhaps the most common method is the Capital Asset Pricing Model. With CAPM, the cost of equity is the sum of the risk-free interest rate and the risk premium for the market portfolio, which is multiplied by the company's "beta". The beta reflects the relative sensitivity of the company stock return to market returns variability (and the risk premium is the required additional return for holding equity rather than risk-free assets such as government bonds).

The difficulty of estimating the equity risk premium has been debated at length. To illustrate the range of opinions, the average equity risk premium in the US over 60 years has been about 6 per cent. However, some analyses suggest the correct measure should be based on the expected risk premium, as measured at each point in time, rather than on the actual, realized value. Using the former method yields a value of about 3 per cent. Assuming a risk-free rate of 6 per cent, this means a difference of 50 per cent in the estimated cost of equity for the average US company.

In addition to issues of estimating the equity risk premium, the validity of the CAPM has been debated. Under other models, such as Arbitrage Pricing Theory, the cost of equity also considers the exposure of the company's stock returns to additional macroeconomic factors or company's characteristics.

Another delicate issue is the time-varying discount rate of companies, particularly in their early years of development or in the early stage of development in their industry. The sensitivity of companies to market conditions may change over time, not only because of changes in the environment but also because of the age of the company and its size in its industry. Altering the discount rate can have a dramatic effect, in particular for companies where most of their valuation stems from the distant future. Simulation tools can help (see the next article).

Conclusion

This article presents highlights of the commonly used methods of valuation. It also explains the principles of the ARI model, including some required adjustments to the balance sheet and income numbers. Though relevant for any company, these have special relevance for companies that rely heavily on intellectual property, many of them in the technology industry. The next article highlights the importance of real options in different stages of company and industry development, and discusses simulations and how they are used in valuation. It will also discuss the valuation impact of network effects, cost structure and strategic partners.

Copyright © Oren Fürst and Nahum Melumad 2002

Further reading

Fletham, G. and Ohlson, J. (1995) "Valuation and clean surplus accounting for operating and financial activities", *Contemporary Accounting Research*, Spring, 689–731.

Fürst, O. and Geiger, U. (2002) *From Concept to Wall Street*, FT-Prentice Hall.

Ohlson, J. (1995) "Earnings, book values and dividends in equity valuation", *Contemporary Accounting Research*, Spring, 661–87.

Penman, S.H. (2001) *Financial Statement Analysis and Security Valuation*, McGraw-Hill Higher Education.

Penman, S. and Sougiannis, T. (1995) "A comparison of dividend, cash flow, and earnings approaches to equity valuation", *Contemporary Accounting Research*, Spring, 661–87.

Valuing companies:
simulations, options and partnerships

In the previous article **Oren Fürst** and **Nahum Melumad** outlined common ways of valuing businesses. Here they consider additional tools and environmental factors.

Oren Fürst is the co-director of the Technology Valuation Executive Program at Columbia Business School and Managing Director of Strategic Models LLC.

Nahum Melumad is the James L. Dohr Professor of Accounting, co-director of the Technology Valuation Executive Program and chairman of the accounting division at Columbia Business School.

When valuing companies, investors face a challenge in choosing the parameter values to use in their forecasts, as they are forced to make assumptions about, say, the revenue growth rate or gross margin. Most tend to verify their forecasts by examining a few values for the main parameters. Scenario analysis is an established method for assessing the nature of strategic risks. It involves probing a company's structures and processes, and the wider market, and examining a range of possible futures in detail. It is particularly important for managers and investors in volatile markets, such as technology industries. However, although financial forecasting involves assumptions regarding the relations between parameters, investors typically do not consider the variability in these relations.

For example, if a company enhances its capital base, its customers may put more trust in its future success and increase its growth rate. However, that relation may differ for different levels of capital in different industries. Think of a software company providing outsourcing services for accounting systems. It is hard to believe that its customers would be willing to hand over vital data and account management systems if they were not confident of the company's future viability. Thus the operating growth rate of the company will depend on its financial stability.

However, even if the parameters in the valuation model incorporate relations with other parameters and scenario analysis is conducted, its results tend to be limited in volatile environments. In particular, simple scenario analysis does not incorporate random behaviour in the relationship between variables or information regarding the distributions of possible parameter values. For that, we need more sophisticated simulation tools.

Simulation is a powerful tool for gauging the impact of uncertainty on a company valuation.

How is a simulation carried out? Instead of assuming a few values for the main parameters of the model, investors can instead make assumptions about the distributions of outcomes of some of those parameters. For example, an analysis suggesting an expected sales growth of 5 per cent gives no indication that the likelihood of its being 7 per cent is greater than the likelihood of its being 10 per cent. Instead of examining numerous scenarios with a range of likely outcomes, simulations allow us to input our assumptions about the variability of the growth rate. In this case, sales growth may be given by a normal distribution with a mean of 5 per cent and standard deviation of 2 per cent.

In addition, simulation tools allow investors to incorporate uncertainty about the correlation between parameter values over time. For example, when the price of PCs declines, the price of computer servers also declines. However, the strength of this relation has a high degree of uncertainty associated with it. If we can calculate a level of correlation for it, we can incorporate this in our model and make assumptions about its degree of variability.

Simulations indicate parameter values based on assumptions of the parameters' distributions and correlations, and examine the results of our financial model for each of these draws. They give us a much clearer picture of the variability of the results and their sensitivity to uncertainty than simple scenario analysis can provide. Further, they can cause the ranking of companies and projects to change dramatically, thereby altering investment decisions.

Real options

Standard valuation methods do not allow information that arises later to be incorporated into the calculation. Suppose there is a company whose sole asset is its access to a project that costs £20 and can yield immediately either £30 or £10, depending on the environment at the time of investment. Using traditional methods, the net value of the project is either a profit of £10 or a loss of £10. Assuming the likelihood for both environments is similar, the expected value (the mean value of its outcomes) is zero. However, if the investment decision can be delayed until the environment is known, the valuation will change. Since the project option will not be taken up if the environment is adverse, the valuation will be positive. In other words, the value of the company is the value of an option to receive an asset worth £10 with a 50 per cent probability.

A company can be analyzed as a set of options, all of which reflect the flexibility to make a decision when new information arrives. The applicability of common methods for valuing financial options to options related to real projects is debatable. Investors typically should use tailored models with numerical estimates and simulations of various scenarios and parameters.

Certain options, such as the ability to use technology owned by a company for new purposes, could be even more valuable than the current activities of the company. Does this mean the company's current choice of activities is wrong? Of course not. For example, think of a company with patents covering the ability to connect home appliances to the internet. The first application the company chooses might be connecting refrigerators to the internet, to keep your local grocery store updated with your inventory of goods. This choice may have been driven by research showing interest in that application in the immediate future, as opposed to the much larger market that will materialize only a few years later. However, when we value such a company, the option to use the patents in other markets, based on developments in those markets and on the success in the test market, is potentially much more valuable than the original application.

Naturally, valuing a company includes valuation of many options and requires the use of elaborate models. The value of most options depends on the same parameters: the expected cash flows from the project, the required investment, the length of time to exercise the option, the uncertainty in the environment and the prevailing interest rate. In contrast to the static value of the underlying assets, which typically decline with higher uncertainty, the value of options increases with uncertainty.

However, when valuing companies with significant growth opportunities, such as technology companies, care is needed in evaluating options. While we need to be wary of broad claims regarding the generality of the products or processes, we should not dismiss such claims out of hand. An important difference between many successful investors and their average counterparts is the ability of the former to see the value of options when other investors miss them. This is no different from any other estimate of parameters, which investors will approach in different ways.

Network and standard effects

The network effect refers to the change in value of a service to each user as a result of changes in the size of the user base. Think of the telephone. Would you buy a telephone if no one else had one? The fact that you buy one adds to the attractiveness of the telephone to other users, and as a result, also to yourself. This is crucial in technology; in many cases, most of a company's value can be attributed to potential network effects.

Rather than using arbitrary formulas, such as Metcalfe's law (originally developed based on the number of connections between users on a network), investors should examine the industry and the impact of the acceptance of a specific technology. This may govern the value of a service to its users and, as a result, their willingness to use and pay for it. One needs to understand how the value per user increases as the number of users grows. The impact should be reflected in the willingness of each customer to pay and in the growth rate of the customer base. The fact that this growth rate accelerates in certain circumstances runs counter to traditional assumptions about decreasing economies of scale.

In evaluating a company, investors should be careful about assumptions regarding the ability to transform non-paying customers into paying customers. History shows that most companies suffer when dramatically changing their pricing regime. Only creative pricing schemes can build on the driving forces underlying the success of the previous model. At that point, though, it is important to consider the identity of the investor – can he affect the pricing decisions of the company and if not, can he assume the company's management will make the correct choices?

The network effect (along with the production learning curve) also explains why some companies are willing to sell goods initially at below cost. The more a product is accepted, the more valuable it becomes to users. For example, selling games consoles below cost expands the user base, which increases incentives for content creation (games), which in turn enhances royalties from games. This is what Sony and Nintendo have done for years, and what Microsoft is expected to do with its XBox console. In forecasts of valuation, the network effect is mainly reflected in the growth rate of the users and in their willingness to pay.

Cost structure

Many companies have similar operational characteristics, such as prices, technology and management, but differ significantly in their cost structures. For example, decisions regarding the outsourcing level of production significantly alter the effect of economic conditions on profitability. Consider an oil company that buys oil to sell at its petrol stations and compare it with a competitor that also owns refineries. The latter should reap higher rewards from sales at its service stations because it retains value added in refining the oil. However, the company has to bear the high fixed cost of operating the refinery.

The above example does not consider the ability of the company to refine fuel for other companies. However, the principle is always the same: in almost any managerial decision, there are many cost structures to choose from. Each of these would affect the sensitivity of the company to changes in the environment in a different way.

Companies that increase fixed costs and hence reduce the variable costs of production are more sensitive to market conditions. This "operating leverage" means in good times they increase profitability quickly and in bad market conditions they lose money more quickly than companies with a more flexible cost structure. In addition, cost structure decisions are based on a company's core competences and on the competitive environment. Nike, for example, focuses on the design and distribution of its shoes, benefiting from stiff competition among manufacturers, and reducing its exposure to capital expenditures for production.

The impact on valuation depends on the assumptions made about future market conditions. Investors typically try to understand the cost structure choices made by a company and incorporate them in forecasts. If they are active investors, they might incorporate into the forecasts their view on the optimal cost structure and the likelihood of it being taken up, given their involvement.

Strategic partners and buyers

Partnerships vary in levels of formality and their impact on the profitability of a company should be examined carefully. Many companies, but particularly those in the technology sectors, rely heavily on strategic partnerships, some of which are in fact long-term outsourcing agreements.

In recent years, many alliances have involved equity investments (an investor–investee relationship) and commercial transactions (a buyer–seller relationship). These are difficult to disentangle for valuation purposes because they are often structured to provide the seller (typically the investee) with much-needed revenue. Assuming the reporting of the transactions complies with reporting rules, there is nothing wrong conceptually with such transactions. However, they may not be representative of the revenue potential of the company. One can rarely extrapolate the potential for similar transactions with unrelated parties.

Finally, consider the impact of exit strategies. Investors always consider how easy or difficult it might be to extract their capital by, say, selling out in the stock market or as part of a merger or acquisition. When valuing a stock one needs to look at the fundamentals of the company as a sole entity, but many investors rely on market conditions to provide an exit strategy, even though this might be misaligned with business fundamentals. For example, in 1999 and the early part of 2000, many investors bought stocks they considered overvalued, simply on the premise that the stocks would continue to be overvalued, but to a larger degree.

Mergers and acquisitions (M&As) provide investors with another mechanism for valuing a company. The value of a potential deal, adjusted for the probability of it materializing, should always be incorporated into the valuation. For technology companies, this value may be much greater than the value of the company alone. M&A value is crucial in particular for companies in their early stages, although this can last a relatively long time.

The notion of value at its best use should be part of every valuation. This allows us to think of the company as potentially part of another company, benefiting from cost synergies, unique technology and a larger customer base, or with better management skills. So the valuation process needs to assume that exit options exist and that they are valuable. It can never be assumed that these options will happen, because the rights to exercise them are owned by external parties. Yet investors should try to value such options and estimate the likelihood of them being exercised.

Conclusion

In this article and the previous one we have highlighted some of the main components in valuing the equity of any company and shown how the importance of some of these components differs across types of companies and industries. The effects of some components in the business model have been discussed. Maximizing the value of companies relies on their ability to combine the components of their business models in a perfectly orchestrated manner. The formulation of these components and their combination into a business model affect the company's ability to create value to its shareholders.

We have also described various methodologies for implementing valuation. While the approaches rest on the same principle – that a company's value equals the sum of its discounted expected dividends – in practice they would often produce different results. These differences have to do with the models' implementation: the information requirement for estimation, the forecasting period chosen, and the company's managerial discretion over the forecasted items.

As most analysis is focused on the first few years of forecasts as a foundation for the complete valuation (when the company may be in rapid growth), the methodology used can have enormous impact. We described Adjusted Residual Income, a method focused on the excess profits created for shareholders. It works well in most situations, and can help in particular with technology-related companies, as well as for other companies that have significant components of intangible assets or that are in their high-growth period.

However, regardless of the business model of the company, its industry and age of development, the same building blocks of valuation exist. What changes is the degree of relevance and importance of these building blocks for a specific industry and company. However, these adjustments and tailoring are what makes valuation an art.

Copyright © Oren Fürst and Nahum Melumad 2002

Further reading

Brynjolfsson, E. and Kahin, B. (eds) (2000) *Understanding the Digital Economy*, Cambridge, MA: MIT Press.

Dixit, A. and Pindyck, R.S. (1994) *Investment Under Uncertainty*, Princeton, NJ: Princeton University Press.

Fürst, O. and Melumad, N. "Outsource even what you do best", working paper, Columbia Business School.

Fürst, O. and Geiger, U. (2002) *From Concept to Wall Street*, Prentice Hall–Financial Times.

Ohlson, J. (1995) "Earnings, book values and dividends in equity valuation", *Contemporary Accounting Research*, Spring, 661–87.

Penman, S.H. (2001) "Financial statement analysis and security valuation", McGraw-Hill Higher Education.

Tirole, J. (1988) *The Theory of Industrial Organization*, Cambridge, MA: MIT Press.

Intangibles:
not seen but must be heard

Accounting-based value metrics have become very popular but are finding it increasingly hard to measure value, says **Chris Higson**, and things are not going to get any easier.

Chris Higson is a professor in the accounting group at London Business School.

A notable feature of the past decade was the growth of value-based management. Companies adopting this discipline use "value metrics" to assess the performance of their business units and as a basis for managers' pay. A value metric is an accounting measure of return on capital that is compared with the cost of capital to signal the creation and destruction of value.

Some companies use traditional measures such as return on equity for this, but most favour proprietary metrics promoted by consultants, such as Economic Value Added (EVA) and Cash Flow Return on Investment (CFROI). (Principles are discussed in Box 1.) Many investors have adopted the same metrics to screen and rank companies when selecting stocks, and this article discusses the use of metrics by investors.

The performance of an investment is judged in two ways. The internal rate of return is the yield of the expected cash flows on the invested capital. Value is created when the internal rate of return is greater than the cost of capital. Equivalently, net present value measures the amount of value created as the difference between the present value of future cash flows and the invested capital.

The use of accounting return on capital to measure economic returns, and of the price-to-book ratio as a proxy for net present value, depends crucially on the quality of the accounting data. The prevailing view, encouraged by some consulting firms, is that accounting is not up to the job, indeed that its standards are downright foolish in many cases, but that these can be fixed. So implementation of value metrics usually involves an energetic, and costly, reworking of accounting conventions.

As stock prices became apparently disconnected from fundamental value in recent years, some commentators concluded that there must be a new financial paradigm in which economic

Box 1 Value metrics

In some guises, a value metric measures accounting return on capital. This becomes clear when we relate measures such as EVA to traditional measures of return on capital such as return on operating assets and return on equity.

$$\text{Return on operating assets} = \frac{\text{Operating profit}}{\text{Operating assets}}$$

$$\text{Return on equity} = \frac{\text{Earnings}}{\text{Shareholders' funds}}$$

The income that a company delivers to shareholders has been subject to corporation tax and the investors' required return is set in terms of after-tax income. Since earnings are after-tax, return on equity can be benchmarked against the cost of equity capital. However, an "enterprise" or "entity-level" measure of return on capital is benchmarked against WACC, which is the weighted average of the costs of the loan and equity capital that make up capital employed. But operating profit and thus return on operating assets are measured pre-tax. Net operating profit after tax (Nopat) resolves this problem by deducting the tax charge from operating profit, adjusted for the tax effects of interest paid and received. If T is the corporate tax rate:

Nopat = Operating profit − (Tax + Net interest paid × T)

The resulting measure of after-tax operating return, commonly known as return on invested capital (RoIC), is:

$$\text{After-tax operating return} = \frac{\text{Nopat}}{\text{Operating assets}}$$

Imagine a business with the following data:	
Operating profit	100
Interest received	10
Interest paid	(30)
Profit before tax	80
Tax	25
Earnings	55

Assume average operating assets are 500, so its operating return is 100/500 = 20%, and the local corporate tax rate (T) is 35%. To find Nopat, we need to know the tax on the operating profit. The actual tax paid is 25, but this reflects the fact that the company received a tax deduction at 35% on its net interest payments of 20; a deduction of 7. So tax on operating profit must have been 25 + 7 = 32, and Nopat is 100 − 32 = 68.

Although the statutory tax rate is 35%, the average tax rate is not 35%, and 32 is not 35% of 100. The Nopat calculation reasonably assumes that interest paid (received) is deducted (taxed) at the marginal, statutory, rate and that the tax breaks that reduce the effective tax rate relate to operating profit.

In this example, if WACC was 8% we would conclude that the after-tax operating return of 13.6% reflected superior performance. The difference between return and the cost of capital is often called spread. In the example, spread was +5.6%. The same data can be presented in a different way. If we make a charge against Nopat for the cost of using the capital employed in operating assets during the year, the surplus is economic profit.

Economic profit = Nopat − Operating assets × WACC

Continuing the example, if Nopat is 68 and assets 500, and WACC is 8%, economic profit is 68 − 500 × 8% = 28.

Economic profit is also known as Economic Value Added, although the term economic profit is used quite loosely in financial analysis and is also commonly applied to spread. The term "EVA" was coined by the consulting firm Stern Stewart. Its version of EVA also incorporates a number of accounting adjustments, designed to correct perceived shortcomings of actual accounting. In simple terms, when we ask whether a company is earning a return greater than the cost of capital, we are asking whether

> **Nopat/(Operating assets) > WACC**
>
> Multiplying both sides by capital, the question becomes whether
>
> **Nopat > Operating assets × WACC**
>
> Moving the right-hand side over to the left casts the question in terms of whether economic profit is positive:
>
> **Nopat − Operating assets × WACC > 0**
>
> So the statement that a company has positive economic profit is logically identical to the statement that it is earning a return greater than its cost of capital. Given the accounting, one measure contains neither more nor less information than the other.
>
> CFROI is an accounting return measure with two distinctive features. The denominator uses gross assets revalued using a general price index (i) rather than using historic cost net assets as do both traditional measures and economic profit. The numerator takes gross cash flow and deducts "sinking-fund" depreciation (Ds) of the inflated gross assets instead of the accountant's, usually straight-line, depreciation (Da). (Sinking-fund depreciation is that necessary payment each period that, if invested in a fund earning the cost of capital, will yield the initial investment by the end of the asset life.)
>
> $$\text{Cash flow investment on return} = \frac{(\text{Nopat} + \text{Da} - \text{Ds})}{(\text{Gross operating assets} \times i)}$$

fundamentals no longer matter for value. Of course, the bottom line is unchanged – in rational markets a company must still generate economic value to survive and be valued.

Yet there are reasons to believe that a company's financial performance will look different in the future and that best practice in equity analysis will need different tools. Some changes in the economic landscape radically alter the profile of business profitability and business risk. Investors need to understand these changes and to adapt mental models and ways of working in response.

Data integrity

In a properly conducted investment appraisal, all the assets and claims used and created by an investment project are accounted for, and all the cash flows are identified. To give the same data integrity when calculating value metrics, income must be comprehensive and the balance sheet needs to give a complete list of assets and claims, measured at their opportunity cost. This is a tall order. Though it is conventional to make adjustments to the accounting when calculating value metrics, the adjustments that outsiders such as investors are able to make, using published accounting data, typically fall short.

The prime focus of the income statement is to describe the profit the company makes from its operations. For example, part of the return that a company delivers to its investors may be in the form of unrealized holding gains on assets such as property. These may or may not be recognized. But even when they are, they will rarely be passed through the income statement. Earnings will not be comprehensive if balance sheet changes such as gains and losses on foreign exchange are taken direct to the profit and loss reserve in the balance sheet rather than being passed through earnings. Investors do not usually adjust for these items.

Balance sheets usually do not carry intangible assets. Accounting practice requires the costs of intangible assets such as reputation, human capital, intellectual property and research to be charged as incurred. Acquired, rather than built, intellectual property assets are sometimes carried in the balance sheet, though these are never subsequently revalued. Investors now commonly capitalize research expenditures but no other elements of intangibles expenditure, and these assets are not usually revalued.

Companies that grow by takeover may make very large investments in goodwill, which is the difference between the cost of an acquired company and the balance sheet assets acquired. Internationally, goodwill is amortized over widely varying periods. Hence accounting returns look very different between companies that grow organically and those that grow by acquisition, and also between acquirers in different countries. It is now common practice to add back written-off goodwill into capital employed when calculating value metrics, but this is rarely revalued.

There will be unrecorded assets and liabilities when the company has written contracts to keep current assets "off balance sheet", for example by factoring the sales ledger or using consigned inventory. Some adjustments by analysts do enhance the completeness of the balance sheet, the most common being the capitalization of operating leases. But devices such as factoring are much harder for the outside analyst to observe and there is usually no attempt to adjust for these.

The main divergence from current value is for tangible fixed assets. Although the balance sheet is usually complete in tangible fixed assets, these are by default carried at their historic costs, which, particularly for long-lived assets such as land and buildings, may bear little relation to current values. Internationally, revaluation of fixed assets is either not permitted, as in the US, or has unfavourable tax consequences. In the UK, revaluations are allowed, but they are found predominantly in property-rich sectors such as hotels and drinks, are occasional and are partial, with not all assets necessarily being revalued.

Visions

The internet is significantly increasing the transparency of off-line and online markets by reducing the buyer's search costs. One vision of the future is that falling search costs will dramatically intensify competition. Gary Hamel and Jeff Sampler (1998) put it thus: "Imagine a world in which you put your weekly grocery shopping out to bid ... Customer ignorance – about prices and relative product performance – has been a profit centre for many companies. But consumers are about to get much, much better informed – and the consequences will be awe-inspiring." They continue: "Let's be clear: in frictionless capitalism, nobody makes any money!"

So, on this "competitive wasteland" view, substantial excess returns will be implausible in most markets. The key to the delivery of superior economic value in the new world will be achieving competitively superior rates of growth, while ensuring that return on capital remains above the cost of capital (albeit only slightly).

The world of intangibles

At the same time, there is a widespread view that the reason for soaring corporate price-to-book ratios in recent years, aside from possible over-valuation by stock markets, is the increasing importance of intangible assets. Intangibles are resources such as intellectual property and knowledge assets, brands, alliances, human and organizational capital. Conservative accounting rules mean that such investment is written off as it is incurred. As a result the "book" in price-to-book is understated. But what is more interesting is the impact of intangibles on "price".

Intangibles are increasingly seen as holding the key to value creation. Their potential in enabling companies to earn and sustain a return that is significantly above the cost of capital comes from their uniqueness and scalability. Most tangible assets, and all financial assets, are commodities in that there are other assets in competitive supply that can provide the same service. Intangibles tend to be unique and, unlike tangibles or financial assets, the use of an intangible at one place and time does not preclude its use elsewhere; intangibles are scalable for relatively low costs. Once the investment in Viagra has been made and protected, the marginal cost of producing the goods is small.

The so-called "network effect" is simply an extreme case of this. It describes a world where not only can you "scale" but where scale brings additional rewards because each customer values the product more as more customers use it. The returns to scale are exponential rather than linear. A direct implication of the scalability of intangibles is that the winner takes all. With scalability, the product with a small advantage in performance can scoop the market. Indeed, if there are potential network effects, beliefs about who will win the battle, rather than objective functionality, may be enough to tip the market.

Shifting terrain

The economic landscape is undergoing fundamental change, triggered in large part by economic deregulation in the final decades of the past century and the transforming power of information technology. In the face of these forces, companies are restructuring in ways that will have a radical effect on risk and on return on capital.

In the new economic order sketched by writers such as John Hagel and Marc Singer (1999), companies are moving away from growth-restricting vertical integration in favour of specialization along resource lines. They see companies reengineering and reconfiguring into three types: product development, infrastructure and logistics, and customer-facing. Each of these business types has a different tangible/intangible asset profile. Whereas an infrastructure business may be capital-intensive in a conventional way, the main asset for product development is likely to be intellectual property, and for the customer-facing business, brand equity. Moreover, the span of resource control increasingly extends beyond conventional ownership to include extended supply and networks of complementary businesses.

Academic Baruch Lev (2001) provides the example of Ford. He argues that the potential for economies of scale in manufacturing is largely exhausted and that excellence in manufacturing has been widely mimicked. So manufacturing production has become commoditized. Increasingly, a company such as Ford must look to innovation and to developing brand equity to build competitive advantage. As a result, Ford sees little use in owning manufacturing assets and is busy pushing manufacturing, and ownership of relevant assets, to third parties. Technology allows Ford to manage these network relationships tightly and efficiently.

A prevalent feature of the modern economy is the shifting of asset ownership out of the corporation by using leasing, factoring, franchising and similar contractual devices. Since these arrangements often replace borrowing, a financial motive for off-balance sheet financing may be to flatten the debt ratio, leading many governments to require companies to bring "off-balance sheet" assets back into the balance sheet. Rules that limit the use of operating leases are also in line with the practice of financial analysts in capitalizing operating leases.

However, a very different motive for off-balance-sheet financing is to shift out assets which others may have greater competency in managing and which are not strategic resources of the business. Outsourcing is not new. For example, companies frequently leased their fleet when they did not wish to maintain in-house skills in fleet management, insurance and repair, and access to second-hand vehicle markets. What has changed is the growing willingness, and the energy, with which companies are applying this logic to reconfiguring their resource systems, and the use of networks, rather than ownership-like contracts, to provide resources.

Airlines have long mixed outright ownership with capital leasing and operating leasing of planes. But in addition, British Airways operates a number of routes through franchised affiliates. These operators fly planes that bear the BA livery but, as independent airlines, their assets do not appear in the BA balance sheet. Planes are clearly core assets to airlines in a way that the executive car fleet is usually not. Nonetheless, planes are not a strategic resource for an airline; airlines all use much the same planes and planes are in competitive supply. A list of the resources that confer competitive advantage on airlines would include control of sites and slots, reputation for safety and service quality, membership of strategic alliances, code-sharing arrangements and reservation systems. None of these appears in the balance sheet.

Coca-Cola's bottlers are analogous to BA's franchises. At a further remove still are networks of software developers commanded by Microsoft. Microsoft is itself a major software developer, but the platforms it has created support many other developers. Most relevant for this discussion, those developers support the Microsoft platform. They comprise a resource that adds value to Microsoft by leveraging the demand for Microsoft's own products.

Performance analysis

Other things being equal, we expect a value-creating business to earn a return on capital that is greater than the cost of capital. Over the past two decades, value-management consultants have refocused companies on this basic logic and investors have been refining investment processes along the same lines, even adopting some of the consultants' metrics. The use of some measure of return on capital is now central to equity analysis practice, both as a metric, to rank companies, and in modelling, by assuming a return on capital that converges on the cost of capital.

The above changes are having a major effect on the return-on-capital profile of companies, an increasing proportion of which do not have a return on capital that can sensibly be measured because they do not directly use capital. Strategic resources or intangible assets do not figure in the balance sheet, while tangible assets that are needed may be held off-balance sheet or held in another company within a network or alliance.

Take Dell Computer, which can be classed as an old or a new economy stock according to taste. Since 1997, Michael Dell has reengineered the business model, and thus the balance sheet, of Dell. Energetic use of internet selling and of IT to manage a network of suppliers gave Dell negligible inventory and net credit. Fixed assets are largely operating leased. Dell's other creditors are more than sufficient to finance the small amount of on-balance sheet operating assets, so Dell's net operating assets became negative. In consequence, an operating margin of 10–12 per cent combined with an infinite asset turn to give an infinite return on capital at Dell.

Hitherto, practical difficulties in implementing the return-on-capital model have usually been blamed on accounting. In the future, it is unlikely that return on capital-driven valuation models will be reliably immunized by some menu of accounting adjustments. In the case of Dell, the response of analysts (and of government standard setters) might be to capitalize operating leases and perhaps the relatively small amount that Dell has spent on research and development (R&D), and this would doubtless yield a finite return on capital. But these adjustments miss the point. Capital is not the scarce resource at Dell, nor is it the appropriate measure for the company's performance.

Just as exploitation of intangible assets offers a way to differentiate, it will also make the world more risky. The uniqueness and scalability of intangibles creates a winner-take-all environment, which brings corresponding risk. Increasingly we see companies making large bets on uncertain outcomes. An unsuccessful investment in an intangible, unlike some unsuccessful tangibles, has little value in another use. Worse, even when an intangible is successful, rights in it are harder to police. These risks are likely to be "unsystematic" – they will not affect the cost of capital. But they have profound implications for equity analysis.

Copyright © Chris Higson 2002

Further reading

Hagel, J. and Singer, M. (1999) *Net Worth*, Boston: Harvard Business School Press.

Hamel, G. and Sampler, J. (1998) "The e-corporation: more than just web-based, it's building a new industrial order", *Fortune*, 12 July, 80.

Lev, B. (2001) *Intangibles: Management, Measurement and Reporting*, Washington DC: Brookings Institution Press.

Trading **and prices**

3

Contents

The past, present and future of trading stocks 100

Lawrence Glosten, Columbia Business School and **Charles Jones**, Columbia Business School

In the past decade there have been dramatic changes in the way stocks are traded – and in the cost of trading. What are the challenges facing exchanges?

The role of equity trade costs in investment results 107

Donald Keim, University of Pennsylvania and **Ananth Madhavan**, Investment Technology Group

This article distinguishes between explicit costs such as commissions and bid-ask spreads, and implicit costs such as those stemming from trade difficulty and market design.

Equity loans: how to sell what you do not own 113

Christopher Geczy, University of Pennsylvania, **David Musto**, University of Pennsylvania and **Adam Reed**, University of Pennsylvania

In the US, the lender of a shorted stock can benefit from controlling the interest payments on the borrower's collateral.

Consolidated limit order book: future perfect or future stock? 118

Kenneth Kavajecz, University of Pennsylvania

This article describes the debate surrounding CLOB, a mechanism that enables greater transparency between investors.

Introduction to Part 3

To the outsider, financial markets can appear confusing and chaotic places, with an impenetrable vocabulary and a plethora of specialized roles. At the simplest level, markets exist to put lenders in touch with borrowers. At another level, they connect the potential buyer of a stock or bond with its seller. Originally, these transactions took place in the physical location of the stock market; now they are more likely to occur across an electronic network. Financial centres nonetheless retain their importance, as these authors show, and differ significantly in the way they effect transactions.

The past, present and future of trading stocks

Competition is driving the evolution of exchanges. **Lawrence Glosten** and **Charles Jones** look at how they work and the potential for consolidation.

Lawrence R. Glosten is S. Sloan Colt Professor of Banking and International Finance at Columbia Business School.

Charles M. Jones is Class of 1967 Associate Professor of Business at Columbia Business School.

Economists like to make idealized assumptions. When it comes to financial markets, they often assume a frictionless market where demand and supply curves interact to generate equilibrium prices and trades. This abstraction is useful, but actual trading mechanisms may not achieve this ideal. For one thing, they require resources, human and otherwise. That means trading costs. Also, each trading venue approaches the ideal differently. This means trading venues are, to a greater or lesser extent, in competition and it means that trading mechanisms are constantly evolving.

This article explores the evolution of this industry. Developments in trading technology and securities exchange organization are considered and linked to the costs of investing.

Exchanges and markets

First, we should be clear about what we mean by the trading industry and what it supplies. If an investor wants to buy or sell, the brokerage function delivers an order with the specified terms to an exchange or other trading venue. At the exchange, buy and sell orders are executed according to execution rules. Finally, the clearing function ensures both sides of a transaction honour their commitments – the buyer delivers cash and the seller delivers securities. Thus, there are several outputs of the trading industry. Transactions are the first output. Simultaneously, a second output is created – prices. The final output is an insurance policy that guarantees the transaction. The customer pays for outputs in two ways. The brokerage commission covers order delivery and clearing (clearing fees are paid indirectly through the broker). The customer also pays for immediacy via the bid-ask spread (the difference between the price at which dealers are prepared to sell a share and the price at which they are prepared to buy). In return for a quick transaction, a buy order usually pays the higher asked or offer price, while a sell order receives the lower bid price.

The oldest form of exchange is the pure dealer market. In a dealer market, designated individuals called dealers or marketmakers are the counterparties to every trade. Dealers quote bid and offer prices at which they are willing to, respectively, buy and sell. Buyers use a broker to locate the dealer with the lowest offer and customers who wish to sell locate the dealer with the highest bid.

Nasdaq in the US and the London Stock Exchange are the canonical examples, although neither is a pure dealer market. Another example is the Nouveau Marché in Paris, a market for new and smaller publicly traded companies.

At the other extreme from the pure dealer market is the electronic open limit order book. This exchange has no designated marketmakers – the quotes come from limit orders submitted to the limit order book. Customers of this exchange who wish to trade, but are patient, submit limit orders specifying buy or sell, number of shares and a price. The highest limit buy orders become the market bid and the lowest limit sell orders form the market offer. Individuals who wish to trade immediately submit market orders that trade with the limit orders.

Examples of this type of market abound – Tokyo, Toronto and Paris were the first, and many European exchanges, including Frankfurt and Stockholm, have moved to this form. Electronic limit order books have also sprung up in the US in the form of electronic communication networks (ECNs). Instinet and Island are prominent examples.

The electronic open limit order book has the advantage of efficiently concentrating competition between "liquidity suppliers" who quote. In contrast, there have been concerns that dealer markets are prone to non-competitive behaviour which have led to antitrust investigations. But there are lingering concerns that an electronic open limit order book may provide less liquidity than a dealer market during volatile times, or for less frequently traded stocks. So it is not obvious that one system is superior to the other.

The New York Stock Exchange's (NYSE) trading floor is a hybrid of the two systems. Floor traders and the specialist (an individual designated by the exchange to manage the trade in a security) sometimes act as brokers and sometimes act as dealers, buying and selling for their own account. Nevertheless, the NYSE has an active limit order book, largely because it has become so easy to submit orders electronically.

Some commentators claim that trading floors are dinosaurs. But defenders counter that hybrid markets such as the NYSE can be all things to all investors. The limit order book provides for cheap execution of small orders and floor broker/dealers handle larger institutional trades. However, trading floors are concentrated in the US (the NYSE and smaller regional exchanges, as well as futures and options exchanges) and Asia. Most European exchanges are virtual.

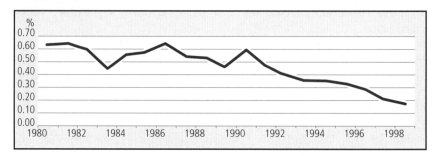

FIGURE 1 Proportional bid-ask spreads on DJIA stocks

Costs

Trading costs around the world have fallen dramatically. The US is a case in point.

Figure 1 reports average quoted bid-ask spreads (as a percentage of price) on the 30 stocks in the Dow Jones Industrial Average since 1980. It has not been an uninterrupted ride downwards, but spreads in 1998 averaged 0.175 per cent of the share price, less than a third of the 1980 figure.

Commissions follow an even steeper downward curve. Figure 2 estimates overall commission rates for NYSE stocks since 1980, based on the commission revenue of NYSE members relative to total NYSE trading. One-way commissions were about 0.55 per cent in 1980, five years after deregulation in the US. They then plunged to about 0.10 per cent by 1998. Commissions for institutions have dropped most dramatically, but retail commissions have fallen sharply as well.

Tick size

Competition between brokerages and increases in trading volume probably explain the decline in trading costs. But the way trading is conducted matters as well. A good example is the minimum price increment or minimum tick.

Before 1997, the minimum tick in the US was, for the most part, an eighth

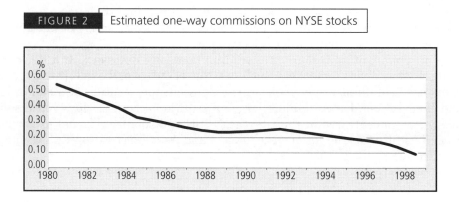

FIGURE 2 Estimated one-way commissions on NYSE stocks

of a dollar, or $0.125. In the spring of 1997, US exchanges adopted sixteenths, halving the minimum tick. In 2001, eighths and sixteenths disappeared from the NYSE, the American Stock Exchange and regional US exchanges, replaced by decimal prices. Nasdaq finished converting to decimals in April and equity options switched as well. Toronto Stock Exchange adopted decimals in 1996 and Tokyo Stock Exchange, already decimalized, reduced its tick size in 1998. Does this matter to investors?

First, decimals themselves are not the story. From a trading cost point of view, the key variable is the minimum tick. Toronto and US exchanges set a penny ($0.01) as the minimum tick in their respective currencies, so the tick is more than 12 times smaller than it was five years ago. Why a penny? Mostly because it is the simplest increment, but it may not be the ideal size.

Smaller ticks have some benefits. Bid-ask spreads shrink. For example, pennies have lowered NYSE spreads by 20–30 per cent. This is good news, especially for investors who submit small market orders. Unfortunately, smaller ticks are not good news for every investor. A study by academics Charles Jones and Marc Lipson (2001) found that when the NYSE went from eighths to sixteenths (data are not available on pennies yet), trade became more expensive for institutions. Total one-way institutional trading costs rose from 0.68 per cent under eighths to 0.85 per cent under sixteenths. A possible reason: liquidity is supplied more slowly with smaller ticks, because narrow ticks give floor participants an advantage over electronic limit orders. For example, someone on the floor can jump in front of a limit order by improving the price just 1 cent. So electronic orders often miss out and get filled only when floor traders decide to pass. Economists call this adverse selection; traders call it "penny jumping" or "getting pennied".

On an electronic exchange, with neither floor nor designated dealers, "pennying" is not possible. Yet evidence from the Toronto exchange (which is electronic) is that while the spread has shrunk for small trades, it may be more costly to complete a large trade. In fact, the NYSE is reviewing the move to trading on pennies, largely because of complaints from institutional traders.

Evidence is pointing towards the conclusion that the tick can be too small. Exchanges and regulators outside the US need to trade off the benefits of a smaller tick against its subtle costs. End-users should care, too. When the tick size shrinks, investors need to think carefully about using a market or a limit order. It may make sense to switch to the former.

Market fragmentation

Market fragmentation refers to the splintering of order flow that occurs when several exchanges are available to execute a trade. It is especially pronounced for Nasdaq stocks. Twenty years ago, almost every trade in a Nasdaq stock was over the phone with a dealer. Nasdaq dealers still make markets, but now there is a dizzying array of alternatives. Most prominent are ECNs, the computerized limit order books mentioned earlier. There are other types of trading systems as well, each with its target audience.

Fragmentation is much maligned. The main argument against it is that information and search costs are lower if all the buyers and sellers for Microsoft, for example, are gathered in one physical or virtual place. In economists' jargon, there are network externalities associated with a single exchange.

It is clear, however, that there is demand for different types of trading systems. A good example is Posit, a crossing network run by ITG. Seven times a day, institutional orders are aggregated and traded at a prevailing midpoint price. The idea is to concentrate liquidity by executing trades at discrete points in time rather than continuously. The concept is not new; gold trades in London in a similar fashion. Posit does not have a huge market share, crossing about 30m shares a day in 2000 compared with about 1bn a day on NYSE or Nasdaq. But institutions like the system for two reasons. First, if their orders execute, they avoid paying the bid-ask spread. Second, the system is anonymous. No broker sees, for example, that a pension fund is trying to buy 1m shares of IBM. That means no broker is able to buy IBM in advance and drive up the price before the pension fund's order is executed. Avoiding such "front-running" has obvious appeal for the pension fund.

Another example is the Paris Bourse and the London Stock Exchange. Paris has an electronic limit order book, while London has a dealer market similar to Nasdaq. Many stocks are listed on both. Compared with London, Paris has narrower spreads between bid and offer, but quotes are good for fewer shares. This is attractive to the retail trader. London, on the other hand, is the trading venue of choice for institutional traders. The market is deep (a trader can buy or sell a large number of shares) and negotiations between dealer and trader often provide price improvement from the relatively wide quoted spreads.

The point is that different traders (or the same trader at different times or for different stocks) may have different needs. A small retail trader may value the small spread of the electronic limit order book in one stock. An institutional trader may value the anonymity of Posit for one trade and the ability to negotiate for another.

How can one obtain this competitive benefit of fragmentation without the problems? The answer lies in having an information system that effectively connects the various trading venues. First, traders need to know not only the quoted terms of trade at any time for each venue but also all the transactions that have occurred. Second, to exploit network externalities, there needs to be an efficient means of transferring excess supply in one exchange to excess demand in another. That is, the fragmentation needs to be consolidated.

The provision of information about quotes (ex-ante transparency) is standard around the world. The extent of ex-post transparency (information about trades) varies a great deal. We can expect considerably more ex-post transparency as investors force exchanges around the world to provide the timely trade information required in US markets. The final step – consolidating order flow across exchanges – is more problematic. But resolving the fragmentation issue may depend on what happens in the way of joint ventures, alliances and mergers of exchanges.

Ownership structure

There has been much talk of exchange mergers and joint alliances. Nasdaq and the American Stock Exchange (Amex) merged in 1999. The French, Dutch and

Belgian bourses have merged into Euronext, now the second largest European exchange. On the other hand, merger talks between the Frankfurt Exchange and the London Stock Exchange broke down in 2000. Both Nasdaq and the NYSE have frequently spoken of alliances with European and Asian exchanges but nothing substantive has been implemented.

Still, the economics of liquidity provision point towards further ownership consolidation. There are economies of scale in providing exchange services. This is most obvious for clearing (guaranteeing trades). Greater synergies come from the ability of a single organization to provide a common technology that will allow separate trading venues to communicate efficiently. If this happens, investors will reap the rewards of competing trading architectures without losing the network externalities of consolidated trade.

The future

What might happen in the next decade? The NYSE has a strong franchise and has been executing well lately, especially on the technology front. There are questions about how much value specialists add, but the NYSE is working hard to automate some of the specialists' simpler tasks, freeing them to focus on larger trades and the bigger picture of maintaining and allocating liquidity across market participants. Nevertheless, the trading floor is the NYSE's most valuable asset. No other exchange handles large trades as effectively and the floor is the reason. The network externalities in stock exchanges are strong and the NYSE would have to stumble badly to lose out to a competitor.

There will probably be an ECN shakeout in the US. Because of the network externalities in trading stocks and the similarities between ECNs, this is a winner-takes-most arena. In two years, there may be just two ECNs left. The winner or winners will likely battle with Nasdaq's traditional marketmakers for market share, with no clear winner for some time, if ever.

Moving to the global market, the trend for increased cross-listing of stocks is likely to continue. This is mostly a time-zone phenomenon. It is much easier for a New Yorker to trade Siemens during NYSE trading hours than to wait for Frankfurt to open.

What will this do to investors' trading costs? Consolidation of exchange ownership could lead to efficiencies in clearing and information costs. Further competition from electronic brokerage, electronic exchanges and other technological improvements could bring more reductions in commissions and bid-ask spreads.

However, technological and regulatory changes are not the only determinants of transaction costs. Over the course of the 20th century, when the market went up, trading costs usually went down and vice versa, and that should continue. Looking back, big market moves in either direction often spur changes from without (regulation) and changes from within (innovation in good times, wrenching reorganizations in bad times). Stock returns and volume growth are likely to be more modest in the coming decade and capital markets will not fund new entrants as generously as they did in the 1990s. As a result, the next 10 years are unlikely to be as dramatic as the last.

Copyright © Lawrence Glosten and Charles Jones 2002

Further reading

Glosten, L.R. (1994) "Is the electronic open limit order book inevitable?", *Journal of Finance*, 49 (4), 1127–61.

Jones, C.M. and Lipson, M.L. (2001) "Sixteenths: direct evidence on institutional execution costs", *Journal of Financial Economics*, 59 (2), 253–78.

The role of equity trade
costs in investment results

Better understanding and control of trading costs could significantly improve investment managers' performance, say **Donald Keim** and **Ananth Madhavan**.

Donald B. Keim is John B. Neff Professor of Finance at the Wharton School of the University of Pennsylvania.

Ananth Madhavan is managing director of research, Investment Technology Group.

Transaction costs are near and dear to most investors, especially institutional investors. But only recently have detailed data become available, prompting systematic studies of trading costs. The findings have implications for policymakers and investors worldwide.

Trading costs

Evidence shows execution costs can be large, often enough to substantially reduce or even eliminate the notional return on an investment strategy. So it is important to measure, analyze and control trading costs. The key is to distinguish between the major components: explicit and implicit costs.

Explicit costs are mainly brokerage commissions but also include fees, stamp duties and so on, for which there is an explicit accounting charge. Commissions vary, averaging 0.20 per cent of trade value overall, and have been declining. They vary by price, market mechanism and broker type. For example, crossing networks (where natural buyers and sellers are matched at predetermined prices without intervention by a marketmaker) charge as little as 2 cents a share, whereas commissions on difficult trades executed by specialized brokers may be as high as 10–15 cents. Explicit costs are generally higher (as a fraction of total costs) outside the US.

Trades are also subject to implicit costs, which are more difficult to measure. They comprise bid-ask spreads, price impact and opportunity costs.

Bid-ask spreads

The quoted spread between bid price and ask price is the

marketmaker's compensation for providing liquidity, analogous to the broker's commission. This bid-ask spread varies depending on the stock's liquidity. Quoted spreads vary widely, from less than 0.3 per cent for the most liquid (largest market capitalization) stocks to 4–6 per cent for the least liquid (smallest market capitalization) stocks.

Quoted spreads often overstate true bid-ask spreads because trades are often executed inside the quoted spread, especially for exchange-listed stocks, by traders on the exchange floor. Also, bid and ask prices tend to rise after a buy order (or fall after a sell order). To eliminate the effects of these biases, researchers study actual transaction prices to measure "effective bid-ask spreads" that approximate the true spread more closely. Studies confirm that effective spreads are, on average, lower than quoted spreads.

Price impact

Institutions make large trades and demand increasing liquidity from markets. As a result, their trades often move prices in the direction of the trade, resulting in "market impact" or "price impact". The price impact of large trades varies with trade size and market capitalization. One study of US markets found that the market impact of large (block) transactions for illiquid stocks in the smallest 20 per cent of market capitalization ranged from 3.04 per cent for the smallest blocks to 6.21 per cent for the largest blocks.

In contrast, a study of block trades in very liquid Dow Jones Industrial Average 30 stocks found relatively small price impacts, ranging from 0.15 per cent to 0.18 per cent. Finally, costs vary by time of day. Some studies document systematically higher costs at the close, a period when imbalances are often large and dealers are reluctant to carry inventories overnight.

Opportunity costs

Opportunity costs are associated with missed trading opportunities. Trades are often motivated by information whose value decays over time. Opportunity cost is incurred when an order is filled only partially or is not executed at all, as well as when an order is executed with a delay, during which the price moves against the trader.

These costs are difficult to measure and depend on the discretion a trader has to execute orders. One accepted method computes opportunity cost by measuring the difference in performance between a portfolio based on actual trades and a hypothetical portfolio whose returns are computed with the assumption that transactions were executed at prices observed at the time of the trading decision. The difference is called "performance shortfall".

Cost determinants

Trade costs are influenced by such factors as trade difficulty or the availability of a particular stock and investment styles. Trade difficulty relates to how liquid a stock is and, consequently, how difficult it is to find ready buyers or sellers. At a basic level, trade difficulty can be represented by trade size and the market capitalization of the stock being traded. Large orders demand more liquidity and so have higher trade costs than small orders. Averaged over all market capitalization levels, the round-trip (purchase and sale) trade costs of exchange-listed shares were 2.32 per cent for the largest trades and 0.64 per cent for the smallest.

Trade costs are inversely related to market capitalization, a proxy for liquidity. We found the average round-trip cost for the smallest market-cap quintile of exchange-listed stocks to be 3.81 per cent. The same cost for the largest market-cap quintile was 0.57 per cent. Trading costs tend to be larger for Nasdaq stocks than for exchange-listed stocks, but differences have narrowed because of regulatory changes and competition from electronic communications networks.

Allowing for trade difficulty is vital in assessing broker performance. For example, a full-service broker, who slowly "works" an order for an illiquid stock, may incur explicit costs of 0.9 per cent and implicit costs of 2 per cent. Compare this with a discount broker dealing with a highly liquid stock, who may incur explicit costs of 0.2 per cent and implicit costs of 0.4 per cent. Without allowing for trade difficulty, one cannot conclude that the broker with the higher total costs is a worse performer. What if the assignments were reversed? Using a full-service broker for a liquid stock might be as bad as using a discount broker for an illiquid stock.

Investment style (such as active or passive, index or momentum) also affects trading costs because it proxies for unobservable factors, such as the trader's time horizon or aggressiveness. Aggressive traders, such as those who chase short-run price movements and some indexers, have high expected costs because they demand (and pay for) immediacy. Less aggressive traders, such as value managers whose strategies are based on fundamental analysis, have lower turnover and lower costs because their longer investment horizon allows them to trade patiently.

Our research indicates estimated round-trip costs of 0.45 per cent for value traders, 1.09 per cent for index traders and 2.04 per cent for momentum (or technical) traders. Even within a particular investment style, differences in order-submission strategy may affect costs. For example, two traders, both using value-based strategies, may have significant differences in the number of trades needed to fill an order, which may translate into cost differences.

A study of 22,000 block trades in DJIA stocks found strong evidence that traders' reputation also affects trading costs. Traders who have a reputation for liquidity trading may be able to obtain better prices because the adverse-selection costs associated with their trades are likely to be minimal. This advantage is especially likely for trades that are negotiated away from the exchange floor, because this "upstairs" market is less anonymous than the exchange floors or Nasdaq.

Policy implications

Recent research findings on trading costs have broad implications in several areas, one of these being best execution. "Best execution" is generally interpreted as trading at the most favourable price available. However, it may be misleading if it is applied without regard to the type and circumstances of specific orders.

For small trades, explicit costs dominate. Such trades rarely incur significant price-impact costs and if they are executed in a single market order, the opportunity costs (from timing and failure to execute) are also negligible. Institutional orders tend to be much more complicated than retail orders. First, institutions typically follow dynamic order-placement strategies and break up orders into several component trades. As a result, best price at the time of a trade must be defined in the context of the overall order-placement strategy – especially because market movements make price-impact costs difficult to measure in a dynamic environment. Further, confidential information about the reasons for buying or selling may leak to the market throughout the trading period and can significantly affect measured price impacts.

Second, large differences may exist between costs measured at the individual trade level and those measured at the total order level. These differences arise from timing and opportunity costs, which are typically ignored in computations of best execution.

Third, institutions vary greatly in their willingness to bear costs. For example, active, momentum-based institutions that demand immediacy are willing to balance higher execution costs against the expected performance from their investment ideas. A trader who expects a 10 per cent appreciation in a stock within a matter of a few days may willingly bear substantial costs to ensure the execution of large trades of that stock within a short period. In contrast, a trader with no private information who simply seeks a position for liquidity reasons may be patient and seek lower costs. Thus, higher-cost trades do not automatically translate into poorer execution. "Best execution" for an informed trader is not identified solely by lower cost.

In assessing the quality of a trade we must consider its cost measured relative to a benchmark that incorporates the difficulty of the trade, the market environment, and the investment style and objectives motivating the trade. Given these complexities, the most effective source of assurance of "best execution" is competitive market pressure.

Alternative market systems

It is natural to use estimates of trading costs to make inferences about the relative efficiency of trading systems. There are many different systems, including pure dealer markets (London Stock Exchange, Nasdaq), hybrid specialist-auction models (NYSE, Frankfurt, Amsterdam), matching systems (Japan) and automated limit order books (Paris, Toronto), the latter being the most common.

Automated systems are cheaper to build and operate than the dealer- and floor-based systems prevalent on more established markets, hence a large percentage of such systems operating today is based in emerging markets. Automated markets are also prevalent in much of Europe. Such systems, by virtue of reduced operating costs and the possibility of eliminating the need for dealers or specialists to intervene, might reduce trading costs. However, this may not be the case for such systems in emerging markets, which exhibit higher costs on average, even after controlling for reduced liquidity and so on. Developed markets with automated auctions, however, are among the lowest-cost trading systems in the world.

The rapid growth of electronic crossing systems, such as Posit, Instinet's system, and the NYSE's after-hours system, are designed to reduce transaction costs. The transactors themselves provide liquidity without middlemen. Typically, they do not provide independent price discovery because buyers and sellers trade at prices that are predetermined. The benefit of crossing systems is that they offer lower execution costs than traditional exchanges. Commissions are usually 2 cents a share, much less than the charge of full-service exchange brokers. Moreover, participants also obtain substantially lower implicit costs because of the lack of any bid-ask spread (because traders themselves provide liquidity) and the lack of any impact cost (because the trade price is independent of order size).

However, crossing systems do not guarantee that an investor's order will be executed and this non-execution risk is associated with potential opportunity costs. Overall, low-cost crossing systems allow institutional traders to trade with one another without adversely affecting primary market liquidity. The growth of such systems can be viewed as a competitive response to an environment with different traders who have diverse needs.

Investor implications

Active managers try to exploit market inefficiencies and tend to trade more frequently, demanding more immediate execution compared with passive managers. As a result, trading costs are substantially higher for active managers than for passive managers. Therefore, when transaction costs are considered, passive indexing strategies might dominate active management strategies even if active managers can add value by identifying mispriced securities. Given the difficulty of implementing an active portfolio strategy, especially in less liquid stocks, there is considerable value in devoting resources to understanding and reducing trade costs.

Constructing an indexed portfolio

Most index funds attempt to hold all stocks in the underlying index. Fund inflows or outflows give rise to trades as the portfolio quickly adjusts to "track" the benchmark. Duplication helps minimize tracking error but could result in significant transaction costs. We found one-way trade costs for index managers were 0.37 per cent for "buys" and 0.38 per cent for "sells".

Trade costs may not be very important for passive portfolios indexed to liquid securities (such as the S&P 500), but portfolios indexed to illiquid securities (small-cap stocks or some value indexes) can incur costs large enough to affect performance significantly. Instead of "pure" indexing, some passive index funds have performed better by allowing minor deviations from the underlying index, thereby reducing the volume of trading and corresponding trading costs.

A recent study of a small-cap index fund is instructive. The fund was willing to provide liquidity in the upstairs (block) market by offering to sell stocks that had moved out of its universe and buy those that had moved into its universe. Consequently, it earned the price concession paid by the liquidity demander, although with some tracking error. In the small cap universe of the fund, comprising the bottom 20 per cent of NYSE stocks by market capitalization, this strategy added 2 per cent return a year.

Predicting costs

Two factors complicate the estimation and prediction of trading costs. First, although some cost elements are predictable, others (for example, opportunity and timing costs) vary with the trader's investment style and market conditions. Second, variability in implicit costs is related to factors that are difficult to quantify, such as trader reputation, skill, investment objectives and subtleties of the trading process (such as upstairs trading).

Our capabilities for predicting costs are improving with better electronic systems and as we advance our understanding of costs. Sophisticated tools estimate the cost of trading, given style and other factors, and recommend the best way of breaking up a block into smaller transactions.

Conclusion

The following findings on equity trading costs appear important.

- Studies must measure both implicit and explicit costs at the level of the entire order (not by individual trades).
- Implicit costs are economically significant relative to explicit costs and relative to realized portfolio returns.
- Costs vary with trade difficulty and order-placement strategy. Market design, investment style, trading ability and reputation also play a part.

For policymakers and investors, the concept of "best execution", especially for institutional traders, is better left to market competition because it is difficult to measure or enforce. Comparisons among trading systems must recognize differences in their structures and objectives. Even with similar systems, one should not rely solely on comparisons of trade costs, especially not on explicit costs alone.

For investment managers, better understanding and control of trade costs could improve their performance and results.

This article is based on "The costs of institutional equity trades", *Financial Analysts Journal*, July–August 1998.

Copyright © Donald Keim and Ananth Madhavan 2002

Further reading

Bruce, B. (ed.) (2001) *Transaction Costs: An Institutional Investor Investment Guide*, New York: Institutional Investor Inc.

Domowitz, I. and Steil, B. (2000) "Automation, trading costs and the structure of the securities trading industry" in Litan, R.E. and Santomero, A.M. (eds) Brookings-Wharton Papers on Financial Services 1999, Washington DC: Brookings Institution Press.

Equity loans:
how to sell what you do not own

The market for lending equities is obscure and privately negotiated, but the benefits are substantial. **Christopher Geczy**, **David Musto** and **Adam Reed** explain.

Christopher C. Geczy is an assistant professor of finance at the Wharton School of the University of Pennsylvania.

David K. Musto is an assistant professor of finance at the Wharton School of the University of Pennsylvania.

Adam V. Reed is a doctoral student at the Wharton School of the University of Pennsylvania.

Behind the scenes of the world's stock markets we find the equity-lending market. To appreciate its role we must step back from the usual perspective on equities, that of a potential buyer. Long trades, that is, trades that involve buying today and selling later, constitute only half the possibilities available to traders. They can also "short", or sell today and buy later, so that returns improve as prices drop.

It is tempting to view a short trade as simply the opposite of a long one, but the logistics are different and sometimes difficult or even impossible. The reason is that the short-seller must deliver like any other seller – but does not have what is sold.

Loan pricing

The problem of delivering shares one does not have is solved by equity lending. Executing a share loan requires access, such as any US brokerage would offer, to equity loans. An equity loan is best thought of as a temporary swap of legal ownership. The lender transfers ownership of some shares to the borrower, who is then free to pass the ownership on to someone else. At the same time as the shares are transferred, the borrower transfers ownership of collateral, usually cash. In the US, the standard collateral is cash amounting to 102 per cent of the value of the shares, to be adjusted daily as their value fluctuates.

So, to borrow 20,000 shares of a company trading at $50 a share, the borrower would remit $1.02m to the lender and would pay in or get back collateral as the shares rise or fall respectively. The loan is closed out when the borrower transfers the 20,000 shares back to the lender, who simultaneously returns the collateral.

But who gets the interest on the collateral? This is the key to pricing the loan. The lender invests the collateral and collects the interest, and the standard investment is a minimal-risk overnight instrument earning close to the Federal Funds rate (this being the inter-bank lending market where repayment is almost certain). If the lender simply kept all interest, the loan's cost and the lender's gross revenue would be as follows. Assuming the loan lasts n days, the lender would receive n days of interest on the collateral at the Fed Funds rate, that is:

$$1.02 \times \text{security value} \times \text{Fed Funds rate} \times (n/360)$$

For the example earlier, this would be $992 for seven days (assuming the Fed Funds rate is 5 per cent and the price stays at $50 a share). But the lending market is not so kind to lenders; they have to give back most of this interest.

Rebates

The loan contract will specify a rebate rate, which is the interest the lender must repay to the borrower. This rebate is usually almost everything. Securities that are not scarce in the lending market – which includes most stocks on a given day and almost always the large ones – have the same rebate rate, known as the general rate.

The general rate is around 20 basis points below the going overnight rate (one basis point being 0.01 per cent), so the rebate in the loan described above would not be 0 per cent but more like 4.8 per cent. This implies a cost to the borrower and gross revenue to the lender of just $40. It is important to note that these are wholesale terms for large loans; retail brokerage customers get a much smaller rebate because of the proportionately larger fixed costs they incur on each loan and the intermediary layers they encounter. But even the big wholesale customers see their rebates shrink as the security gets scarce.

When supply of a stock is small enough relative to its borrowing demand, lenders negotiate lower rebates. A stock in this situation is said to be "on special" and the shortfall in its rebate is called its specialness. Why would a stock go on special? For one thing, it probably started there.

Stocks are notoriously hard to borrow in the first days after their initial public offering (IPO). In our research we find IPOs to be invariably on special at first, with an average specialness of more than 300 basis points. Specialness gradually settles down to mature-stock levels, in particular after the insider-selling restrictions end at 180 days. Once a stock emerges from the initial shortage it is usually not scarce unless a new event associated with widespread shorting occurs.

The major event associated with borrowing scarcity is merger arbitrage. When one company proposes to absorb another, arbitrageurs such as hedge funds often wish to buy the target and short-sell the acquirer. This generally pays off if the merger goes through and loses if it does not. An example is At Home's acquisition of Excite, which made At Home very expensive to borrow. Another example was the proposed merger of Office Depot with Staples, which made Staples extremely expensive to borrow, compounding the losses to arbitrageurs when the deal fell through. Specialness in these situations can sometimes reach 90 per cent. This means the arbitrageur's profit net of borrowing costs can be much lower than it first appears.

Lending revenue

It also means lenders can make a lot of money. The lender can potentially earn the gross return of the hedge funds' speculative position by selling its stake in the acquirer and buying the target; or it could simply lend the shares and thereby accrue some of the trade's gross return with none of its risk. This source of income, often called hypothecating income, can offset the expenses of managing certain portfolios.

Portfolios in the best situation to benefit from lending are index funds, especially those that contain many small stocks. Indexing brings two related benefits. The index's low turnover implies low turnover for the fund, so the fund can lend with little fear of needing the shares back soon, which would happen if the fund needed to sell. Also, the fund's mandate to track – rather than outperform – the index encourages it to hold even those index constituents that others are shorting, and not to withhold shares from the lending market on the theory that short-selling would hurt the price. The virtue of small stocks is simply that they are more likely to grow scarce, other things being equal.

Consider, for example, Vanguard's Extended Market Index Fund, a $5bn, 3,055-stock fund tracking the Wilshire 4500 index. The company's 2000 annual report shows security lending income of $10.5m (about 20 basis points) and total expenses of $13m (about 25 basis points). So the income from lending shares offsets 80 per cent of expenses. The report also shows that only 3 per cent of the fund's year-end value was out on loan ($164m of $5.3bn).

Similarly, Vanguard's 1,896-stock Small-Cap Index Fund shows 10 basis points of lending revenue, against 20 basis points of expenses, with only 2 per cent out on loan. The implication is that the fund's shareholders achieve net returns much closer to those of their target indices than their expense ratios, taken in isolation, would suggest, while lending only a small fraction of shares – presumably just the specials. Once we move beyond small-cap index funds, though, this revenue mostly dries up. Within Vanguard we find only 0.4 basis points of lending revenue for the Mid-Cap Index Fund, and 1 basis point for the Windsor I Fund, which is actively managed.

Efficient markets

Lending revenue is one way that investors in general, and not just short-sellers, benefit from equity lending. There is also the less tangible but more general benefit of increased market efficiency. By facilitating short sales, the lending market transforms negative information into negative demand, speeding its incorporation into prices.

For example, stocks that are not specials, and so are relatively easy to short, respond relatively less well to negative earnings announcements than do the specials, although their response to positive news is normal. So when scarcity in the lending market makes a stock hard to short, the market is more surprised by the publication of bad news than it is by good news. The implication is that investors who already know or suspect bad news before its publication have relatively less success trading on it with the specials, and so incorporate less of it into the pre-publication price (see Reed, 2001). By contrast, trading on good news is not a problem. Bad news will eventually have its effect; society's benefit from equity lending is that this happens sooner, reducing the likelihood that some investors might buy at prices that other investors know to be high.

Legal issues

The research organization Robert Morris Associates estimated the value of US equities on loan as $104bn at the end of 2000. The figure for European equities was $43bn. In spite of its size, this market is far from centralized. An equity loan arranged by a broker might be made up of shares from another account at the brokerage, or from a mutual fund lending its portfolio, or from a custodian bank lending from its clients' portfolios, as the clients permit. The whole variety of institutional accounts participate, and in contrast to the visible and publicly available market for equities, the market for equity loans is obscure and privately negotiated.

Every day, lenders have borrowing prices for all stocks but they do not report them, even to the *Financial Times*, and they do not systematically make them available to all investors. For example, our research found that at least three out of four IPOs can be borrowed on their respective first days, but retail investors hoping to short IPOs should expect much less success; their brokers will likely report that the trade is simply not possible.

There is a dimension of equity lending that is driven not by short-selling but by the seemingly technical distinction between legal and beneficial share ownership. If A loans B a share on Monday and gets it back on Tuesday, then B is the share's legal owner at the close of Monday trading. That means B receives any benefit that accrues to legal owners. For the loan not to interfere with A's enjoyment of the benefits of ownership, however, B is generally required to reimburse to A whatever accrues to Monday's legal owners, so A remains the share's "beneficial" owner. The usual benefit would be a cash dividend, but it could be a stock dividend or some other distribution. If Monday was the record date of such a distribution, B owes it to A. (There is an exception to this rule in corporate votes. If Monday is the record date of a vote, B gets the right to make the vote, not A.)

These distribution issues may seem like technicalities but they can be the primary reason for equity loans. That is, investors borrow not because they shorted and need to deliver but because they value the distributions they get more than the reimbursements they give.

To see how this could occur, consider dividend tax credits. Many countries (such as Canada, France, Germany and Italy) give some sort of credit to their tax-paying citizens for the dividend income they receive from domestic corporations. One way to get this credit is to borrow a domestic company's shares for a dividend record date. The dividend coming in is taxable but qualifies for the tax credit and the reimbursement going out is a deductible expense. The net effect (roughly) is zero cash flow at dividend time, with the dividend matching the reimbursement, plus zero taxable income, net of the deduction, plus the credit. The opacity of the lending market makes it hard to gauge the intensity of this sort of activity, but the incentive is large. An investor not eligible for the credit, such as a foreign citizen, cannot earn it directly but can get some of it indirectly, via the pricing of the loan.

Conclusion

The equity-lending market is obscure but vital. By facilitating short-selling it extends the opportunity to sell an equity beyond the group of investors already holding it. This is not only a direct service to investors interested in negative exposure to the equity but also an indirect benefit to everybody because it enlarges the set of information that the equity's price reflects.

Consumers may also benefit, without realizing it, from equity-lending income earned on their pension or mutual funds. This income can be so large that it offsets most of the funds' expenses, and it might not result from short-selling. Finally, in certain situations, such as dividend days for some countries' equities, loans are popular simply for the legal ownership – potentially leading to tax credits – that they confer.

Copyright © Christopher Geczy, David Musto and Adam Reed 2002

Further reading

Geczy, C.G., Musto, D.K. and Reed, A.V. (2001) "Stocks are special too: an analysis of the equity lending market", working paper (http://intranet.kenan-flagler.unc.edu/faculty/reeda/gmr.pdf).

Reed. A.V. (2001) "Costly short-selling and stock price reactions to earnings announcements", working paper (http://intranet.kenan-flagler.unc.edu/faculty/reeda/reed_paper.pdf).

"Securities lending transactions: Market development and implications (1999)", Bank for International Settlements (http://www.bis.org/publ/cpss32.pdf).

Consolidated limit order book:
future perfect or future shock?

Trading systems vary and there is a debate raging in the US about whether to standardize on a consolidated limit order book system. **Kenneth Kavajecz** summarizes the arguments.

Kenneth A. Kavajecz is an assistant professor of finance at the Wharton School of the University of Pennsylvania.

Many different trading systems make up the landscape of today's global equity market. These include specialist systems such as the New York Stock Exchange, competitive dealer systems such as Nasdaq and Seaq, and pure limit order markets, for example Electronic Communication Networks, the Paris Bourse and the Toronto Stock Exchange. Given their diversity, it is not surprising that there is a debate as to which trading system is best for investors and what best actually means.

Arthur Levitt, former chairman of the US Securities and Exchange Commission, sparked the debate by calling for research into the possibility of creating a consolidated limit order book for US equities. Under a consolidated limit order book system, or CLOB, limit orders would be collected into a central electronic system and displayed according to price-time priority. This is in contrast to the existing fragmented system, whereby limit orders are maintained by individual exchanges and dealers. The concept produced strong reactions from a wide range of market participants.

To appreciate the arguments, as well as how a CLOB is likely to affect investors, we must first understand the nature of limit orders and limit order books. Broadly speaking, traders can choose between using a market order or a limit order. A limit order specifies the side of the market (that is, "buy" or "sell"), the quantity to be traded, the length of time the order is active and the worst price the trader is willing to accept. For example, an investor may submit a limit order to buy 500 shares of a stock, where the order is active until the close of trading that day and the investor is willing to transact at any price less than or equal to the limit price of $20.875.

In submitting a limit order, an investor runs the risk of delayed execution as well as the risk that the order is never executed. Because active limit orders stand ready to trade at the discretion of other market participants, they are thought of as supplying liquidity to the market, in much the same way as a marketmaker stands ready to buy shares when investors want to sell and to sell when investors want to buy.

In contrast, a market order, which merely specifies the side of the market and the quantity, represents an implicit agreement to transact at the best available price when the order arrives at the trading venue. For example, instead of a limit order, the same investor could have submitted a market order, which guarantees execution, to buy 500 shares of XYZ stock; however, the trade price is not known in advance. The need to trade immediately requires liquidity from the market; therefore market orders can be thought of as demanding liquidity.

Given that limit orders may not be executed immediately when they are submitted, at any time there are active limit orders awaiting execution or further action (such as amending or cancelling the order) by the submitting investor. A limit order book is the current set of active limit orders that is sent to, and maintained by, an exchange or dealer. Orders on a limit order book are arranged first by price and then by time, with low-priced sell orders and high-priced buy orders having the highest priority. Within a set of limit orders with the same limit price, they are arranged so that orders submitted earlier (oldest orders) have priority over later orders.

Figure 1 is an example of a limit order book for a hypothetical stock XYZ on April 10, 2001 at 11.30 am that is maintained by a particular marketmaker or

FIGURE 1 Limit order book for stock XYZ on 10 April, 2001 at 11.30 am

Date	Time	Side	Duration	Shares	Price					
04-04	9:38:18	Sell	GTC*	800	30.000					
03-30	14:21:01	Sell	GTC	100	29.875					
03-29	10:15:55	Sell	GTC	200	29.500					
04-09	12:02:34	Sell	GTC	100	27.500					
04-05	15:36:28	Sell	GTC	500	26.000					
04-09	9:22:25	Sell	GTC	200	24.000					
03-30	15:07:51	Sell	GTC	100	24.000					
04-10	11:11:07	Sell	Day	200	23.500					
04-09	13:00:34	Sell	GTC	1,000	23.500					
04-10	10:19:44	Sell	Day	300	23.000					
04-10	9:30:17	Sell	Day	1,000	22.875					
04-10	11:04:31	Sell	Day	500	22.500					
04-10	11:28:03	Sell	Day	100	22.375					
04-10	11:04:59	Sell	Day	2,000	22.375					
Marketmaker quote			Offer depth 2,500		Offer 22.375	Bid 22.125	Bid depth 500			
						22.125	500	Day	Buy 11:26:47	04-10
						22.000	1,400	Day	Buy 11:21:53	04-10
						20.875	500	GTC*	Buy 8:50:38	04-10
						20.000	200	GTC	Buy 9:39:57	03-28
						20.000	100	GTC	Buy 10:06:40	04-04
						20.000	100	GTC	Buy 10:06:40	04-04
						20.000	500	GTC	Buy 11:27:59	04-05
						19.875	100	GTC	Buy 13:57:42	04-02
						18.000	100	GTC	Buy 12:02:40	03-26
						17.750	200	GTC	Buy 9:51:30	01-08
						Price	Shares	Duration	Side Time	Date

*GTC means good-until-cancelled orders; Day means limit orders that expire at close of trading

trading venue. The upper left panel displays sell limit orders arranged by increasing price-time priority, while the lower right panel displays buy limit orders arranged by decreasing price-time priority. Investors typically are not able to view the limit order book at a given trading venue. Instead, most trading venues disseminate the marketmaker's quotes, which are shown in the centre of Figure 1.

A descriptive way of viewing a limit order book is in its cumulative depth form. Cumulative depth at a given limit price measures the number of shares available at or below that limit price for sell limit orders and the number of shares available at or above that limit price for buy limit orders. For example, Figure 1 shows that there are 2,100 shares available for sale at \$22.375; thus, the cumulative depth at \$22.375 is 2,100 shares. Correspondingly, the cumulative depth at \$22.875 is 3,600 shares (2,100 at \$22.375, 500 at \$22.500 and 1,000 at \$22.875). By adding all the limit order shares that are available for execution at successively distance limit prices, the cumulative depth of the limit order book can be constructed.

Figure 2 displays the cumulative depth for the XYZ limit order book presented in Figure 1. The shares on the left represent the limit orders to buy and the shares on the right represent the limit orders to sell. Consequently, the cumulative depths represent the current demand and supply schedules for XYZ shares. The space in the centre of Figure 2 represents the current bid-offer spread on the XYZ limit order book.

The example in Figures 1 and 2 represents a limit order book at a particular time, which is maintained by a particular marketmaker or exchange. Each trading venue that makes a market in XYZ stock maintains its own limit order book; therefore, there are several limit order books in the market at any time.

The importance of maintaining links among these competing trading venues motivated an amendment in 1975 to the Securities and Exchange Act of 1934, which mandated the creation of a National Market System (NMS). While the goal of the NMS has been the integration of trading activities on the separate systems, the current platform, that is, the Intermarket Trading System (ITS), displays only best prices and corresponding depths at each of the trading venues rather than the entire limit order book.

Various facts about structure and linkages between these trading venues provide the backdrop for the CLOB debate. First, order flow and liquidity

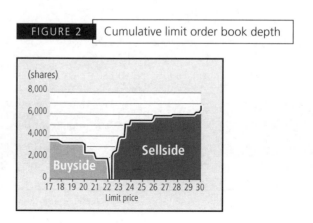

FIGURE 2　Cumulative limit order book depth

provision are fragmented among these competing exchanges. Second, because the ITS system reports only the best prices and depths at each venue, it does not maintain price/time priority across trading venues even though the limit order books adhere to price/time priority within each trading venue. Third, the existence of trading floors that are not completely electronic (such as the NYSE, the American Stock Exchange and regional exchanges) implies that not all available liquidity is necessarily displayed within a venue's quotes.

CLOB proponents

In general, proponents of a consolidated limit order book argue that the current system fails in two respects. It does not afford equal treatment of all liquidity providers. In addition, the current system fragments liquidity among competing venues so it is costly to trade large numbers of shares at a single venue.

The argument that the current system does not afford equal treatment of liquidity providers is based on the fact that competing limit order books are not integrated with respect to time. As a result, limit orders sent to remote trading venues often do not receive the same exposure as limit orders sent to larger trading venues. For example, assume that the NMS best bid and offer (NBBO) is $22.125 bid and $22.375 offer, with 500 shares at both the bid and offer. Consider two limit orders, sent at the same time, to buy 500 shares of XYZ at $22.125. One is sent to the Boston Stock Exchange and the other to the NYSE. Suppose a sequence of market sell orders arrives at the NYSE that induces trading to occur at $22.125 such that the NYSE limit order and many other similarly priced, but younger, limit orders are executed. If the market were to move subsequently to $22.250 bid and $22.500 offer, the limit order sent to the Boston Stock Exchange would go unexecuted, while younger NYSE limit orders would be executed.

Under another scenario, the Boston limit order could be the only order determining the NMS bid, yet market sell orders are executed on the NYSE at $22.1875, giving a $1/16 improvement on the Boston quote. The presence of floor brokers at a trading venue allows some liquidity to remain undisplayed as orders are worked by hand rather than submitted electronically. This undisplayed liquidity may be executed at a limit price of $22.125 or better, while the Boston limit order again goes unexecuted.

These possible scenarios arise because the NMS links these competing trading venues only by price and not by time. Proponents of a CLOB argue that the aggregation of all limit orders into a single trading venue would provide a level playing field, in that all limit orders would be subject to a single price/time priority ordering. The internal consistency of a single limit order book would ensure that all limit orders and all liquidity providers (limit orders traders, brokers and marketmakers) were treated in the same way. A CLOB would eliminate the possibility that newer orders could be executed in advance of, or instead of, older orders with the same limit price.

Moreover, the collection of all limit orders into a common electronic book alleviates undisplayed liquidity since the absence of a trading floor would necessitate that all liquidity providers post their trading interest by limit orders rather than using floor brokers. As a result, consolidation would not only eliminate the possibility of undisplayed liquidity stepping in front of standing limit orders but would also make it easier for liquidity demanders to be exposed to the entire set of liquidity supplied for that security.

Finally, there is support for a CLOB from a theoretical perspective. In a 1994 study, Professor Lawrence Glosten presented a stylized model of various trading systems competing to supply liquidity. Glosten argued that an open electronic limit order book system, unlike other liquidity provision mechanisms, would not invite competition from alternative trading systems. Furthermore, he argued that an open CLOB would provide at least as much liquidity as any competing system within both normal and extreme trading environments.

CLOB opponents

In general, opponents of a CLOB centre their arguments on the idea that mandating a single liquidity provision system stifles competition to supply liquidity, making it difficult to innovate. They also argue that creating a CLOB presupposes that all orders and all market participants have the same implicit goals. This "one-size-fits-all" structure may mitigate the process of specialization within the market to provide liquidity. For example, market participants often have different ideas of what constitutes good execution: day traders require speed of execution while others, such as fund managers, need to trade large blocks of stock.

Moreover, a CLOB may have other costs associated with the behaviour of limit order traders. For example, reductions in the minimum price variation (tick size), from an eighth to a sixteenth in 1997 and more recently to pennies, have reduced dramatically the cumulative depth on limit order books.

Professor Michael Goldstein and the author (2000) show that in 1997, the cumulative depth on the NYSE limit order books was reduced by between a quarter and a half after the tick size reduction. The reduction in cumulative depth resulted in transaction cost increases for liquidity demanders trading large blocks or trading infrequently traded shares. The reaction by limit order traders was because a small minimum price variation makes it less costly for limit order traders to compete on price. This allows competing limit orders to step in front of less aggressive limit orders with only a small price concession. A limit order trader gives away the right to determine when an order is executed. In this sense, limit orders are like options. Reducing the minimum tick size effectively reduces the premium that limit order traders are able to extract for their option, thereby making them less willing to give the option away (by displaying liquidity via posting a limit order).

Another potential concern is that a CLOB may make prices more volatile. Unlike some designated marketmakers, limit order traders have no obligation to constantly supply liquidity. Consequently, limit order traders may be more sensitive to the costs of supplying liquidity than designated marketmakers. This sensitivity could manifest itself in more volatile CLOB prices or, in the extreme, lower liquidity due to the scarcity of, or even absence of, limit orders.

Finally, a study by the author and Professor Elizabeth Odders-White (2001) showed that on the NYSE, prices on limit order books tend to be more volatile than quoted or transaction prices. Also, evidence suggests limit order traders may react more dramatically than other liquidity providers to extreme market movements.

Conclusion

The arguments both for and against a CLOB, strike a chord with investors because each side has a fundamental principle as its foundation: equal treatment of all market participants on the one hand and the need for unfettered competition on the other. It is clear that a CLOB would place all limit orders on a level playing field. However, it is not clear that limit order traders would care to "play" to the same extent after the field is level.

Markets are designed to bring together buyers and sellers, liquidity demanders and liquidity suppliers. A successful market dictates that both sides of a trade be willing to participate. Therefore, markets must be designed to weigh the needs of liquidity demanders and suppliers properly. The proper weighting of these needs is difficult.

Economic agents who are free to pursue their self-interest in an environment where competition and innovation are left unobstructed will gravitate towards institutions that provide the right service at the lowest cost. Commensurate with this ideal, the Securities and Exchange Commission (SEC) enacted regulation requiring exchanges to publish regularly statistics on execution quality. The goal is to inform market participants about the quality of the liquidity provision service so that they may make informed choices about where and how to trade. The hope is that institutions providing poor execution quality are likely to lose order flow to institutions providing the best quality.

In summary, while a consolidated limit order book system has both merits and costs, it is difficult to determine an optimal market structure given the speed with which circumstances change, technology advances and innovations are born. Even if a CLOB is an optimal liquidity provision structure, simply mandating its creation bypasses the critical process by which a market arrives at a particular structure. The preferences and demands of market participants shape, and are shaped by, the ability of other market participants to step in and satisfy those demands. Since markets are set up to facilitate this interaction, they become the forum by which liquidity demanders and suppliers learn about each other as well as the common structure that best suits their needs over time.

Copyright © Kenneth Kavajecz 2002

Further reading

Glosten, L.R. (1994) "Is the electronic open limit order book inevitable?", *Journal of Finance*, 49, 1127–61.

Goldstein, M.A. and Kavajecz, K.A. (2000) "Eighths, sixteenths and market depth: changes in tick size and liquidity provision on the NYSE", *Journal of Financial Economics*, 56, 125–49.

Kavajecz, K.A. (1999) "The specialist's quoted depth and the limit order book", *Journal of Finance*, 54, 747–71.

Kavajecz, K.A. and Odders-White, E. (2001) "Volatility and market structure", *Journal of Financial Markets*, 4, October.

Asset **allocation** 4

Contents

How to mix assets to match needs 128
Suresh Sundaresan, Columbia Business School

Different kinds of investors choose different balances of assets. Risk preferences, funding priorities and ease of investment or withdrawal are important factors in the choice of asset mix.

Asset allocation and the importance of active investment strategies 135
Craig MacKinlay, University of Pennsylvania

This article confronts the view that asset allocation is everything, and finds value in active management.

The equity premium puzzle 141
Rajnish Mehra, University of California Santa Barbara

Historical data show that stocks have delivered better returns than bonds. Investment theories suggest, however, that the difference should be much smaller. This article looks at possible explanations for the discrepancy.

Working hard for better returns 147
John Heaton, University of Chicago Graduate School of Business and **Deborah Lucas**, Kellogg Graduate School of Management

Investors have learnt that diversification is good for returns. How does the concentration of labour income, property and small businesses affect investment theory?

Investing with death in mind 153
Charles Kindleberger, Massachusetts Institute of Technology

This article gives advice on investing wisely and reducing risk when facing a short investment horizon.

Stocks and bonds in the portfolio lifecycle 157
Steven Davis, University of Chicago Graduate School of Business and **Rajnish Mehra**, University of California Santa Barbara

This article assesses the conventional wisdom that says we should switch out of equities into safer bond-related investments as we age.

Introduction to Part 4

How should investors spread their assets to reduce risk? They can choose from a multitude of asset classes, including equities, treasury bonds, derivatives and property. The act of selecting an appropriate mix of assets to hold is known as asset allocation and, for individual investors, is greatly influenced by age, working status and aversion to risk. As writers in this part explain, asset allocation also deals with how investors should alter the mix of securities over time to take account of economic changes.

How to mix assets to match needs

Suresh M. Sundaresan is Chase Manhattan Bank Foundation Professor of Financial Institutions at Columbia Business School.

Suresh Sundaresan outlines a basic framework for asset allocation to reflect the different funding priorities of households and institutions.

The term "asset allocation" encompasses two concepts: first, the mix of assets, such as stocks, bonds, certificates of deposit or real estate, that an individual, household or institution decides to hold; and second, the manner in which the mix is varied over time in response to changes in the economy and individual circumstances.

Households and institutions analyze their investment opportunities and make asset allocation decisions to meet goals that reflect their preferences for risk and return, their tax environment and their future funding needs. The following illustrations show how this occurs.

Example A: the young household

A relatively young family with children may allocate savings to a mix of stocks and bonds, so that the annual income from the portfolio will fund the future expenditures associated with schooling and college education. In this case, the household may accept a lower growth rate in the investment to ensure sufficient annual income to fund the recurring expense of education. This may call for a greater emphasis on high-quality bonds, which provide a stable income, and less emphasis on stocks, which can fluctuate dramatically in market value over time.

If the household is wealthy enough to meet the costs of education solely from its earnings, the asset allocation picture may change. The household may emphasize stocks in the portfolio to provide for growth for the children, as the portfolio is not expected to meet recurring costs such as education. If there are tax incentives that promote savings in less risky assets to fund future educational expenses, that will tilt the asset allocation in favour of bonds.

This example suggests that the level of earnings, tax incentives and the cost of education can all influence the way households choose to allocate their assets.

Example B: the pension plan

Corporate sponsors of pension plans select professional portfolio managers to manage a mix of stocks and bonds on their behalf. Their objectives are to meet the obligations in benefit payments associated with retired employees and the future obligations of active employees with vested pension benefits. A company that has a mature workforce, where a significant number of employees has vested benefits, may select a portfolio that emphasizes high-quality bonds. The cash flows from the bonds can then be used to fund the benefits.

A company with a significant surplus of assets over projected liabilities may emphasize stocks more in the portfolio because the existing surplus provides a cushion to absorb fluctuations in the value of stocks, but the stocks themselves may provide potentially greater rewards. On the other hand, if a pension plan has a limited surplus it may emphasize bonds to ensure projected funding obligations can be met. The size of the surplus (or deficit) of assets over projected liabilities is an important factor in the asset allocation decision of a pension sponsor.

Further, many countries offer tax advantages to people who have long-term savings (towards retirement, for example). This implies that an asset location decision is also relevant for households. The asset location decision refers to the choice between holding an asset in a retirement or tax-deferred account, as opposed to holding it in an open account, which is subject to normal tax treatment. The tax status of some assets may influence both the asset location and asset allocation decision.

Example C: the money manager

Professional money managers make asset allocation decisions relative to an index, which serves as their performance benchmark. The compensation received by money managers often depends on their ability to "outperform" the index. The idea is that the manager should be able to match the performance of the index by a simple "buy and hold" strategy. Figure 1 shows the Lehman Brothers Index, which is one of the popular indices used to measure the performance of money managers.

Money managers may choose portfolios that give greater weight to certain sectors based on their own beliefs and analysis. Figure 2 shows the asset allocation of a hypothetical money manager. Note that the manager has weighted his portfolio towards the corporate sector, agencies and asset-backed securities relative to the index. The overall interest rate risk and the credit risk of the manager's portfolio will still be held close (but not identical) to the index.

The basic idea is that the money manager is given some discretion in choosing the sectors and securities, but since his performance is measured relative to that of the index, he has an incentive not to deviate "too much"

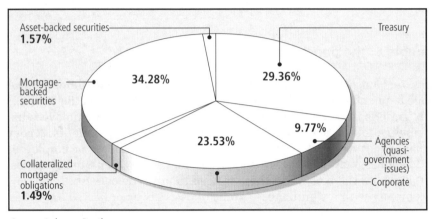

FIGURE 1 Lehman Brothers Index, June 2000

Source: Lehman Brothers

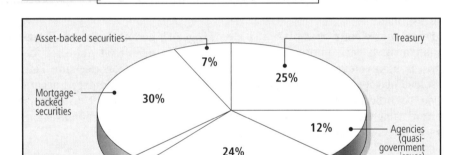

FIGURE 2 Asset allocation of investment manager

from the index. The money manager will have to explain his strategy of deviations from the index to his clients. Further, the clients can specify indices of their choice, such as a small-cap stock index, a high-yield bond index or an emerging market index.

These examples show that asset allocation decisions affect all kinds of investors. How should investors build a basic framework for asset allocation in which their goals reflect their funding priorities?

Framework

A conceptual framework for asset allocation must address a number of factors. The asset allocation decision turns on the trade-offs between the following three choices, which are inter-related:

- risk and return;
- short-term funding priorities and future growth;
- liquid versus illiquid investments (the latter might include tax-deferred investment, for example).

Risk-return trade-offs

The trade-off between risk and return is a critical factor in asset allocation. Modern portfolio theory (MPT) suggests that investors will not want to expose themselves to risk that can be diversified away. They will therefore hold diversified portfolios of stocks that carry the so-called "non-diversifiable" or market risk. In other words, MPT suggests that investors should hold broad stock market portfolios, such as index funds. With such portfolios, their main risk is that the entire market may go down – hence such risk is called market risk.

Risk-averse investors will allocate part of their wealth to this diversified stock portfolio and the rest to risk-free bonds. In this framework, the more risk-averse the investor, the more of their wealth they allocate to risk-free bonds. To use academic terminology, the investor maximizes the expected return (mean returns) on the portfolio while keeping the risk (measured by the variance of returns) at a level that is consistent with their risk aversion. The resulting portfolio is sometimes referred to as the "mean-variance efficient portfolio" – the mix of assets that gets the best return given the investor's preference for risk.

The practical implementation of this scheme has been well understood. Professional investment companies specialize in selecting mean-variance efficient portfolios from an array of assets. The MPT framework is a useful place to start but is too simplistic or parsimonious: it does not take into account dimensions such as funding needs or liquidity requirements. We need to modify the MPT to get a better guide to real-life asset allocation problems, where such requirements do play a prominent role.

Moreover, the MPT relies on a static, fixed time horizon in which investors do not have to worry about revising their decisions. In reality, funding priorities, liquidity needs and the liability structure may all change in important ways. But the framework is rich enough to accommodate the changes needed to make the asset allocation model sufficiently realistic.

Funding priorities and growth

We mentioned earlier that funding priorities might influence asset allocation. In particular, the optimal portfolio, which includes funding priorities, may well differ from the mean-variance efficient portfolio, which applies to a fixed time horizon. To show how, consider the problem facing a corporate pension sponsor. Note that corporate pension assets in developed countries constitute a significant part of the overall assets of a company. A successful asset allocation strategy can make a big difference to overall profitability. At one extreme, if a company were to ignore pension liabilities, it would have selected a mean-variance efficient portfolio consistent with the risk aversion exhibited by its senior managers. Managers can be very risk averse if a significant percentage of their wealth and compensation depends on the performance of their portfolio. (For the purposes of this example we are ignoring the fact that pension asset management is customarily delegated to professional money managers.)

At the other extreme, if the company were to focus only on its future funding needs, it would buy a portfolio whose cash flows exactly matched those needs. This is sometimes called a "liability-replicating portfolio". For example, if the pension liabilities are projected at £10m a year, the liability-replicating portfolio may simply be a portfolio of government bonds whose cash flows amount to £10m a year. This is a matched funding strategy.

In reality, the choice of asset allocation will be neither a mean-variance efficient portfolio nor a liability-replicating portfolio. The pension sponsor may have an incentive to pursue strategies whereby the value of pension portfolio exceeds the pension liabilities – in other words, to create a surplus of pension assets over pension liabilities. For example, a pension surplus reduces future funding needs and provides an internal source of capital. In fact, the extent to which the sponsor may have such an incentive depends on accounting and tax treatment of the surplus and the ability of senior managers to access the surplus for purposes unrelated to the pension.

If surplus assets can be accessed for corporate purposes without any penalties, there is a strong incentive to build them up. There may be strategic reasons for doing this. For example, pension surpluses have been used for financing mergers and buyouts. Typically, however, the pension contributions made by the company to the pension plans are tax-deductible. Hence it is very likely that the pension surplus (built with such a tax subsidy) will not be available to the sponsor without significant tax penalties.

How does the corporate pension manager build up the surplus and how does this affect the allocation of assets in the portfolio? Mainly, the manager would raise the level of equity investment, since equity has outperformed other investments in the long term. But this return comes at a risk. Too much emphasis on equity may leave the pension assets vulnerable to short-term fluctuations in stock values, which in turn could lead to a potentially disastrous shortfall in funding requirements. Note that the S&P 500 index, which provided returns ranging from 21 per cent to 37.5 per cent during 1995–99, lost 9.1 per cent in 2000. The latter risk will tilt the portfolio towards high-quality bonds; bond indexes tend to have a more stable performance.

For a pension sponsor who has built up a large surplus, the risk of not meeting the funding requirements is low and such a sponsor may pursue an asset allocation policy close to the mean-variance efficient portfolio. For a sponsor whose pension surplus is insignificant, the optimal policy may be the liability-replicating portfolio. For most other sponsors, the optimal portfolio is a combination of the two portfolios. The extent of current and desired surplus will determine whether the sponsor sails closer to the mean-variance efficient portfolio or the liability-replicating portfolio.

The analysis presented here generalizes easily for other investors. For example, insurance companies design their asset portfolios to reflect their liabilities. They may issue annuities, which they hedge by purchasing high-quality bonds of similar duration.

Liquid versus illiquid assets

The investor also needs to decide how liquid or illiquid the asset mix should be – in other words, how easy it is to buy and sell the constituent assets. A liquid portfolio allows investors to move quickly to change the asset mix, yet illiquid assets can often be advantageous.

To illustrate this trade-off, let us examine the typical household that we introduced earlier. During the peak of his working career, the householder enjoys growing wage income and prospects of even higher wages in the future. This suggests he can afford to invest in assets that may have high growth prospects but may be relatively illiquid or even inaccessible until retirement. He may instead decide to focus on high-growth assets such as stocks in pension plans or in tax-deferred accounts. Typically, assets placed in pensions or other tax-deferred accounts are either entirely inaccessible until retirement or accessible earlier only with a significant penalty. Quite aside from explicit penalties, accessing them prematurely will also bring tax liabilities.

Such a decision has several costs and benefits. By locating an increasing amount of assets in a pension plan or a tax-deferred account, the householder accepts that the assets are unavailable to meet consumption (or funding) needs until retirement or the terminal date by which assets can be accessed without penalty. One might think of this as an opportunity cost. On the other hand, by locating assets in such plans the householder may be able to reduce the present value of tax liabilities. Research shows that the manner in which the householder chooses between tax-deferred accounts and open accounts may depend on factors such as age, wealth and the nature and magnitude of capital gains in the portfolio held by the household.

The liquidity issue also bears on other investment forms. A local government body, for example, may have to fund the construction of major roads and requires capital expenditures of $20m every year for the next five years. The body may fund a project by buying a portfolio of safe bonds. Such a portfolio may not be very liquid but it is unlikely to carry any default risk. By choosing illiquid bonds the council may actually reduce its funding costs – it has no need to sell these bonds at short notice but only needs to avail itself of the cash flows the bonds provide.

By contrast, consider a national bank. It may often have to engage in open market operations at short notice. It would therefore need very liquid securities that can be bought or sold at a narrow bid-offer spread. If the investor needs to withdraw cash periodically at certain times that can be predicted reasonably accurately, the asset allocation decision can be designed to meet that requirement by placing funds in safe bonds. However, if the cash flow needs cannot be predicted, the asset allocation decision must emphasize liquid, short-term assets. This will often erode the growth potential of the portfolio.

Tax and accounting

As the foregoing analysis suggests, the tax and accounting environment often affects decisions on asset location and allocation. In many countries, bonds issued by central and local governments enjoy some tax advantages. Such securities tend to attract certain kinds of buyers. For example, in the US, a significant percentage of tax-exempt municipal bonds is held by wealthy households, mainly because the marginal tax brackets of such households are very high. Likewise, inflation-protected government bonds are typically held in tax-deferred accounts, as the inflation-related gains in such bonds are taxable in the US. By locating them in tax-deferred accounts, such tax liabilities can be minimized. In the UK, a significant proportion of inflation-indexed bonds is held by pension funds, which are tax exempt.

Corporate tax and accounting treatments affect pension asset allocation decisions, as noted. At the household level, the asset mix may be influenced by the treatment of estate taxes and the availability of "step-up" basis to the surviving beneficiaries. Step-up basis refers to the fact that when stocks that have appreciated significantly are passed as gifts to beneficiaries, they can use the "stepped-up" (or appreciated) price as the basis (the purchase price) in their tax calculations.

Conclusion

Investors' asset allocation decisions are invariably determined by their aversion to risk, their funding needs and their liquidity needs. Recognition of these linkages leads to important modifications to the mean-variance efficient portfolio that is suggested by portfolio theory as the optimal portfolio. In addition, tax and accounting factors may play an important role in the choice of the asset mix. Finally, the time horizon and the state of the household (age, working status and so on) play a powerful role in the asset allocation decision.

Copyright © Suresh Sundaresan 2002

Further reading

"Asset allocation in a changing world" (1998) Association for Investment Management and Research (AIMR).

Asset allocation and the
importance of active investment strategies

Which is more important for investment returns: the initial choice of assets or the way the asset mix is altered over time? **Craig MacKinlay** enters the debate on active management and challenges some established assumptions.

A. Craig MacKinlay is Joseph P. Wargrove Professor of Finance at the Wharton School of the University of Pennsylvania.

Over the past decade, there has been considerable debate about the importance of active strategies in the investment process. The debate has been driven by the claim that asset allocation (that is, the decision that initially determines which kind of assets to invest in and how much of each to hold) accounts for more than 90 per cent of an investor's performance while "active investment strategies" contribute far less.

Much of this claim is based on evidence presented in two influential articles – one published in 1986 by Gary Brinson, Randolph Hood and Gilbert Beebower, and an update published in 1991 by Brinson, Brian Singer and Beebower. In the first, the authors state: "Although investment strategy can result in significant returns, these are dwarfed by the return contribution from investment policy – the selection of asset classes and their normal weights." Investment "strategy" refers to the idea that the mix of assets is actively managed with frequent adjustments based on views of the future directions of financial market prices. It is in contrast to investment "policy" – the approach of long-term adherence to a pre-determined weighting among asset classes.

Although it was not the intention of the authors, the implication drawn from the two studies is that investors should concentrate on determining the appropriate long-run asset allocation and not allocate significant resources to active management. While this implication may have some merit, this article, drawing on some simple examples, shows that such an implication does not follow from the cited research.

The rationale for turning away from active management is based primarily on two empirical findings: first, the policy return (the return on a passive portfolio invested using the long-run allocation) explains more than 90 per cent of total return, and second, on average, managers using active strategies do not add value. The latter finding does not seem particularly informative because over time one would expect that the performance of actively managed portfolios on average must be close to that of passive benchmarks.

For this not to be the case, there would need to be a segment of investors who consistently underperform these benchmarks to effectively subsidize the active managers. The existence of such a segment seems unlikely. Transaction costs and other expenses make superior performance on average even more difficult. The former finding deserves closer examination. As noted above, it has widely been interpreted to imply that there is not much of a role for active management. However, such an interpretation is not warranted.

Much of the confusion can be traced to the focus on a specific statistical measure, the R^2, in statistical analyses of the relation between total return and policy return. Proponents of the argument that policy is the primary determinant of return have relied on high R^2 for the regression of total return on policy return. This measure, R^2, is a statistical measure of correlation and can be interpreted as an indicator of the extent to which "variability" in one factor is related to "variability" in another factor. (To be precise, the R^2 is the statistical correlation squared.) Many in the investment community have, however, misinterpreted the high R^2 in regression analyses between total returns and investment policy. The common interpretation is that the high R^2 indicates that the magnitude of the total return is very similar to the magnitude of the policy return. This article explains the fallacy of this interpretation using simple examples.

Components of return

To understand the thrust of the debate, it is useful to break the total return of a portfolio into parts and then examine the empirical importance of the differences in return arising from various policy mixes (long-run asset allocations). These differences can be contrasted with the differences that can arise from the use of active management. The total return of a fund has three components, as indicated by the equation:

$$\text{Total return} = \text{policy return} + \text{return from active asset allocation} + \text{return from asset selection}$$

In this equation, "policy return" refers to the return on a passive position invested using the long-run allocation, "active asset allocation" refers to the process of ongoing changes made to the long-run allocation, and "asset selection" refers to the process of picking individual stocks within equity classes and bonds within fixed income classes.

The debate centres on the importance of the first component, policy return, relative to the others. From historical returns, we can see the importance of the policy mix for explaining differences in total return. Table 1 presents average returns over more than 30 years for various policy mixes of three US asset classes – stocks, bonds and Treasury bills.

Over the whole period, the average annual return of a portfolio entirely consisting of equity investments was 12.6 per cent. A portfolio consisting

TABLE 1 Average annual returns for various policy mixes (%)

	All Equity	All bonds	All Treasury bills	Mix (equity/bonds/bills) 80/20/0	60/40/0	40/40/20
Jan/1971–Apr/2001	12.6	8.8	6.8	12.1	11.4	10.3
Jan/1971–Dec/1980	8.4	5.5	6.9	8.0	7.5	7.3
Jan/1981–Dec/1990	13.9	13.1	8.8	14.0	13.9	13.0
Jan/1991–Mar/2001	15.6	8.1	4.9	14.2	12.8	10.6

Notes: Returns rebalanced quarterly. Benchmarks used: S&P 500 for equities; Lehman Aggregate Bond Index from January 1976, before this an equal combination of the CRSP SBBI government and corporate indices; return from investing in three-month Treasury bills

entirely of Treasury bills gave 6.8 per cent. The difference was substantial, almost 6 percentage points. However, comparison of the returns of the 100 per cent equity position with that of a more balanced position – 60 per cent stock and 40 per cent bonds – reveals a considerably smaller difference in average annual return of only 1.2 percentage points. This difference is sensitive to the time period considered. For the decades beginning in January 1971 and in January 1981, the return differences between policy mixes are small, which we can attribute to the weak performance of the equity market in 1973 and 1974 and the strong bond market in the 1980s. In contrast, from January 1991 to March 2001 the return differences across policy mixes are larger because of the strong performance of equities. Generally, historical numbers tell us that long-term asset mix is an important component of return, but that the differences between policies are not as large as some might think.

What about the importance of active strategies? We can get a rough idea by using results for different asset mixes and different stock portfolios published periodically by financial newspapers. For example, consider *The Wall Street Journal*'s "Who has the best blend?" chart. The chart published on 17 February 2000 reports the returns from following the recommended blends of various investment houses for a balanced position over five years ending on 31 December 1999. The five-year returns differ substantially. The recommended blend of the top performing investment house provided an annual average return of 22 per cent. In contrast, the annual average return of the recommended blend of the worst performer was 15.3 per cent. This difference, of almost 7 percentage points per year, strongly suggests that active asset allocation can play an important role.

Similar conclusions about asset selection can be drawn from an examination of the same newspaper's chart "Brokerage houses stock-picking prowess" of 12 February 2001. It reports the return from investing in the recommended lists of stocks over five years ending on 31 December 2000. Over the period, the annual average returns across brokerage houses differ by as much as 12.3 percentage points. The annual average returns for the top performing list and the worst performing list were 22.5 per cent and 5.0 per cent, respectively. This annual difference is huge given the five-year horizon. (This difference is not adjusted for risk, but it is very unlikely that risk can explain the magnitude.) Such differences emphasize the importance of asset selection. Given the return spreads between active positions, the dismissal of an important role for active management seems premature.

R^2 and the active components

The most commonly quoted number supporting the idea that policy return is the primary determinant of total return is the R^2 of a regression of the total return on the policy return. This number exceeded 90 per cent for both Brinson and Beebower studies, leaving little total return to be explained by the other components of the return (active asset allocation and asset selection). Such an interpretation of R^2 evidence, however, is flawed. As stated earlier, the R^2 is a measure of the variability of the total return that is explained by the variability of the policy return. It does not tie the level of the policy return to the level of total return. This can be illustrated with two simple hypothetical examples.

Masterful active asset allocation

Consider a case in which we have three asset classes: stocks, bonds and Treasury bills. Assume a long-run policy mix of stocks at 70 per cent, bonds at 30 per cent and no Treasury bills. The equity benchmark is the Standard & Poor's 500 index, the bond benchmark is the Lehman Brothers Aggregate Bond index, and the Treasury bill benchmark rolls over three-month Treasury bills. Applying this mix from April 1991 to March 2001 gives a policy return of 13.8 per cent a year.

Now consider adding in active asset allocation. Suppose that the investor has the ability to forecast months in which the equity benchmark underperforms the Treasury bill benchmark. In these months the equity proportion is reduced to 50 per cent and 20 per cent is allocated to Treasury bills, giving a 50/30/20 asset allocation. What is the average annual total return for this investor who actively manages asset allocations? As might be expected, it is substantially higher than the passive policy return at an average of 17.4 per cent a year.

However, when the above data are subject to statistical regression analysis, some might find it surprising that the R^2 is 99 per cent (using quarterly observations of the total return on the policy return). Thus, a focus on R^2 might lead one to conclude that policy return appears to determine total return almost completely. But we know that active management of the portfolio is adding over 350 basis points of value a year. Figure 1 presents a

FIGURE 1 | Value of policy position versus value of active position

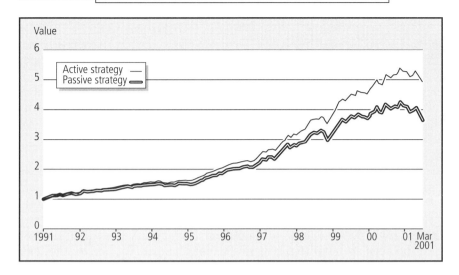

plot of the growth of the passive position and of the active position over the 10-year period.

Observe that the values of the active position and the policy position move together – this explains why the R^2 is high. However, in the months when the equity proportion is reduced, the total return exceeds the policy return, leading to the large value for the active asset allocation component.

Superior stock selection

Now consider a case in which the portfolio consists entirely of equities. The equity position is managed actively and very successfully. Its manager is consistently able to outperform the equity benchmark by 50 basis points each quarter after costs, which means stock selection skills add more than 200 basis points of value every year.

If we run a regression of the total return on the policy return for this portfolio, what will the R^2 be? 100 per cent! Yes, 100 per cent – because the portfolio's total return keeps varying consistently with the equity benchmark. The total return variation is completely explained by the policy return variation. However, it would be foolish to conclude that active management is unimportant. In this case, because the active management does not add any variability to the policy return, the policy return completely explains the total return.

Although the above examples are unrealistic, that does not mean they have little practical relevance. It is a simple matter to find active funds that, at least historically, have both a high R^2 and significant value added or lost. Clearly a high R^2 does not imply that policy return is the primary determinant of total return. Instead, it is correct to say that a high R^2 means that the policy return explains the variability of the total return, not necessarily its level. In short, the R^2 is a measure of diversification, not a clear indicator of the driver of the level of investment performance.

Is R² the wrong indicator?

It should be clear that R^2 does not fully characterize the effect of active management on the total return. This is not due to issues related to scaling of the R^2, the horizon used to measure returns, the costs of active management, or the technique used to come up with long-run allocations. It is simply due to the fact that R^2 is an indicator of variability, not value. Does this mean R^2 is not relevant to the value added from active management? No. For a given level of value added, the higher the R^2, the more valuable is that value added. To put it another way, given a high R^2, the manager is introducing very little idiosyncratic risk while delivering the value added.

Where does this leave us with respect to the importance of active management? The bottom line is that R^2 does not answer the question. The answer depends on one's ability to identify active managers who can, with some consistency, add value. If one believes that such managers are impossible to identify, the role for active management is minimal. On the other hand, if one can uncover successful active investment managers, active management can play a key role in adding value.

Thus, any decision on the use of active management should hinge on one's ability to identify managers whose performance will be superior and not on the extent to which policy return explains the variability of the total return.

Copyright © Craig MacKinlay 2002

Further reading

Brinson, G.L., Hood, R. and Beebower, G. (1986) "Determinants of portfolio performance", *Financial Analysts Journal*, July–August, 39–44.

Brinson, G., Singer, B. and Beebower, G. (1991) "Determinants of portfolio performance II: an update", *Financial Analysts Journal*, May–June, 40–7.

Ibbotson, R. and Kaplan, P. (2000) "Does asset allocation explain 40, 90, or 100 per cent of performance?", *Financial Analysts Journal*, January–February.

Jahnke, W. (1997) "The asset allocation hoax", *Journal of Financial Planning*, February, 109–13.

MacKinlay, A.C. (1998) "Asset allocation and stock selection: on the importance of active strategies", *Journal of Investment Consulting*, December, 18–21.

Singer, B. (1997) "Asset allocation, hoaxes, and the creation of straw men", *Journal of Financial Planning*, October, 14–15.

The equity premium puzzle

Investment theories state that stocks should give a higher return than bonds in the long term. But the historical difference is far greater than expected, says **Rajnish Mehra**.

Rajnish Mehra is a professor of finance at the University of California Santa Barbara and a visiting professor at the Chicago Graduate School of Business. He is also a senior investment adviser to Vega Asset Management Group.

There is a wealth of evidence that for more than a century, stock returns have been considerably higher than those for Treasury bills. The average annual real return (that is to say, the inflation-adjusted return) on the US stock market over the past 110 years has been about 7.9 per cent. Over the same period, the return on a relatively riskless security was a paltry 1 per cent. The difference between these returns – 6.9 per cent – is called the equity premium. This statistical difference has been even more pronounced since the second world war, with the premium being almost 8 per cent.

Further, this pattern of excess returns on equity holdings is not unique to US capital markets. Equity returns compared with the return to debt holdings in other countries also exhibit this historical regularity. The annual return on the UK stock market was 5.7 per cent since the war, a 4.6 per cent premium over the average bond return of 1.1 per cent. Similar differentials are documented for France, Germany, Italy and Spain.

Academic Jeremy Siegel (1998) has analyzed data on US stock and bond returns going back to 1802 and found a similar, though somewhat smaller, premium in place for the past 200 years. Table 1 summarizes the data.

The dramatic investment implications of these different rates of return can be seen in Table 2, which maps the capital appreciation of $1 invested in different assets from 1802–1997 and from 1925–2000. As this shows, $1 invested in a diversified stock index yields $558,945 against a value of $276, in real terms, for $1 invested in a portfolio of Treasury bills for the period 1802–1997, while for the 75 years between 1925 and 2000, the corresponding values are $266.47 and $1.71. (This table assumes that all payments to the underlying asset, such as dividend payments to stock and interest payments to bonds, are reinvested and no taxes are paid.)

| TABLE 1 | US stocks and bond returns |

	% real return on a market index	% real return on a relatively risk-free security	% risk premium
	Mean	Mean	Mean
1802–1998	7.0	2.9	4.1
1889–1978	6.98	0.80	6.18
1889–2000	7.9	1.0	6.9
1926–2000	8.7	0.7	8.0
1947–2000	8.4	0.6	7.8

Sources: 1802–1998 from Siegel (1998); 1889–1978 from Mehra and Prescott (1985); author's estimates

This long-term perspective underscores the remarkable wealth-building potential of the equity premium. It should come as no surprise that the equity premium is of central importance in portfolio allocation decisions and estimates of the cost of capital. Also, it is central to the debate in the US about investing social security funds in the stock market.

In putting together an investment portfolio, investors choose among different assets such as stock, real estate and corporate bonds. Typically an investor chooses a portfolio by assessing the relative risk characteristics and expected returns of various options. The risk premium spells out the differential return an investor can expect from different assets.

Are stocks riskier?

Why have stocks been such an attractive investment compared with bonds? Why has the return on stocks been higher than on relatively risk-free assets?

| TABLE 2 | Capital appreciation over 200 years |

	Terminal value of $1 invested in:			
Investment period	Stocks		Bills	
	Real	Nominal	Real	Nominal
1802–1997	$558,945	$7,470,000	$276	$3,679
1925–2000	$266.47	$2,586.52	$1.71	$16.56

Sources: Ibbotson (2001) and Siegel (1998)

One answer is that because stocks are "riskier", investors seek more reward. Indeed, the standard deviation of the returns to stocks (about 20 per cent a year historically) is larger than that of the returns to Treasury bills (about 4 per cent a year), so obviously stocks are considerably more risky. But are they?

To deepen our understanding of balancing risk and return in pricing assets, let us look at why different assets give different rates of return. The theory prices assets so that the "incremental loss of well-being" in sacrificing current consumption when buying an asset is equal to the "incremental gain in well-being" from the increase in consumption anticipated when the asset pays off. The essence here is the "incremental loss or gain of well-being due to consumption", which is different from "incremental consumption". In other words, the same amount of consumption may result in different degrees of well-being at different times. (A five-course dinner after a heavy lunch yields less satisfaction than a similar dinner when one is hungry.)

Hence assets that pay off when times are good and consumption levels are high – that is, when the incremental value of additional consumption is low – are less desirable than those that pay off an equivalent amount when times are bad and additional consumption is more desirable and more highly valued. This can be illustrated by considering the standard model of modern finance, the Capital Asset Pricing Model. This postulates a linear relationship between an asset's "beta" (a measure of its risk) and expected return. Thus, high beta stocks yield a high expected rate of return. In the CAPM, good times and bad times are captured by the return on the market. The performance of the market as captured by a broad-based index acts as a surrogate indicator for the state of the economy.

A high beta stock tends to pay off more when the market return is high, that is, when times are good and consumption is plentiful. As discussed earlier, such a stock provides less incremental well-being than a security that pays off when consumption is low, and hence is less valuable and consequently sells for less. To use the jargon of modern asset pricing theory, an asset that pays off in states of low marginal utility will sell for a lower price than a similar asset that pays off in states of high marginal utility. Since rates of return are inversely proportional to asset prices, the latter class of assets will, on average, give a lower rate of return than the former.

Another way of looking at asset pricing is to realize that economic agents prefer to smooth out patterns of consumption over time. Assets that pay off a relatively larger amount when consumption is high "destabilize" these patterns of consumption, whereas assets that pay off when consumption levels are low "smooth out" consumption. Naturally, the latter are more valuable and thus require a lower rate of return to induce investors to hold these assets. (Insurance policies are a classic example of assets that smooth consumption. People willingly purchase and hold them, in spite of their low rates of return.)

To return to the original question: are stocks that much riskier than bills so as to justify a 7 per cent differential in their rates of return?

The puzzle

Stocks and bonds pay off in approximately the same states of nature (economic scenarios where consumption is similar). Hence, as argued earlier, they should command approximately the same rate of return. In fact, a 1985 paper by this author and Edward Prescott showed that stocks on average should command at most a 1 per cent return premium over Treasury bonds. However, for as long as there was reliable data (about 100 years), the mean premium on stocks over bonds was considerably and consistently higher, so we realized we had a puzzle on our hands.

It should be stressed that the equity premium puzzle is a quantitative puzzle. Standard theory is consistent with our notion of risk that, on average, stocks should return more than bonds. The puzzle arises from the fact that returns predicted by the theory are very different from those that have been historically documented. The puzzle cannot be dismissed lightly, since much of our economic intuition is based on the very class of models that fall short so dramatically when confronted with financial data. It shows that concepts central to financial and economic modelling fail to capture the single characteristic that appears to make stocks comparatively so risky. It also questions the viability of using this class of models for a quantitative assessment, say, to gauge the welfare implications of alternative stabilization policies since the costs and benefits associated with these polices are now suspect.

For these reasons, finance specialists and economists have made repeated attempts to solve the puzzle over the past 15 years or so. Most research falls into two camps. Some have proposed modifications of the utility functions that are typically used to model investors as being highly averse to risk. Others have proposed explanations based on market imperfections, transactions costs, potential disaster states, selection bias, and the inability to insure against risk and disaster scenarios.

Two recent approaches to resolving the puzzle appear promising. The first, expounded by academics John Campbell and John Cochrane (1999), incorporates the possibility of economic recession as a variable in the calculations. In this approach, the risk aversion of investors rises dramatically when the chances of a recession become larger. The second approach, proposed by George Constantinides, John Donaldson and this author (2001), incorporates consumer heterogeneity and departs from the representative agent model. In their approach, equity thus is no longer a homogenous asset; it has a very different investment characteristic for the middle-aged, who typically have stable employment and salaries, than for the young person, whose future wage income is uncertain.

In this model, an economy consists of three overlapping generations: the young, the middle-aged and the old. The consumption and investment decisions of each generation affect the demand for, and thus the prices of, assets in the economy. The young are restricted from participating in the stock market because they face a binding borrowing constraint. Hence stocks are priced not by the young, for whom they are an attractive asset, but by the middle-aged, for whom stocks tend to be far less attractive. For the young, stocks and wages are not highly correlated and thus stocks are a potential hedge against wage fluctuations. The middle-aged, however, have no significant future wages and so the fluctuation in their consumption arises directly from fluctuations in the value of their holdings of stocks.

At this stage of the lifecycle, equity income is highly correlated with consumption and it no longer helps to diversify the effects of risky human capital. Hence, for middle-aged and older people to hold equity, it must offer a higher rate of return. That is, in equilibrium it must command a large premium over safe securities. This new approach is called the lifecycle approach to asset pricing.

Another form of heterogeneity, proposed by academics George Constantinides and Darrell Duffie, captures the notion that consumers are subject to idiosyncratic income shocks that cannot be insured away. Simply put, consumers face the risk of job loss, or other major personal disasters that can be neither hedged away nor insured against. This means equities and cyclically related investments exhibit the undesirable feature that they drop in value when the probability of job loss increases. In economic downturns, consumers need an extra incentive to hold equities and other similar investment instruments. The equity premium is thus rationalized as the added incentive needed to make equities palatable to investors.

There is also another point of view, held by a group of academics and professionals who claim that at present there is no equity premium and by implication no puzzle. To address these claims we need to differentiate between two different interpretations of the term "equity premium". One is the ex-post or realized equity premium. This is the actual, historically observed, difference between the return on the market, as captured by a stock index, and the risk-free rate, as proxied by the return on government bills. It is this interpretation that Edward Prescott and this author addressed in the 1985 paper.

However, there is a related concept – the ex-ante equity premium. This is a forward-looking measure of the premium, that is, the equity premium that is expected to prevail in the future or the conditional equity premium given the current state of the economy. To elaborate, after a bull market, when stock valuations are high relative to fundamentals, the ex-ante equity premium is likely to be low. Nonetheless, it is precisely when the market has risen sharply that the ex-post or the realized premium is high. Conversely, after a major downward correction, the ex-ante (expected) premium is likely to be high, while the realized premium will be low. This should not come as any surprise because returns to stock have been documented to revert to a mean over time.

Which of these interpretations of the equity premium is relevant for an investment adviser? Clearly this depends on the planning horizon. The 1985 paper referred to very long investment horizons. It has almost nothing to say about what the premium will be over the next few years. The ex-post equity premium is the realization of a stochastic process over a certain period and it has varied considerably over time, as shown in Figure 1. Further, the variation depends on the time horizon over which it is measured. There have even been periods when it has been negative.

Market watchers and others who are interested in short-term investment planning will wish to project the conditional equity premium over their planning horizon. This is not a simple task. However, even if current market conditions suggest that the conditional equity premium is small (and there seems to be a general consensus that it is), this in itself does not mean that it was obvious that either the historical premium was too high or that the equity premium has diminished. The data used to document the equity premium over

| FIGURE 1 | Realized equity risk premium a year 1926–2000 |

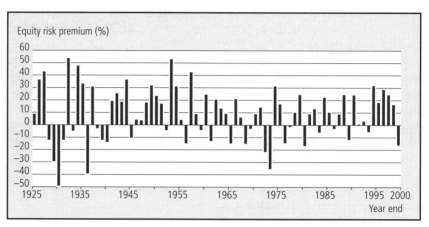

Source: Ibbotson (2001)

the past 100 years are probably as good as any economic data we have and 100 years is a long series when it comes to economic data. Before we dismiss the premium, we not only need to have an understanding of the observed phenomena but also know why the future is likely to be different.

In the absence of this, we can make the following claim based on what we know. Over the long horizon the equity premium is likely to be similar to what it has been in the past and the returns to investment in equity will continue to substantially dominate those in bonds for investors with a long planning horizon.

Copyright © Rajnish Mehra 2002

Further reading

Campbell, J.Y. and Cochrane, J.H. (1999) "By force of habit: a consumption-based explanation of aggregate stock market behaviour", *Journal of Political Economy*, 107, 205–51.

Cochrane, J.H. (1997) "Where is the market going? Uncertain facts and novel theories," *Economic Perspectives*, 21, 3–37.

Constantinides, G.M., Donaldson, J.B. and Mehra, R. (2001) "Junior can't borrow: a new perspective on the equity premium puzzle", *Quarterly Journal of Economics*, February 2002, 17, 269–96 (http://www.econ.ucsb.edu/~mehra/junior.pdf).

Ibbotson (2001) *Stocks, Bonds, Bills and Inflation: 2000 Yearbook*, Chicago: Ibbotson Asociates.

Kocherlakota, N.R. (1996) "The equity premium: it's still a puzzle", *Journal of Economic Literature*, 34, 42–71.

Mehra, R. and Prescott, E.C. (1985) "The equity premium: a puzzle", *Journal of Monetary Economics*, 15, 145–61.

Siegel, J. (1998) *Stocks for the Long Run*, 2nd edn, New York: Irwin.

Working hard
for better returns

Finance theories tend to ignore risks arising from labour income, property or small business ownership. **John Heaton** and **Deborah Lucas** consider how these risks affect investors and their required rates of return.

John Heaton is James H. Lorie Professor of Finance at the University of Chicago Graduate School of Business and a research associate with the National Bureau of Economic Research.

Deborah Lucas is chief economist at the Congressional Budget Office and Donald C. Clark/Household International Distinguished Professor of Finance at the Kellogg Graduate School of Management.

Underlying all classical asset-pricing theories, from the workhorse capital asset pricing model (CAPM) of investment textbooks to more modern consumption-based models, is the tenet that investors (or at least those large enough to influence market prices) finance their consumption from well-diversified portfolios. Any other source of income risk, such as labour income risk or the risk of owning a small business, is assumed to be insignificant or insured away. These assumptions underlie the elegant, and very practical, conclusion that while investors demand compensation for unavoidable market risk, idiosyncratic or company-specific risks can be diversified away and hence command no additional return.

The presumption that investors, particularly large investors, would choose to diversify is a logical consequence of the apparently large gains from diversification and the seemingly low cost of doing so. An investor who sells a single-share portfolio and invests the proceeds in one with five randomly chosen shares approximately halves the risk of his annual stock return. Moving to a mutual fund that mimics the Standard & Poor's 500 index halves that risk again. Not only are the risk-reduction benefits of diversification great, but the costs of diversifying are modest. Investment vehicles such as stock market mutual funds and the demise of fixed commissions have lowered the cost of diversification considerably. Investors have taken this message to heart and are increasingly trading in their individual share holdings for more diversified mutual or pension funds.

Yet a closer look at investors' portfolios suggests a pervasive lack of diversification when one looks beyond shares and bonds. Uninsured "background risks" such as labour income risk, small business or entrepreneurial risk and concentrated property investments call into question the underpinnings of both portfolio and asset pricing theory, and suggest new explanations for the observed behaviour of asset prices.

In this article, we review evidence on the types and magnitude of background risks faced by stock market investors and how these should influence their portfolio choices. We then turn to the ramifications of background risks for asset pricing theory.

Risky human capital

The single most important asset that most people have is their human capital, developed through investments in education and from experience. One of the fruits of those investments is a stream of future wages and salaries, or dividends and capital gains on privately held businesses. These cash flows are typically quite variable and may be highly correlated with stock and bond market returns. For example, for corporate executives and small business owners, the value of their human capital tends to decline with share prices during recessions.

Unlike stock market risk, diversifying human capital risk can be expensive. Establishing a speciality maximizes the value of experience, but also puts workers at risk if their skill set loses value in the market. For entrepreneurs, investing heavily in their own businesses may be the only alternative when outside financing is extremely costly or unavailable. Grants of shares and share options are valuable in helping to align an executive's incentives with those of other shareholders, but put executives doubly at risk to the extent that their job security and investments are highly correlated.

Because a judiciously chosen portfolio of financial assets can be used to offset these risks, choosing an optimal portfolio becomes a more complicated and idiosyncratic exercise. Ideally, an investor will find a portfolio of shares that tends to pay a high return in circumstances in which his human capital is likely to decline, diversifying his human capital risk. For example, an entrepreneur specializing in support services to internet start-ups may want to hold a portfolio that avoids shares of high-tech companies. This reduces the probability of a decline in portfolio value just when the demand for the entrepreneur's services is waning.

Diversification and returns

In theory, human capital risk affects the required return on financial assets because investors' attitudes towards financial market risk are influenced by their overall risk exposure. For example, a tenured university professor with an assured income stream will still be in a relatively secure financial position if she decides to invest in the stock market, in marked contrast to a small business owner whose livelihood is likely to be much less certain. As a result, the professor can be expected to demand a lower return for holding stocks, everything else being equal. To the extent that the return on human capital tends to be positively correlated with returns on the stock market, the required return premium on equity can be expected to be higher still.

As a practical matter, share holdings are very concentrated in the portfolios of wealthy investors. Even in the US, where the democratization of stock holdings has perhaps been the greatest, the wealthiest 10 per cent of the population holds about 80 per cent of publicly traded stocks. To understand the likely practical importance of human capital and other background risks for asset returns, it is important to look at the risk profiles of those households which invest heavily in the stock market.

The authors have investigated the risk exposure of shareholders and found strong evidence that, for people who have significant stockholdings, income from entrepreneurial ventures represents a large source of risk that is positively correlated with stock returns. Although entrepreneurs represent a small fraction of the overall population and only 25 per cent of shareholding households, entrepreneurs with a business value of at least $10,000 accounted for a third of total shareholdings in 1992. Shareholders also invest heavily in the companies for which they work, on average placing 10 per cent of their shareholdings in their own companies. Property also represents a large share of wealth for shareholding households, but it appears to be a less important source of risk.

This evidence supports the idea that shareholders are exposed to considerable background risk, which therefore may have a measurable impact on financial asset returns. Incorporating a factor representing entrepreneurial income risk into an otherwise standard empirical asset-pricing model was found to significantly improve the performance of that model. Whether further refinements of such risk measures will have practical value for asset-pricing models is an intriguing, but as yet untested, possibility.

The equity premium puzzle

The significant exposure of the typical stock market investor to background risk, and the fact that until recently it seems that most investors did not diversify their portfolios, may help to explain the notoriously intractable "equity premium puzzle". This puzzle, as discussed in the previous article, refers to the difficulty of using economic theory to explain the high average rate of return on stock market investments relative to government securities historically. Adjusted for inflation, the average annual return on the US stock market over the past 110 years has exceeded the real return on comparatively safe securities such as government bonds by 6.9 per cent.

Most attempts to solve the equity premium puzzle maintain the assumption that investors hold well-diversified portfolios and have no significant exposure to background risk. Early investigations incorporating background risk, such as those by academics Deborah Lucas (1994) and Chris Telmer (1993), considered only labour income risk. Because of the low correlation between average labour income growth and share returns, and because labour income can actually moderate overall risk exposure relative to that of an investor who holds only financial assets, these investigations did not lead to a simple resolution of the puzzle.

Although the presence of background risk does not in itself solve the equity premium puzzle, lack of diversification may provide a partial explanation. Due to the underlying structure of most of the models in which the equity premium puzzle arises, solving the puzzle requires establishing that investors are exposed to the risk of experiencing very low consumption.

Under the assumption that investors hold well-diversified portfolios, historical experience suggests that the probability of such a catastrophic loss is negligible. After all, even during the Depression of 1929 to 1939, a well-diversified investor who continued to reinvest his dividends in the stock market would have seen his stock portfolio fall by only 18 per cent. This implies that it is hard to come up with plausible scenarios under which the consumption of well-diversified shareholders drops precipitously enough to generate the observed average premium.

By contrast, there is a significant probability of a catastrophic outcome in a poorly diversified portfolio. The recent experience of day traders holding a select few internet stocks is a case in point and looking at the statistical properties of poorly diversified portfolios confirms this impression. When the typical investor is assumed to hold only a few shares, the standard model predicts an equity premium in keeping with historical outcomes.

Is lack of diversification the solution to the equity premium puzzle? Although we would like to declare victory, this answer is not altogether satisfying. This is because it fails to address why investors would choose to hold poorly diversified portfolios in the first place. Although the transaction costs associated with diversification were higher in the past, if the theoretical models are correct, the gains from diversification would likely have outweighed the costs of doing so. To the extent that poor diversification is part of the reason for the historically high equity premium, the puzzle becomes one of why investors did not choose to diversify.

Changing risks

The current high valuation of the US equities market relative to dividends or earnings has led many observers to speculate that perhaps the equity premium has fallen. That is, investors have bid up stock values because their required return in future is lower than in the past.

Recent studies, one by academics Eugene Fama and Kenneth French (2001), attempt to calculate the market's anticipation of the equity premium. Using recent experience and the historical record of stock returns and dividends, they find that the equity premium may have fallen to less than half of its historical average. While a decline in the equity premium is consistent with the high valuation of the equities markets, the source of this decline is less clear. One possible explanation is an increase in the willingness of the typical investor to bear risk. This increase in risk tolerance could arise for any number of reasons. For instance, academic Annette Vissing-Jorgensen (1999) argues that wider stock market participation has improved risk sharing, thereby lowering required returns. A related explanation is that improved portfolio diversification has increased risk tolerance. Others have pointed to the taming of the business cycle or to demographic factors such as the ageing of the baby-boom generation.

In further research, we examined some of these hypotheses to explain the shrinking equity premium in the context of a calibrated consumption-based asset-pricing model. Here again, we found that the most promising risk-related explanation for the share price run-up was based on increasing portfolio diversification. While historical data on individual portfolio composition is scarce before the past two decades, anecdotal evidence suggests that investors rarely held portfolios of more than half a dozen stocks. In recent years, the trend out of individual stocks and into highly diversified funds has accelerated, at the same time that the forward-looking equity premium appears to have fallen.

Conclusion

In this article we have argued that considering the impact of the widespread lack of diversification is important for our understanding of portfolio decisions and the behaviour of asset prices. For example, recent work has shown that consideration of the risks of entrepreneurial activity and the correlation of these risks with returns helps explain why some shares have historically had higher returns than others. Over time, exposure to diversifiable risks is likely to decline as new financial products are developed and as the costs of accessing and using financial markets continue to decrease.

The effect on the behaviour of asset prices could be substantial. For example, the increased marketability of entrepreneurial ventures could reduce the risk of this factor in future. A substantial change that has already occurred is an increase in the diversification of the typical investor's portfolio. We believe this has already had an important effect on financial markets by raising the general level of stock prices.

Copyright © John Heaton and Deborah Lucas 2002

Further reading

Davis, S. and Mehra, R. (2001) "Stocks and bonds in the portfolio life cycle", Mastering Investment, *Financial Times*, 4 June.

Fama, E. and French, K. (2001) "The equity premium", working paper 522, Center for Research in Security Prices, University of Chicago (http://gsbwww.uchicago.edu/fac/finance/papers/newequity.pdf).

Heaton, J. and Lucas, D. (2000a) "Asset pricing and portfolio choice: the role of entrepreneurial risk", *Journal of Finance*, 55, 3 (June), 1163–98.

Heaton, J. and Lucas, D. (2000b) "Stock prices and fundamentals" in B.S. Bernanke and J.J. Rotemberg (eds) *NBER Macroeconomics Annual*, 14, 213–42, Cambridge: MIT Press.

Lucas, D. (1994) "Asset pricing with undiversifiable income risk and short sales constraints: deepening the equity premium puzzle", *Journal of Monetary Economics*, 34, 3 (December), 325–41.

Telmer, C. (1993) "Asset-pricing puzzles and incomplete markets", *Journal of Finance*, 48, 5 (December), 1803–32.

Vissing-Jorgensen, A. (1999) "Limited stock market participation and the equity premium puzzle," working paper, University of Chicago (http://www.src.uchicago.edu/users/viss).

Investing
with death in mind

Financial advice is generally directed at people with 5–30 years in which to see their investments come to fruition. For the 90-year-old, the time horizon is considerably shorter, says **Charles Kindleberger**.

Charles P. Kindleberger is Ford International Professor of Economics, Emeritus, at Massachusetts Institute of Technology. He wrote *Manias, Panics and Crashes* (Wiley, 2000) and *A Financial History of Western Europe* (OUP, 1989).

Financial writers in newspapers and magazines often discuss cases of young couples, perhaps in their thirties or forties, contemplating how much they have to save to live comfortably, or at their customary standard, in retirement at the age of 55, 60, 65 or 70. Social security payments, a company pension or tax-deferred funds enter the discussion, and in the US, the proposal from President George W. Bush that part of the social security deduction from income be invested by the prospective recipient in his or her choice of investments. Newspapers carry occasional sections on retirement which deal with these issues, particularly when to retire and how much to save in advance.

Retirement is one thing. Death is another. No financial adviser to my knowledge tackles how a single person, widow or widower, should invest at the age of 90. Such a person – I take an upper-middle-class example – may turn the problem over to a trust company or financial consultant, which or who presumably follows much the same course as if dealing with a sophisticated, long-retired businessman. Our subject will have social security payments, a pension, some assets, little if any debt and a place to live, but a limited life expectancy.

Assume grown children, themselves close to retirement, grandchildren and possibly even great-grandchildren to whom he wants to leave something. He may seek immortality by a substantial charitable donation, endowing a named professorship or financing a building with his name over the door. Most 90-year-olds are past wanting more toys, playing endless golf, tennis, bridge, chess or travelling to new places. They have already travelled the world and the airports are now too crowded. The question is: how should this 90-year-old handle his money?

Investment horizon

In a 2001 article, Mark Kritzman compares the risk of equities declining by a stipulated percentage at any time during a specified period with the risk of a decline at the end of the horizon – taken here to be death. Tables are produced showing the risk of a 10 per cent or 25 per cent loss in stock values, calculated over 5, 10 and 25 years. Chances of loss are higher, to be sure, at any time within a period, and lower at the end.

As an illustration, the likelihood of a 10 per cent loss over five years is 61 per cent and 65 per cent over 25 years within the period, but only 14 per cent at the end of five years and 2.5 per cent at the end of 25 years. For a 25 per cent loss in equity values, the comparable figures are 24 per cent and 31 per cent during the five- and 25-year periods respectively and 6.4 per cent and 1.5 per cent at their ends. A 1.5 per cent chance of a 25 per cent loss at the end of 25 years signifies reversion to the mean. The results justify advice to buy equities for the long haul and hang on to them.

But the investment horizon of a 90-year-old person is less than five years. In my guess it is closer to 1.5 years. For example, in my secondary school class of 1928, which contained 42 males, only 10 are still alive, and two have died within the past year. Some time ago, I read that the percentage of equities in a portfolio should be 100 minus one's age. For a 90-year-old, therefore, it should be 10 per cent. In this calculation I ignore the type of equities or other assets – old economy, high-tech, large-cap or small-cap. Elsewhere, I find that a distinguished economist, indeed a Nobel Laureate, asserts that the proportion of equities be the same at all ages. This strikes me as irrational, or at least super-sophisticated.

Normal life, unless cut off by disease, accident or extreme conditions of some kind, follows a Gompertz or S-shaped curve, from childhood, adolescence, adulthood, through to old age. Countries themselves follow the same trajectory, though they do not die over the age of 70 and sometimes get a second birth. What investments one should hold at 90 depends on one's time horizon, one's life expectancy (though variance is high) and income, lifestyle, health, insurance, appetite for consumption, taxes, dependants and their needs and lifestyles.

Needs and costs

For the purpose of illustration, let us consider a single person of 90, say a widower, living in a retirement community, with health services and one good meal a day in the general fee, and health insurance covering all medical expenses. The living quarters may be rented, bought or acquired through an advanced payment, 90 per cent of which is paid to the estate after death. Social security payments continue, along with pension payments. In the US one might also be tempted to consider the income from any 401(k) plan – a contribution plan that allows investors to set aside tax-deferred income for retirement purposes. However, US tax law requires any 401(k) payments to be taken back on a schedule that reduces the investment to zero several years before the age of 90 (and taxed).

If social security and pension cover the monthly fee, income is still needed for other meals, entertainment beyond that which is provided, additional medical expense and travel. Most 90-year-olds in my experience stay with the old car (if in fact the children do not take away the keys), stop accumulating clothes, household articles and furnishings unless forced to by heavy depreciation. The worst outcome is the need for care beyond that provided by the nursing home or "assisted living" (help in the chores and requirements of day-to-day living). Such needs can vary widely, depending on hours per day, number of days per week and cost per hour. At its height, three persons a day at eight hours each, seven days a week for a year, at, say, $12 an hour, plus one or more meals, the total sum could come to more than $100,000. It is likely to be much less, but some capital should be kept on hand in case of deep trouble.

For the elderly, travel can have several purposes: to visit children or grandchildren, to take grand tours, cruises, summers in the mountains or at the shore to escape cabin fever. But travel appeals less and less to most nonagenarians, especially if they have seen a bit of the world already. *The New York Times* publishes a supplement several times a year called "The Sophisticated Traveller" – presumably one prepared to spend considerable amounts of money to visit attractive or interesting places. A 90-year-old sophisticate is often one who stays at home. The *Financial Times* produces a weekend section called "How to Spend It". Invariably the elderly think in terms of how to get rid of it – not money, but things, before cleaning up after them devolves on children. They seek to dispose of what economists call "negative goods" or stuff collected over many years with little utility for others.

Taxation

The US press these days is full of discussion of the estate tax, known to well-to-do conservatives as the "death tax". The phrase "double taxation" also arises, since one pays a tax first on income, then a second on amounts unspent. Many want it abolished, though it is paid by only a small percentage of the population. With substantial inflation since the second world war, the level at which the tax takes hold has been raised continuously. It is now $675,000 and scheduled to rise in 2009, a date that holds little interest for most 90-year-olds. Special higher levels have been established for family farms and small family businesses, so that the death of the owner does not require the sale of the business for tax purposes.

One can reduce one's estate while alive by gifts, with a limit of $10,000 a year above which a gift tax is applied (£3,000 in the UK). One can also leave money, tax-free, to charities. An argument against abolishing estate tax made by some wealthy people, such as investment experts Warren Buffett and George Soros, is that it would reduce charitable giving. Some buy life insurance to pay the tax, but for the very elderly the rates climb to roughly equal to tax rates.

Death is an interesting subject, not least in financial terms. One tactic occasionally mentioned in the press (more often in novels) is to skip a generation and leave assets to grandchildren. These may lend them to parents.

But private loans within families must pay interest at close to market rates; if not, they are likely to be considered tax evasion rather than tax avoidance. A loan to a child to buy a house should use a formal mortgage, which becomes part of the estate. The inheritance of that person can include cancellation of the mortgage.

If a spouse has a revocable trust, it can be kept open after his or her death. This means the size of the remaining person's estate on his or her death is reduced and possibly held below the tax limit. If a family mortgage is in the revocable trust and is receiving interest, it, rather than the surviving partner, pays income tax. Life is complex and so is death.

Former US Senator John Kerrey has said that those approaching retirement should shift to lower-risk investments. I would amend his advice for the very elderly to suggest investments with minimal risk, such as money market fund or certificates of deposit with maturities of less than a year. Income is likely to be limited – one is tempted to write derisory – but the risk of dying in a financial crisis with losses in risky assets for heirs and consigns is broadly eliminated.

As one who has written about the history of financial crises, I should perhaps be able to forecast the course of asset prices over the next few years, possibly even its shape: a V- or U-shaped curve, or an extended curve after the long decade of high levels just ended. I cannot. For investors at the ages of 80 and 90, therefore, I strongly recommend risk aversion.

Copyright © Charles Kindleberger 2002

Further reading

Kritzman, M. (2001) "The equity risk premium puzzle: is it misspecification of risk?", *Economics and Portfolio Strategy*, 15 March, Peter L. Bernstein Inc.

Stocks and bonds
in the portfolio lifecycle

Conventional wisdom advises that investors move into bonds as they grow older. **Steven Davis** and **Rajnish Mehra** review this thinking.

Steven J. Davis is a professor of economics at the University of Chicago Graduate School of Business and a principal of Chicago Partners LLC.

Rajnish Mehra is a professor of finance at the University of California Santa Barbara and a visiting professor at the Chicago Graduate School of Business. He is a senior investment adviser to the Vega Asset Management Group.

Conventional wisdom holds that investors, as they age, should shift from equities to bonds. This prescription is sometimes justified by claims about lower risk from longer-term stock ownership. Another rationale stresses that stocks are riskier than bonds and that older investors have lower tolerance for risk. Lower risk tolerance for older investors makes sense, if they have less ability to recover from a financial shock by working longer.

In contrast to conventional wisdom, the standard theory of portfolio allocation does not recommend that investors shift towards bonds as they age. Standard theory holds that the optimal portfolio is a combination of a broadly diversified equity fund and safe, risk-free securities. The optimal share of equity in a portfolio depends on an investor's risk aversion, according to standard theory, but not age. This prescription for an equity share that is constant with respect to age emerges from a theoretical framework that ignores labour income.

In reality, labour income accounts for about two-thirds of national income and human capital is the largest component of wealth for many households. Human capital refers to the energy and skills that a worker brings to the labour market. The value of human capital derives from the current and future labour income the worker expects to earn. Because future labour earnings are uncertain, human capital is a risky asset. Recent research on portfolio allocation and asset pricing gives risky labour income a major role in the standard theory. This approach recognizes two important facts. First, dividends and wages affect consumption and portfolio decisions. Second, the share of wealth in the form of human capital declines as a worker ages.

We have pursued this lifecycle approach with academics George Constantinides, John Donaldson and Paul Willen. In this article, we apply the approach to portfolio allocation and asset pricing. We consider portfolio allocation and then turn to asset pricing and the "equity premium puzzle" discussed earlier in this part.

Portfolio allocation

Younger and middle-aged households have large, illiquid claims on income streams that flow from human capital and small business ownership. The claims are illiquid because they cannot readily be traded in capital markets in the same way as stocks and bonds. The value of this income fluctuates with news about wages and employment (for workers) and profits (for small business owners). In addition, the value of human capital decreases with age for workers and business owners. As retirement draws closer, the value of expected future labour income declines, eventually reaching zero.

To see how these facts matter for portfolio choice, start from first principles. From an investor's perspective, the desirability of an equity security depends on the relationship between the investor's future consumption and the future returns on the security. If the security is likely to pay off when consumption is low, the investor will look more favourably on it. Why? Because the marginal utility of consumption – the incremental improvement in well-being from a unit increase in consumption – varies inversely with consumption. So, investments that pay off when consumption is high are less valuable, other things being equal, than those that pay off when consumption is low.

Imagine a security that pays high returns in circumstances that also put the investor's job in jeopardy. For example, an energy crunch is often good news for oil company stock returns but bad news for workers who make and sell gas-guzzling cars. For such worker-investors, oil stocks tend to pay off well when labour income and consumption are low and the marginal utility of consumption is high. Hence, in this example, oil stocks are relatively attractive investments for workers in the car industry.

Risky human capital

This line of thinking has important implications for portfolio choice. In particular, investors should structure their portfolios with due regard for the relationship between asset returns and shocks to the value of risky human capital. Other things being equal (such as expected returns, tax consequences and transaction costs), worker-investors should curtail or eliminate exposure to risky financial assets that do well in times of good news about their own labour income and raise exposure to financial assets that do well in times of bad news about their own income.

This principle is expressed using the concept of "covariance", which measures how closely two variables move together. That is, investors should load up on risky securities that have a negative covariance with the value of their own human capital and shy away from securities that have a positive covariance. Exercising this principle requires solid information about the relevant covariances. Sometimes the requisite knowledge is evident, for example when an executive holds restricted equity in the company for which he works. Clearly, this manager has illiquid wealth tied up in a form that does well precisely when the company stock performs well. He is well advised to structure the discretionary parts of his portfolio to offset this high exposure to company stock.

More often than not, however, the requisite knowledge is not evident. Consider a 40-year-old steelworker. What is the relationship between the value of the steelworker's human capital and equity returns at the aggregate, industry and company level? In principle, careful empirical research can uncover the requisite knowledge by investigating the covariance between the returns on financial assets and the value of human capital. Unfortunately, such research has only begun to provide an empirical foundation for better portfolio choice.

Research to date offers two messages. First, the correlation between equity returns and the value of human capital rises with the education level of the worker. Available evidence suggests that this relationship to education holds for aggregate equity returns, own-industry equity returns and, perhaps, own-company returns as well. This evidence resonates with the view that the financial interests of capitalists are more closely aligned with highly educated professional workers than with less-educated, blue-collar workers. The portfolio implication is that less-educated workers should hold a larger fraction of financial wealth in aggregate and own-industry equity than otherwise similar workers with more education.

Second, and contrary to the views of many, it need not be foolish or risky for a worker-investor to hold stock in his own company or industry. Economic theory and empirical evidence both suggest that this portfolio strategy reduces risk for some workers. To see why, consider the steelworker again. If the ups and downs of steel stocks mainly reflect shocks to the demand for steel, then capital and labour rise and fall together. In this case, the steelworker is well advised to curtail exposure to steel industry stocks and other financial assets that move in sympathy. However, if the ups and downs of steel stocks are dominated by developments that shift the relative demand for capital and labour – such as labour-saving technological innovations or wage-bargaining conflicts that alter the division of a fixed pie – equity returns covary negatively with the value of human capital. In this case, the steelworker is well advised to load up on steel stocks.

To recap, bringing risky human capital into financial theory yields a clear principle for portfolio choice, but one that requires a strong empirical foundation for its application. As yet, our knowledge about the covariance between asset returns and human capital is sketchy. Better information in this regard offers potentially big rewards – for savvy worker-investors and for society at large. Pension fund management, mutual fund design, the creation of new securities and institutions that support individualized social security accounts could all be improved by better knowledge of the covariance between asset returns and the value of human capital.

Ageing advice

What does this analysis imply about portfolio allocation over the lifecycle? In particular, does it support the prescription that investors should shift towards bonds as they age? Yes, but only under conditions that apply to some, not all, workers, and for reasons quite distinct from those put forth by the conventional wisdom on ageing and portfolio allocation.

To see the logic, consider two 40-year-old investors: a tenured professor of history at a financially sound college and a factory worker for a car company. Labour income has quite different risk characteristics for these investors. The professor can anticipate a very stable earnings path until retirement, with considerable protection against firing and salary cuts. His labour income path shares much in common with the cash flows generated by a long-term coupon bond. The factory worker faces a different prospect. The car industry is highly cyclical, tending to rise and fall with the aggregate economy. When new car demand drops off in a cyclical downturn, the factory worker faces the threat of layoff or reduced hours. A downturn might also precipitate early retirement. In contrast, an upswing sharply lessens layoff risk and may bring heavy overtime and a big jump in earnings. In this regard, it is important to observe that the stock market also tends to rise in cyclical upswings and fall in cyclical downturns. Hence, the labour income path for the car factory worker shares much in common with the returns generated by a broad-based equity fund.

In short, by virtue of his job, the factory worker implicitly holds an "asset" – human capital – that is much like equity. The tenured history professor implicitly holds an asset that is much like a bond. More generally, think of a worker-investor's total portfolio as the sum of financial holdings plus the holdings implicit in his human capital. Thus, for a tenured history professor, ageing involves a gradual reduction in human capital that progressively reduces an implicit position in bonds. In consequence, it makes good sense for the professor to offset the reduction in human capital by gradually increasing the share of bonds in his portfolio of financial assets. But for a carworker, ageing involves a reduction in human capital that progressively lowers his implicit position in equity. Hence, it makes good sense for the factory worker to offset the drop in human capital by gradually increasing the share of equity in his financial portfolio.

The general principle is now clear: investors should rebalance their financial portfolios as they age so as to maintain a balanced total portfolio, which includes the value of human capital. For some worker-investors, this principle requires a declining share of financial wealth in equities, but for others it requires an increasing share. So, conventional wisdom gives the right prescription for some, but not all, workers.

There is another problem with the conventional wisdom. After retirement, a worker no longer earns a return on human capital, so the rationale for rebalancing a financial portfolio toward bonds (or equities) no longer holds. Yet financial planners routinely recommend that retirees continue to shift portfolio investments into bonds as they age. In this regard, the conventional wisdom about ageing and portfolio composition is a prescription in search of a principle.

The premium puzzle

A lifecycle perspective also helps us understand the celebrated equity premium puzzle. To recap, average stock returns have greatly exceeded average bond returns over recorded financial history. Adjusted for inflation, the average annual return on the US stock market in the past 110 years has been 7.9 per cent. Over the same period, the real return on comparatively safe securities like government bonds was 1 per cent. The difference of 6.9 per cent is the "equity premium". It is puzzling because it defies easy explanation in theories of asset pricing.

Consider a young person who anticipates uncertain future wage and equity income. An important fact in this regard is that risky human capital is the major form of wealth for most young people. Another important fact is that equity returns are positively correlated with aggregate consumption and wages, but not highly so. Given a low correlation between aggregate equity returns and aggregate wages, the high return on equities suggests they are attractive investments for the average young worker. That is, equities appear to offer high returns and good diversification benefits for most young workers. On both counts, it seems the average young worker should have a high demand for equities. But if this analysis were correct, millions of young workers would hold large equity portfolios. Collectively, they would drive up the price of equities, lower equity returns and cut the equity premium. This doesn't happen.

Ideally, young workers would like to smooth lifetime consumption by borrowing against future wage income, consuming a part of the loan and investing the rest in equity. In practice, most young people are effectively shut out of equity markets by the high cost of borrowing against future wage income. For most young households, the cost of funds is the interest rate on unsecured credit, which is typically high. A 7.9 per cent return on equities has little lustre for an investor whose cost of funds is 12.9 per cent!

As a result, what initially looks like a high demand for equities by the average young worker becomes a zero or near-zero demand. The reason for this is not hard to see. Human capital is risky and highly illiquid. The deeper reasons involve moral hazard, adverse selection and enforcement problems in lending markets without secure collateral. In any event, the consequence is that most young workers have little or no participation in equity markets.

Who then holds equities and how are they priced? Here again, the lifecycle perspective is helpful. Equities are mainly held by middle-aged and older persons who have accumulated financial wealth (possibly in a pension fund) over the lifecycle. Their wage uncertainty has largely been resolved. After retirement, future "wages" are either zero or a fixed amount. At this stage of the lifecycle, equity income is highly correlated with consumption and it no longer helps to diversify the effects of risky human capital. Hence, for middle-aged and older people to hold equity, it must offer a higher return. That is, in equilibrium it must command a large premium over safe securities.

We conclude that there is something of a "free lunch" for young people with substantial financial asset holdings. For a young person in this happy circumstance, equity remains a desirable asset. Moreover, since equity is priced by older people, our happy young investor can reap high equity returns but with less impact on consumption risk.

Copyright © Steven Davis and Rajnish Mehra 2002

Further reading

Constantinides, G.M., Donaldson, J.B. and Mehra, R. (2001) 'Junior can't borrow: a new perspective on the equity premium puzzle", *Quarterly Journal of Economics* (http://www.econ.ucsb.edu/~mehra/junior.pdf).

Davis, S.J. and Willen, P. (2001) "Risky labor income and portfolio choice", in Bodie, Z., Hammond, B. and Mitchell, O.S. (eds) *Innovations for Financing Retirement*, University of Pennsylvania Press (http://gsbwww.uchicago.edu/fac/steven.davis/research).

Davis, S.J. and Willen, P. (2000) "Using financial assets to hedge risky labor income: estimating the benefits", working paper, University of Chicago Graduate School of Business (http://gsbwww.uchicago.edu/fac/steven.davis/research).

Jagannathan, R. and Kocherlakota, N.R. (1996) "Why should older people invest less in stocks than younger people?", Federal Reserve Bank of Minneapolis Quarterly Review, Summer.

Mehra, R. and Prescott, E.C. (1985) "The equity premium: a puzzle", *Journal of Monetary Economics*, 15, 145–61.

Global **investment** 5

Contents

The logic that lies behind overseas diversification 166

Robert Hodrick, Columbia Business School

How much of an investor's portfolio should be concentrated in his or her home country, and how much distributed throughout other markets?

Taking stock with foreign exchange 173

Robert Aliber, University of Chicago Graduate School of Business

Investors have traditionally stuck to what they know. However, international investing may confer real advantages.

An open and shut case for portfolio diversification 179

Ian Cooper, London Business School

This article identifies a number of potential difficulties with international portfolio diversification, but shows how the benefits outweigh the dangers.

Room for improvement in protecting investors 186

David Beim, Columbia Business School

Strong institutions and profits, as well as growth, are vital for success, but foreign investors can find it difficult to assess the risks.

Introduction to Part 5

Nearly all investors agree that assets are safer when diversified. However, geography plays a big part in the level of diversification of portfolios. For instance, a French investor will know more about French companies, or a US investor about US companies, and be more likely to invest in them than in those of other nations. Even among institutional investors there is widespread disagreement about the ideal ratio of foreign to domestic stocks in a portfolio. In this part writers explore some of the factors involved in global investment, including the effects of foreign exchange fluctuations and differences in investor protection regimes.

The logic that lies behind
overseas diversification

Robert Hodrick assesses the reasons behind holding overseas stocks as part of an investment portfolio and shows how a rational judgement can be made.

Robert J. Hodrick is Nomura Professor of International Finance at Columbia Business School and Columbia University's School of International and Public Affairs. He is also a research associate of the National Bureau of Economic Research.

How internationally diversified should a portfolio be? Advice varies widely. In February 2001, *The New York Times* reported that Merrill Lynch advises a limit on foreign stocks of 5 per cent, down from 35 per cent. The article noted that Goldman Sachs advises 15–20 per cent and Morgan Stanley 25–35 per cent. Stefano Cavaglia, a global equity strategist at UBS Brinson, advises US investors to hold half of their portfolio in foreign equity. Who's right?

The case for diversification begins with the fact that investors must make decisions in an environment of uncertainty. Because future returns cannot be known, smart investors will assess the uncertainty of returns by specifying probability distributions (see Box 1). These distributions, which reflect the subjective views of an investor, describe the expected values and variances of the returns, as well as correlations between returns. Investors are rational when their subjective views coincide with what is objectively true. Unfortunately, objective probability distributions are not published anywhere, so differences about diversification can be traced to differences of opinion about the probability distributions of future returns. One way to generate these distributions is to estimate them using historical data, assuming the future will look like the past. Let's suppose this is true.

Table 1 gives statistics for dollar-denominated excess returns on 12 country portfolios. The raw data are the Morgan Stanley Capital International total monthly returns for each country in excess of the return on a eurodollar deposit, which is a reasonable proxy for the risk-free return. Mean monthly excess returns are annualized and standard deviations are calculated to correspond to an annualized holding period. The highest average is Sweden's 11.2 per cent and the lowest is Italy's 3.3 per cent. The US average is 5.7 per

> **Box 1 A statistical refresher**
>
> - A probability distribution lists the values returns may take and the probabilities associated with different possible returns.
> - The expected value of a future return is also called the mean of the probability distribution and is calculated as the probability-weighted average of the possible future values of that return. This is the sum of the probabilities of the events times the values of the return if those events occur.
> - The variance of the distribution of a future return is the probability-weighted average of the squared deviations from the mean return.
> - A related concept is standard deviation, which is measured in the same units as returns because it is the square root of variance.
> - The covariance of two returns describes how the possible realizations of these returns move together. It is measured by the probability-weighted average of the deviations from the mean for one return times the deviations from the mean of another return.
> - A related concept is the correlation coefficient – the covariance of two returns divided by the product of the two respective standard deviations. Correlations range between −1 and +1. If two returns are perfectly correlated, the correlation is +1; if they are not at all correlated, the correlation is 0; and if they are perfectly negatively correlated, the correlation is −1.

cent. Standard deviations range from a low of 15.3 per cent a year for the US to 30.9 per cent for Singapore. Because returns are in dollars, the return for any country other than the US contains both the local currency equity return and the change in the value of the US dollar relative to the local currency, which provides an additional source of volatility.

After assessing the probability distributions, the rational investor must consider preferences for risk and return. It is uncontroversial to assume that an investor likes high expected returns on a portfolio and dislikes variance in future returns. What trade-offs between risk and return do financial markets offer?

For a US investor with a US portfolio, there is a trade-off in terms of how much the expected return rises with an increase in the portfolio's standard deviation as the investor moves from risk-free assets to equities. This trade-off can be calculated using the mean return and standard deviation statistics in Table 1. In the case of the US portfolio, the trade-off is $5.7/15.3 = 0.37$. So for each percentage point increase in the standard deviation of a US portfolio, the investor is compensated with a 0.37 per cent increase in expected return. Depending on their tolerance for risk, investors will choose a portfolio, for example, two-thirds in US equities and a third in risk-free securities. However, this analysis ignores a key issue, which is the potential improvement in the trade-off between risk and return that comes from diversifying internationally.

Now, suppose our US investor is willing to add British equity to the portfolio if doing so improves the trade-off between risk and return. Some investors might look at the ratio of British expected excess return to British standard

TABLE 1   Statistics from annualized excess returns by country

US dollars; 1970–2000

Country	US	JP	GB	FR	DE	IT	NL	BE	CH	SE	AT	SG	
Mean	5.7	8.8	7.8	7.6	6.7	3.3	8.4	8.9	7.3	11.2	3.5	10.9	
Standard deviation	15.3	22.9	23.9	23.0	20.4	26.4	18.8	17.8	19.0	22.3	25.1	30.9	
Correlation	1.00	0.27	0.50	0.45	0.38	0.25	0.42	0.57	0.49	0.43	0.47	0.47	US
		1.00	0.36	0.39	0.36	0.35	0.40	0.42	0.42	0.38	0.29	0.34	JP
			1.00	0.54	0.43	0.34	0.51	0.64	0.56	0.42	0.47	0.48	GB
				1.00	0.61	0.44	0.66	0.61	0.61	0.40	0.37	0.28	FR
					1.00	0.39	0.64	0.69	0.68	0.47	0.30	0.28	DE
						1.00	0.41	0.37	0.37	0.36	0.23	0.19	IT
							1.00	0.66	0.63	0.42	0.30	0.31	NL
								1.00	0.71	0.47	0.41	0.41	BE
									1.00	0.50	0.39	0.37	CH
										1.00	0.40	0.36	SE
											1.00	0.42	AT
												1.00	SG

US = United States
JP = Japan
GB = Great Britain
FR = France
DE = Germany
IT = Italy
NL = Netherlands
BE = Belgium
CH = Switzerland
SE = Sweden
AT = Australia
SG = Singapore

Note: The means and standard deviations are measured in per cent per annum. The raw data are MSCI monthly country returns in excess of the eurodollar rate (which averaged 7 per cent).
Figures are annualized by multiplying the mean monthly returns by 12 and the standard deviation of monthly returns by the square root of 12.

deviation – which from Table 1 is 7.8/23.9 = 0.33 – and conclude they should not diversify because the British trade-off of 0.33 is worse than the US figure of 0.37. This conclusion is wrong.

Underlying logic

To see why, one should recognize that the expected excess return on a portfolio of US and British equity would be the weighted sum of the expected excess returns on the two country returns, where the weights are the shares of wealth invested in each of the two countries (see Equation 1).

The variance of the portfolio is the squared weight on the US return times the variance of the US return, plus the squared weight on the British return times the variance of the British return, plus two times the product of the two investment weights times the covariance between the two country returns (see Equation 2).

From differential calculus we know that the effect of adding British equity to the expected portfolio excess return is simply the British expected return, while the effect on the variance of the portfolio is given by the covariance of the British return with the US return. Thus, the ratio of expected portfolio return to the variance of the portfolio return goes up if the ratio of the expected return on British equity to its covariance with the US is larger than

EQUATIONS

Equation 1
Expected portfolio excess return = (% invested in US x expected US excess return)
+ (% invested in GB x expected GB excess return)

Equation 2
Variance of portfolio return = [(% invested in US)² x (variance of US excess return)]
+ [(% invested in GB)² x (variance of GB excess return)]
+ [2 x (% invested in US) x (% invested in GB) x (covariance of US excess return and GB excess return)]

Equation 3
Risk-return trade-off improves if:

$$\frac{\text{expected GB excess return}}{\text{covariance of US excess return and GB excess return}} < \frac{\text{expected US excess return}}{\text{variance of US excess return}}$$

the ratio of the expected return on the US to the variance of the return on the US (see Equation 3).

We can rephrase the argument in terms of expected returns and standard deviations by recognizing that the covariance is the correlation coefficient times the product of the two standard deviations. So, US investors should add British equity if the ratio of British expected return to standard deviation divided by the correlation between the US and British returns is greater than the ratio of US expected return to its standard deviation. The British statistics produce a result of $7.8/(23.9 \times 0.50) = 0.65$. This easily exceeds the US figure of $(5.7/15.3) = 0.37$. A similar result comes out for the other countries, except Australia which comes out lower, at 0.30.

The average correlation between the US return and returns on the other countries is 0.43. It is this low correlation between country returns that generates a significant improvement in the risk-return trade-off. Let's see how our US investor can use this to generate a portfolio that has an optimal risk-return trade-off.

An optimal portfolio

Figure 1 has expected return on the vertical axis (equal to the excess return from Table 1 plus the eurodollar rate, which averages out at 7 per cent) and standard deviation of return on the horizontal axis. Points corresponding to expected returns and standard deviations from Table 1 are labelled with the country codes. The upper half of the solid curved line represents the efficient frontier, that is the minimum standard deviation of a portfolio of the 12 country returns that can be achieved for a given level of expected return on the portfolio. The dashed line represents the efficient frontier for a US investor who invests only in G5 countries (US, Japan, Great Britain, France and Germany). The point labelled MVE, the mean-variance efficient point, corresponds to the point of tangency between a straight line starting from the risk-free return on the vertical axis and the efficient frontier. The MVE point corresponds to a specific portfolio investment in the 12 countries that I'll call the global portfolio.

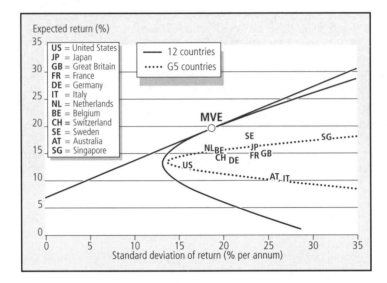

FIGURE 1 Mean standard deviation frontiers 1970–2000

An investor with no equities gets the risk-free return, which averaged 7 per cent during this sample period. Increasing investment in the global portfolio moves the investor to the top right along the straight line, increasing expected return and risk. Because the expected excess return of the global portfolio is 12.6 per cent and the standard deviation of the global portfolio is 18.6 per cent, the trade-off between the expected excess return and standard deviation for the global portfolio is 12.6/18.6 = 0.68.

Notice that for the same standard deviation as the US equity portfolio – 15.3 per cent – the global investor can have an increase of almost 5 per cent in expected return, from 12.7 per cent to 17.6 per cent. Alternatively, the investor can accept the same expected return as the US portfolio while reducing the standard deviation of the portfolio to below 10 per cent. Investing only in G5 countries also offers an improvement in the risk-return trade-off for a US investor, but the improvement is not as great as from the global portfolio.

This analysis uses historical data from 1970 to 2000 to estimate true expected returns, variances and covariances. Why might it misrepresent the case for diversification? First, estimating expected returns is difficult, so average excess returns are measured with substantial error. In choosing a sample period, it is important to include several good and bad periods to avoid bias. For example, calculating average returns from 1980 to 2000 would substantially overstate the true expected excess returns because this period does not contain sufficiently problematic experiences, such as recessions and major wars, that are associated with poor equity performance. Omitting the 1970s, the average excess returns on equities exceed the average returns in Table 1 by anywhere between 1.5 per cent and 5 per cent, depending on the country.

One can also use theory to help determine an appropriate expected return. When academic Jacob Thomas and analyst James Claus (2001) combine analysts' earnings forecasts for major countries with a financial valuation model, they find expected excess returns of just 3 per cent.

Second, some past returns are probably poorer representations of what to expect than others. Japan's average excess return of 8.8 per cent represents very good performance in the 1980s, yet is poor for the 1990s. What should we expect going forward? Is Japan mired in recession or is a return to growth around the corner?

Third, the analysis does not constrain all the portfolio positions in the different countries to be positive, and the MVE portfolio takes short positions in 5 of the 12 countries. Many investors avoid short positions in portfolios. Allowing only long positions reduces, but does not eliminate, gains from international diversification. For example, the risk-return trade-off for a global portfolio whose weights correspond to the average market capitalizations of the 12 countries during the sample period is 6.9/14.0 = 0.49.

Fourth, there is evidence that correlations of country returns are increasing, especially in down markets. As technology progresses and markets become more integrated, we should expect correlations to increase. The average correlation between returns for the US and the other countries calculated for the last five years of the sample is 0.58, substantially above the 0.43 for the full sample period. Could future correlations be even higher?

The New York Times article cited earlier indicates that correlations calculated over three-year rolling intervals between the US market and developed foreign markets were as low as 0.15 in early 1987 and now stand slightly below 0.8. Further, academics François Longin and Bruno Solnik (2001) have demonstrated that correlations across countries are especially large when the US market experiences a large drop. Thus, exactly when US investors have the greatest need for the benefits of diversification, they do not materialize. Does this evidence indicate that international diversification is unwarranted?

Academics Andrew Ang and Geert Bekaert (2000) have found that correlations across countries do increase in highly volatile markets, confirming the findings of Longin and Solnik. Yet Ang and Bekaert still find substantial value from international diversification because correlations fall when equity markets are doing well and volatility is lower. It seems unlikely that the world economy is so integrated that future correlations are going to remain as high as they may now seem. There is simply too much diversity in government policies and business cycles to think otherwise.

It is also possible to diversify internationally by choosing the equities of a country based on some measurable criterion and not just by their geographic location. Investment managers often use the ratio of a company's book value to its equity market value (the B/M ratio) to classify companies as "value" stocks (ones with high B/M) and "growth" stocks (ones with low B/M).

Academics Eugene Fama and Kenneth French (1998) found that value stocks in the US and major countries in MSCI's EAFE index had substantially higher average returns than growth stocks between 1975 and 1995. Fama and French rank companies in the MSCI index of a country by B/M. This ranking produces a high book-to-market portfolio (HB/M) of companies in the top 30 per cent of B/M and a low book-to-market portfolio (LB/M) of companies in the lowest 30 per cent. Differences between country portfolios are substantial, from Japan's 9.9 per cent to Italy's –7.0 per cent; with the US at 6.8 per cent and the UK at 4.2 per cent. There is also benefit from diversification because the correlations of returns across countries on portfolios that long the HB/M companies and short the LB/M companies of a country are low. For example, the average correlation of returns on the high and low portfolios for these countries with the equivalent US portfolio is 0.10.

These arguments suggest there is ample opportunity for a US investor to form a globally diversified portfolio that improves upon the risk-return trade-off from investing only in the US. However, knowing the right percentage of foreign equity is difficult. A world market portfolio would require US investors to put half of their investments in foreign equity because US equity represents about half of the world economy. This is the UBS Brinson advice. Will US investors diversify that much? Probably not, because the US did very well in the 1990s and correlations of returns across countries are high. Even so, this author is uncomfortable with Merrill Lynch's 5 per cent level. The US has not always produced the best returns. I also expect future correlations to be low enough to give a substantial benefit from international diversification.

Copyright © Robert Hodrick 2002

Further reading

Ang, A. and Bekaert, G. (2000) "International asset allocation with regime shifts", National Bureau of Economic Research working paper 7056 (http://www.columbia.edu/~aa610).

Fama, E.F. and French, K. (1998) "Value versus growth: the international evidence", *Journal of Finance*, 53, 1975–99.

Longin, F. and Solnik, B. (2001) "Extreme correlation of international equity markets", *Journal of Finance*, 56, 2, 649–76.

Thomas, J. and Claus, J. (2001) "Equity premia as low as three per cent? Evidence from analysts' earnings forecasts for domestic and international stock markets", working paper (http://www.columbia.edu/~jkt1/research.html).

Taking stock
with foreign exchange

A prime reason for investing in foreign companies is the expectation of higher returns from faster-growing overseas economies. **Robert Aliber** examines the merits of the argument.

Robert Z. Aliber is professor of finance at the University of Chicago Graduate School of Business.

In the 1920s the economist John Maynard Keynes concluded that foreign investment did not pay for British investors – that the promised returns were not realized because of exceptional losses. He used British ownership of shares in the New York City subway as an example; if the subway had failed, the shares held by British investors would have become worthless and the owners of the subway's bonds would have acquired control as a result of debt-for-equity conversion.

Two assumptions central to his conclusion are puzzling. One is that British investors owned the equity rather than the debt of the subway, the other is that higher rates of return on the British foreign investments that did not go bankrupt were insufficient to compensate for losses on the investments that failed.

International investment occurs in waves. British foreign investment surged in the last three decades of the 19th century, as did US foreign investment in the 1920s and the 1960s. Japanese foreign investment increased rapidly in the 1980s. US companies being bought by competitors with headquarters in Europe has been a feature of the past four or five years.

Traditionally, investing has had a local bias; some countries still have two or three regional stock exchanges as well as a dominant national exchange. Residents of most countries, even small, internationally open countries such as the Netherlands and Switzerland, still have a strong home bias in selecting bonds and shares and hold most of their wealth in securities denominated in their local currency.

Growth

The basic argument for acquiring foreign securities is that rates of return will be higher than on domestic securities, primarily because of their more rapid rates of growth. The economic intuition is that higher rates of economic growth are associated with more rapid increases in corporate earnings and hence in share prices. A secondary argument is that their inclusion with domestic securities will reduce the overall risk of a portfolio. Changes in the prices of foreign securities, it is said, are not perfectly correlated with domestic securities.

In the 1980s, Japan became the prime example of higher returns from global portfolios following the surge in share prices in Tokyo and the sharp increase in the foreign exchange value of the yen. At the end of the 1980s, the returns on a global portfolio exceeded those of a portfolio of US shares, largely because of higher US dollar rates of return on Japanese shares. (The flip side of this statement is that Japanese investors were better off than if they owned only domestic shares.) Economic growth in Japan had been rapid in the 1950s and 1960s as the country rebounded from the devastation of the second world war. Growth slowed in each of the next decades but was still higher than in most other industrial countries.

The higher US dollar rates of return on Japanese shares – despite the unhappy experiences of many US owners of Tokyo shares since 1990 – reflects the two primary factors that explain why the rate of return on foreign securities will be higher than the rate of return on domestic securities. The first is that some countries – typically those that have only recently begun to industrialize – may realize more rapid rates of economic growth as they "catch up" with countries that achieved rapid growth earlier. The second is that for an extended period many national share markets were "segmented" – cut off from the global market by portfolio regulations and exchange controls. Investors who wanted to buy the shares of Japanese companies and shares of companies based in numerous other countries were prevented from doing so by formal and informal procedures. As controls have eased, the valuation of domestic shares has increased to more nearly correspond with the valuation of shares on the New York Stock Exchange. Segmentation is a transitional argument, since much of the liberalization occurs over three to five years. The catch-up story is also transitional, although the period of rapid growth may be 20 years or more.

Evaluation

Keynes's proposition that foreign investment does not pay can be evaluated by comparing the rates of return on a portfolio of US shares, for example, the Standard & Poor's 500, with returns on comparable share prices in other countries over a variety of holding periods. Three comparisons can be made: local or own-currency returns (for example, returns to a US investor on US shares), US dollar returns when the foreign exposure is not hedged, and US dollar returns when the foreign exposure is hedged.

These comparisons are made from the viewpoint of US residents. The non-

TABLE 1	Rates of return on share price indices		
	Holding period		
	1969–99	1979–95	1989–99
Local currency returns			
US	9.0	11.5	14.0
Australia	10.7	13.1	10.5
Canada	11.9	14.8	–
France	14.4	14.5	13.0
Germany	10.0	11.4	12.0
Great Britain	14.6	18.6	12.3
Italy	12.1	18.0	12.9
Japan	8.8	9.9	–5.3
Netherlands	14.5	18.0	18.0
Spain	13.5	19.2	16.0
Sweden	18.9	25.4	19.3
Switzerland	10.3	12.6	16.7
US dollar returns (brackets indicate exchange exposure hedged)			
US	9.0	11.5	14.0
Australia	8.0	12.1	6.5
Canada	10.8	8.3 (5.5)	9.2
France	12.8	13.1	10.9
Germany	11.7	12.7 (13.1)	9.0
Great Britain	12.7	15.9 (15.8)	11.6
Italy	7.6	13.3 (9.2)	7.1
Japan	13.0	15.9 (13.1)	–2.9
Netherlands	15.8	19.3	14.9
Spain	9.8	14.7 (12.2)	10.2
Sweden	16.4	21.8 (20.2)	14.2
Switzerland	13.5	14.8 (16.0)	15.3 (19.2)

Source: Morgan Stanley Capital International. Exchange rate data from International Financial Statistics

US investor may draw the inverse conclusion: for example, the Japanese yen rate of return on the US share price index differs by an amount equal to the difference between the dollar rate of return and the yen rate of return on the Japanese index.

Table 1 shows rates of return on share price indices for various countries (excluding dividends). A basic problem is choosing the most representative holding period for comparison. There is a view that longer periods are preferred to shorter periods, yet critics claim that exceptionally high rates of return on US shares in the second half of the 1990s skew the results. In the table, 1969 was selected as the base year for the long holding period, even though US share prices were flat from 1969 to 1982.

The local currency rates of return on the foreign share price indices generally were higher than the rate of return on US share price indices between 1969 and 1999. Moreover, the local currency rates of return on US share price indices and most foreign indices generally were higher between 1989 and 1999 than in longer periods. However, the rates of return for the UK, Japan and Australia were lower in this recent 10-year period. Surprisingly, the rates of return from about half the countries were higher than the US dollar rate of return in this recent period.

The data on US dollar rates of return assume that at the beginning of the holding period US residents bought foreign currency and shares, and at the end of the period sold foreign shares and bought US dollars. Now part of the return to US residents involves the change in the price of the dollar relative to each of these foreign currencies between the beginning and the end of the holding period. As a result of the introduction of the exchange rate factor, US dollar rates of return are higher than the local currency rates of return on the share price indices of those countries whose currencies appreciated relative to the US dollar – Japan, Switzerland, Germany and the Netherlands. A significant part of the excess dollar return on foreign share prices indices was due to the appreciation of foreign currencies as opposed to there being a higher local currency return than the return on US shares.

The third comparison involves the US dollar rate of return on foreign indices when the foreign currency exposure is continuously hedged. The US investor buys the foreign currency in the spot exchange market and at the same time sells this currency in the forward exchange market with delivery in a year's time. This comparison involves several simplifying assumptions. One is that at the beginning of the holding period the investor knows what the value of the foreign share holdings will be at the end of the period and buys the corresponding amount of US dollars in the foreign exchange market. (An alternative assumption would be that the investor hedges only the amount of the initial purchase of the foreign shares and the change in the value of the share portfolio is not hedged. The results do not differ materially.) A second is that the one-year forward exchange contracts are "rolled over", that is, when the forward contract matures, the investor buys a new one-year forward contract.

The US dollar rates of return on the foreign share price indices when the foreign exchange exposure is hedged, shown in brackets in Table 1, are generally lower than the unhedged rates. But the hedged US dollar rates of return are higher on the German and Swiss share price indices. The implication is that forward exchange rates are downward-biased relative to the spot exchange rate on the dates that the forward exchange contracts mature for those currencies that have depreciated relative to the US dollar. Conversely, the forward exchange rate is upward-biased for currencies that have appreciated relative to the dollar. Either investors have over-estimated the rate of depreciation and appreciation or they prefer to hold currencies that they believe are unlikely to depreciate.

The ranking of countries by rate of return is sensitive to the choice of holding period. The difference in the rankings weakens the rationale for a global portfolio based on the assumption that rates of return will be higher on shares available in emerging market countries. Rates of return are high on these indices when their markets become less segmented from global markets and when they stabilize their economies. But there is little evidence that rates of return in these countries are higher over extended periods.

A significant part of the higher rate of return that US residents would have earned on their purchases of foreign shares results from the appreciation of a handful of currencies relative to the US dollar. In the 1970s the Japanese yen, the German mark and several other European currencies appreciated after a period of undervaluation in the 1960s. Some foreign currencies are likely to appreciate relative to the dollar in the future and US investors can buy these currencies directly without buying (exposure to the) foreign equities.

Japanese investors had a lower currency rate of return than residents of these other countries, which seems paradoxical given the high rates of domestic economic growth in the 1970s, 1980s and even in the first half of the 1990s. Moreover, if Japanese investors had purchased foreign share price indices they would have found that the excess of the local currency rate of return in these other countries over the local currency rate of return in Japan was smaller than the average rate of appreciation of the yen.

It is risky to make projections over 10 or 20 years for returns on share indices using past rates of return. Such rates reflect both the observed rates of economic growth and the reduction in segmentation of national markets. The experience with buying Japanese shares is a strong reminder of the sensitivity of the results to the choice of the holding period. In the 1980s Japanese share prices increased more than twice as rapidly as US prices. By the end of the 1990s Japanese shares had declined to their mid-1980s level.

Conclusion

Rapid economic growth is associated with high rates of return on shares and often with currency appreciation. Rates of return on non-US share price indices were higher than the rate of return on the US share index in part because the rates of economic growth in these countries were higher than in the US after the second world war. In some cases rates of return were higher because share price indices increased when local markets became more open to foreign investors.

Keynes might well have concluded that British investors would have obtained a higher rate of return on investments in those foreign countries that had higher rates of economic growth and greater success in achieving a low inflation rate than Britain. He would have been mindful of the benefits of diversification and sceptical about how large a share of the excess returns on foreign investments would have been captured by financial intermediaries.

Copyright © Robert Aliber 2002

Further reading

Berryessa, N. and Kirzner, E. (1993) *Global Investing: The Templeton Way*, Homewood, IL: Business One Irwin.

Kalb, S.E. and Kalb, P.E. (1998) *The Top 100 International Growth Stocks*, New York: Simon & Schuster.

Solnik, B. (1996) *International Investments*, Reading, MA: Addison-Wesley.

An open and shut case
for portfolio diversification

There are various arguments put forward against buying international securities, but none of them holds any water, says **Ian Cooper**. Only the degree of investment is unclear.

Ian Cooper is a professor of finance, chair of the finance faculty and director of the Institute of Finance and Accounting at London Business School.

Other articles in this book state three fundamental principles of portfolio optimization: diversify to reduce risk, deviate from full diversification only if you have superior information or particular motives arising from tax, liquidity or hedging, and adjust to get the desired level of risk by mixing fixed income and equity, not by reducing the diversification of your equity portfolio. These principles lead to the conclusion that most portfolios should have at their core a highly diversified equity fund. This raises the question of what "highly diversified" means.

Two perspectives can be taken. One is to diversify within the investor's local stock market. This is the logic behind funds such as FTSE tracker funds in the UK and Standard & Poor's index funds in the US. The alternative is to treat the global market as the natural universe. Then full diversification means holding an internationally diversified portfolio. This article is about the case for the latter perspective.

Global gains

The prime motive for holding a global equity portfolio is to obtain the benefits of international diversification. The first article in this part by Robert Hodrick discussed this. He showed how to combine estimates of risk and return for countries to give an optimal international portfolio. Unfortunately, the construction of an optimal international portfolio requires estimates of expected return and risk for all assets considered. This is not an easy task, and the estimates are subject to considerable error. Academic Mark Britten-Jones (1999) has shown that relatively small errors in inputs can produce large errors in the portfolio selected.

TABLE 1   Annualized return and risk in the US, 1970–2000

Country	Excess return (%)	Standard deviation (%)	Sharpe ratio
France	7.6	23.0	0.33
Germany	6.7	20.4	0.33
Japan	8.8	22.9	0.38
UK	7.8	23.9	0.33
US	5.7	15.3	0.37
Global market portfolio	6.0	14.1	0.43

Data: MSCI monthly equity index returns, excess returns relative to Libor

So, although it is clear that international diversification is valuable, the appropriate degree is unclear. As a result, discussions of international investing are often couched in terms of adding a modest amount of foreign securities to a largely domestic portfolio, as if the domestic portfolio is close to optimal and requires only a slight adjustment.

There is an alternative perspective, which Table 1 illustrates. It shows the historical average return and risk for various countries' equity markets between 1970 and 2000. The average risk premium has been computed by subtracting the London interbank offered rate (Libor) from average returns. Risk is measured by the standard deviation of returns. The risk premium for a unit of risk, called the Sharpe ratio, is also shown. A higher Sharpe ratio indicates a more favourable investment.

The individual countries in the table have similar Sharpe ratios. However, one portfolio dominates all five major countries listed, in the sense that it has the highest Sharpe ratio. This is the global market portfolio, with holdings proportional to the capitalization of different markets. It dominates because international diversification results in a much lower level of risk without sacrificing excess return, on average.

The logic behind focusing on the global market portfolio as a plausible holding is the same as that for using domestic market indices as benchmarks. If you have no special information, you should hold the "average" portfolio. For domestic assets, this average is the market index. But the "average" portfolio for the world is the global market portfolio. Table 1 shows that this is a better starting point for building equity portfolios than are the market portfolios of the individual countries listed.

The source of gains

Diversification comes from holding investments that have unrelated returns. Global diversification results from the relatively low correlations between the returns on different countries. It is difficult to intuitively grasp the size of these diversification effects. However, Steven Heston of Goldman Sachs and academic Geert Rouwenhorst (1994) have provided a useful benchmark. They examined returns to see how international diversification compared with diversification within a single country. They found that "diversification across countries within an industry is a much more effective tool for risk reduction than industry diversification within a country". In other words, according to them, the first and most important dimension of portfolio diversification is internationalism.

In light of this it is ironic to hear fund managers complain that concentration of their home market in a few companies limits diversification. If a domestic portfolio is held, this is indeed true. For example, John Gillies of US fund management company Frank Russell estimates that the top 15 companies account for more than three-quarters of the relevant FTSE index in Austria, Belgium, Denmark, Germany, Italy, the Netherlands, Norway, Portugal, Spain and Switzerland. In Australia, Canada, France and the UK they account for over half. This limits the diversification that can be obtained within a domestic portfolio. However, the top 15 companies account for little more than 10 per cent of the FTSE world index. So the diversification problem disappears once a global perspective is taken. Global diversification not only improves the risk/return characteristics of the portfolio, it also solves the practical problem of concentrated equity markets.

Home-loving

These benefits of international diversification have been well documented since the 1960s. Yet many investor portfolios remain highly concentrated in their home markets. Table 2 shows holdings of foreign securities of pension funds. German and US pension funds hold almost all their assets in domestic securities. Even UK funds, which have the most international holdings, invest less than a fifth of their money in foreign securities.

This behaviour may not seem surprising to some readers. But one would be amazed if Scottish pension funds invested almost all their money in Scotland and Welsh funds all their money in Wales. That would be irresponsible behaviour that ignored diversification. Yet such behaviour is apparently not considered unusual when the economic entity is Germany, the US or the UK, rather than Scotland or Wales.

TABLE 2 Pension fund holdings of securities issued by non-residents

Country	%
Germany	5.0
Japan	9.0
UK	19.8
US	5.7

Source: IMF, International Capital Markets, September 1998

So the empirical evidence is strongly in favour of global diversification. Yet many portfolios are highly concentrated in domestic equities. The contrast between the gains from international diversification and the actual portfolios that many investors hold raises the question of whether there are negative aspects of international investment that offset these gains.

Problems

One perceived problem with international investing is currency risk. However, this is not as great a difficulty as is often claimed. Work by academic Philippe Jorion (1989) has shown that the extra risk from currency fluctuations is small for international equity portfolios. Furthermore, such risk can be hedged at low cost. So the gains from diversification outweigh these currency concerns.

Another reason sometimes given for concentrating pension funds locally is that domestic equities are a good hedge against inflation. The goal of defined benefit pension funds is to match pension liabilities that rise with inflation. So holding assets whose returns rise with inflation is desirable for these funds.

With my colleague Evi Kaplanis, I have tested whether domestic equities provide such inflation protection. The evidence is strong that they do not. We tested the relationship between equity returns and inflation for the nine largest stock markets and found that high inflation is not matched by high equity returns. So this motive is not a good reason to forgo the benefits of international diversification.

A recent focus of research has been whether international diversification benefits disappear in risky times. Evidence suggests that international stock markets become more related to each other when markets are volatile. These are the circumstances when risk reduction is needed most, so such effects reduce the gains from international diversification. Academics Sanjiv Das and Raman Uppal (2001) tested how much this should affect the degree of international diversification. They found that the effect was small and that investors should still hold highly international portfolios even when this effect is taken into account.

A final argument against international investing comes from the notion that foreign markets are intrinsically risky. This argument cannot generally be true. It is not possible for the US to be a highly risky foreign market for UK investors and, at the same time, the UK a highly risky foreign market for US investors. The risks of the markets are the same for both sets of investors. Each market has its own level of risk and this is taken into account in Table 1. This leads us to the conclusion that global portfolios are beneficial.

How to diversify

It may be, however, that some international markets are illiquid, costly, unfamiliar and generally disadvantageous to trade in. For instance, in some markets foreign investors have poorer access to information. Academics Michael Brennan and Henry Cao (1997) have found evidence of this. Avoiding foreign markets would be the wrong response, however. These problems do not negate the value of international diversification. They simply mean that all ways of achieving it are not equally desirable. One should choose carefully the markets and instruments used. The goal should be diversification at low cost.

Moreover, international diversification does not require investment in all foreign markets. Investments in a limited number of foreign countries can achieve most of the benefits. Holdings can be allocated to markets with transparent market structures. Within these markets, the instruments chosen can represent passive portfolios. These are increasingly available for foreign markets through index funds, index futures, passive mutual funds, swaps, index participation products and a variety of other devices. Active funds such as hedge funds also offer a wide range of international strategies.

Further efficiency can be gained by concentrating foreign holdings in industries that are less correlated with the investor's domestic market. For example, there is little point in diversifying an Australian portfolio first into international resource stocks, whereas this may well be the right move for a Japanese portfolio. Similarly, it is not necessary to increase the weighting of mobile phone makers in a Finnish portfolio.

A home-bias puzzle

In these ways the gains from international diversification are increasingly available at low cost to any investor with a reasonably sized portfolio. Yet equity portfolios remain stubbornly concentrated in domestic markets. Indeed, International Monetary Fund statistics show the proportion of the US equity market owned by foreigners fell between 1998 and 2001 from just over to just under 7 per cent. This leaves us with a puzzle for which no one has provided a convincing solution. It is called the home-bias puzzle.

One suggestion is that the benefits of international investment have been overstated. It could be the case that increasing integration of economies has reduced the benefit of international diversification. If this were true, it would be reflected in increasing correlations between international equity markets. Bruno Solnik (2000) of Groupe HEC has tested this. He finds correlations fluctuate over time, but there is no trend towards increasing correlation.

Another way to resolve the puzzle is if indirect holdings of foreign investments through global companies, investment trusts, country funds, cross-listing of securities, hedge funds and derivative trades are very substantial. If this is the case, the available data on international portfolio holdings could mask a very high degree of international diversification being achieved through these mechanisms. However, this is unlikely to be the answer. The data examined above include international companies and so the gains reflect any international investments held through companies. In addition, pension funds generally make very limited use of derivatives, so it is unlikely that they are achieving international diversification in that way.

The past and the future

All attempts by financial economists to explain home bias in terms of modern portfolio theory have failed. It may be, however, that the explanation is more institutional. Twenty years ago the barriers to international investing were, indeed, substantial. There were few derivatives to hedge currency risk, many restrictions on cross-border holdings, complex tax barriers, poor information flows, fewer cross-border investment funds and limited passive country index investment vehicles. So, at that time, the costs of achieving international diversification may well have offset the benefits.

Most of these costs have been swept aside. International capital markets over the past 20 years have evolved quickly, but the evolution of governance structures of some investment funds has been relatively slow. For instance, many funds retain prohibitions on the use of derivative trades, one of the most efficient ways to achieve international diversification. Paradoxically, many of them invest in other funds that use such strategies.

Similarly, despite the accessibility of a global universe of investments, many funds still measure their performance against a largely domestic benchmark. It might be difficult to be the one fund manager holding a globally diversified portfolio in a year when the domestic market outperforms the global market. On the other hand, it is not so bad being one of many who match the domestic benchmark in a year when the global market has outperformed the domestic market. So it is natural that fund managers' strategies cluster around the benchmark chosen, even if it is the wrong one. An identical issue arises in the definition of fiduciary prudence, where international diversification is viewed in some countries as increasing rather than reducing risk.

These institutional rigidities may be one explanation for the relatively slow move towards global portfolios. But the future is relatively clear. Barriers and costs to international investing are falling systematically. Mechanisms to get around the remaining obstacles are continually being found. Information flows are becoming ever faster. Trading and issuing systems are converging. Tax systems are being harmonized.

All these make it less and less natural for UK investors to choose BP automatically if they want to invest in an oil stock and Vodafone if they want an investment in a mobile operator. It may be that they choose these companies, but the reason should be that they offer the best investments in their sectors rather than that they have their headquarters in the same country as the fund. Twenty years or less from now the challenge will be not "the case for global investing" but "why deviate from a globally diversified equity portfolio?"

Copyright © Ian Cooper 2002

Further reading

Brennan, M. and Cao, H. (1997) "International portfolio investment flows", *Journal of Finance*, December.

Britten-Jones, M. (1999) "Sampling error in mean-variance efficient portfolio weights", *Journal of Finance*, April.

Cooper, I. and Kaplanis, E. (1995) "Home bias in equity portfolios and the cost of capital for multinational firms", *Journal of Applied Corporate Finance*, Fall.

Das, S. and Uppal, R. (2001) "Systemic risk and international portfolio choice", working paper, London Business School (http://www.london.edu/ifa).

Heston, S. and Rouwenhorst, G. (1994) "Does industrial structure explain the benefits of international diversification?", *Journal of Financial Economics*, June.

Jorion, P. (1989) "Asset allocation with hedged and unhedged foreign stocks and bonds", *Journal of Portfolio Management*, Summer.

Solnik, B. (2000) *International Investments*, Reading, MA: Addison-Wesley.

Room for improvement
in protecting investors

David O. Beim is a professor of finance and economics at Columbia Business School.

Strong institutions and profits, as well as growth, are vital for success, but foreign investors can have difficulty assessing the risks, says **David Beim**.

Investors in emerging financial markets were filled with enthusiasm in the early 1990s. Later in the decade, despair predominated. What does the future hold? Many people imagine that investors have fled emerging markets and capital flows have reversed, but Figure 1 shows this is not true. The flow has slowed and for 1998–99 was negative in Asia, but investors have continued

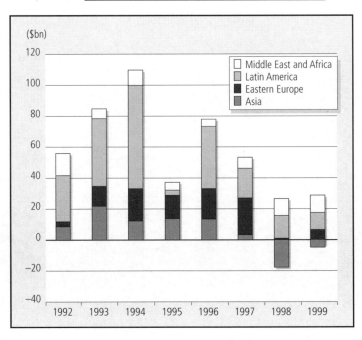

to make net investments. Foreign direct investors (that is, companies buying plants and businesses) show an even stronger pattern of continuing investment.

Developing countries typically have excellent growth opportunities but weak institutions: imperfect rule of law, poor financial regulation, banks saddled with non-performing loans and so on. Investors enter these markets with expectations of high returns but often with little understanding of the problems. As a result, prices are bid up to unrealistic levels in good times and often followed by financial crisis and institutional collapse.

Investors learned a great deal in the 1990s and have become more selective. It is no longer appropriate, if it ever was, to buy a cross-section of the whole emerging market asset class. Rather, one must select certain countries. In particular, for investments in shares and bonds to be rewarding, three things must hold:

- selected countries and companies must be growing at strong, sustainable rates;
- growth must be profitable;
- profits must be shared with outside investors.

In a perfect world, these issues would be reflected in the prices of securities. Investors, however, have great difficulty in understanding and assessing the sources of sustainable growth and the risk from weak institutions. Only when that risk has become obvious, as now, are emerging market securities priced at levels that can provide high future returns.

Sustainable growth

Investment in emerging financial markets is based on a simple idea: that developing countries have better growth opportunities than industrialized countries. For this theory to work, there must be real, sustainable growth in the economy. Unless citizens are getting richer, it is unlikely that outside investors will get richer either, at least over the long term. Indeed, if investors got rich while citizens got poorer, it is likely that institutional rules would be changed.

Table 1 shows that real gross domestic product per head is growing more rapidly in most emerging markets than in the industrial world, even in the crisis-laden period 1995–99. Of course, many experienced negative growth in the 1990s, particularly in Africa and eastern Europe. But some developing countries have grown very rapidly over an extended period of time. A good example is Korea. Just 30 years ago Korea had the same standard of living as many countries in Africa. In 1970 Korea had a GDP per head of $267, a figure similar to Ghana ($257) and Ivory Coast ($271). However, by 1980 it was $1,512, comparable with Poland's $1,533 and Syria's $1,501. By 1990 it had reached $4,422, pressing close to Portugal ($5,318) and Greece ($5,794). Meanwhile, in 1990 Ghana stood at $216 and Syria at $1,462.

How did Korea do it? Fundamentally, the country set out to join the global economy, committing itself to improving technical knowledge and growing

TABLE 1 Data on 25 emerging markets (with US, UK and Japan for comparison)

Country	Real growth of GDP/head 1995–99 (%)	Freedom from corruption	New business procedures	Private ownership of banks (%)	Financial disclosure	Rule of law	Shareholder rights	Creditor rights	Quality of financial regulation	Stock market capitalization /GDP	Private credit /GDP	Bond market capitalization /GDP
China	9.4	3.1	7	1	3.7	4.9	n.a.	n.a.	3.8	0.18	0.93	*
Poland	5.2	4.1	10	16	5.2	6.1	n.a.	n.a.	4.3	0.07	0.16	0.19
Taiwan	n.a.	5.5	8	23	5.4	6.9	6.0	5.0	4.8	1.04	1.55	*
Greece	3.1	4.9	13	22	5.2	6.0	2.0	2.5	3.9	0.24	0.34	0.82
Brazil	3.1	3.9	15	68	5.1	4.6	6.0	7.5	4.1	0.30	0.30	0.35
India	3.1	2.8	10	15	4.9	5.3	4.0	5.0	4.3	n.a.	n.a.	n.a.
Korea	3.0	4.0	11	75	4.7	6.9	4.0	2.5	3.9	0.22	1.43	0.42
Malaysia	2.4	4.8	6	90	5.2	6.7	6.0	5.0	3.9	2.08	1.45	0.67
Chile	2.4	7.4	12	80	6.0	7.2	6.0	10.0	5.4	0.92	0.68	*
Singapore	2.2	9.1	10	78	5.6	8.9	6.0	5.0	5.9	1.34	1.14	0.37
Philippines	2.2	2.8	10	73	4.8	4.8	8.0	5.0	4.6	0.70	0.56	*
Israel	2.1	6.6	5	35	5.4	6.9	6.0	5.0	4.9	0.41	0.71	*
Hungary	2.0	5.2	11	63	5.0	6.4	n.a.	n.a.	3.9	n.a.	n.a.	*
Median	1.9	4.0	11	63	5.0	5.6	5.0	5.0	4.0	0.30	0.56	0.36
Peru	1.9	4.4	14	74	5.0	4.0	4.0	5.0	5.0	0.23	0.20	*
Indonesia	1.6	1.7	7	57	3.9	3.2	4.0	5.0	2.4	0.30	n.a.	*
Czech Republic	1.5	4.3	11	48	4.3	6.1	n.a.	n.a.	3.1	0.29	0.60	*
South Africa	0.9	5.0	15	100	5.5	4.3	8.0	7.5	5.2	1.92	1.39	0.19
Egypt	0.8	3.1	10	11	4.7	5.3	4.0	5.0	4.1	0.23	0.42	*
Mexico	0.3	3.3	15	64	5.3	4.1	0.0	5.0	3.6	0.33	0.16	*
Argentina	0.0	3.5	13	40	5.1	5.6	8.0	7.5	4.4	0.16	0.18	0.19
Turkey	-0.5	3.8	15	44	5.0	5.0	4.0	10.0	3.5	0.24	0.18	*
Thailand	-0.5	3.2	12	83	4.7	5.8	6.0	2.5	3.0	0.39	1.50	*
Jordan	-2.1	4.6	11	74	n.a.	6.4	2.0	0.0	n.a.	0.70	0.75	*
Venezuela	-4.2	2.7	16	42	4.1	3.7	2.0	2.5	3.6	0.14	0.10	*
Russia	-8.7	2.1	15	67	3.6	3.6	n.a.	n.a.	2.3	0.19	0.08	0.11
For comparison												
United States	1.3	7.8	4	100	6.4	7.5	10.0	7.5	6.4	1.22	1.89	1.57
United Kingdom	1.7	8.7	7	100	6.3	8.4	8.0	5.0	6.3	1.47	1.20	0.59
Japan	0.7	6.4	11	100	5.3	7.8	6.0	5.0	5.3	0.63	2.04	1.10

n.a. data not available; *too small

Sources: *International Financial Statistics* (IMF), Transparency International website (www.transparency.org). "The regulation of entry" (NBER working paper 7892), "Government ownership of banks" (NBER working paper 7620), *Global Competitiveness Report* (World Economic Forum), "Law and finance" (*Journal of Political Economy*, 1998, 106, 2, 1113–55), *A New Database on Financial Structure and Development* (World Bank)

exports through products of increasing complexity. By competing, Koreans forced themselves to perform at ever-higher levels and achieved a far higher standard of living.

A contrasting case is Argentina. In the 1930s it had a European standard of living, but since then it has tended to coast. In the 1990s Argentina made great strides in reforming its monetary and financial system, but it still relies on commodities such as wheat, beef and hides, and has not modernized the sources of its wealth.

Embracing the world economy tends to accelerate growth because of convergence: when people, ideas, goods, services and money can flow easily across borders, and companies from all countries compete in a global marketplace, countries become more like each other. This means that countries with lower GDP per capita are likely to catch up with others by growing more rapidly. Convergence works very well when borders are fully open. For example, the US in the late 1880s showed large internal differences in wealth: southern states were the poorest and western states the richest. But with wide-open internal borders, the southern states grew more rapidly than the average and western states more slowly, so they converged.

Those who demonstrate loudly about the supposed evils of globalization would do well to ponder this fact. In the modern era no country has grown richer without embracing the outside world. Those that have tried to isolate themselves from global ideas and influences have stagnated or become poorer.

Investors, then, should begin with a country's openness to global markets and global ideas. This quickly shows up in its real growth rate. Of the eight top-growth countries for 1995–99, four represent the export-driven "East Asian model". A fifth (India) has been more tentative about openness and reform, but starts from such a low base that even moderate reforms plus great strength in technical education have made it one of the fastest-growing markets in the set.

Greece is enjoying the fruits of convergence within the European Union. Poland represents the most thoughtful and successful transition from communism to capitalism; its superior growth in the late 1990s reflects its commitment to strong legal and financial infrastructure as well as convergence with the neighbouring EU. Brazil is a unique country that has aggressively embraced technology. Also, it has the most sophisticated financial markets in Latin America and promotes exports.

Is growth profitable?

The next requirement is that the growth be profitable. GDP is a top-line concept: a company's contribution to its country's GDP is, roughly, its sales (less its purchases of intermediate goods from other companies). To say that a country's GDP is growing is to say that most companies' revenues are growing. However, investors know (or should have learned from the dot-com mania) that a growing top line does not necessarily guarantee a growing bottom line. A growing bottom line requires efficiency and productivity – getting the most output possible per unit of input. Economist Paul Krugman once observed that productivity is not everything, but in the long term it is almost everything. This is because inputs are invariably limited. Only by constantly upgrading ideas, technology and processes can companies and their owners get richer, and economies keep growing. What gets in the way of this process?

Sadly, the answer is often government. In developing countries, government is much more intrusive in the economy than is the case in Europe or the US and this typically damages profitability and efficiency. The first issue is corruption, in which government officials seek private enrichment from the private sector for permits, contracts and so on. Bribery acts like a substantial tax, reducing companies' profitability and altering their incentives in highly unproductive ways. Corruption is a problem almost everywhere, but seems to be especially acute in much of the developing world. It is now being measured, mainly by survey data, and studied by economists to document its effects. Table 1 shows how these measures compare in a number of developing countries, in this case documented by Transparency International, a German non-profit organization.

A related issue is the bureaucracy that governments impose. India, for example, was burdened for decades by the "licence raj", which meant companies could not make even minor changes in assets or business without a licence. The resulting cost, delay and inefficiency held back growth.

The Peruvian writer Hernando de Soto (1989) raised the difficulty of legally starting a business, even a simple one, in developing countries such as Peru. The process can drag on for years, serves no evident social purpose and is highly correlated with corruption. Table 1 shows the result from a study into the number of procedures required to start a new business.

More broadly, governments often like to allocate capital directly rather than allowing this to be done by markets. Government is about power, and the ability to allocate capital resources is a major component of such power – either directly by owning banks or indirectly by giving "guidance" to banks and companies. A good example is the Korean government's push, in the late 1970s, towards heavy and chemical industries, which resulted in over-investment, excess capacity and losses. Government officials probably believed they knew better than companies what would be good for the economy. Unfortunately, government choices are often driven more by politics – favouring certain individuals, regions or companies – than by concern for economic performance. The consequence is usually growth of the top line but losses on the bottom line.

Table 1 also shows the fraction of bank assets directly controlled by the private sector, as a proxy for the extent of private allocation of capital. Where this measure is 100 per cent or nearly so, financial markets are most fully trusted to make capital allocation decisions, which should result in the greatest efficiency.

Investors need to look not just at top-line growth but also at bottom-line productivity and efficiency. They will do well to avoid countries where the government is too intrusive. Table 1 gives an indication of where such problems are particularly severe.

Are profits shared?

Table 1 shows that the Chinese economy has grown very quickly, thanks largely to an export-driven growth policy and a burgeoning private sector. Capital has been provided by wealthy Chinese businessmen in Hong Kong and throughout southeast Asia. However, none of this guarantees that outside investors will do well in China.

In the industrial world it is taken for granted that profits are shared by outside providers of capital, but in many countries this cannot be assumed. Things can go wrong on two levels: managers may steal from owners and inside investors may steal from outside investors. Managerial theft was most obvious in the transition of formerly communist countries in central and eastern Europe. Enterprises were controlled by state-appointed managers who saw the transition from communism as a golden opportunity to appropriate wealth. They did this most readily by selling assets of established enterprises, which they controlled, to smaller ones that they actually owned, at prices far from fair market value. This practice, called "tunnelling", was blatant in Russia and widespread in many other transition countries.

In most developing countries, however, companies are controlled by individuals and families playing active managerial roles, so that abuse of owners by hired managers is less common. The greater temptation is for inside owners/managers to abuse outside owners and lenders. This is often done through complex conglomerate structures, making it hard for outside investors to understand exactly who has how much interest in which assets. These structures are deliberately opaque and are often used to divert profits from outside investors.

It is said that sunlight is the best disinfectant and investors should put their funds only in countries and companies where financial disclosure meets certain standards. Since most businesses do not want to reveal their affairs, government must require some level of disclosure. There must also be a decent respect for the rule of law, so that insiders feel an obligation to share profits appropriately with outside suppliers of capital.

Table 1 has a column on financial disclosure and another column that ranks countries' respect for the rule of law. When a country such as China grows rapidly but has very weak financial disclosure and very weak rule of law, someone will get rich but it is unlikely to be foreign investors. If a government wants to strengthen capital markets, it will pass laws giving rights to outside owners and lenders. Research has focused on the quality of shareholder and creditor rights. It shows these rights are generally strongest in countries whose legal systems derive from the Anglo-Saxon tradition and weakest in those following the French tradition.

Shareholder rights include measures such as the right to have one vote for each share, the right to cast such votes with a mailed-in proxy, freedom from the need to deposit shares before voting and so forth. These rights are used for Table 1.

Creditor rights mainly concern bankruptcy procedures. Can lenders force a company into bankruptcy or are there severe restrictions? In bankruptcy, are secured interests protected by the value of their collateral? Does secured debt get paid first? Do managers remain in control during bankruptcy or does a court take over?

Moreover, investors need more than laws. They also need a regulatory agency to enforce the laws. Foreign investors are uniquely vulnerable. Their interests are likely to be ignored unless a local securities commission looks after them. One indicator for external investors is the size of internal financial markets relative to GDP. It is no accident that stock markets are large relative to GDP in countries such as Taiwan and the Philippines, which score 6–8 on shareholder rights. Where internal investors seem well treated, external investors should be safer.

The future

There will be no euphoria over emerging markets for some time, but we can expect progress in some countries. Developing countries need external capital, so as investors become more demanding, countries will have incentives to reform.

Many developing countries will undoubtedly grow faster than the economies of Europe and the US, particularly if their growth strategies are export-driven and their private sector is vigorous and competitive. But investors need to see more than rapid growth. In addition they need a good infrastructure of law, information, regulation and governance. This is hard to build, but the need for capital will be an enduring incentive and we have reason to hope for some solid success stories.

Further reading

de Soto, H. (1989) *The Other Path: The Invisible Revolution in the Third World*, New York: Harper & Row.

de Soto, H. (2000) *The Mystery of Capital: Why Capitalism Triumphs in the West and Fails Everywhere Else*, New York: Basic Books.

de Thorsten Beck, T., Demirge-Kunt, A. and Levine, R. (1999) "A new database on financial development and structure", World Bank (http://econ.worldbank.org).

de Johnson, S. and Shleifer, A. (1999) "Coase v. the Coasians", National Bureau of Economic Research, working paper 7447 (http://papers.nber.org).

Djankov, S. *et al.* (2000) "The regulation of entry", National Bureau of Economic Research, working paper 7892 (http://papers.nber.org).

La Porta, R. *et al.* (1998) "Law and finance", *Journal of Political Economy*, 106, 2, 1113–55.

La Porta, R., Lopez-de-Silanes, F. and Shleifer, A. (2000) "Government ownership of banks", National Bureau of Economic Research, working paper 7620 (http://papers.nber.org).

Hedge funds 6

Contents

Optimizing returns in a risk-conscious world 196

Kaveh Alamouti, Optimum Asset Management Limited

Increased investment in hedge funds has raised the competitive stakes in the industry. Which strategic priorities should hedge fund managers worry about?

Getting an edge from flexibility 201

Majed Muhtaseb, Global Fund Analysis

The argument here is that hedge funds perform better because their managers can seize on opportunities more easily.

Creative funds that have come into their own 207

Vikas Agarwal, London Business School and **Narayan Naik**, London Business School

Hedge funds can take various forms. This article identifies some of the problems that investors face in trying to evaluate their performance.

Introduction to Part 6

Hedge funds have a 50-year history and have become increasingly popular in recent times. They are a broad class of assets and are therefore hard to define, but commonly are managed by a firm or individual with much greater freedom in deciding the course of investment strategy than other more traditional instruments, such as mutual funds. Hedge funds are not simply about hedging: managers can sell short, use gearing or leverage and employ derivatives in order to secure the best returns. However, they are also controversial: in 1998 the hedge fund LTCM collapsed, leaving debts that destabilized the world's financial system. Here writers and practitioners discuss the attractions and dangers of this growing asset class.

Optimizing returns
in a risk-conscious world

Dr Kaveh Alamouti is chief executive of Optimum Asset Management Limited, a hedge fund management company.

Consistency is just as important as good returns on a portfolio. **Kaveh Alamouti** shows how both can be achieved.

Hedge funds are increasingly attracting the attention of institutional investors. Falling and volatile equity markets, low bond yields and crisis-prone emerging markets are prompting investors to search for new destinations for their assets. According to Tass, a research organization, hedge funds attracted a net inflow of $6.9bn in the first quarter of 2001. This compared with a total of about $8bn invested during 2000.

Institutional interest has encouraged an emphasis on analyzing performance and selecting managers. Typically, criteria used to assess performance include managers' experience, the length of time they have worked together, the management structure of the firm, audited public track record of the managers, and statistical analysis of the risk and return of the fund. The common factor is the managers' competence in managing operational and market risk.

Operational risk in the context of hedge funds refers to potential losses resulting from inadequate systems, management failure, faulty controls, fraud or human error. The assessment criteria are often expressed in terms of risk-adjusted returns. For example, a hedge fund manager might say "premium returns (12–20 per cent) with acceptable risk (8–15 per cent) with low correlations with other asset classes". This focus on risk does not imply that hedge funds operate in a more risk-averse world. Rather, investors are more risk-conscious and this has far-reaching implications for managers. Moreover, as more hedge funds are established to satisfy demand, the industry is becoming more competitive. Competition can alter the risk-return characteristics of trades and the attractiveness of market opportunities. The question facing hedge funds is how to optimize returns in a competitive environment where there is more focus on the risk assumed by managers in pursuit of returns.

Consistency

The objective of optimizing the long-term returns of a hedge fund can best be achieved by assigning nearly as much importance to consistency as to the returns themselves. Consistency over time is rewarded enormously. Institutional investors and their advisers prefer consistent lower returns to volatile higher returns. Consistency and predictability reflect the quality of returns and should be ingrained in a manager's trade selection and decisions. One can assess hedge funds' quality of returns and compare them with major asset classes by estimating how much excess return they generate per unit of risk they take.

Hedge funds are expected to show returns of higher quality because they can hedge general market risks and focus on specific risks and trading opportunities in which they have expertise. Table 1 shows the attractions of hedge funds and their risk-return profile compared with other asset classes.

Capital preservation

While consistency is a major consideration in hedge fund management, preservation of the fund's capital is also a central concern. The risk/return trade-off for a hedge fund business is not linear. In other words, the long-term rewards for achieving, say, a 30 per cent return in a year are not as great as the damage inflicted on the business by a 30 per cent loss.

This has a major impact on a fund's risk profile and trade selection strategies. In the longer term, it can also greatly hinder or help the progress of a fund. For example, if a fund is down 10 per cent in the first quarter of a trading year, its capacity to take risks is constrained and it may not be able to take full advantage of opportunities. Moreover, because performance fees are paid only on new capital appreciation, a manager's profitability for a given period is doubly affected by the increase in the value of the fund from the beginning of the period. Thus the rational approach is to try to "hit singles" – in other words, only risk capital on low-risk trades, take profits quickly and cut losses even more quickly, at the start-up of a fund or the beginning of a year. Once profits are in, one can take bigger risks.

TABLE 1 Returns from various asset classes, 1998–2000

	Compound annual return	Sharpe ratio (%)
VAN Global Hedge Fund Index	17.9	1.4
MSCI World Equity Index	9.1	0.3
S&P 500	16.7	0.9
Lehman Brothers Aggregate Bond Index	8.5	0.8

Hedge fund returns are net of fees. The Sharpe ratio, named after Noble laureate Prof. William F. Sharpe, is the return-risk-free rate divided by the standard deviation of returns. The higher the ratio, the better the quality of returns.
Source: VAN Hedge Fund Advisors International

Some banks and financial intermediaries have now taken this idea a step further and provide "capital insurance" or "principal protection" for investors. As long as investors keep their investments for a minimum period (typically five years or longer), their original investment is protected. This has proved to be popular and particularly suitable for new investors. For hedge fund managers, capital preservation is the prime objective. Funds that achieve this, alongside the criteria of consistency, premium returns and low correlation with other asset classes, become very attractive.

Diversification

These criteria shape the framework for managing the assets of a fund. Successful operators implement trading and investment strategies within a framework that encompasses many different kinds of risk. Given that most trading opportunities are probabilistic (there are not many pure arbitrage opportunities available), the only sensible approach to optimizing returns within such a risk framework is through diversification.

Even a narrowly focused fund should adopt diversification as a way of reducing the impact of random events in the markets on returns and improving the quality of its earnings. Each trading opportunity should be assessed not only in terms of its risk/return profile but also with reference to its correlation with the existing portfolio of trades and its marginal impact on the performance of the portfolio. Efficient use of diversification can significantly increase the manager's edge over the market and his competitors.

Sophisticated analytical and statistical tools are increasingly used to help build diversified portfolios and monitor their risk. The most widely used technique is the Value-at-Risk (VaR) methodology. This uses historic data and projected correlation of market variables to estimate the size and probability of future changes in the value of a portfolio. It should be noted that VaR and other techniques are there to help managers make decisions. They do not supplant managers' judgement and trading knowledge, which are the main inputs of portfolio management.

Diversification can enhance performance in two ways. First, it reduces variability by incorporating many trades and strategies. Second, it can help through timing. The best entry and exit points for most trading opportunities are not obvious. Many arbitrage or relative value trades may eventually be profitable, but in the interim would show significant losses relative to the market benchmark and would damage the consistency of the fund's reported profits and losses. Timing diversification on entry and exit can significantly improve performance and reduce the effect of random market fluctuations (see Box 1). I estimate that a combination of portfolio and timing diversification can increase the staying power (the ability to withstand temporary adverse market movements) by a factor of three to five times.

It should be noted that diversified portfolios are not constructed and then left to drift in the market; they are actively managed in response to economic changes and market events. In particular, the correlation between different asset classes and trading opportunities may change over time, requiring associated changes in the portfolio. For example, a portfolio that was well

> **Box 1 Timing diversification**
>
> A good example of timing diversification is the case of the Ecu basket convergence trade. It was known that the Ecu would be replaced by the euro on 1 January 1999. As investors increased their exposure to the Ecu in anticipation of the strengthening of the single currency, the Ecu's value rose in relation to the basket of its 15 constituent currencies. The relationship between actual and theoretical Ecu had been traded by currency arbitrageurs for many years. However, there was now a known and almost definite end date. Moreover, if the single currency were to be delayed, the Ecu's value would collapse in relation to the theoretical basket, as investors reduced their exposure.
>
> This was an irresistible opportunity for arbitrageurs. Traders shorted the Ecu and bought the theoretical basket, benefiting from an almost guaranteed convergence profit, plus windfall profits should the euro be delayed. In mid-1998 the Ecu was trading at around 0.40 per cent higher than the theoretical basket (quite a large spread in the eyes of arbitrageurs). The spread widened to as much as 1.8 per cent towards the end of the year, as market turmoil and distress among many hedge funds and banks' proprietary trading groups resulted in an imbalance of supply and demand and a cascade of loss-cutting trades. Traders who committed all their risk capital in mid-1998 to such a "sure" trade would have had to cut their losses and unwind the trade well before convergence. The trade became progressively more attractive as the end of the year approached. Had timing diversification been used, one would have had a much greater chance of profiting from the eventual convergence on the eve of the introduction of the single currency.

diversified at the beginning of a quarter can become a lot riskier at the end of that quarter because of some global macro event or a market-specific shock. If the cause of increased risk is a truly unanticipated shock, such as a war in the Middle East, there is little the manager could have done to protect a portfolio. However, most instances of increased correlation risk are extended over time and provide alert managers with plenty of opportunities to distinguish themselves. Management of the correlation risk and anticipation of changes in correlation structure can have as much of an impact on performance as the balance and selection of assets in the initial portfolio.

Leverage

Another factor that directly affects the performance of a fund is leverage. Leverage is the capacity of a fund to increase its position by borrowing from market intermediaries such as banks, using the fund's assets as collateral. Leverage magnifies profits and losses. Hedge fund managers must make a conscious decision about the size of leverage the fund requires. It is widely recognized that the higher the volatility of the underlying asset or trade, the lower the requirement for leverage is. Thus leverage should be inversely proportional to the risk of the underlying portfolio strategy.

Directional futures trading and emerging market investments should not require any leverage as they are already volatile activities. Fixed-income arbitrage and relative value trading, on the other hand, benefit from leverage, as it allows managers to hedge general market movements and the trades are based on relatively small movements.

Judicious use of leverage can enhance performance significantly. However, if used excessively it can lead to disastrous losses. Many hedge fund disasters (such as LTCM in 1998) and market collapses (such as the bond market collapse of 1994) have been the direct result of excessive use of leverage.

Size matters

For most investment styles and hedge fund strategies, there is an optimum fund size. Once a fund grows beyond that size, performance is likely to deteriorate. There are several reasons for this: there is only a finite number of opportunities, managers lose flexibility and mobility as the fund grows, dealing costs rise for larger transactions, and the fund may lose its focus. The long-term profitability of a hedge fund is maximized by operating optimally sized funds as opposed to maximizing the capital under management in each fund. This is in sharp contrast to the objective of traditional fund managers who seek to maximize the size of assets under management. Hedge funds aim to generate consistent long-run results.

Having too much capital to manage can be just as damaging to long-run performance as, say, using excessive leverage. The usual practice is to close the fund to any new money once the optimum size is reached. Alternatively, if market conditions change and there are no longer sufficient opportunities to accommodate all of the fund's capital, then capital should be returned to investors. Moore Capital, one of the largest hedge fund managers, follows this principle and has enhanced its reputation with investors in the process.

Finally, one should not ignore the single most important attraction of investing in a hedge fund: the expectation of positive absolute returns in any market environment. The risk management principles discussed above – diversification, preservation of capital, control of leverage and optimum size – matter only if the hedge fund can generate positive returns in a consistent way.

Copyright © Kaveh Alamouti 2002

Further reading

Peltz, L. (2001) *The New Investment Superstars*, New York: Wiley.
Risk Management: A Practical Guide (1999) RiskMetrics Group.
Soros, G. (1994) *Alchemy of Finance*, New York: Wiley.

Getting an edge from flexibility

Greater freedom to invest, such as the ability to sell short, should help hedge funds perform better than mutuals, argues **Majed Muhtaseb**.

Majed R. Muhtaseb is a senior analyst at Global Fund Analysis, a London-based fund research and consulting company.

Hedge funds are difficult to define because they come in many different forms and are not distinguished by their investment in a traditional class of assets but rather by the strategies their managers use. Hedge fund managers have much more freedom than their mutual fund counterparts in the investment styles they choose and in the activities they can undertake on behalf of investors. First, they can sell short, enabling them to exploit bearish expectations in the market. Second, their use of gearing allows them to make more aggressive bets on undervalued securities and capture small returns from fixed-income arbitrage opportunities. Third, derivatives can make funds more efficient, allowing managers to hedge systematic risk. Finally, they can be more flexible in market timing.

The pay of active fund managers is usually tied to the size of assets under management. The pay of hedge fund managers, on the other hand, is normally based on a combination of a size-based management fee and fund performance. This usually includes a high watermark and a hurdle rate. The former ensures a fund manager is paid performance fees only if a fund's value exceeds the investor's initial value. The hurdle rate is the return above which a manager qualifies for performance fees. It may be 5–10 per cent. Many hedge fund managers set it equal to some short-term rate.

Performance record

Does the strategic flexibility or different pay scheme of hedge funds give them an edge in performance? And how can hedge funds be judged against each other? The vast differences between hedge funds make it difficult to evaluate performance, because like cannot be compared with like. Also, hedge funds are secretive about their strategies and are reluctant to report negative results. Data banks include only existing hedge funds. This creates a distortion called "survivorship bias" – in other words, only the better-performing (surviving) funds appear in performance results.

However, research has tried to compare hedge fund and mutual fund returns. Results show that most active traditional portfolio managers do not outperform major benchmarks. Academic Shervin Hanachi (2000) found that typically the average mutual fund underperformed an appropriate benchmark, allowing for size and style. In a UBS Warburg report, Alexander Ineichen (2000) studied hedge funds and mutual funds in quarters when the Standard & Poor's 500 fell on average. He found that the sum of returns in negative quarters for mutual funds was –43.8 per cent compared with –0.2 per cent for hedge funds.

Active managers, while they construct many different portfolios, are limited to going long (betting on a rise in prices) on the future of a market, sector or style. As a group, it would be difficult for them to outperform the market while it is falling. To do so, they would have to allocate significant parts of the fund to cash, which is contrary to any fund's investment strategy or mandate. Table 1 shows the relative performance, not adjusted for risk, of hedge funds and mutual funds. Table 2 shows that in absolute terms some US hedge fund categories outperformed US shares, bonds and international equities. On a risk-adjusted basis, hedge funds pursuing relative value, event-driven and long-short strategies have significantly higher Sharpe ratios than US stocks, bonds and international equities. That is, they generated higher excess returns for a unit of total risk.

Investors are lured into investing in risky funds because of the potential of a high rate of return – at the very least, a rate higher than the risk-free rate or minimum acceptable return (MAR). The higher rate of return brings with it risk in the form of volatility, that is, variability in the rate of return. Volatility can be good and bad. Volatility above MAR is good; below it is bad. The latter is measured by downside deviation, which is the variability of each return that falls below a minimum acceptable return. The smaller the downside

TABLE 1 Best and worst performing hedge funds and mutual funds

	Hedge funds (%)	Mutual funds (%)
Top 10	62.2	51.5
Top 10 per cent	46.3	27.2
Top 25 per cent	36.3	20.3
Bottom 25 per cent	6.4	5.6
Bottom 10 per cent	0.7	4.0
Bottom 20	–4.4	–16.1

Based on five-year net compound annual returns, Q1 1995 to Q4 1999.

Source: Ineichen/Van Money Research

TABLE 2 Performance of hedge funds and traditional asset classes

January 1990–March 2000	Relative value	Event driven	Long/short equities	Global asset allocators	Short sellers	S&P 500	Treasury bonds	EAFE equities
Returns (%)	10.7	13.8	22.1	18.7	–3.3	18.0	7.6	7.1
Volatility (%)	3.4	5.4	10.3	11.1	22.1	13.7	4.0	17.1
Sharpe ratio at 5%	1.6	1.5	1.5	1.2	–0.3	0.9	0.6	0.2
Downside deviation at 5%	2.6	3.6	5.1	4.8	14.1	8.5	2.5	11.9
Correlation coefficient								
Relative value	1.00							
Event driven	0.43	1.00						
Long/short equities	0.27	0.55	1.00					
Global asset allocation	0.12	0.00	0.12	1.00				
Short sellers	–0.13	–0.60	–0.65	0.10	1.00			
S&P 500	0.04	0.49	0.58	0.10	–0.74	1.00		
Treasury bonds	–0.09	0.03	0.07	0.24	–0.11	0.34	1.00	
EAFE equities	0.14	0.30	0.45	–0.02	–0.43	0.54	0.15	1.00

Source: Beerman, D. et al. (2000) "Evolution of asset class: absolute return strategies", *Journal of Investing*, Winter, 9, 24/Deutsch Asset Management

deviation, the lower the downside risk. Except for short sellers, the downside deviation of each of the four other hedge fund categories is significantly below that of the S&P 500 and EAFE (an MSCI index covering Europe, Australia and the Far East). In other words, hedge funds are generally less risky in stagnant or falling markets than traditional US and international share portfolios.

In addition, investors can construct more efficient portfolios by investing in both hedge funds and other asset classes because hedge funds have a low correlation with other assets. An efficient portfolio is one that is expected to earn the highest return for a given level of risk. Of the five hedge funds categories in Table 2, long-short equities has the highest correlation (0.58) with the S&P 500. It compares with that of the S&P 500 and EAFE (0.54). One ramification is that US investors do not need to invest outside the US to reap the benefits of international diversification.

Hedge funds may perform even better in markets with no predominant overall trend. From January to December 2000, hedge funds of funds (a fund made up of many hedge funds) had an average return of 9 per cent – in sharp contrast with the S&P 500 and Nasdaq Composite indices, which were down 10.5 per cent and 36.2 per cent respectively. This refers to 2000 when markets were very volatile. Markets reached an all-time high in March–April and dropped significantly towards late summer and the end of the year.

A 2001 study by academics Thomas Schneeweis and Richard Spurgin examined the monthly performance of hedge fund strategies, the S&P 500 and the Lehman Brothers Bond index for 1990–2000. It found that all hedge fund strategies, except for bond hedge funds and systematic global asset allocators, produced higher Sharpe ratios than those of either index.

Researchers Richard Grinold and Ronald Kahn (2000) found that the long-short hedge funds do not demonstrate greater levels of risk than long-only strategies. Their study indicates that the performance of long-short strategies is little affected by overall movement in the market. That is, a hedge fund combined with traditional asset classes can contribute significantly to the efficiency of a portfolio.

Advantages

Hedge fund managers are better positioned to take advantage of market inefficiencies or mispricing opportunities. Aside from the characteristics mentioned at the beginning of this article, they are not bound by the restrictive regulations on conventional investment vehicles and can change their positions quickly. The fact that hedge fund strategies generally diverge from those of the market may be one explanation for their purported low correlation with major market averages – and their lower volatility and downside deviations.

In addition, many hedge funds attempt to deliver absolute returns, in other words, returns that are independent of fluctuations in the major market indices. To claim such returns, a hedge fund manager should not base that claim exclusively on a low correlation with the market. As well as looking at the correlation of returns over a specified period, analysts should examine returns during falling and stagnant markets within that period and the correlation of the volatilities of the fund and the market index. This author found that the volatilities of many hedge funds are negatively correlated with those of the market and/or benchmark.

Evaluation

Evaluating the performance of a hedge fund against a benchmark such as the FTSE 100 or S&P 500 gives a cursory result at best. In essence, market indices reflect the performance of portfolios consisting solely of long positions. Hedge funds' regular use of gearing, short-selling and derivatives limits the value of such benchmarks.

Alternatively, one can construct benchmarks for hedge funds. These have obvious limitations. The huge variation in hedge fund strategies makes it necessary to construct many indices. Comparing performance of the fund against a narrow index may be inadequate for investors who are interested in comparisons with a broad benchmark. Even funds pursuing similar strategies could implement them very differently. For example, two market-neutral, long-short funds could use different amounts of gearing, which can change over time. These challenges do not obviate the need for a benchmark. The goal of the investor is to gain an insight into the fund manager's ability over a reasonable period. In selecting a benchmark, investors face a trade-off. A benchmark such as the S&P 500 or FTSE 100 is too broad and so different from a hedge fund that it offers little value as a comparison. On the other hand, using a very narrow benchmark (one that makes comparisons based on a specific strategy) will contribute little to a general performance evaluation.

What should be done? The answer may be to use both. A broad benchmark shows how the fund performed relative to an aspect of the market (equities, bonds and so on) that investors know and understand. Second, they want to find out how well a fund manager performed relative to his similarly skilled peers. This helps investors determine the skill level of the manager compared with the overall skill level of fund managers pursuing the same strategy. One way of accomplishing this is to calculate M^2 for the fund, based on a broad market benchmark and based on the style or strategy of the fund. M^2 is a risk-adjusted measure of performance, which defines risk in terms of the variability of a fund's returns. The M^2 of the fund is the theoretical return that the investor would have realized if the fund's risk had been modified to match that of the benchmark. A third method for evaluating a hedge fund manager is to find a comparable peer group from a reputable data bank. The group's members must be comparable in terms of strategy, asset size, gearing, age and geographical diversification.

For the most part, hedge funds are based outside the larger investment houses. They tend to be relatively small, specialized boutiques. There are more than 6,000 hedge funds managing in excess of $1,000bn on $400m capital, which implies a gearing ratio of 150 per cent. About half of hedge funds manage capital of less than $25m and 80 per cent are smaller than $100m. Because of the recent surge in demand for hedge funds, they are constantly evolving. Therefore investors should be vigilant in conducting due diligence before investing.

Research groups such as Global Fund Analysis, Hedge Fund Research, MAR Hedge and TASS Tremont have constructed many indices for the industry. Their websites are given on the next page.

Many hedge funds have been secretive. However, they are subject to minimal regulatory oversight in the US and Europe and most do disclose some information to serious investors. They send either monthly or quarterly reports to current investors, but levels of disclosure vary. However, the industry is making progress towards greater transparency. The credit ratings agency Fitch rated two hedge fund shops and two hedge funds of funds in 2000. The ratings provide an independent assessment of the viability of hedge funds. They also enable hedge funds to diversify their funding sources. Hedge funds can benefit from greater disclosure and compliance with a performance presentation standard such as the Global Investment Performance Standards sponsored by the Association for Investment Management and Research.

Conclusion

Hedge funds have had a great influence on world markets. Their drive in seeking alpha returns causes markets to become more efficient – making it more difficult to extract such returns. In competing to identify and exploit price deformations, hedge funds will continue to contribute to market efficiency. However, hedge fund investors should recognize that such opportunities will not evaporate.

Direct and indirect indexing by pension funds and mutual funds, coupled with the unwarranted sell-side research bias towards buy recommendations, create new pricing inefficiencies in the market and reinforce old ones. Mutual funds have the appetite but not the flexibility to exploit those inefficiencies, which leaves a great deal of money on the table for skilled hedge fund managers.

The Economist recently characterized hedge funds as "spectacularly wealthy, secretive and prone to dramatic losses". This author would argue that hedge funds are spectacularly wealthy because their managers have sought, investigated and exploited investment opportunities for huge gain and have the freedom to make good investment decisions in both rising and falling markets.

Copyright © Majed Muhtaseb 2002

Further reading

Grinold, R. and Kahn, R. (2000) "The efficiency gains of long-short investing", *Financial Analysts' Journal*, 56, 6, 40–53.

Hanachi, S. (2000) "Can the average US equity fund outperform the benchmarks?", *Journal of Investing*, 9, 2, 45–52.

Ineichen, A. (2000) "In search of alpha: investing in hedge funds", Global Equity Research, UBS Warburg.

Muhtaseb, M. (2000a) "Adherence to stricter uniform performance standards can avert severe market discipline" in *Global Fund Analysis Yearbook*, London: Global Fund Analysis.

Muhtaseb, M. (2000b) "What can hedge funds do to enhance transparency without disclosing proprietary information?", *Journal of Performance Measurement*, 4, 4, 6–13.

Schneeweis, T. and Spurgin, R. (2001) "The benefits of hedge funds", working paper, CISDM/Isenberg School of Management, University of Massachusetts, Amherst, MA.

Websites

www.marhedge.com
www.hfr.com
www.tremontadvisers.com
www.globalfundanalysis.com

Creative funds that
have come into their own

They may have been around for a long time, but hedge funds have grown dramatically in the past decade, say **Vikas Agarwal** and **Narayan Naik**.

Vikas Agarwal is Fauchier Partners' Research Scholar in the doctoral programme in finance at London Business School.

Narayan Y. Naik is an associate professor of finance and director of the Centre for Hedge Fund Research and Education at London Business School.

Most investors regard hedge funds as a recent phenomenon, yet they have existed for 50 years. Alfred Winslow Jones, a journalist, sociologist and fund manager, is credited with starting the first hedge fund in 1949. Jones used a long-short strategy to hedge market risk. In other words, he took a long position in undervalued securities and a short position in overvalued securities. Initially, his fund failed to attract much attention. However, a 1966 article in *Fortune* magazine highlighted his spectacular performance and ignited interest in hedge funds.

In the following two years the hedge fund industry grew rapidly, only to suffer significant losses during the bear markets of 1969–70 and 1973–74. As a result, hedge funds went out of fashion. They remained unpopular until 1986, when the financial press revealed the spectacular performance of Julian Robertson's Tiger fund in the US. Founded in 1980 with $8m, this fund had shown an annual return of 43 per cent during its first six years.

The investment styles of hedge funds have changed significantly over time. Today, many do not hedge in the strict sense of the term. In fact, in this context, the term "hedge" is something of a misnomer. There is no universal definition of hedge funds. However, they can be broadly described as private investment vehicles where the manager has a significant personal stake in the fund and can flexibly employ a broad spectrum of strategies involving derivatives, short selling and leverage to enhance returns and better manage risk.

Industry size

It is difficult to estimate the size of the industry because the

Securities and Exchange Commission restricts advertising and reporting of performance by US hedge funds. Van Hedge Fund Advisors International estimates the number of hedge funds (excluding fund of funds) increased from about 1,400 in 1988 to more than 5,500 (both domestic and offshore) by 1998. The volume of assets managed also grew in that time, increasing from $42bn to about $300bn. Another hedge fund advisory company, Hedge Fund Research, estimates that assets under management grew from $39bn in 1990 to $487bn in 2000.

Furthermore, these figures represent only the capital account balances of investors and not the amounts deployed in the markets. With certain strategies investing in a highly levered way, some believe the total invested exceeds $1,000bn. A large majority of hedge funds are either based in the US or in an offshore territory. However, the past few years have seen a rapid growth in hedge funds in Europe. A survey of investors and hedge fund managers by Goldman Sachs projected a growth rate of 60 per cent in 2001, taking assets under management to $73bn.

Wealthy individuals form the largest group of investors in hedge funds. A 1998 study by RR Capital Management Corporation and KPMG Peat Marwick found that 80 per cent of the assets under management come from private investors, with the balance from institutional investors. The study projects an annual growth rate of about 26 per cent to over $500bn of assets by 2001 and a 10-fold increase to $1,700bn in 10 years.

Classifying funds

Although the term "hedge fund" came from the long and short strategy originally used, the new definition covers many different strategies. Unlike traditional investment, there is no accepted classification system for hedge funds. However, most people tend to categorize them by domicile or according to their trading strategies.

The domicile category consists of onshore and offshore hedge funds. Onshore funds domiciled in the US are usually limited partnerships, where the manager is the general partner and the investors are limited partners. Because hedge funds are private investment partnerships, the SEC for a long time limited the number of their investors to 99, at least 65 of whom had to be "accredited". To encourage investment in hedge funds, however, the law changed in 1996 to allow up to 500 investors (including the general partner) without any registration and disclosure requirements. Recently, the SEC has further broadened the appeal of hedge funds by removing this limit altogether for "qualified investors". To qualify, the individual investor's net worth must not be less than $5m and institutional investors, such as pension funds, should have capital of at least $25m.

In contrast, offshore funds are established in tax-neutral jurisdictions such as the British Virgin Islands, the Bahamas, Bermuda, the Cayman Islands, Dublin and Luxembourg, allowing investors to minimize their tax liabilities by investing outside their own country. One offshore innovation that allows offshore and onshore investors to band together is a passive foreign investment company. Here, the offshore fund can accept both types of investor but must ensure that at least half of the assets in the fund are from offshore investors. This structure allows the manager to hold a single portfolio and not be concerned about allocating trades among offshore and onshore accounts.

When analyzing hedge funds according to trading strategies, they can be segregated into two broad categories: non-directional and directional. The former do not depend on the direction of any specific market movement and are commonly referred to as "market-neutral" strategies. It is important to note that the non-directional strategies are neutral only to the first moment, that is to say, expected returns. They are not neutral to the second moment, that is, standard deviation, since in volatile periods liquidity dries up, convergence (the return of the asset prices to equilibrium level) is not always obtained and "arbitrage-based" strategies can make losses.

Non-directional strategies are usually designed to exploit short-term market inefficiencies and pricing discrepancies between related securities while hedging as much market exposure as possible. Due to the reduced liquidity inherent in many such situations, they often run smaller pools of capital than their directional counterparts. In contrast, directional strategies hope to benefit from broad movements in the market. Table 1 gives a list of strategies but it is by no means exhaustive. In addition, some of the strategies mentioned have different names in other databases.

Hedge funds and mutual funds

Hedge funds differ from traditional investment vehicles such as mutual funds in the nature of their strategies, their return objectives, correlation of returns, co-investment opportunities, compensation structures, liquidity and transparency. Most mutual funds are restricted in their investment options. In contrast, hedge funds have more flexibility in where and how they can invest. They can use leverage, sell securities short and invest across different asset classes. Hedge funds can use leverage either explicitly or implicitly. Explicit leverage can be seen from the balance sheet and refers to the ratio of their assets to net worth. Implicit leverage refers to the leverage that hedge funds can achieve by buying securities on margin, through the use of short positions and derivatives and/or using collateralized borrowing in repurchase, or repo, markets. With the flexibility of leverage, hedge funds can multiply their returns (and risk) on arbitrage opportunities in the market.

The downside of flexibility is that it can reduce investors' ability to monitor a fund manager. Some managers trade in and out of positions so frequently that direct oversight may be logistically fraught and ultimately ineffective. It can be exceedingly difficult to monitor whether the manager is diverging from his or her stated strategy, inappropriately using derivatives or leverage, or engaging in other behaviour that may cause the fund to lose money or even go bankrupt.

Unlike mutual funds regulated by the SEC, hedge funds are largely exempt from disclosure and regulation, as they cater to individuals and institutions through private placements. In addition, the minimum investment is usually much higher, ranging from $100,000 to $20m. However, this figure can be substantially lower if one invests through a fund of funds – the term for a fund

TABLE 1 Classification of hedge funds

Non-directional strategies	
Fixed-income arbitrage	Having long and short bond positions via cash or derivatives markets in government, corporate and/or asset-backed securities. The risk varies with duration, credit exposure and the degree of leverage.
Event-driven	A strategy that hopes to benefit from mispricing arising from different events such as merger arbitrage or restructuring. Managers take a position in an undervalued security that is anticipated to rise in value because of events such as mergers, reorganizations or takeovers. The main risk is that the predicted event does not happen.
Equity hedge	Investment in equity or equity-like instruments where the net exposure is generally low. The manager may invest globally, or have a more defined geographic, industry or capitalization focus. The risk relates primarily to the risk of specific long and short positions.
Distressed securities	Buying and occasionally shorting securities of companies which have filed for creditor protection under Chapter 11 in the US and/or ones undergoing reorganization. The securities range from senior secured debt to common stock. Liquidation of a financially distressed company is the main source of risk.
Merger arbitrage	Buying the securities of a company that is being acquired and shorting that of the acquiring company. The risk associated with such strategies is more of a "deal" risk rather than market risk.
Convertible arbitrage	Buying and selling different securities of the same issuer (such as convertibles or common stock) and seeking to obtain low volatility returns by arbitraging the relative mispricing of these securities.
Directional strategies	
Macro	Seeking to capitalize on country, regional or economic change affecting securities, commodities, interest rates and currency rates. Asset allocation can be aggressive, and leverage and derivatives may be used. The method and degree of hedging can vary significantly.
Emerging markets	A strategy that employs a "growth" or "value" approach to investing in equities with no shorting or hedging to minimize inherent market risk. These funds mainly invest in the emerging markets where there may be restrictions on short sales.
Equity non-hedge	Similar to equity hedging with significant net long exposure.
Short selling	Selling short over-valued securities, with the hope of buying them back at a lower price.

Source: Hedge Fund Research

that invests in several hedge funds. Also, the industry has recently moved closer to lowering the investment threshold to make hedge funds available to a wide range of investors. In contrast to most mutual funds, hedge funds typically impose restrictions on the withdrawal of funds by clients. They usually require a lock-up period of up to 12 months or more. This gives the flexibility to invest in relatively illiquid securities for a longer term than normal.

Hedge fund managers argue that they should be evaluated on absolute performance, as opposed to the relative performance measures applied to traditional active managers. Mutual fund managers, for example, are evaluated on their performance relative to a benchmark.

In mutual funds, fees are based largely on the size of assets under management. Hedge funds carry stronger incentives as managers' fees are based on the performance of the fund. The incentive fee ranges between 5 per cent and 25 per cent of yearly profits, that is, over and above the annual management fee, which can be between 1 per cent and 2 per cent. In addition, hedge funds typically have features such as "hurdle rates" and high watermark provisions that can help align the interests of managers and investors. (A hurdle rate is the minimum return a manager needs to claim any incentive fee. "High watermark" provision refers to the fact that a manager cannot collect incentive fees until any losses have been made up. In other words, the cumulative return of the manager has to be above the hurdle rate. High watermark provision and hurdle rate are independent criteria, since the purpose of the watermark is to recuperate losses whereas the hurdle rate is used for collecting incentive fees.)

Understanding funds

In recent years, the hedge fund industry has been in the limelight. After the near bankruptcy of Long Term Capital Management in 1998, regulators were concerned about the threat hedge funds could pose to financial stability of world markets. Politicians such as Malaysian prime minister Mahathir Mohamad have accused hedge fund managers of destabilizing markets. Active institutional investors such as the California Public Employees' Retirement System are increasing their allocation to hedge funds.

Meanwhile, the hedge fund industry is changing. Two of the most famous managers, George Soros and Julian Robertson, have wound up their flagship funds at a time when traditional fund management houses are launching new hedge funds. In general, investors seem to be attracted by the combination of equity-style returns and bond-like volatility that some hedge fund strategies offer. However, the near-collapse of Long Term Capital Management, the liquidation of several hedge funds during the latter half of 1998 and various fraud cases have left many investors demanding a better understanding of different hedge fund strategies. The events in the second half of 1998 prompted a study of hedge funds by the US president's working group on financial markets. Unfortunately, less stringent disclosure requirements (especially for offshore hedge funds) and the reluctance of managers to divulge information mean hedge funds have often been shrouded in secrecy.

Historically, returns from hedge funds have had little correlation with traditional asset classes, such as equities, currencies, commodities and bonds, because of their dynamic trading strategies. The dynamic nature of the strategies arises from the frequent change in risk exposures and the continuous movement between different asset classes. This is often associated with the use of short selling, derivatives and leverage.

Supporters of hedge funds make their case by describing the diversification benefits offered by using the mean-variance framework. By virtue of the low correlation between hedge funds and stocks or bonds, inclusion of hedge funds in a portfolio can reduce the standard deviation of the total portfolio and improve the risk-return trade-offs. However, it is not clear that low linear correlation can be interpreted as low systematic risk. Hedge fund returns have option-like features and hence systematic risk can be of non-linear form. For example, hedge funds, especially those using non-directional strategies, may show low betas on an equity index such as the Standard & Poor's 500. Their returns may be non-linearly related to the S&P 500 due to their use of derivatives or the nature of their opportunistic trading. In addition, mean-variance analysis relies on the normality of asset returns and assumes that the investor cares only about the mean and standard deviation of returns.

We know that hedge funds have generated very high or low returns more often than has been predicted by a normal distribution. Hence their returns may not be normal and the use of optimization techniques based on mean variance may understate the risk in hedge funds. Finally, during market declines, the correlation between hedge funds and stocks can increase, reducing or eliminating the advantage of diversification. Thus, results based on mean-variance analysis need to be treated with caution.

Lack of information means academic research has relied on style analysis to estimate the risk exposures of hedge funds and to understand the sources of returns. The task of performance attribution is challenging considering that returns data are usually available monthly, which does not provide enough information to capture the dynamic nature of the trading strategies used by hedge funds. Further, the use of dynamic trading restricts the applicability of the traditional performance attribution and style analysis techniques that split a manager's returns into the part attributable to the market or systematic factors and the part attributable to the manager's skill. It has been shown that, compared with mutual funds, the hedge fund manager's skill contributes a significant proportion of overall returns. Hence, manager risk is one of the most important risks associated with hedge funds.

Finally, various biases, including survivorship bias and self-selection, contaminate performance data. Survivorship bias occurs if a survey reports only on surviving funds. This can result in overstating the performance of hedge funds. However, well-performing funds may also stop reporting as they have no incentive to attract new investment; some researchers call this self-selection bias. Selection bias occurs if the funds covered are not truly representative of the hedge fund universe. This is largely due to voluntary reporting by fund managers.

Regulation of hedge funds has been vigorously debated, as they have been accused of disrupting financial markets and posing a threat to stability. Research seems to suggest there is not enough evidence of hedge funds engaging in herding and positive feedback trading to cause potential threats to market stability. Moreover, the number of offshore funds would make regulation extremely difficult. One plausible approach is that banks and financial institutions need strict guidelines on lending to hedge funds.

Academics and practitioners have tried to estimate the risk-adjusted performance of hedge funds. Various studies have compared hedge fund performance with that of the S&P 500 index. However, considering that some hedge funds have little exposure to the S&P 500, it is unclear whether the index can serve as an appropriate benchmark for adjusting for systematic risks. Hence, there is a need to design an appropriate benchmark. The hurdle rates, such as the risk-free rate, suggested by hedge fund managers (by claiming their market neutrality) for collecting incentive fees may not always be appropriate. The heterogeneity among different hedge fund strategies and different hedge funds within a particular strategy makes it a challenge to understand the nature of risks involved and determine their risk-adjusted performance. In addition, research has asked whether features such as incentive fees, hurdle rates and high watermark provisions have a significant impact on performance. In this regard, one issue is related to the relationship between performance and size. In this argument, the limited number of profitable opportunities in the market makes it difficult for a hedge fund to invest a large amount of money over the medium term. So performance should be negatively related to the size of the assets under management.

However, it is not clear whether this is the case for all hedge fund strategies and whether the relationship between size and performance is strictly linear. On one hand, it can be argued that there is a positive association between size and performance as large funds can have administrative and legal economies of scale. On the other hand, returns can decrease with larger funds because they may not be able to exploit small-scale opportunities, or managers may find it difficult to move in and out of different positions and capacity constraints may hinder large trades in niche markets. Thus, arguments about size seem to suggest that the association between size and performance is non-linear.

Finally, hedge fund managers' compensation deals are designed to align the interests of the manager and the investor. Can such contracts discourage managers from taking excessive risks? On the face of it, one would imagine that managers are tempted to take more risks to increase their chances of earning higher incentive fees. However, evidence suggests that managers are discouraged from taking excessive risks by the potential damage to a fund's reputation.

The future

Because profitable opportunities are limited, it is going to be difficult for the ever-increasing number of hedge fund managers to consistently provide the high returns that investors seek. Given the considerable freedom available to the manager to use dynamic trading strategies, arguably the main risk in the case of hedge funds is manager risk. Hence, it is important to monitor this risk continually as well as to diversify risks generally.

One way of accomplishing this is to invest in a fund of hedge funds. This can provide relatively easy access to a large number of hedge funds with low minimum investment requirements. However, their services are accompanied by an additional layer of fees and investors need to understand that the performance of the fund of funds is only going to be as good as the investment skill and monitoring ability of its manager.

Quantitative analysis, by its very nature, tells an investor what has happened in the past. However, the risk of any investment lies in the future. Therefore, whenever we invest in hedge funds, rigorous and robust quantitative analysis must be accompanied by due diligence and monitoring to optimize the trade-off between risk and return.

Copyright © Vikas Agarwal and Narayan Naik 2002

Further reading

Crerend, W.J. (1998) *Fundamentals of Hedge Fund Investing: A Professional Investor's Guide*, New York: McGraw Hill.

Lavinio, S. (2000) *Hedge Fund Handbook: A Definitive Guide for Analyzing and Evaluating Alternative Investments*, New York: McGraw Hill.

Lederman, J. and Klein, R.A. (1995) *Hedge Funds: Investment and Portfolio Strategies for the Institutional Investor*, Burr Ridge, IL: Irwin.

President's Working Group on Financial Markets (1999) "Hedge funds, leverage and the lessons of long-term, capital management", Washington DC.

Social Science Research Network (http://www.ssrn.com), quick search on "hedge funds" for relevant articles.

Risk 7

Contents

A formal approach in a risky business 218

Christopher Culp, Chicago Graduate School of Business

Risk management enables investment managers to judge whether the risks they are taking in the portfolio are precisely the ones they want to take. There are benefits to a rigorous and centralized risk management policy.

The varying nature of volatile forces 224

Menachem Brenner, New York University

This article examines the nature of volatility and its prevalence in various markets.

Too much being left to chance by personal investors 231

Greg Elmiger, RiskMetrics

Risk management tools are moving from Wall Street to the High Street.

A model approach to using technology 237

Terry Marsh, Haas School of Business and **Paul Pfleiderer**, Stanford Business School

This article shows how investors can take account of many kinds of information when identifying the best mix in their portfolio.

Introduction to Part 7

Investors take risks, and good investors are rewarded by their judgement in calculating and spreading risk. Decades ago such judgements consisted of little more than unsupported opinion and rules of thumb. Today risk managers use statistical analysis and probability theory, backed by massive computing power, to try to limit the downside on any investment. In this part writers explore various aspects of investment risk, from modern portfolio management to the possibilities offered by the latest technology.

A formal approach
in a risky business

Dr Christopher Culp is an adjunct associate professor of finance at the Chicago Graduate School of Business and is managing director of CP Risk Management LLC.

Portfolio managers are meant to take risks, so why invest in systems that appear to second-guess their decisions? **Christopher Culp** examines the benefits.

Following high-profile losses in the 1990s at respected funds such as Long Term Capital Management and the Orange County Investment Pool, risk management has come into vogue for investment managers. Nevertheless, there is still an inherent tension between risk management and the primary mandate to invest in risky assets to earn excess returns or fund a liability stream. A typical investment management organization selects portfolio managers largely based on their ability to achieve consistently good risk-adjusted returns. Why should it set up an internal process that second-guesses those managers' decisions?

In fact, risk management does not necessarily mean refusing new transactions all the time. This article explains that risk management for asset managers is not about deciding how much risk to take – classical investment management requires that. Risk management, by contrast, analyzes whether or not the risks a fund is taking correspond to the risk preferences of its investors.

Traditional methods

Classical investment management aims to invest capital in financial instruments whose combined expected return and risk reflect the risk preferences of investors. No single return-to-risk trade-off is "correct"; the right combination of risk and return for one investor may not be the same for another. A hedge fund manager whose objective is to "make money" for clients, for example, can take more risks than the manager of a defined-benefit pension plan whose sponsor expects assets to fund pension liabilities without any further contribution.

Fund managers try to achieve the target risk-return profile of their investors in a three-stage process: asset allocation, security selection and market timing. The first stage allocates capital into broad asset classes such as fixed income and domestic equity. Once target portfolio weightings have been defined for broad asset classes, managers select securities to hold within the prescribed allocation for each class. Finally, market timing refers to the tactical decisions of managers to try to buy or sell securities at the most advantageous times.

A major challenge is determining the investors' risk tolerances. This is done in many different ways. Some managers rely on marketing literature to attract "a certain type of customer" and do not try to quantify investor risk tolerances. Others determine target risk and expected return levels subjectively or based solely on external factors. A defined-benefit pension plan, for example, must typically invest in assets whose expected return is at least as high as the actuarial growth rate in its liabilities. Some plans stop there and constrain their risks to be whatever risks are required to get an expected return that is equal to or slightly greater than the actuarial return – but no more.

At the other extreme, some asset managers adopt a more quantitative approach to matching their actual investment decisions with a target trade-off between risk and reward. This assessment usually occurs in the first part of the investment management process – asset allocation – and uses "portfolio optimization" methods. The same portfolio optimization methods could be applied to security selection decisions, but often are not purely to keep computational costs down. Portfolio optimization uses mathematical techniques to determine asset class weightings that characterize the set of "efficient" portfolios, defined as those combinations of asset classes for which expected returns can only be increased by taking additional risks. The classic portfolio optimization model, developed by Nobel laureate Harry Markowitz, assumes that the variance or volatility of a portfolio's return is an adequate measure of its risk. A "minimum variance frontier" is then identified mathematically as those asset class weightings that minimize portfolio variance over a range of expected returns.

Having defined the minimum variance frontier, the investor must then identify the minimum-variance-efficient frontier: the set of asset portfolios for which a higher expected return cannot be achieved at a given volatility, or for which risk cannot be reduced to earn the same expected return. Defining the efficient set of portfolios, however, is only the first part of the asset allocation process. Next, the asset manager must choose which portfolio of asset classes on the efficient frontier to hold. This can only be done by assessing the tolerance of investors, constituents or beneficiaries of the fund for trading off expected return against risk.

Using hypothetical "utility functions" that link different expected return and volatility combinations with "units of happiness", economists generate what they call "indifference curves" to represent this risk-return trade-off for investors. The "optimal portfolio" is found at the point where such indifference curves meet the minimum-variance-efficient frontier.

Defining risk

The classic asset allocation and portfolio optimization model has much to recommend it, but it has limitations. Perhaps most obviously, investors rarely have enough information to link realistically the risk/reward preferences of their constituents to the type of indifference curves demanded by the model. Instead, investors usually opt for more qualitative methods, such as risk questionnaires, to try to identify the portfolio that most closely corresponds to what seem to be investor preferences for trading off risk and reward.

Another major limitation of classical mean-variance portfolio optimization is the use of the variance or volatility of returns as a sufficient measure of the risk of an asset or portfolio. Variance is used so often mainly because it is easy to compute and because of the way it relates to the "normal" or bell-shaped "distribution" or the relation between returns to the frequency with which those returns are expected to occur.

Specifically, the normal distribution is symmetric, which means that a return of –R per cent below the average is just as likely to occur as a return of +R per cent above the average. As long as returns are normally distributed, variance can also be used to make specific probabilistic statements about portfolio returns, such as: "The probability of achieving a return that is more than 1.65 standard deviations above the average return is less than 5 per cent."

When returns on an asset are not symmetric or normally distributed, however, variance can be a very imprecise measure of risk. Especially when returns are "negatively skewed", the probability of a large decline in portfolio value exceeds the probability of an increase in portfolio value of the same magnitude. In this case, investors may be more concerned about "downside risk" than just volatility. If a portfolio manager considers variance too simplistic as a measure of risk, the asset allocation decision can be refined using different statistical measures of risk. Downside semi-variance, for example, can be a useful alternative to variance in portfolio optimization models where investors are concerned about downside risk. Asset allocation in that case involves generating a minimum-downside-semi-variance-efficient frontier, and the optimal portfolio occurs at the tangency point between that frontier and indifference curves defined in expected return/downside-semi-variance space. Complex, but possible.

In theory, all risks about which investors are concerned can be addressed in this way in the classical investment management process. As long as the decisions of an institutional investor achieve the desired risk/return, and risk is completely and exhaustively defined, the need for more formal risk management is questionable. But in practice, risk is not always defined exhaustively in advance. And because optimization is usually undertaken at the level of asset allocation but not security selection or market timing, the investment decisions of managers may well not achieve the target risk/reward optimum. As such, risk management as a formal process can play an important role for institutional investors.

The process

"Risk management" can be defined as the formal process by which investors try to ensure that the risks to which they are subject in their portfolios are the risks to which they want to be subject. Clearly, risk management requires that investor tolerances for risk versus returns have already been specified. Risk management thus does not tell investors when they are taking "too much" or "too little" risk in some absolute sense; rather, it tells investors when they are taking too much or too little risk relative to their risk tolerances.

As a process, risk management typically includes several components:

- identification of risks to which the fund is subject;
- measuring, monitoring and reporting risk exposures relative to pre-defined risk tolerances;
- controlling deviations between actual and desired risk exposures;
- governance of the whole process.

Risk management as a separate process can make sense for an institutional investor in several situations, in the first instance as a pure compliance function. Investment policies may explicitly prohibit certain activities or place parameters around other activities, but a diagnostic risk management function may be required to identify deviations from those policies. Second, when decisions made by individual portfolio managers fail to consider the aggregate risks facing an investor, a centralized risk management function can add value.

Many managers of international debt and equity portfolios, for example, are given discretion whether or not to hedge exchange rate risk. But exposures across different portfolios often either offset or exacerbate individual portfolio exposures. In this situation, a centralized and formal risk management process can play a constructive role by, say, guiding the proper use of what is known as an FX "overlay programme", or a hedging programme that covers net foreign exchange risks across all portfolios in a fund.

Formal risk management can also serve as a catalyst for stimulating discussions between managers and executives whose strategies and tactics might otherwise be reviewed only during asset allocation. During asset allocation, however, risk management can provide a healthy venue for the discussion of tactical portfolio shifts, the use of new financial products, and other investment decisions that could otherwise fall between the cracks of the fund's investment policy and compliance function.

A related benefit of formal risk management is to provide a diagnostic tool to assist in its portfolio management decisions. As an example, an investor's asset allocation decision may need rebalancing, but the timing may be discretionary. Comprehensive and independent risk management can give managers additional information about actual risk exposures relative to tolerances to help define the best times for such rebalancings. These benefits usually can be accomplished fairly easily by creating an appropriate risk management policy and making a few organizational changes, such as the creation of risk or compliance officers and possibly a risk management committee. The changes required can be undertaken at a reasonably low cost and often make a great deal of sense. Importantly, none of the above necessarily requires substantial investment in a risk measurement system.

Nevertheless, in principle, another benefit of risk management can be realized when the definition of risk used for ex-ante asset allocation decisions is incomplete. In this case, monitoring a more comprehensive measure of portfolio risk can make sense, but investors must exercise a good deal of caution in weighing the benefits with the costs.

Dos and don'ts

Measurement of market risk for control purposes can take many forms, ranging from the simple to the complex. Simple measures of market risk include, for example, basic summary risk measures for portfolios such as average duration, or even just static reports of nominal exposures, such as pounds at risk or exposed to changes in value when exchange rates move.

More general and forward-looking measures of risk such as "value at risk" have become popular recently. Measuring risk using VaR allows investors to make statements such as: "We do not expect losses to exceed £1m in more than one out of the next 20 months." In its simplest form, VaR is calculated by assuming that all portfolio and asset returns are distributed normally. As in the Markowitz portfolio optimization model, this allows managers to use volatility as the basis for all risk calculations. Although VaR is intended to capture "extreme" market movements, the classical way to measure VaR is, in fact, little more than a scaled version of variance.

VaR can also be measured without assuming that underlying return distributions are normal or symmetric. Using advanced statistical methods, most types of portfolio return distribution can be accommodated in the context of VaR. Unfortunately, the more complex the distribution, the more expensive the system required. In addition, exotic financial instruments and illiquid securities such as private placements are often expensive and difficult to model without implementing a complex – and expensive – VaR measurement system.

The degree to which an institutional investor can make use of risk measurement methods such as VaR often depends on how the investor is measuring risk in the asset allocation decision. An investor using variance as a base measure of risk in allocating assets into asset classes, for example, will gain little from implementing a volatility-based VaR measurement system. The VaR, after all, would simply be telling the investor what they already knew from their portfolio optimization model. But a VaR model that captures the downside risk of a portfolio whose returns are negatively skewed could provide an important additional tool for investors whose asset allocation assumes that variance is an adequate measure of risk.

Some investors go much further with risk measurement systems and use VaR as the basis of limits or even "risk budgets" in which the asset allocation of the fund is redefined based on VaR. In a VaR-based risk budget, a fund's aggregate VaR is allocated to different managers who are then obliged to remain within their prescribed risk limits. Transactions that push a manager's VaR above the risk budget are forbidden, and market movements that cause VaR to exceed a risk budget would force security sales or hedging.

Risk budgeting is attractive to some because it obviates the need for discretionary approval of specific transactions by senior managers or directors and allows the senior asset manager to evaluate regularly the risk-adjusted value that particular managers add. But to implement a risk budget using VaR, the system must be able to process all financial instruments and asset classes, and should not rely on as many assumptions as simpler systems. This can quickly drive up the cost of a full-blown VaR system to a staggeringly high amount.

Conclusion

Risk management can play an important role for institutional investors, but only to the extent that it complements rather than replaces or circumvents the classical investment management process. Institutional investors should engage in some form of risk management, if only to ensure through compliance and monitoring that the risks to which funds are actually exposed match the risks to which investors believe they are exposed. More elaborate risk management systems that rely on sophisticated measures of market risk, however, should be carefully evaluated on the strength of their costs and benefits.

Copyright © Christopher Culp 2002

Further reading

Culp, C.L. (2001) *The Risk Management Process: Business Strategy and Tactics*, New York: John Wiley.
Culp, C.L., Mensink, R. and Neves, A.M.P. (1998) "Value at risk for asset managers", *Derivatives Quarterly*, 5, 2, Winter.
Rahl, L. (ed.) (2000) *Risk Budgeting*, London: Risk Books.
Zask, E. (ed.) (1999) *Global Investment Risk Management*, New York: McGraw-Hill.

The varying
nature of volatile forces

Financial markets have seen dramatic fluctuations in the past couple of years. **Menachem Brenner** asks whether there are more to come.

Menachem Brenner is a professor of finance at the Stern School of Business, New York University.

Volatility is a pervasive force in financial markets. On 14 April 2000, the Dow Jones index displayed a low of 10,202 and a high of 10,923, fluctuating by more than 700 points (7 per cent) in a trading period of six-and-a-half hours. This range was about five times the average daily range of about 1.5 per cent. An investor in an index fund would have faced the alarming prospect of seeing the value of an investment fluctuate within a range of 7 per cent in a day.

Is such an event uncommon or can we expect more of the same in the future? Before we can deal with this question we must first understand the significance of volatility and its role in financial analysis and markets. Volatility influences almost every facet of finance. Box 1 gives a selection of the most important. Using data on US shares and bonds from 1926 to 2000, research company Ibbotson and Associates provides estimates of volatility for the following financial assets: large company shares, small company shares, long-term government bonds and Treasury bills. Table 1 sets out estimates based on historical asset prices.

On average, the volatility of shares is more than twice that of government bonds. This reflects the greater risk of holding an equity portfolio compared with a bond portfolio. This difference is even more pronounced if one looks at the high and low range of rates of return. During the period covered, investors in large company shares saw the value of their portfolios decline by as much as 43 per cent in a single year. The worst decline suffered by holders of government bonds was only 9.2 per cent. Further analysis shows that smaller companies were riskier than large ones (volatility was 33.6 per cent compared with 20.1 per cent) and that long-term bonds had a much higher volatility than short-term Treasury bills (9.3 per cent compared with 3.2 per cent). In portfolio selection, investors

Box 1 **Influences on finance**

- Security analysis and valuation: modern methods of security analysis depend on estimates of volatility to gauge the risk of investing in a particular asset.
- Portfolio selection (asset allocation): every investor who chooses a combination of financial assets to suit his risk tolerance opts for the risk and return profile inherent in these assets. Volatility is a quantitative description of risk in this selection process.
- Option valuation and strategy: volatility plays a major role in pricing options, securities with option features, and in strategies involving options and related products.
- Hedging commodity or currency risk: this requires an estimate of volatility to determine the required hedge ratio (that is, the proportion of risk that should be hedged) and risk of the hedged position.
- Risk management methods: for example, Value-at-Risk computations, which measure the one-day (or one-week) expected maximum loss faced by an institution, require estimates of volatility.
- Investment projects: corporate investment decisions require estimates of cash flow volatility.
- Market-making: the volatility of asset prices is an important determinant of the bid-ask spread.
- Macroeconomic policy decisions: in conducting monetary policy, central banks use volatility estimates to assess price stability.

TABLE 1 Volatility of US bonds and shares (1926–2000)

	Standard deviation	1920–2000 Low rate of return	High rate of return	1930s Standard deviation	1950s Standard deviation
Large company shares (%)	20.1	−43	54	41.6	14.1
Small company shares (%)	33.6	−58	143	78.6	14.4
Long-term government bonds (%)	9.3	−9.2	40	5.3	4.6
Short-term (Treasury bills)	3.2	0	3.9	0.2	0.2

Source: Ibbotson Associates

examine such estimates in deciding how to allocate funds between shares and bonds.

Average estimates do not tell the whole story. Since the early 1970s, in contrast to the tranquil 1950s and 1960s, volatility has grown steadily. In broad terms this observed increase can be attributed in part to the global trend towards more competitive, open economies. In the "old" days, greater government involvement and regulation reduced observed volatility – the price for such stability being less efficient, lower-growth economies. Other, more recent factors may have contributed to volatility, such as a growing proportion of funds channelled to highly risky investments, the unprecedented linkages between markets (evident during the crash of 1987) and moves to electronic trading and information.

However, studies show that financial innovation – particularly risk management in the form of options and futures – has counterbalanced this trend. Hopefully, the use of derivatives alongside developments in trading technology and communication will result in levels of market volatility that more closely reflect the determinants of risk in the economy. As discussed later, behavioural economists argue that these developments have a limited impact compared with the influence of investor psychology.

International trends

The past decade has witnessed an increased trend towards international investment. Table 2 presents volatility estimates for five leading stock markets between 1990 and 2001. In this period, the FTSE 100 index had the lowest volatility, less than 15 per cent, while the Nikkei had the highest at about 23 per cent. The volatility of the Standard & Poor's 500 was very close to that of the FTSE, while the Dax and the CAC each had a volatility of about 20 per cent.

Tables 1 and 2 describe the past but may not be very useful in forecasting the future, especially if levels of volatility change. The same tables show that volatility can change drastically. The average annual volatility during the

TABLE 2 Volatility of five stock market indices (Jan 1990 to Apr 2001)

	S&P 500	Dax	CAC	Nikkei	FTSE
1990–2001					
Average (%)	15.15	20.08	19.43	23.45	14.85
Minimum (%)	4.77	4.69	7.03	7.85	6.04
Maximum (%)	41.6	53.13	50.48	55.35	36.39
1990–95					
Average (%)	11.79	18.08	18.18	24.27	13.27
1995–2001					
Average (%)	17.35	21.53	20.36	22.79	15.98
1995–98					
Average (%)	13.15	17.45	17.50	22.02	12.09
1998–2001					
Average (%)	21.64	25.88	23.57	23.77	19.95

Source: Datastream

1930s and 1950s is given in Table 1. For shares, the difference is very large, especially for small companies. In Table 2, volatility in all markets, except for Japan, increased from low levels in the first five years, 1990–95, to higher levels in the last four years. For example, the volatility of the S&P increased from 11.8 per cent to 21.6 per cent.

It is interesting to note that in the past 80 years there were two periods with relatively high volatility, which occurred under very different economic conditions. The levels of the last four years – especially of Nasdaq shares – recall the depression years, especially in respect of smaller shares. In the 1990s, as in the 1930s, we observe highly "stochastic" volatility, that is, volatility itself fluctuated from about 4.8 per cent to 41 per cent. In recent years, bursts of extremely high volatility were associated with economic crises, for example, the Asian crisis in the summer of 1997 and the collapse of the Long Term Capital Management hedge fund in the autumn of 1998.

This observed increase may be partly explained by the notion of "excess" volatility advanced by academic Robert Shiller and other behavioural financial economists, who claim that investors' psychology, not necessarily linked to the economic fundamentals of the markets, contributes to the volatility of financial assets. The steady increase in the number of households that invest in the stock market over the past three decades may have been a factor, especially in a period when the economy was undergoing significant changes.

Forecasting

To forecast volatility it is important to know more about the way volatility changes over time. For example, is it related to past volatility? Does it increase on days that the market drops? Numerous empirical studies have been conducted using innovative statistical methods. Their main findings are summarized in Box 2.

Several models incorporating some of these properties have been proposed and implemented. In general, they estimate volatility conditional on past information. A simple method used by risk measurement specialists RiskMetrics is the "exponential smoothing" method. It uses exponentially decaying weights, where more recent observations carry a higher weight than earlier ones. This method uses ad-hoc weights and does not take into account most of the phenomena mentioned above, such as mean reversion or the negative relationship between volatility and price changes.

The Arch-Garch class of models, pioneered by academic Robert Engle and extended by Tim Bollerslev, Daniel Nelson and others, builds on the fact that volatility varies over time and is persistent. In particular, the Garch model specifies a relationship between current volatility and both past volatility and past squared returns. The parameters used to forecast the next volatility are estimated from past data. The most popular Garch model is the Garch (1,1) which is conditional on the last period where the previous day's volatility impounds all previous information. Unlike the RiskMetrics model, it accounts for volatility reverting to the mean over time.

> **Box 2 Changing over time**
>
> - Fat tails: extreme events, reflected in extreme rates of return, are seen more often than is expected from a bell-shaped normal distribution curve. Volatility estimates understate the occurrence of such events.
> - Mean-reversion in returns: returns tend to revert towards the long-run mean and should dampen long-run volatility estimates.
> - Mean-reversion in volatility: volatility itself tends to revert to a long-run mean. For example, after a sharp increase during the crash of October 1987, volatility fell back in the next six months. However, this was not the case in the US Depression of 1930–39.
> - Leverage-like effects: in 1976 academic Fischer Black noted a negative relationship between volatility and price changes. This phenomenon became more pronounced after 1987.
> - Volatility spill-over: in today's global economy, price changes in one market affect other markets, especially if the economies are closely related. That may explain why patterns of volatility are similar in the US and UK, and in France and Germany.
> - Volatility and trading: studies show that volatility is higher during trading periods than non-trading periods, which has led to the practice of using only trading days (252) when annualizing daily volatility.

Implied volatility

Although these models attempt to incorporate all available statistical information, they do not use information from options markets. Option prices are determined by volatility, among other factors, so we can use the market price of the option to deduce the volatility implied by this price. In other words, the price of the option reflects the perception of market participants of the future volatility of the underlying asset. Since the introduction of option markets, implied volatility has been used extensively. Although it is derived from the Black-Scholes option-pricing model and relies on the assumptions of that model, it is used in various applications, including volatility forecasting.

The extent to which implied volatility is a good predictor of future volatility can be seen in Figure 1, which plots implied volatility versus realized volatility. In the lower part of the figure, realized volatility of the S&P 100 and S&P 500 are depicted along with the implied volatility from options of the S&P 100. Although during most of the 1990s implied volatility is slightly higher than the realized volatility, the pattern looks remarkably similar. This was also true in the 1980s, in particular after the crash of 1987.

If implied volatility is strongly related to actual volatility, we should observe phenomena similar to those reported earlier. For example, the inverse relationship between volatility and price has been examined by academic David Weinbaum using the S&P 100. He finds that an increase in implied volatility is strongly related to a decrease in market price and vice versa. Also, the volatility implied from long-term options is, most of the time, lower than the volatility implied from short-term options, which is consistent with mean reversion.

FIGURE 1 | Implied and realized volatility of shares and indexes

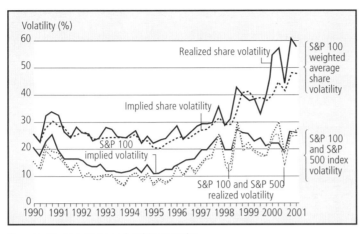

Sources: Reuters, Fame and Goldman Sachs

Volatility options

In the past decade, the realization that volatility is itself volatile has affected not only forecasting but also option valuation and risk management under such conditions. Little has been done to suggest how to manage risk under these conditions. This author and Dan Galai (1989) have proposed making a volatility index and introducing volatility options and futures to hedge against changes. Recently, the French futures and options exchange Monep introduced a volatility index based on this methodology. The idea is to construct an index that implies the volatility that will prevail in the next 30 days by averaging across options with different maturities.

Another implied volatility index is VIX, introduced by the Chicago Board Options Exchange. The *Financial Times* publishes relative volatility indices from RiskMetrics for bond and equity markets from Tuesday to Friday. The next step should be the introduction of options on volatility that could be useful to hedge against unexpected changes in the volatility of share and bond portfolios as well as option portfolios.

Conclusion

First, is the increase in volatility here to stay? To try to answer this question, Figure 2 presents two implied volatility indices created by the Chicago Board Options Exchange: VIX, which represents the S&P 100 index, and VXN, which represents the NDX index (the 100 largest Nasdaq shares). Both show that implied volatility increased substantially between 1998 and 2001 (as was true for realized volatility).

It should be noted, however, that the volatility of Nasdaq shares has increased far more than that of the S&P 100 shares and the volatility itself has become much more volatile. This may be a feature of the technology revolution and/or the behavioural "excess volatility" aspect caused by the increased participation of

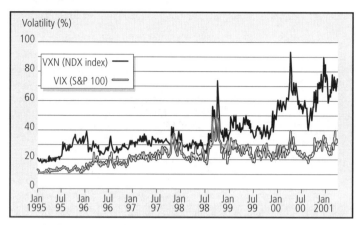

FIGURE 2 Implied volatility of S&P 100 and NDX indexes

Source: Chicago Board Options Exchange

individual investors in financial markets. If the current wave of economic change should slow and household participation does not increase, then volatility will stabilize or even decline. Currently, volatility implied from longer-term option is about 2–3 per cent lower than that implied from short-term options. The market expects a decline in the coming year.

Second, although many variations of statistical volatility models, including the use of high-frequency data, have been proposed, it appears that the use of implied volatility is gaining a stronger hold and is spreading into new areas. Several central banks (such as the Bank of England, the Bank of Israel and the Bank of Sweden) have been using implied volatilities from financial assets to get an indication of price stability for use in their decisions on monetary policy.

Volatility plays a major role in financial theory and in practice. The changing nature of this phenomenon makes its study an interesting and challenging task. A better understanding of volatility and how to estimate it should improve decision-making in finance and economics.

Copyright © Menachem Brenner 2002

Further reading

Andersen, T.G. and Bollerslev, T. (1998) "Answering the skeptics: yes, standard volatility models do provide accurate forecasts", *International Economic Review*, 39, 885–905.

Brenner, M. and Galai, D. (1989) "New financial instruments for hedging changes in volatility", *Financial Analysts Journal*, 45, 61–5.

Mayhew, S. (1995) "Implied volatility literature review", *Financial Analysts Journal*, 51, 8–20.

Schwert, G.W. (1989) "Why does market volatility change over time?", *Journal of Finance*, 44, 1115–53.

Too much being left
to chance by personal investors

Information on most aspects of investing is just a mouse click away, says **Greg Elmiger**, but individuals need better awareness and professional tools for assessing risk.

Greg Elmiger is retail risk product specialist at RiskMetrics, a New York-based company that specializes in risk measurement.

Conventional wisdom would have us believe individual investors couldn't have it any easier. Since the mid-1970s, we have witnessed a shift away from an insider community of money managers to a more open and transparent network, where access to financial markets is a mere mouse click away. High-speed transmission of information has driven the brave new world of personal finance. Modern-day investors have almost everything at their disposal – no matter how profound or prosaic.

This free flow of information has replaced a guarded and opaque financial system that previously restricted accessibility and skewed the playing field. Investment services now cater for every imaginable interest and all levels of net worth. The divide separating high- and low-end investors has never been narrower. Retirement and tax planning are ubiquitous services offered over the web at a fraction of their customary costs.

But while individuals have tremendous financial opportunities in this new environment, they also face new responsibilities. Demographic changes and the shift away from government provision for old age have made people more dependent on their personal investments. This in turn has placed a premium on understanding and controlling risk.

Markets matter

The difference between investing today and in years past is not only the ease with which individuals access information and build a portfolio but the fact that financial markets are more intricately tied to our blueprints for the future. Whether it is recognized or not, the markets matter because financial portfolios are replacing more traditional means of savings as the primary way of saving for retirement. Gone are the days when governments or employers took care of people's long-term finances and pensions. Because people are living longer, current and future investments will have a significant impact on their lives in retirement. It is the success of these investments that will eventually determine the standard of living we will have in the future.

Our futures will be shaped by a host of factors. Some will be personal, such as our time to retirement and aversion to risk, while others will be beyond our control, such as the final rate of return or the pace of inflation. The good news is that technology offers everyone far more access to information than ever before. As financial decisions are becoming more important, technology is providing more tools to help make those decisions in a smarter way.

These changes are taking place around the world. Self-directed investing is charging ahead across the world, even in areas where capital markets are still not fully developed. In fact, as *The Economist* wrote in 2000: "The stock market with the highest proportion of internet trading is not, as you might think, in New York, but in Seoul." After all, the article added, the 1990s will be remembered as the decade of the internet and when the world was introduced to shares. The capitalization of stock markets around the world reached 110 per cent of global gross domestic product by 2000, up from 40 per cent in 1990. Solvency questions about government pension systems are being raised everywhere and being answered in part by an increased reliance on individual saving and asset accumulation.

The irony is that the availability of information has sometimes created confusion, not clarity. Rather than making investment choices easier, the wealth of information has made making decisions more difficult for many. Information overload has become a common affliction among investors. Yet isn't technology supposed to simplify our lives? Even technology, which can bring streams of the latest market information on command and execute trade orders at all hours of the day, cannot suspend the fundamental relationship between risk and return. Some people have wrongly assumed that because trading is so effortless – getting in is easy, getting out should be easy too – risk can somehow be forgotten as well. Many have confused the simplicity of making a trade with the seriousness of investing. In this vein, technology has been both a boon and a poisoned chalice for investors.

The current generation of investors faces a conundrum. Without prudent investing, preparations for a secure financial future will fall short. So where does this leave us? Whether we accept it or not, the markets will continue to have a growing impact on our lives. As a result, the principles of risk management will grow in importance as individuals are encouraged to invest savings in markets. As professional risk managers know, making sense of markets requires a significant amount of research and reflection, and an ability to synthesize not just one aspect of investing but an entire picture of risk and return. Simply put, a healthy approach to investing in the markets requires a systematic and rational approach that can balance risk and return in an optimal way. Finding a systematic approach that works is the first main step to building a portfolio.

Risk in personal investing

As more investors begin to participate directly in financial markets and have greater assets at stake, there is a greater need for risk awareness. Many investors pay a great deal of attention to performance and not enough attention to risk. An example is the intense interest many investors take in mutual fund performance in choosing among funds and the role recent performance plays in fund ratings. In fact, it is well documented that this year's above-average stock or fund is likely to be among next year's underperformers.

Why do people generally pay so little attention to risk in personal investing? After all, we are generally conscious of risk in most areas of our lives. We assess risk carefully in making most personal and financial decisions, such as changing jobs. The insurance industry has become one of the world's largest for that reason. One part of the answer is that there is as yet only limited public awareness that risk is an important investment issue. A casual survey of websites devoted to the needs of individual investors turns up little discussion of risk. In spite of the volume of information on the web, risk remains a neglected aspect of personal investing.

But perhaps a more important reason for the lack of interest in investment risk is that it is difficult for people to assess risk accurately even when they focus on it. One part of this is that most investors lack an objective view of how well situated they are to judge the risks and opportunities of investments. There is a widespread predisposition among investors, for example, to overestimate their ability to select stocks or time the market. (An example from outside the financial world is a finding that 90 per cent of Swedish drivers consider their driving abilities to be above average.) One result is that there is a much higher volume of trading than if investors were more conscious of how unlikely they are to pick winners. These natural "comfort zones" lead investors to pay too little attention to risk. Investors may feel more comfortable with a portfolio containing a few blue-chip stocks than a well-diversified portfolio of smaller companies, even though the blue-chip portfolio is objectively riskier.

Investors tend to pay more attention to losses than gains: when presented in certain ways, they emphasize potential losses over the potential opportunities that risk presents. Compare, for example, how you would react to a 10 per cent discount on cash purchases and to a 10 per cent mark-up on credit card purchases if the prices were identical. If you find this example unconvincing, think about how you react when a company cuts its dividend and when a company refrains from increasing its dividend.

One consequence of aversion to loss is that investors are more inclined to take profits than realize losses. Studies in behavioural finance have shown that investors are far more distressed by prospective losses than they are made happy by equivalent gains. Investors typically consider the loss of £1 twice as painful on an emotional scale as the pleasure they would receive from a £1 gain. After a time, portfolios end up very different from what investors would have chosen had they focused on risk and opportunity as well as performance. Another tendency is for people to focus on the part rather than the whole.

Perhaps this helps explain why investors around the world tend to hold most of their portfolios in local stocks, even when holding a globally diversified portfolio could reduce risk.

These examples could be multiplied indefinitely. It is difficult to make decisions in a complex and unfamiliar environment without some rules of thumb. Many investors therefore use rules of thumb that come naturally. They would be better served by looking at objective measures of risk and opportunity.

Hence risk management is poised for growth. With a combination of intriguing tools, research, advanced technology and the blessings from regulators, risk management is on the verge of crossing over from large institutions into the mainstream investment market. After all, who needs the tools more? One could argue that when emerging economies mismanage risk and Nobel laureates fall, the International Monetary Fund and the banking community will rush in with aid. But when an individual investor mismanages a portfolio, retirements are pushed back and a family's quality of life is jeopardized.

Risk and return tools for individuals

The best defence against these tendencies of people facing decisions under uncertainty is an array of accessible tools, readily understandable by most people but grounded in quantitative analysis. This, after all, is how professional investors control risk: they rely on their expertise, but subject themselves to disciplines such as benchmark targets, stop-loss levels and Value-at-Risk limits, which provide a measure of the total risk facing a bank or portfolio.

What tools should individual investors have available to carry out a disciplined investment planning process? There is no definitive answer, since experience will show the way and we are at the beginning of a new era. But much can be learned from the experience of institutional investment and risk management, and from the portfolio approach they use.

For individual investors as for institutional managers, portfolio diversification can be as important in determining the performance of their investments as finding individual securities or funds with the highest possible return. Similarly, risk management concepts such as VaR and stress testing are as important for individual investors as for banks and brokerages (see Box 1). In fact, the idea of stress testing is intuitive to most investors: how much can I lose in a short space of time if markets move against me, or if a dramatic market event of the recent past were to be repeated?

As more individuals accumulate assets and become more dependent on personal assets to meet retirement goals, it will become more important for basic financial understanding, including the risk concepts that are relatively new even to the professional financial community, to become common knowledge.

There is a responsibility on risk and investment advisers at all levels to take on a role as educators. The retail investment world has until now been focused almost exclusively on recent returns of funds and stocks. The end of each

> **Box 1 RiskGrades: making VaR relevant**
>
> To make risk management tools available to the typical investor, the concepts on which they are based need to be brought out of their original context. For example, RiskGrades, produced by the RiskMetrics Group, measures volatility and the VaR of a portfolio against the level of volatility of the world market. A portfolio with the same level of risk as a market-weighted global index fund has a RiskGrade measurement of 100.
>
> A table of volatility for bond and equity markets worldwide is published on the international Capital Markets page of the *Financial Times* from Tuesday to Friday (see example below).
>
> **RISKGRADE™ VOLATILITY**
>
> | Bond markets | 4 Jun | Day change | Month ago | 52 wk high | 52 wk low |
> |---|---|---|---|---|---|
> | Europe | 28 | −1 | 26 | 34 | 20 |
> | Americas | 51 | −1 | 53 | 57 | 28 |
> | Asia | 27 | −1 | 34 | 40 | 17 |
> | Global | 56 | 5 | 59 | 62 | 29 |
> | *Equity markets* | *4 Jun* | | | | |
> | Europe | 100 | −2 | 121 | 137 | 78 |
> | UK | 98 | −1 | 107 | 122 | 63 |
> | Americas | 108 | −2 | 130 | 143 | 68 |
> | Asia | 132 | −2 | 157 | 177 | 93 |
> | Global | 120 | −2 | 142 | 155 | 88 |
>
> RiskGrades are calculated daily by RiskMetrics. They are designed to measure the riskiness of today's global market returns. A RiskGrade of 100 corresponds to the average volatility of the international equity markets during normal market conditions. Data shown is one day in arrears. More information is available at www.riskgrades.com

quarter sees the publication, even in the high-quality financial press, of remarkably narrow reviews of the past three months that are meant to be read by self-directed investors with horizons of a quarter of a century. What the world needs is more focus on diversification, risk and the long term. To make that happen, the level of financial literacy of investors and advisers will need to be significantly enhanced.

The future

What can we look forward to in the next generation? We can only conjecture how rapidly personal finance will progress. If the past two decades are any indication, the next 20 years will bring many new conveniences and pitfalls. Already, we are seeing the first signs of one-stop shopping materializing at larger online brokerages. These efforts are bringing more sophisticated wealth-planning applications and financial advice on to existing trade execution platforms. It can be argued that the current wave is simply another chapter in the evolution of personal finance. Now more than ever, individuals must gain an understanding that investing is a grown-up business.

It is likely that investing will be further automated in the not-too-distant future. As a result, investment accounts will instantaneously reflect the latest personal statistics including income, tax and household adjustments. Each investment decision will be immediately factored against other objectives, thereby optimizing longer-term priorities. Individual investing will be driven by the four pillars of personal finance – multi-goal planning, asset selection, balancing risk with return and tax awareness – which are the fundamental components of a full-scale solution.

As people increasingly opt to do it themselves, they will find it necessary to carefully plan, frugally preserve and appropriately harvest their gains to reach investment goals. It is clear that the tools of financial risk management will play a central role in this process.

This article is adapted from a forthcoming book, written with Ethan Berman and Steve S. Kim, *RiskGrade Your Investments: Measure Risk and Create Wealth*, published by John Wiley.

Copyright © Greg Elmiger 2002

Further reading

Bernstein, P.L. (1998) *Against the Gods: The Remarkable Story of Risk*, Chichester: John Wiley.
Bogle, J.C. (2000) *Common Sense on Mutual Funds: New Imperatives for the Intelligent Investor*, Chichester: John Wiley.
Graham, B. (1997) *The Intelligent Investor: A Book of Practical Counsel*, London: HarperCollins.
Malkiel, B.G. (1997) *A Random Walk Down Wall Street*, New York: W.W. Norton.

A model approach
to using technology

Technological advances now allow investors to incorporate an array of factors in their calculations when planning their portfolio. **Terry Marsh** and **Paul Pfleiderer** outline the important developments.

Terry Marsh is an associate professor of finance at the Haas School of Business. He is a principal of Quantal International, a company specializing in investment management technology.

Paul Pfleiderer is the William F. Sharpe Professor of Financial Economics at the Stanford Business School. He is a principal of Quantal International.

The interplay and aggregation of basic building blocks is an important theme in science. For example, the folding sequences in chains of amino acids that make up proteins are thought to occur because of specific patterns of attraction between sets of nearby amino acids. In addition, even the architecture of supercomputers that can be used to analyze such patterns involves aggregating processors, sub-processors and memory. The scale on which the units of amino acids and sub-processors are defined and the level at which they can be aggregated generally depend heavily on measurement technology and guiding models.

In the same vein, investment portfolios are simply aggregates of assets. The technology that, at its simplest level, makes portfolio construction possible involves understanding how these assets "aggregate". Its users include institutional fund managers, enterprise risk managers and private client investment advisers.

Asset allocation

The current technology for assisting with the asset allocation decision – the split of investment capital among equities, fixed-income securities, commodities and so on – is, alas, quite rudimentary. Take, for example, the oft-quoted rule that an investor with no market-timing ability and no special information should allocate $(100 - x)$ per cent of her funds to equities, where x is her age. The typical rationale is that if an investor is young and takes a big hit in her investments, she has more years in which to recover. However, as economist Paul Samuelson pointed out, she also has more years in which to take further hits.

In the following sections we use two examples to show how

portfolio technology can help manage equity funds. We focus on equity portfolios, but the technology we describe applies equally to pools of any assets or economic units.

The socially responsible portfolio

Consider an investor who does not believe that he can beat the market and, in the absence of special preferences, would index his holdings to the FTSE 100. However, the investor has chosen not to invest in five industries he considers undesirable: aerospace and defence; tobacco; oil and gas; forest products and paper; and chemicals. In substituting for stocks in these industries in his portfolio, the investor wants to minimize the risk of underperforming the FTSE 100.

On 11 June, we created a $100m portfolio that minimizes the investor's risk of underperforming the FTSE 100 index given the industry exclusions and very few additional restrictions (this was created using Quantal Pro, a system co-developed by the authors). The optimizer substitutes with stocks that are similar to the stocks in the excluded industries in so far as they tend to move predictably with them. The optimal portfolio has a predicted tracking error of 130 basis points in relation to the FTSE 100; for comparison, the predicted (annualized) volatility on 11 June for the FTSE 100 is 20.5 per cent.

Table 1 shows the estimated sensitivities (betas) of the portfolio to industry returns. Notice that the portfolio has almost identical exposures to the excluded industries as the FTSE 100 index, but contains none of the stocks in those excluded industries.

This example is similar to what is typically called "enhanced indexing", where a manager bears a slight risk of diverging from a benchmark index as a trade-off for the expectation of outperforming the index by, say, 100 or 200 basis points. The manager might, for example, buy stocks a few days before they are added to a benchmark, or trade on private information.

Investors can use similar technology to "home brew" their own custom portfolios. Suppose that an investor is impressed with the technology sector in, say, France and Germany, but does not think the potential benefits of the technology are yet reflected in stock prices. Typically, he might simply invest in a mutual fund that contains pan-European technology stocks. To apply the principle above, however, one would select a European universe and either exclude non-French and non-German technology stocks or express a bullish opinion on technology stocks in France and Germany.

The long-short equity hedge fund

How could technology improve the construction of a hedge fund portfolio containing paired trades, in which the manager buys an undervalued stock and pairs it with a short position in a closely related stock? Conventional pairs trading faces a number of difficulties. First, pairs are often chosen from the same industry, yet the industry grouping of stocks is not generally the best way of controlling risk, since companies whose stocks are classified as being in the same industry often barely resemble each other. Consider the mishmash of computer-related stocks in industries typically labelled "business services".

Second, industry pairing also has the disadvantage that a model being used

TABLE 1	Estimated sensitivities to industry returns		
Industry	Index beta	Portfolio beta	Beta difference*
Aerospace & defence	0.45	0.45	0.01
Auto manufacturers & parts makers	0.60	0.60	(0.00)
Banks	0.86	0.86	(0.00)
Building materials & components	0.55	0.56	(0.00)
Business and public services	0.67	0.67	(0.00)
Chemicals	0.77	0.77	0.00
Cosmetics & personal care	0.87	0.87	(0.00)
Electric utilities	0.96	0.97	(0.01)
Energy sources	0.69	0.64	0.05
Entertainment and leisure (all)	0.70	0.71	(0.00)
Fixed-line communications	0.51	0.51	(0.00)
Food & beverage makers	0.76	0.76	(0.00)
Forest products and paper	0.40	0.40	0.00
Home construction & furnishings	0.43	0.43	(0.00)
Industrial – diversified	0.66	0.67	(0.00)
Industrial equipment	0.40	0.40	(0.00)
Industrial transportation	0.25	0.25	0.00
Insurance	0.71	0.72	(0.00)
Machinery & engineering	0.81	0.81	(0.00)
Media	0.59	0.59	(0.00)
Mining & metals	0.30	0.30	(0.00)
Oil & gas	0.29	0.29	(0.00)
Real estate	0.45	0.46	(0.00)
Retailers (all)	1.10	1.10	(0.01)
Speciality finance	0.58	0.58	(0.00)
Technology – hardware & equipment	0.30	0.30	(0.00)
Textiles & apparel (all)	0.27	0.27	(0.00)
Tobacco	0.53	0.52	0.01
Travel	0.32	0.32	(0.00)

*Values may differ because of rounding errors

for judging which stocks are undervalued or overvalued at current market prices (in practice, these are referred to as stocks with positive or negative alpha, respectively) is also being used as a model for risk control. For example, based on a fundamentals analysis of Nokia, which often partly involves industry comparison, Nokia looks attractive to a portfolio manager. She buys Nokia and hedges by shorting Ericsson, which is classified in the same industry. In the future, Nokia's price drops because of a decline in sales of hand-held devices. Meanwhile, Ericsson's price falls only slightly because it is doing well in its network infrastructure area, where Nokia's presence is limited. The reason Nokia looked profitable is that the original analysis did not account for differences within the industry.

Third, a portfolio of paired trades could contain systematic but unintended exposures, such as a tilt towards value or small-cap stocks. Finally, if the objective of pairs trades is to create a market-neutral portfolio, it is an unnecessarily constrained way of doing so. All that should be required is that the aggregate long side of the portfolio be "paired" with the aggregate short side, so that the portfolio as a whole is market-neutral.

Let us suppose that the manager's universe is the S&P 500, and that the manager has alphas for the first 100 stocks in the index. To generate this example, we randomly assigned "over-perform" and "underperform" alphas across the 100 stocks. On 11 June, when we constructed the portfolio, the forecasted volatility for the S&P 500 was approximately 23 per cent and the information-neutral expected return was around 12 per cent. Our calculation produced a long-short portfolio with 54 longs and 48 shorts, a predicted volatility of around 5.6 per cent that will be almost entirely caused by company-specific events, and a predicted beta of –0.0014. The portfolio is constructed to have zero net exposure to the systematic risk factors identified by the authors' linear factor model. The portfolio's industry exposures are also relatively low, though of course it is over-weighted in industries with high alpha stocks and underweighted in industries with low alpha stocks.

Complications arise when using this technology. First, when markets make large moves, the risk exposures may not remain constant. Second, even if predicted equity risks turn out to be accurate, the ways in which the alphas are derived may mean that the long-short strategy "pays off" unevenly across market scenarios. For example, if the strategy tends to do best when the market suffers, in this respect it resembles a put option on the market. Third, we need to be mindful of the prediction error in conditional risk exposures.

Risk models

Risk is a key ingredient in the investment technology used to construct portfolios. If the portfolios contain only equities and derivatives such as exchange-traded funds, futures and swaps with payoffs that are linear in equity prices, then the distribution of daily or weekly returns on these portfolio components will be reasonably symmetric. (This ignores dynamic rebalancing strategies that induce non-linearities.) This means that the only way to limit downside risk in the portfolio is to limit its volatility, and thus its upside potential as well.

To forecast the volatility of an equity portfolio conditional on information up to the current time, we need to know the forecast of the variances and covariances of all the equity securities that could possibly be included in the portfolio (the "investment universe").

Even for a relatively narrow universe of securities, such as the S&P 500, the number of parameters required is large and would be impossible to estimate directly from available data. As in other scientific fields, the best approach is to identify the most important factors using a model, here a factor model of returns. If, say, there are 15 common factors explaining most of the movements across the 500 stocks, the problem boils down to estimating each stock's exposures to these factors, plus the 500 stock-specific risks. In this way, a factor model for stock returns becomes a core ingredient of portfolio management. Factor models for equities are generally linear; in other words, the equity return on each stock is a linear function of the common factors and an additive "left-over" stock-specific contribution. As a general rule of thumb, some half to two-thirds of the variation in a typical stock's return can be explained by the common factors.

There are three broad classes of factor models:

- models in which stock returns are explained by macroeconomic factors such as interest rates, term structure spreads and rates of growth in industrial production;
- models in which stock returns are explained by a company's attributes, such as the industry in which it is classified, its size and its leverage;
- a returns-based factor model in which common factors manifest themselves as clustering among stocks when looking at the stocks' recent returns.

The first two models are called structural models, while the last is a reduced-form model. In principle, if one has a perfectly specified structural model of a process, it will always produce better forecasts than a reduced-form model. In a real financial setting, however, even when the first two models are perfectly specified, they do not afford dramatically better portfolio decisions than the third – even on a good day, it is hard to explain more than 5 or 8 per cent of stock price variation with macroeconomic variables. And when the structural models are misspecified because some factors are missing or the ones that are included are measured improperly, they are substantially inferior to the returns-based model.

A big advantage of a returns-based factor model over the structural model is its potential for staying up to date. If the factor structure is shifting over time, a daily returns-based conditional risk model will update much more readily than a model that must await changes in industrial classifications or needs quarterly or annual accounting data going back as far as five years.

The three classes of factor model are all linear, which is consistent with our earlier notion that daily or weekly stock returns tend to be symmetrically distributed. One might think that we should be able to find companies whose earnings/dividend growth rates and stock prices respond asymmetrically to the changes in business conditions that are impounded in the prices of other stocks. For example, some businesses appear to have operating leverage and substantial "real options" to exploit their technology under good business conditions.

Moreover, even without real options, we would expect that the stock of a highly leveraged company would have option-like payoffs as a function of the company's earnings and dividend stream, even if the latter were linear with respect to common factors across stocks. However, we have found that, while it is relatively easy to find instances of historical asymmetry in stock returns, it is extremely difficult to predict such behaviour reliably over the normal daily, weekly or monthly rebalancing intervals. Perhaps even a non-linear generating model for returns would be approximately linear over these shorter intervals.

It is helpful to bring technology to bear when constructing an optimal portfolio of assets that incorporates various objectives, as well as opinions about which stocks will under- and over-perform the market, constraints, trading costs or tax considerations. Investment technology can help the active manager whose objective is to beat the market by exploiting his insights and private information.

Copyright © Terry Marsh and Paul Pfleiderer 2002

Further reading

Fedrigo, I., Marsh, T. and Pfleiderer, P. (1996) "Estimating factor models of security returns: how much difference does it make?", working paper (http://www.quantal.com).

Marsh, T.A. and Wagner, N. (2000) "Return-volume dependence and extremes in international equity markets", working paper 293, U.C. Berkeley, (http://papers.ssrn.com/sol3/papers.cfm?cfid=793106&cftken=67448518&abstract_id=235536).

Investment psychology   8

Contents

Investors seek lessons in thinking 246

Nicholas Barberis, University of Chicago Graduate School of Business

Finance theory takes the idea that investors are rational as one of its fundamental conditions. In practice, people are subject to psychological biases and make habitual errors that affect the quality of their decisions.

In search of money for nothing 252

Francisco Gomes, London Business School

This article describes how the arbitrage principle helps us price complicated assets and investigates the mechanics of arbitrage of professional investors

The perils for investors of human nature 257

Simon Gervais, University of Pennsylvania and **Terrance Odean**, University of California

People tend to attribute success in any activity to their own skill or experience and put failure down to unpredictable events outside their control. What are the market implications of over-confidence?

The curious case of Palm and 3Com 261

Owen Lamont, University of Chicago Graduate School of Business

Investors should beware: the law of one price might not give a true picture of market activity.

The art and craft of reading the market 267

Bruce Kamich, Rutgers University

The interpretation of market movements is part art, part science. Yet there seems to be a strong future for the acquired skills of technical analysis.

Introduction to Part 8

Much investment theory is based on common-sense assumptions about human nature, such as the principle that, when faced with two identical goods selling at different prices, buyers will choose the cheaper one. By and large these assumptions are well founded: price disparities tend not to last long in any market, least of all financial markets. However, human beings often exhibit traits of behaviour that are not strictly rational or are, indeed, systematically erroneous. Behavioural finance, the subject of this part, is the study of how financial markets are affected by these traits, such as overconfidence and conservatism.

Investors seek lessons in thinking

Nicholas Barberis is an associate professor of finance at the University of Chicago Graduate School of Business.

The theory that irrational behaviour distorts stock market prices is gaining ground over the established efficient markets hypothesis. **Nicholas Barberis** examines the case for human error.

The dominant framework used by academics to study stock movements used to be the efficient markets hypothesis. This was developed at the University of Chicago in the mid-1960s and says that price reflects fundamental value, defined as the best possible forecast, given available information, of a security's future cash flows, discounted at a rate that is appropriate for the risk of those cash flows.

Over the past decade, another view of financial markets known broadly as "behavioural finance" has emerged. Proponents argue that investors can make systematic errors in forecasting cash flows or in setting the discount rate and these errors can push stock prices away from fundamental value for extended periods of time.

The stratospheric rise in the value of US equities and of the technology sector in particular during the late 1990s has shaken many observers' belief in efficient markets, and drawn many to the behavioural finance view. This raises the possibility that behavioural finance will replace the efficient markets hypothesis as the dominant model, a prospect that strikes fear into the hearts of financial economists who have built careers on the efficient markets hypothesis.

Researchers in behavioural finance spend a good deal of time studying work by psychologists trying to understand the biases that affect decision-making. Some of these ideas can provide a useful way of looking at financial markets. This article summarizes the more important cognitive errors, as well as the insights they may offer investors.

Over-confidence

In general, people significantly over-estimate the accuracy of their forecasts. For example, we might ask an investor to forecast a company's earnings a year from now and to provide a range, such that he is 95 per cent certain that earnings will fall within that range. Studies have found that the ranges people give are far too narrow: actual earnings fall into the range only 60 per cent of the time.

Over-confidence may be due, at least in part, to an error known as self-attribution bias. This refers to investors' tendency to ascribe any success they have picking stocks to their own insight and any disasters to bad luck. Persistent application of such a rule will lead an investor to the pleasing but inaccurate conclusion that he is a genius; put differently, he will become over-confident about his ability. Over-confidence may also be related to optimism. For example, in one study 80 per cent of drivers believed themselves to be above-average in ability. About half of my MBA students believe they will be among the 20 per cent to receive a top grade.

One manifestation of over-confidence in financial markets may be excessive trading, for which there is much evidence. A 2000 study by researchers Brad Barber and Terrance Odean found that after taking trading costs into account, the average return of the individual investor client base of a large US discount brokerage firm was significantly below market benchmarks. Put simply, these investors would have been better off if they had traded less. The behavioural finance interpretation of these findings is that investors are over-confident about the value of information they uncover: they believe they have information worth trading on, whereas in fact they do not. They trade too much and the trading costs lower their average return.

Over-confidence may also explain investors' love affair with actively managed funds, in spite of overwhelming evidence that such funds do not, on average, beat market indices. Many investors appear to believe they can pick money managers who are going to beat the index, even though only a few investors will actually be able to do this.

Representativeness

When evaluating the probability that an object A comes from a class B, people typically base their judgement on the extent to which A is representative of B, in other words, the extent to which A reflects the essential characteristics of B. For example, consider the following: "Steve is very shy and withdrawn, invariably helpful, but with little interest in people or in the world of reality. A meek and tidy soul, he has a need for order and structure, and a passion for detail." Studies find that when asked to guess whether Steve is a librarian or a lawyer, people are much more likely to guess librarian, because, with apologies to librarians, Steve "sounds" more like a librarian; put differently, he is representative of librarians.

Representativeness can be a good rule of thumb, but it can also lead people astray. In the above example, Steve is in fact more likely to be a lawyer. Although he sounds like a librarian, there are far fewer librarians than there are lawyers, making it unlikely that Steve is a librarian, the description notwithstanding.

One possible consequence of representativeness in financial markets is that investors may be too quick to detect patterns in data that are in fact random. If a company reports increased earnings several quarters in a row, representativeness may lead investors to conclude that the company has a high long-term earnings growth rate: after all, past earnings are representative of a high growth rate. However, this conclusion is likely to be premature: investors are forgetting that even though the company "looks" as if it has a high growth rate, even a mediocre company can produce several good quarters of earnings, simply by chance.

Representativeness can therefore explain numerous episodes in which investors appeared keen to buy stocks with impressive earnings histories or simply high past returns, even though these stocks had been declared overvalued by market observers. It can also explain why mutual funds with good past performance attract large inflows of funds, even though past performance is a poor predictor of future returns. Investors may be drawn to funds with a good track record because such funds are representative of funds with skilled managers. However, investors are forgetting that even unskilled managers can post periods of high returns by chance.

Conservatism

Once they have formed an opinion, people are often unwilling to change it, even when they receive pertinent new information. Suppose that, based on its past performance, investors have decided that company A has merely average long-term earnings prospects. Suddenly, A posts much higher earnings than expected. Conservatism predicts that investors will persist in their belief that the company is only average and will not react sufficiently to the good news. The stock price should therefore move too little on the day of the announcement but should gradually drift upwards in later weeks as investors shed their initial conservatism.

This prediction has been confirmed in a phenomenon known as "post-earnings announcement drift" that forms the basis of many investment strategies popular with money managers. Companies that report unexpectedly good (bad) earnings news typically have unusually high (low) returns after the announcement.

Narrow framing

When monitoring their economic well-being, investors should pay attention to changes in their total wealth, because it is this – the value of stock market investments, home and capitalized future salary – that determines how much they can afford to spend on goods and services, which is, ultimately, all they should care about. In spite of this, many investors appear to engage in "narrow framing", namely an excessive focus on changes in wealth that are narrowly defined, both in a temporal and in a cross-sectional sense. Even if they are saving for retirement and so have a long investment horizon, they often pay too much attention to short-term gains and losses. Moreover, they become obsessive about price changes in a single stock they own, even if it represents only a small fraction of their total wealth.

Narrow framing is dangerous because it can lead people to over-estimate the risk they are taking, especially when they are loss-averse, that is, more sensitive to losses than to gains. This is because the more narrowly an investor frames, the more likely he is to see losses: the stock market often has short-term losses, but these are less frequent in the long term. Similarly, individual stocks are more likely to trade at a loss relative to purchase price than a diversified portfolio. If people are loss-averse, narrow framing can make risky investments seem riskier than they are.

This effect has been demonstrated in experiments. Some studies ask people how they would split their money between a riskless and a risky investment. The latter is actually stocks, although participants are not told this. Crucially, some subjects are shown the distribution of monthly returns on the risky investment, while others are shown annual returns. The way data are presented should not matter, but it does. Those shown monthly returns are far less keen to invest in the risky asset. The most plausible explanation for this is that at a monthly horizon, losses are more frequent, scaring anyone who is loss-averse. The broader implication is that investors who focus too much on short-term fluctuations will over-estimate stock market risk and allocate too little of their money to equities.

Another undesirable consequence of narrow framing is the disposition effect, the finding that when investors sell stocks, they typically sell stocks that have gone up in value relative to their purchase price rather than stocks that have gone down. This is not a sensible practice, because on average, stocks display short-term momentum: a stock that has recently gone down in value will, on average, continue to go down even further over the next six months. It is not hard to guess at the underlying cause of the disposition effect: if investors pay too much attention to the gains and losses of individual stocks that they own, it is probably difficult for them to close out their investment in a specific stock at a loss.

Ambiguity aversion

People are excessively fearful of situations of ambiguity where they feel they have little information about the financial gambles they are considering. In experiments, people are much more willing to bet that a ball drawn at random from an urn containing 100 balls is blue when they know the distribution of black and blue balls to be 50:50, than when they know only that the urn contains 100 black and blue balls, but not the proportion of each. In a financial setting, ambiguity aversion suggests that investors will be more wary of stocks that they feel they don't "understand". The flip-side of such aversion is a preference for the familiar, or an excessive liking for gambles about which investors feel they have good information.

Preference for the familiar is a leading explanation of the dramatic under-diversification displayed by many investors. First, there is extensive home bias: over 90 per cent of the equity allocation of investors in the US, UK and Japan is to domestic equities, in spite of the amply demonstrated benefits of international diversification. Other studies have found home bias within countries: investors often hold a disproportionate number of shares in local companies. Finally, studies in the US have found that in their defined contribution pension plans, investors allocate heavily to their own company stock, leaving themselves dangerously underdiversified.

Researchers have tried to find rational explanations of these effects, but with limited success. One explanation, but certainly not a justification, is that an investor's home country, his local region and the company he works for are familiar settings, and he prefers familiar investments.

Exploiting psychology

There are at least two ways that knowing about such bias can be helpful. First, knowing that these mistakes are common will alert investors to the possibility of making them. When about to trade a stock based on some research, investors should stop to consider whether, like so many others, they are over-confident about the analysis. When investors see a string of good earnings announcements from a company, they should be careful not to jump too quickly to the conclusion that this is a company with a high long-term growth rate. Investors with a long investment horizon should avoid worrying too much about short-term fluctuations in the stock market.

Once investors have tried to purge decision-making of such bias, they can take a more aggressive approach and try to design strategies that exploit the hapless investors who are still subject to them. Of course, some care is required here: the more people cure themselves of bias, the less profitable such strategies will be. Nonetheless, some bias is so deep-seated that it may be a long time before investors cure it completely.

As a simple example, consider narrow framing. If people engage in this, they will over-estimate the risk of stocks and insist on a high rate of return to compensate for the risk. Specifically, they will lower their demand for stocks until the price falls sufficiently for them to be able to expect a high rate of return. In fact, the historic rate of return on equities has been much higher than can be explained by standard measures of risk – the so-called equity premium puzzle – and increasingly people believe narrow framing may be the cause. If we believe in narrow framing, we must also believe the future equity premium will be high. For an investor who does not engage in narrow framing and who therefore does not find stocks to be so risky, this higher premium is effectively a free lunch, and one that can be captured by investing more aggressively in equities.

Representativeness, meanwhile, suggests that value strategies will be profitable. Such strategies direct investors towards stocks that trade at low multiples of price to fundamentals such as earnings. If a company reports a series of disappointing earnings, investors who over-use representativeness will come to the premature conclusion that the company is a long-term dud and will push the stock price too far down. Since the stock is now undervalued, a value strategy may earn high returns as the stock eventually corrects to a more reasonable level. In fact, over the past three decades, value strategies have, on average, been highly profitable. An investor who believes this is partly caused by representativeness, and also believes that representativeness is a deep-seated bias, will want to continue pursuing such strategies.

As discussed earlier, conservatism can lead to a post-earnings announcement drift, an effect that can be exploited by investors. Conservatism predicts that prices will not react sufficiently to other kinds of corporate news, such as dividend initiations or announcements of share repurchases, so there should also be a price drift after these announcements that can be exploited. This prediction has been confirmed by US data: dividend initiations and repurchase announcements are, on average, followed by unusually high returns.

A final word of caution. This article has taken the view that many investors suffer from the same kind of psychological bias and that their ill-informed demand pushes prices away from fundamental value, presenting savvy investors with potentially free lunches. There is, however, a significant fraction of academics who, in spite of mounting evidence, believe that prices always reflect fundamental value and that the efficient markets hypothesis holds. These academics often concede that many of the phenomena discussed in this article – the high level of trading, historic profitability of value strategies, the disposition effect and the equity premium puzzle – cannot easily be explained in a world of rational investors. However, they believe that the right way forward is to redouble their efforts within the rational model rather than give in to the potentially undisciplined alternative of behavioural finance where, it is said, it may be all too easy to think up stories that can explain any historical fact.

This academic conflict has important implications for investors. Efficient markets devotees argue that value strategies earn high returns not because they exploit investor bias but because they are riskier. If this is correct, there is no free lunch in value strategies and no reason to favour them over any other strategy. The difficulty with this view is that economists have been unable to find a plausible measure of risk under which value strategies are indeed riskier; nonetheless, it is a possibility that cannot be ruled out.

Ultimately, the battle between efficient markets theory and behavioural finance theory will be decided by each theory's ability to predict phenomena not previously known. Researchers are working on understanding and testing the broader predictions of the two models. If behavioural finance comes through this process successfully, its place in financial economics will be secure.

Further reading

Barber, B.M. and Odean, T. (2000) "Trading is hazardous to your wealth: the common stock investment performance of individual investors", *Journal of Finance*, 55, April.

Shefrin, H. (1999) *Beyond Greed and Fear*, Cambridge, MA: Harvard Business School Press.

Shiller, R. (2000) *Irrational Exuberance*, Princeton, NJ: Princeton University Press.

Shleifer, A. (2000) *Inefficient Markets*, New York: Oxford University Press.

Thaler, R. (ed.) (1993) *Advances in Behavioral Finance*, New York: Russell Sage Foundation.

In search of money for nothing

Francisco Gomes is an assistant professor of finance at London Business School.

In theory, arbitrage opportunities should not exist. The fact that they do and prices can deviate from fundamentals gives investors a powerful tool, says **Francisco Gomes**.

Arbitrage is one of the most important concepts in modern finance theory. An arbitrage opportunity is an investment that requires no net outflow of cash and carries no chance of losing money, yet has some probability of yielding a positive return. The classic example of an arbitrage opportunity occurs when two assets offer the same returns but trade at different prices. Faced with this situation, an arbitrageur will buy the cheaper asset and short-sell the more expensive one. Doing this provides an immediate benefit of cash (the difference in prices) and there is nothing to pay for in the future, because the cash flows associated with the long and the short positions offset each other. Thus the investor gets money for nothing.

What about a strategy that requires an initial investment but guarantees a profit that exceeds this investment at some time in the future? Is this an arbitrage opportunity? After all, the investor knows no money will be lost. In fact, comparing an initial investment with a future return is like comparing apples with oranges and we cannot describe this investment as an arbitrage opportunity without additional information. For example, suppose a default-free government bond is trading at par and will pay a fixed coupon rate at maturity. Buying this bond requires an initial investment but gives a guaranteed higher return at maturity. This is not an arbitrage opportunity as the investor is just receiving a fair compensation for lending money.

The no-arbitrage principle and the law of one price

In the economists' world of perfect markets, arbitrage opportunities are ruled out in equilibrium if we make the plausible assumption that there exists at least one investor who wants more wealth. Suppose an arbitrage opportunity does exist: one stock becomes over-priced relative to another combination of assets that generates exactly the same future cash flows. Then, all rational investors in search of more wealth will hold a short position in this stock and a long position in the alternative assets. These investors make money immediately and are fully hedged. Yet by following this strategy, the rational investors will bid down the price of the expensive asset and bid up the price of the alternative assets, until the two have converged and the arbitrage opportunity is eliminated. Therefore we can rule out arbitrage opportunities just by assuming market equilibrium and the existence of rational investors who want more. As the economists put it: "There is no free lunch."

The absence of arbitrage implies the law of one price: two perfect substitutes must trade at the same price. (Perfect substitutes are products or instruments that are identical in their investment characteristics.) This result is extremely helpful because it allows us to price complicated financial instruments by replication, that is, instead of trying to measure an instrument's true value directly we just need to find a portfolio of perfect substitutes whose price we can directly observe.

One application of the law of one price is the famous Black-Scholes option-pricing formula, derived by professors Fischer Black, Robert Merton and Myron Scholes, which constitutes the basis of modern option pricing theory. They were faced with the task of pricing financial options, which are financial instruments with complicated cash flow structures. They solved the problem by identifying a specific portfolio of stocks and bonds that acted as a perfect substitute for the option. Because we know the prices of the stocks and the bonds, we can easily compute the price of the option. Another application came from the work of academics Franco Modigliani and Merton Miller. They used the arbitrage principle to establish their capital structure irrelevance proposition: in perfect capital markets, making changes to the capital structure of the company does not change the value of the company.

Risk arbitrage

As mentioned above, under perfect capital markets, the condition required for ruling out arbitrage opportunities is that just one investor wants more wealth. Recently, however, financial economists have begun to study a slightly different concept – risk arbitrage. In most financial markets, as pointed out by academics Andrei Shleifer and Robert Vishny (1997), if assets are mispriced and therefore fail to trade at their fundamental value, this does not generate pure arbitrage but "risk arbitrage".

Suppose that an arbitrageur knows that a given asset is over-priced. To take advantage of this opportunity, the arbitrageur must simultaneously sell the asset and buy a perfect substitute that is "correctly priced" – in more technical terms, the perfect substitute is trading at its fundamental value. This perfect substitute must be an asset or (replicating) portfolio that will deliver exactly the same cash flows in the future, so the arbitrageur is fully hedged. In reality, though, such a substitute might be hard to find, depending on the asset one wants to mimic. For example, a perfect substitute for US three-month Treasury bills is easier to find than a perfect substitute for shares of Amazon.com.

When perfect substitutes do not exist, arbitrageurs must face the idiosyncratic risk associated with both the long and the short positions: these positions no longer cancel each other out exactly. The concept of arbitrage relies on the notion of price convergence: the price of the expensive asset will eventually converge to the fundamental price given by the price of replicating portfolio and when this happens the arbitrageur will make money. If the replicating portfolio is not a perfect substitute, the investment strategy is not a pure arbitrage opportunity. The two prices might not converge or they might diverge much more before they converge and the investor might end up losing money.

Even when it is possible to find a perfect substitute, the opportunity for arbitrage might still be limited in certain markets because of restrictions placed on short-selling. And even if there are no such restrictions, short positions are more risky for investors because they carry margin requirements that force them to put down collateral payments. These payments are marked-to-market, which means that every day investors must cover their losses. If the price gap widens, they will be required to increase the margin deposit. As a result, arbitrageurs might need capital to finance their strategies, otherwise they will be forced to liquidate their position at a loss. This is therefore an example of risk arbitrage. Investors do not make money with absolute certainty and may need to invest significant capital before the price convergence eventually occurs.

The technology bubble

Imagine an investor in April 1999 who believes the Nasdaq is substantially over-valued. The tracking stock of the Nasdaq 100 Index (known as "The Qs" for its ticker symbol QQQ) climbs to $60 by July 1999 and the investor decides to sell it short. This immediately presents a problem: what is a perfect substitute for the Nasdaq? How can the position be hedged? One way is to take a position in US Treasury bills, if stocks appear over-valued relative to government bonds. Alternatively, if technology stocks appear over-priced relative to other stocks, the investor can take a position in a value fund – a mutual fund that invests predominantly in "old economy stocks".

Either way will present some idiosyncratic risk. If the investor kept the position until April 2001, there would have been a substantial return as the tracking stock was trading at close to $35. However, before this correction took place, the Nasdaq 100 index was substantially higher, reaching a peak of close to $120 by March 2000. At this point, the investor would have been faced with substantial margin calls and would probably have been required to liquidate the position at a heavy loss.

Professional arbitrage

Under these conditions the arbitrageur's initial investment is limited by the capital that can be raised to meet potential future margin requirements. In perfect capital markets this would not be a problem. As the price gap increases, the arbitrage opportunity becomes even more attractive. Every rational investor would want to lend money to the arbitrageur, knowing it would be paid back after the convergence takes place. In other words, the arbitrageur would have unlimited funds, or alternatively there would be an infinite number of small arbitrageurs. As a result the price convergence would occur immediately as they would bid up the price of the under-valued asset and bid down the price of the over-valued asset.

However, in financial markets arbitrage is commonly conducted by a relatively small number of specialized professionals (such as hedge fund managers), who combine their knowledge with the resources of outside investors. In general, investors do not know or understand the strategies or specialist knowledge of the arbitrageurs (and arbitrageurs have no incentive to reveal such knowledge).

This separation creates an asymmetric information problem, as arbitrageurs and their investors must make decisions based on different degrees of information. If the position of the arbitrageur deteriorates, the investors might attribute this to a temporary increase in the mispricing, or they might attribute it to incompetence on the part of the arbitrageur. If the mispricing has increased, the arbitrageur will need extra money to meet additional margin requirements. It may be in investors' interests to provide the extra money if the arbitrage opportunity is now an even better deal than before.

However, if investors suspect that the bad performance is due to a lack of skill or bad judgement, they may withdraw funds, forcing the arbitrageur to close the position at a loss. Knowing this, arbitrageurs might choose not to explore certain (risky) arbitrage opportunities. This "performance-based arbitrage" is much less effective at preventing prices from deviating from their fundamental values. It is particularly ineffective when prices are substantially far from fundamentals and arbitrageurs are already strongly invested.

Clearly this problem is less severe when the fundamental value of the asset is easy to measure, such as in bond markets when the default risk is small and convergence is guaranteed at the expiration date of the bond. However, it is far harder to measure the fundamental value of a stock or the default risk of a junk bond. Also, in the case of a bond, investors know its terminal value, so the maturity date gives an upper bound for convergence. In the case of a stock, there is no guarantee of how long it will take before it reverts to its fundamental value, prompting the warning: "The market can stay mispriced for longer than you can stay solvent."

Therefore, unlike pure arbitrage, risk arbitrage is not strong enough to correct all sources of mispricing. Further, risk arbitrage might even contribute to the mispricing, as the next example will show.

Destabilizing arbitrage

For individual stocks, one of the strongest predictors of future short-run performance is past short-run performance. This phenomenon is known as the "momentum effect" in stock returns and is usually visible at horizons of three to six months: stocks that have outperformed the market over that period are more likely to do so again in the next three to six months.

One potential explanation for this effect is that investors follow "positive feedback strategies" as they extrapolate future performance from past performance. In other words, they tend to buy more stocks when their price goes up and they sell them when their price goes down. This creates a cycle that continues until prices revert to their fundamental positions.

In the presence of this type of momentum effect, what should an arbitrageur do? When prices are being bid up, the investor knows they will eventually revert and therefore there is money to be made by shorting the underlying assets. As mentioned above, by following this strategy the investor must have enough capital to be able to meet potential margin requirements, in case the over-reaction rises unexpectedly high. However, in this case the investor can do better by "jumping on the bandwagon" – prices are more likely to rise for a while before they revert to fundamentals and so the best strategy is to buy the asset and sell it just in time. The arbitrageur will thus contribute to bidding up the prices, at least temporarily.

Conclusion

Arbitrage is one of the most powerful concepts in financial economics. In a simplistic world with perfect capital markets, pure arbitrage opportunities are ruled out by basic assumptions. Under these conditions we can price complicated financial instruments indirectly, just by identifying portfolios of alternative assets that act as a perfect substitute. Furthermore, we can compute those prices without any information about the risk attitudes of the relevant investors.

In perfect capital markets the no-arbitrage condition must hold regardless of investors' risk aversion. As we consider relevant deviations from this ideal, arbitrage can sometimes be replaced by risk arbitrage. As a result, mispricing can exist in equilibrium.

Copyright © Francisco Gomes 2002

Further reading

Dybvig, P.H. and Ross, S. (1989) "Arbitrage", in *The New Palgrave: A Dictionary of Economics*, Palgrave.

Varian, H.R. (1987) "The arbitrage principle in financial economics", *Journal of Economic Perspectives*, Fall, 55–72.

Shleifer, A. and Vishny, R. (1997) "The limits of arbitrage", *Journal of Finance*, 52, 35–55.

The perils for investors of human nature

People tend to take the credit for success and blame failure on bad luck. The resulting over-confidence can be dangerous, warn **Simon Gervais** and **Terrance Odean**.

Simon Gervais is an assistant professor of finance at the Wharton School of the University of Pennsylvania.

Terrance Odean is an assistant professor of finance at the University of California, Davis.

People constantly learn about their abilities by observing the consequences of their actions. They assess their abilities not so much through introspection as by observing successes and failures. Yet they tend to take too much credit for their own successes. This can lead to over-confidence. Investors, like others, may attribute too much of their success to personal skill and not enough to good fortune. They may become over-confident in their abilities and as a result make investment decisions that are not in their best interests.

This process takes place in most walks of life: a newly graduated lawyer may be uncertain about her cross-examination skills, a teenager entering a new school may not fully appreciate his level of skill in a particular subject, or a footballer may not be able to ascertain precisely the level of success he can achieve as a professional. In these circumstances, people learn by doing, that is, they adjust their views about their ability to perform a given task through their performance of that task.

For investors, the learning process involves taking positions in financial securities and looking at the profits (or losses) that these positions then generate.

Psychologists have shown that there is a self-serving bias in how people learn about their abilities. When successful, people tend to credit success to their abilities. When they fail, they blame failure on bad luck or on others. Self-serving bias can lead people to become over-confident in their abilities and knowledge. Such over-confidence has been observed in many fields. Clinical psychologists, physicians and nurses, investment bankers, engineers, entrepreneurs, lawyers, negotiators and managers have all been observed to exhibit over-confidence in their judgements. Investors, too, may be over-confident.

Effect on investors

Over-confidence is potentially harmful to investors only if it affects their behaviour. This is likely to be the case because over-confident investors believe their ability to profit from analyzing and interpreting financial information is greater than it really is. Over-confidence will affect trading behaviour in a number of ways.

In a 2000 study, researchers Brad Barber and Terrance Odean found that investors at a large discount brokerage held an average of only four to five common stocks. While some gained further diversification through mutual funds, many did not. Over-confident investors may underdiversify portfolios because they are too sure their stocks choices are the right ones. Investors who are sure they are right do not see the point of hedging. Such over-confident investors will invest too much in strategies that they perceive as profitable, underestimating or even ignoring the risks. As a result, their portfolios will tend to be riskier than warranted by the available information and their ability to bear risk.

Over-confident investors tend to trade too much. While an investor who has no confidence in his ability to pick common stocks might buy and hold a broad-based mutual fund, the over-confident investor is likely to routinely buy stocks he feels are winners. By trading too much, over-confident investors add to aggregate market trading volume. Increased trading activity is not necessarily damaging to financial markets (in fact, large trading volume may increase liquidity in these markets); however, unnecessary transaction costs can only be detrimental to investors. Barber and Odean show that, in a sample of more than 60,000 households, the 20 per cent of investors who traded most actively underperformed the 20 per cent that traded least actively by more than five percentage points a year.

What happens to over-confident investors when the positions that they thought were justified by analysis do not pan out? For one thing, they start learning the errors of their ways and readjust their beliefs towards a more objective view of themselves. In the long term, investors who systematically examine the outcomes of their decisions will gain a realistic appreciation of their abilities. The length of time a given investor takes to reach a more reasonable perspective depends on the frequency with which he gets feedback and the perspective and judgement he uses in examining such feedback. This process is likely to be quicker for professional traders whose job is to analyze the market and whose absolute and relative performance is frequently examined. For a casual investor who makes only a few investment bets a year, the process may take longer.

Mature investors are therefore less likely to be over-confident than their younger counterparts or inexperienced investors who have not been trading for long. The relatively short trading history of young investors can make them more prone to errors in their self-assessment, especially if they have an early string of profits. While these profits could have resulted from innate ability, they could also be the product of simple luck. The problem is that it is difficult to distinguish ability from luck in the short term. As a result, investors who are young and lucky are likely to be over-confident.

Over-confidence and markets

The adverse effects of over-confidence on investors are clear, but does over-confidence also affect market prices? This is an unresolved controversy. The extent to which investors affect market prices depends on their willingness and ability to trade. Wealthy investors who are willing to bear risk have more influence than those who are poor or averse to risk. Investors will not necessarily have greater influence on prices simply because they are not over-confident. Wealthy, over-confident investors may influence markets as much as their less over-confident brethren.

Several investors – over-confident or not – may influence prices as much as one wealthy investor if they share the same opinions. If over-confident investors differ in their opinions, they will increase market trading volume but, because their actions are offsetting, have little influence on prices. If, however, a significant group of over-confident investors take aggressive positions in the same securities, they are likely to move prices.

"Don't confuse brains with a bull market," warns an old Wall Street adage. Investors who fail to heed this advice are likely to become over-confident in a bull market. Those who profit from buying small speculative stocks may become convinced that this is the optimal investment for savvy investors such as themselves. They may pour more of their resources into such stocks, even borrowing on margin to do so, and drive prices still higher. Even if other investors realize that their over-confident counterparts are misled, the risks associated with the short positions required to bring prices back to a justifiable level may be too high. Knowing that if prices rise further they may be forced to take losses on short positions may keep reasonable investors from acting. Thus self-attribution bias and over-confidence can contribute to and extend a price bubble.

Some argue that over-confident investors and others who do not behave optimally are of little importance because they will be driven out of markets as more strategic investors exploit their mistakes. If over-confident investors thereby decrease sufficiently in wealth and numbers, they may not affect prices. If, however, success leads investors to become over-confident, many of them will be wealthy. They will be in no immediate danger of being driven from markets. These investors, who trade more aggressively due to their over-confidence and in greater quantities due to their wealth, are likely to affect prices, at least in the short to medium term.

What about the long run? At first, the destabilizing effects of over-confidence seem possible only for short periods: after all, traders do eventually learn about their abilities and over-confidence fades. In a world where no new people decide to participate in financial markets, over-confidence may disappear.

However, every year, securities exchanges welcome new participants who have yet to learn about their abilities to assess the market. Furthermore, it is likely that investors who are fresh entrants to the trading bandwagon are, on average, over-confident at the outset. Over-confidence leads them to believe they can be successful traders. This process, in which new investors continue to stream into the market, leads to the propagation of over-confidence through people and time, with lasting effects on markets, even if the market is competitive.

Just as the over-confidence of an investor is likely to vary with personal experience, so too is the aggregate over-confidence of financial markets likely to vary. Most investors have long positions in financial assets. In a bull market, investors are successful and are likely to become over-confident, so aggregate over-confidence rises. This results in increased trading activity and, possibly, speculative bubbles. Conversely, bear markets tend to reduce aggregate over-confidence.

The extent to which over-confidence influences financial markets is, ultimately, an empirical question. Researchers face a significant challenge in separating the effects of over-confidence from those of other economic factors.

Conclusion

The human tendency to take too much credit for one's own successes while blaming one's failures on bad luck or others can lead successful investors to become over-confident. While successful investors may have more actual ability than others, they are likely not to have as much as they think they have.

Over-confident investors are likely to trade too actively and damage their own financial welfare. They may also buy portfolios that are inappropriately risky simply because they are too sure in their opinions and therefore underestimate their risks. Since successful investors will tend to become both over-confident and wealthy, over-confident investors may have a disproportionate influence on markets. This is particularly likely when such investors hold similar views. An individual investor's over-confidence will not flourish indefinitely; time and experience gradually rid him of it. However, in a market in which new investors are born every minute, over-confidence will flourish.

This article is based on "Learning to be overconfident", published in the *Review of Financial Studies 14*, Spring 2001, 1–27.

Coppyright © Simon Gervais and Terrance Odean 2002

Further reading

Barber, B.M. and Odean, T. (2000) "Trading is hazardous to your wealth: the common stock investment performance of individual investors", *Journal of Finance*, 55, April.

Daniel, K., Hirshleifer, D. and Subrahmanyam, A. (1998) "Investor psychology and security market under- and over-reactions", *Journal of Finance*, 53, December.

De Long, J.B., Shleifer, A., Summers, L.H. and Waldmann, R.J. (1990) "Noise trader risk in financial markets", *Journal of Political Economy*, 98, August.

Gervais, S. and Odean, T. (2001) "Learning to be overconfident", *Review of Financial Studies*, 14, Spring.

The curious case of Palm and 3Com

Market participants should quickly destroy any discrepancies in stock valuations, but this does not always happen. **Owen Lamont** introduces the law of one price and explains how it can be broken.

Owen A. Lamont is an associate professor of finance at the University of Chicago Graduate School of Business.

Former US Treasury Secretary Lawrence Summers once described finance professors as practitioners of ketchup economics: "They have shown that two quart bottles of ketchup invariably sell for twice as much as one quart bottle of ketchup except for deviations traceable to transaction costs ... Indeed, most ketchup economists regard the efficiency of the ketchup market as the best established fact in empirical economics." Summers was right. Arbitrage, defined as the simultaneous buying and selling of the same security for two different prices, is the central concept of modern finance. The absence of arbitrage is the basis of most modern financial theory, including option pricing and corporate capital structure.

In capital markets, the law of one price says that identical securities must have identical prices, otherwise investors could make unlimited profits by buying the cheap one and selling the expensive one. It does not require that investors be rational or sophisticated, only that they are able to recognize arbitrage opportunities. Because arbitrageurs can make profits by enforcing this law, it should be almost impossible to break in a well-functioning capital market. The law of one price is a basic, common-sense condition, so theorists have used it as a minimal condition, a starting point that leads to other implications.

Market disturbance

Unfortunately, something very disturbing happened in US capital markets during the recent technology stock mania. The law of one price was violated. A prominent example is the price of Palm relative to 3Com. On 2 March 2000, 3Com sold part of its stake in handheld computer maker Palm. In this transaction, called an equity carve-out, 3Com sold about 4 per cent of its stake in Palm in an initial public offering and about 1 per cent to a consortium of companies. It kept 95 per cent of the shares. Palm shares were issued at $38. On the first day of trading, Palm immediately went to $150 and later rose to $165, before ending the day at $95.06.

Based on the relative number of shares of Palm and 3Com, a holder of one share of 3Com stock indirectly owned 1.5 shares of Palm stock. Based on 3Com's ownership of Palm alone, at the end of the first day of trading, 3Com shares were worth at least $142.59. 3Com, in addition to owning Palm, held cash and securities worth more than $10 a share, and ran a substantial and profitable network business. Thus one might expect 3Com to trade substantially above $142.59.

In fact, 3Com's value was $81.81 (3Com's stock price actually fell 21 per cent during the day). The "stub value" or implied value of 3Com's non-Palm assets and businesses is the difference between the lower bound of $142.59 and observed price $81.81, or –$60.78. The equity market gave a negative implied value to 3Com's other assets, which is puzzling since stock prices cannot be negative.

Most puzzling of all, 3Com had announced its intention to spin off its remaining shares of Palm, pending a decision from the US Internal Revenue Service on the tax status of the spin-off. The spin-off was expected to take place by the end of the year and a favourable ruling was highly likely. To profit from the mispricing, an arbitrageur would need to buy one share of 3Com, short 1.5 shares of Palm and wait less than a year. In essence, the arbitrageur would be buying a security worth at least zero for –$60.78 and would not need to wait long to realize the profits. As shown in Figure 1, this strategy (if one had been able to implement it with no transaction costs) would have been very profitable. The stub value of 3Com gradually rose until the distribution took place.

This mispricing was not in an obscure corner of capital markets, but in an IPO that attracted frenzied attention. On the day after the issue, the mispricing was discussed in several newspaper articles.

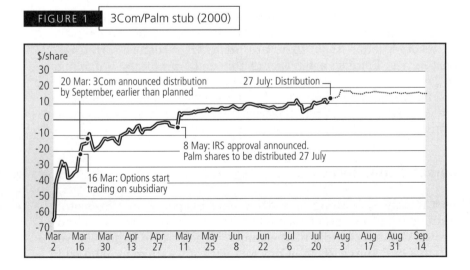

FIGURE 1 3Com/Palm stub (2000)

The 3Com example is not unique. In 1923, for instance, the young Benjamin Graham, later to co-author a classic book on security analysis, became the manager of what would now be called a mutual fund. Graham noticed that Du Pont's market capitalization was about the same as the value of a stake it owned in GM. Du Pont had a stub value of about zero, despite the fact that it was a major company with many valuable assets. Graham bought Du Pont, short-sold GM, and profited when Du Pont later rose in value.

Something is terribly wrong here. This negative implied "stub value" should not be happening. Economists have known about other apparent violations of the law of one price for many years. But these cases have special features that might explain the discrepancy between price and value. While one might be able to dismiss such cases as freakish anomalies, large capitalization stocks trading in Nasdaq should not be mispriced.

Correcting prices

In understanding any violation of the law of one price, there are two questions. First, why don't arbitrageurs correct the mispricing by selling the over-priced security and buying the underpriced security? Second, even if something prevents the arbitrageurs from correcting the mispricing, why would anyone ever buy the over-priced security when they can buy the underpriced security?

The answer to the first question lies in transaction costs. To implement the arbitrage trade, one needs to sell short shares of Palm. Transaction costs arise in two ways: finding shares to short and the cost of holding the short position over time. To be able to sell short a stock, one must borrow it; for institutional reasons, borrowing shares can be difficult or impossible for many equities, especially on the day of the IPO. Even weeks after the IPO, shorting can be difficult. To borrow shares, an investor needs to find a willing lender. Much of this borrowing is typically done through financial institutions, such as mutual funds, trusts or asset managers which lend their securities. In the case of Palm, retail investors rather than institutions held most of the shares, making Palm hard to borrow. For short-sellers who could find shares to borrow, lenders demanded a high payment. This comes in the form of a daily cost to those shorting the stock. In the case of Palm, there were reports of very high holding costs, in the order of 40 per cent a year.

Thus the arbitrage opportunity is more apparent than real, since it is difficult and expensive to sell Palm short. Although not an easily exploitable arbitrage opportunity, this is a case of blatant mispricing. And it's worth noting that some investors did make substantial profits. While these investors did not make infinite arbitrage profits, they were making very high returns on near-arbitrage opportunities. For example, a young finance professor who took advantage of negative stub situations used the proceeds to buy a new car. Finance professors are not generally known for their market savvy or stock-picking success. Compared with institutional investors, they certainly have higher information-gathering and trading costs. So the apparent ability of professors to earn excess returns is troubling for the efficient markets hypothesis.

Evidence from the level of short-selling is consistent with the idea that Palm was over-priced. The level reached an amazing 148 per cent of floating shares, meaning that more than all the available shares had been sold short. This is possible if shares are borrowed, then sold short to an investor who permits the shares to be borrowed again. But it takes time to build this supply of shares, because this shorting market works sluggishly.

Initially, demand for shares was too large for the market to supply via short sales, creating a price that was too high. The upward trend in the stub value of Palm is matched by the upward trend in short sales, so that the graph traces out the demand curve for Palm. As supply of shares grows, we move down the demand curve of Palm investors and the Palm price falls relative to 3Com.

Option prices

The options market offers further evidence on mispricing. Exchange-traded options were introduced two weeks after the IPO. A basic relation that should hold in well-functioning options markets (and another manifestation of the law of one price) is put-call parity. Put-call parity almost always holds (taking into account transactions costs) for most stocks. Without going into detail, put-call parity says that the price of Palm should be the same as the price of a synthetic security, constructed using puts and calls (types of options) on Palm. This synthetic security has the same pay-off as Palm stock, so it should have the same price. Options prices for Palm massively violated put-call parity: puts were very expensive, calls were very cheap. These option prices are consistent with Palm being over-priced but costly to sell short.

We have three ways of inferring Palm's true value: the embedded value reflected in 3Com's share price, the value reflected in options prices, and the actual price. The market for options and shareholders in 3Com seemed to agree: Palm was worth far less than its market price. The direction of the deviation from the law of one price is consistent with the difficulty of shorting Palm. To profit from the difference between the synthetic security and the underlying security, one would need to short Palm and buy the synthetic long. If shorting is costly, then the deviation from the law of one price can be interpreted as the cost of borrowing Palm shares.

By comparing option prices with the actual price for Palm, one can calculate the implied cost of shorting. During 2000, this cost of shorting fell as the stub value rose. The pattern shows that options prices adjust to virtually eliminate profitable trading opportunities. Put differently, the implied cost of shorting falls as the desirability of shorting falls.

Although it is difficult to profit from the mispricing, one can always turn the question around and ask why anyone buys Palm. Options give investors a third way to buy Palm: they can buy Palm directly, buy it indirectly by buying 3Com, or buy it indirectly by buying calls (and selling puts). The second two methods are much cheaper than the first, so it is puzzling why anyone would buy Palm directly.

Why buy Palm?

Putting aside the failure of arbitrage, the second question is why anyone would buy a share of Palm for $95.06 when they could buy a share of 3Com (embedding 1.5 shares of Palm) for $81.81. One superficially appealing explanation for the mispricing is that the price of Palm is high because demand for shares outstrips supply. While undoubtedly true, this does not explain much. Why were Palm shareholders content to pay so much more when cheaper choices were available (such as 3Com stock or Palm options)? At one point when the stub value of 3Com was negative, investors worth more than $2.5bn thought that Palm was a better buy than 3Com.

While it is impossible to say what, if anything, was going through these investors' minds, there are clues. Numerous press reports mentioned that without Palm, 3Com's future growth was expected to be lower. For example, in the week after the IPO, a headline from *The Wall Street Journal* read: "3Com faces bleaker future without Palm." Investors may have simply pursued the idea that Palm was good and 3Com was bad, without pausing to do the calculations.

More generally, early 2000 was a time of great optimism about technology stocks. Between February 1999 and February 2000, the tech-heavy Nasdaq Composite Index more than doubled. One dramatic illustration of this optimism occurred in Hong Kong. In February 2000, chaos erupted when crowds gathered at 10 banks and police were called. Some branches closed and others extended their hours to accommodate the mob. A bank run? Sort of. But instead of fighting to get their money out, people were fighting to get their money in. They were applying to subscribe to the IPO of tom.com, an internet company. According to some sources, 300,000 people queued to apply and more than 453,000 applications were submitted, so that almost 7 per cent of the population subscribed to the IPO.

Market implications

There are two important implications of the efficient markets hypothesis. The first is that it is not easy to earn excess returns. The second is that prices are "correct" in the sense that they reflect fundamental value. This latter implication is, in many ways, more important than the first. Do asset markets offer rational signals to the economy about where to invest real resources? If some companies have stock prices that are far from intrinsic value, they will attract too much or too little capital.

While important, this aspect of the efficient markets hypothesis is difficult to test because intrinsic values are unobservable. That is why the example of 3Com and Palm is important. It demonstrates that market prices can be wrong when transaction costs prevent arbitrageurs from correcting market mistakes. The example casts doubt on the claim that market prices reflect only rational valuations because it is a case that should be particularly easy for the market to get right. If markets are failing this easy test, what else are they getting wrong?

Stock market prices affect the real world. When prices are wrong, the world suffers. The technology stock mania that peaked in 2000 had real consequences. Money, time and talent were poured into ventures that gave little return. Financial economists have regarded "frictions", such as transaction costs, as minor concerns. Using an analogy from physics, the trajectory of a ball thrown in the air can be predicted using a simple formula that ignores complications such as wind resistance; one can pretend the ball has been thrown into an airless vacuum. While all agree that transaction costs, like wind resistance, exist, the traditional view is that these minor deviations are safe to ignore.

This is a misleading analogy. The case of 3Com and Palm shows that frictions are not minor details but are central to understanding how market prices are determined. It is as if the ball, rather than being thrown into a vacuum, were hurled into a tornado. Although one is sure that the ball will eventually return to earth, ignoring complications is not a good idea.

Copyright © Owen Lamont 2002

Further reading

Lamont, O.A. and Thaler, R.H. (2001) "Can the market add and subtract? Mispricing in tech stock carve-outs", working paper, at
http://gsb-www.uchicago.edu/fac/finance/papers/.

Ross, S.A. (1987) "The interrelations of finance and economics: theoretical perspectives", *American Economic Review*, May, 77 (2): 29–34.

Summers, L.H. (1985) "On economics and finance", *Journal of Finance*, July, 40 (3): 633–5.

The art and craft of reading the market

Analyzing the market, rather than the companies whose shares are traded, is a well-established technique. **Bruce Kamich** believes technical analysis has a golden future.

Bruce M. Kamich is an adjunct professor of finance at Rutgers University and Baruch College. He sits on the boards of the Market Technicians Association and the International Federation of Technical Analysts.

Over the past 30 years technical analysis has become an accepted part of making investment decisions. In dealing rooms, brokerage houses and fund companies, traders and sophisticated investors have access to charting packages, websites and proprietary software. Some colleges and universities have trading rooms and a few even have classes in the subject. The Market Technicians Association, a US industry body, defines technical analysis as "the study of data generated by the action of markets and by the behaviour and psychology of market participants and observers. Such study is usually applied to estimating the probabilities for the future course of prices for a market, investment or speculation by interpreting the data in the context of precedent."

Technical analysis looks at the actions of the market itself, as opposed to the goods in which the market deals. Fundamental analysis looks at statistics about a company relating to business conditions.

Benefits

Results from trading or investing can be put into five simple categories: a big gain, a small gain, a scratch or flat result, a small loss and a big loss. The small gain, small loss and scratch will tend to cancel out over time, leaving two results – a desirable large gain and an undesirable large loss. No matter what one's approach to investing, a few basic tools can help avoid the unforgiving large loss. Closing below a key rising line or a longer-term moving average can signal a major reversal before the economic numbers or earnings have actually eroded.

Imagine you own a stock that has been rising steadily for 18 months as investors anticipate increased earnings for six consecutive quarters. A trend line can be drawn with a ruler connecting the troughs in prices as a stock moves higher. If you maintain the chart every day, eventually the price will close below this significant upward trend. To a technician, this is a signal that the trend of the stock price has shifted from upwards to sideways, or possibly downwards. A technician is not concerned with why prices are turning down. Even what might turn out to be a false sell signal should be followed, because the chance of success is greatly increased if you have a plan to limit losses and the discipline to execute it faithfully.

If you come up with a short list of investment candidates through fundamental analysis, why commit money to a stock whose price is experiencing a downward trend? Studies have shown that concentrating on shares that show superior relative strength rankings will enhance performance.

Logic

Technical analysis is based on three or four underlying assumptions.

Market action or prices discount the future. While the market pays attention to day-to-day developments and unexpected events, it also looks at what people believe will happen. The stock market is a leading indicator.

The market has already discounted the news. One of the oldest sayings on Wall Street is: "Buy the rumour and sell the news." The essence of this well-worn advice can also be seen in the lesser-known adage of "news follows the tape". If someone knows or believes something before most people, their buying or selling will show up in the marketplace. The share price will move before the news is reported. Sometimes news does break before prices react, but all too often a market moves and then you see the rush of the media and the business community to explain why. Often a move may happen without a news event because of a crystallization of traders' thoughts and expectations. Consider movements in interest rates – how many times have you seen US Treasury bonds rally ahead of an expected interest rate cut by the Federal Reserve Bank, only to decline when the cut is announced?

History tends to repeat itself. When people are confronted with the same set of circumstances, they tend to react in similar ways. Things may not happen exactly as they did on previous occasions but human emotions swing from greed at the peak of a market cycle to fear at its trough. Patterns of supply and demand in the price action that technicians observed in 1901, 1951 and 2001 have played out in the same way.

Prices move in trends. A casual examination of charts of securities, commodities, interest rates or currencies will show many examples of prices forming discernible trends. A well-known upward trend is a long-term chart of the Dow Jones Industrial Average from the early 1920s, showing a clear upward slope, with some minor dips from left to right. The chart is used in the sales literature of mutual funds and by financial planners to show the benefit of a buy-and-hold strategy. An upward trend is a succession of higher peaks and higher troughs. A downward trend is a succession of lower peaks and lower troughs.

Before such trends begin, stocks go through periods of accumulation and distribution. Accumulation patterns occur at bottoms and distribution patterns at tops. During the accumulation phase, more informed and far-sighted investors are accumulating stock, counting on better conditions six to nine months ahead. Investors tend to resist paying more for a stock than the price that others have recently paid unless the stock keeps going up – giving the investor the hope or confidence that it will continue to go up. In a downward trend, people will resist selling a stock for less than the price that other people have been getting unless the price keeps sliding and fear builds that it will continue to slide.

Imagine you are reliably informed that a company's new product is a commercial success. If you are a shareholder, you are unlikely to sell your shares because the company is doing well. Or you may buy more shares because business is good. By not selling, or becoming a buyer, you keep shares off the market and reduce supply, so the share price tends to rise. At some point, news of the company's success spreads to brokers, other professional investors and perhaps a wider public. New buyers must pay more for the shares they want. This rationale underlies an upwardly moving trend.

Patterns have relationships. Commodity prices can make sharp moves from an unanticipated change in supply or a share price may jump up sharply from a takeover bid. However, large price moves are normally preceded by large sideways consolidations or trading ranges where the market trades up and down in a band and buyers slowly buy shares and reduce supply. These large consolidations represent the period when investors shift their views and alter their investments by gradually buying. Smaller sideways patterns tend to support only shorter rallies or falls and technicians have observed that the market movements have a relationship to one another. This assumption is important but not necessary to operate as a technician and is not a core belief like the first three.

Tools

Technical analysis is part art and part science. Its tools reflect the nature of the craft. Central to most technicians' work is the price chart. Charts can quickly take a series of data points and present them in a graphic form to reveal underlying trends.

Prices can be shown in many ways: bar charts, candlestick charts, point and figure, swing charts, Equivolume, market profile, kagi, three-line break. However, interpreting these movements is a subjective exercise. Finding a pattern and successfully interpreting it can be complicated by its location. On the chart it might look as if the price is peaking, but if it happens at a relatively low price level technicians should be wary of predicting a fall. Inexperienced investors try to find a major peak or trough pattern in a few days or weeks of activity when major patterns should develop over months. Price patterns should also be accompanied by specific volume patterns and greater success in reading chart patterns can come from using volume along with price.

Prices, volume and other market data have been manipulated into various indicators. When we look at price charts we are concerned directly with prices, but indicators are mathematical constructs that are derivatives of price. Analysts should use indicators as a secondary tool to add value to basic chart analysis or to confirm price signals. Indicators can be divided into three rough groups: trend-following indicators, momentum oscillators, and indicators dealing with market structure.

Trend-following indicators trail the price action. They are partly designed to smooth out price fluctuations so that a trend can be seen as a line. The most important of these indicators are moving averages, which include simple, weighted and exponential forms. A moving average is a mathematical smoothing of the closing price to give a line that represents the price trend. Adding the closing prices for IBM over 10 days and dividing the sum by 10 would construct a 10-day simple moving average for IBM. The average moves forward by adding the next observation, deleting the first and dividing by 10 again. A weighted moving average puts more emphasis on more recent prices and an exponential moving average is another form of weighted moving average.

Momentum oscillators measure the speed at which prices change. An oscillator is constructed so that its values move above and below a midpoint line or zero line. Some oscillators have upper and lower boundaries from 0 to 100 or –1 to +1 depending on their construction. Peaks and troughs in the price action will tend to be mirrored by the ups and downs in the oscillator. They are useful in identifying trends but best applied to trading range markets where prices are fluctuating in a horizontal band. The rate of change of a price advance tends to peak before the price itself. Momentum oscillators therefore tend to be leading or coincident indicators. As a move gets under way, the amount by which the price moves in each period will tend to increase, driven by a growing need of market participants to take part in the rally. But as the move matures and more people have completed their purchases, the amount by which the price moves in each period will tend to decrease.

Indicators dealing with market structure include such tools as the advance-decline line, sentiment indicators, contrary opinion, volume analysis and cycles. The advance-decline line looks at the breadth and confidence of a market movement. At a market bottom, investors tend to buy better-known companies, but as the market rises and the economy improves, more companies participate in the rally, the advance broadens and the advance-decline line rises. The lower the number of stocks moving up in a market advance, the greater the probability of a reversal. The longer a price advance extends without the participation of the broad market or the majority of stocks, the more fragile it is. Here, investors examine the number of advancing issues compared with the declining issues.

Technicians have applied the approach to stocks, corporate bonds, commodities and sectors. A strong market has many more advances than declines. This will continue, confirming the rally, but at some point the number of advances will start to decrease before a peak in the price averages such as the DJIA and the Standard & Poor's 500 indices.

The advance-decline line peaks before major averages for several reasons. First, because the market discounts the business cycle, certain leading sectors such as construction and consumer spending will top out ahead of the rest of the market. Second, about 40 per cent of stocks on the New York Stock Exchange are sensitive to interest rates – such as utilities and finance – and because interest rates tend to rise late in the business cycle, these stocks will fall first. Finally, quality companies will be the last to be sold in a bull market.

Looking ahead

Technical analysis is undergoing a transformation. It is being taught in universities and industry practitioners hold academic positions. In *A Non-Random Walk Down Wall Street*, Andrew Lo and Craig MacKinlay showed that predictable components do exist. More business schools will add trading rooms and finance skills.

Hedge funds use sophisticated technical approaches involving chaos theory and modelling. Many Wall Street investment banks arrange private courses on technical analysis for trainees. Traditional commodity markets have used technical analysis for decades; newer power and energy markets are following suit. The golden age of technical analysis may lie just ahead of us.

Copyright © Bruce Kamich 2002

Further reading

Kaufman, S.K. (1990) "A new method of forecasting trend change dates", *Cycles*, September (http://www.pfr.com/pfr/cycles.pdf).
Kirkpatrick II, C.D. (2001) "A test of relative stock values reported over $17^{1}/_{2}$ years" (http://www.mta.org/awards/01/kirkpatricl.htm).
Murphy, J.J. (1999) *Technical Analysis of the Financial Markets*, New York: New York Institute of Finance.
Pring, M.J. (1991) *Technical Analysis Explained*, New York: McGraw-Hill.

Websites

Federal Reserve Bank of St Louis (http://www.stls.frb.org/research/wp).
Laboratory for Financial Engineering, MIT (http://web.mit.edu/alo/www/).

Governance 9

Contents

Seeking value from changes in Europe 276

Rory Knight, University of Oxford and **Deborah Pretty**, independent strategic adviser

This article argues that a company's corporate governance arrangements – in particular the rules governing its duties towards shareholders – substantially affect the performance of the company and its reception in the market.

Disclosure: inside information for all 281

Ewen Cameron Watt, Merrill Lynch Investment Managers

Investors and the companies in which they invest are engaging in more open debate in developed economies. But still the relationship is complex.

The bottom line to a social conscience 287

Geoffrey Heal, Columbia Business School

Do funds that eschew so-called undesirable businesses perform well? And has the popularity of ethical funds had an influence on managers?

Introduction to Part 9

Corporate governance is an important factor in investment performance. When companies are held accountable and their activities documented and communicated to stakeholders, it seems that shareholders benefit from higher performance. In this part writers take different approaches to the topic: they look at the effects of different governance regimes on international performance as well as the stewardship duties of institutional investors.

Seeking value from changes in Europe

The Rhenish business model is on the wane as Anglo-American values begin to hold sway in continental Europe. **Rory Knight** and **Deborah Pretty** look to the future.

Rory F. Knight is dean emeritus of Templeton College, University of Oxford, where he is fellow in finance.

Deborah J. Pretty is an independent strategic adviser on risk and value.

The performance of European equities has recently looked lacklustre, mainly due to the disappointing performance of the euro. As this article discusses, however, seismic changes in corporate governance should provide the discerning investor with considerable opportunities in the coming years. To judge the future of European investment markets on the mid-term performance of the euro would be a serious error.

Governance structures, such as cross-holdings, pyramid structures and strategic (often family) investments, all of which are common in mainland Europe, discourage the discipline of takeover found in the Anglo-American market and reduce the free-float shares available for trading. This does not mean no market exists for corporate control, but simply that it is not centred on value.

The relationship between corporate governance and performance is complex. However, a simple result emerges. If corporate governance arrangements are not focused on shareholders, the share price is discounted. In the case of the Rhenish or mainland European world, this discount burdens companies with a higher cost of capital. Thus there is a strong economic incentive and an increasing political appetite to change the culture of governance in these markets. There is much value to be realized.

Performance

Let us consider the association between governance and performance. The largest 500 companies in North America have on average created $7.50 for every $1 raised in capital markets. The same companies generated a 7.5 per cent return in excess of their cost of capital. This stands in contrast to the top 500 companies in southeast Asia (excluding Japan), which managed to generate operational cash flow at a rate only 0.1 per cent above their cost of capital, creating $4.70 for every $1 in capital. The value multiplier depends on market expectations of future performance. However, the dispersion in value performance reveals something about governance regimes.

Europe, for example, is currently (in 2001) performing better than the US in generating risk-adjusted operational cash flows. However, in the US, performance is being capitalized at an almost 50 per cent greater multiple; 7.5 versus 5.2. The point is made more sharply by comparing Germany and the US. Germany consists of the top 100 German companies in the Europe 500. The US value multiplier is 2.3 times that of Germany. It is difficult to believe that real growth in the US will outstrip Germany to this extent.

The main source of the continental European discount is the fact that managers are subject to different disciplines. US and UK markets place the shareholder at the centre of corporate governance, allowing the sanction of managers relatively easily. Less-regulated Rhenish markets protect managers from the disciplinary effects of hostile takeovers at the price of a higher cost of capital.

Differences

The main distinction between the two systems revolves around regulation. The Anglo-American model is highly regulated, with the contract between shareholders and managers in public companies specified largely by statute and prohibitions. In contrast, the Rhenish model is largely unregulated – companies are much less restricted. The result of this laissez-faire approach is an idiosyncratic regime that is peculiar to the country in which the company resides. There are three major factors that entrench management in Rhenish companies.

Voting restrictions

It is quite common for Rhenish companies to ignore the principle of "one share, one vote". In Germany, for example, companies may place a ceiling of 5 per cent on the vote of any particular shareholder. This means that if a shareholder or predator builds up a stake beyond 5 per cent, all voting rights above this level effectively devolve to management.

Shareholding structures

The corporate cross-holding and pyramid structure, largely outlawed in the Anglo-American world, are ubiquitous in the Rhenish setting. Cross-holdings arise where a company owns the shares in another, which is one of its own shareholders. In a pyramid structure, a company gains control of another indirectly through a series of corporate investments.

They have two main effects. First, they reduce considerably the free float of shares available for trading. This phenomenon has been highlighted by the adjustment of the MSCI and FTSE stock indices. Hitherto these have been based on total market capitalization. Now the weightings are based on the value of shares after adjustment for cross-holdings and pyramid structures.

The companies most affected are all Rhenish-style companies, including Deutsche Telekom, L'Oréal, France Telecom, Allianz and Munich Re. Second, they tend to protect management from the threat of hostile takeover.

Information and transparency

Rhenish systems tend to be much more opaque than their Anglo-American counterparts. Although financial reporting by European companies has improved, the disclosure of shareholdings is still less transparent.

Challenges

The challenges facing all international investors, active and passive, include currency risk in international portfolios, understanding co-movement among different markets and the selection of stocks. Investors tend to hedge out the effect of currency fluctuation, particularly in volatile markets. This is misguided, since deeper investigation reveals that bilateral exchange rate movements have little to do with share price movements. The arbitrary removal of currency risk may actually increase portfolio risk. Currency risk may offset an element of share price risk and removing currency risk via hedging is not only costly but can make the previously offset risk reappear.

Global investors are very interested in the extent to which markets move together. If all markets are subject to the same factors, any benefits from international diversification will be greatly diminished. Second, if a high and increasing degree of co-movement derives from increased integration of capital markets, many global financing strategies will be futile. In an integrated capital market, the cost of funds will be similar across markets, rendering redundant any attempts to raise capital in global markets for the purpose of reducing the cost of capital.

When selecting stocks, a number of pitfalls await the unwary international investor. Do not run to the security of big names. International investors often opt for well-known stocks in foreign markets, such as Nestlé or Volvo. But these companies are big names precisely because they are global companies and are therefore affected by similar factors in the world economy. Skewing a portfolio towards this group inevitably will dilute the benefits of diversification. Never forget: international capital is lumpy. Outside Anglo-American markets, stock markets are highly concentrated. A significant proportion of total market capitalization is contributed by a few companies. This distorts correlation studies that underlie allocation decisions.

Play your active part in governance. The trend towards international investment and passive diversification has resulted in fewer shareholders participating in the corporate governance of the global companies in which they invest. This is unhealthy for two reasons. First, it allows the performance of entrenched managers to escape the spotlight. Second, the diluted effect of the shareholder sanction and the difficulty of communicating effective performance means managers are likely to worry less about share price performance. Share-based incentive schemes are designed to mitigate these effects.

Globalization may mean investors stay at home. The emergence of global companies means that an increasing proportion of what appears to be domestic capitalization is held in internationally diversified assets. A typical example is Swiss pension funds. Traditionally, these hold only Swiss equities – but the largest Swiss companies, such as Nestlé and Novartis, are themselves global. The global company can act as a surrogate for international portfolio diversification. However, the efficiency of this surrogacy remains unproven and is the subject of much argument.

Information on stocks is not uniformly reliable. There are wide variations in accounting and disclosure practices in different markets. These differences can confuse investors trying to evaluate companies across borders and lead them to make blunders.

Global and local

Although many companies are listed on more than one market, surprisingly few of their shares are held outside their home countries. The much heralded listing of Daimler-Benz on the New York Stock Exchange, for example, resulted in only about 3 per cent ownership in the US. The merger with Chrysler created a company that was about half US owned on the day of the merger. Today the US holding is about 20 per cent.

More recently, under the pressure of privatization, other European companies, including Deutsche Telekom and Aventis, have sought equity capital abroad. But it remains hard to find an example of a global company in which the majority of shares are held outside the home country. Since Nestlé permitted foreigners to own registered shares, it is believed that a little more than half of its shares have become foreign-held. Estimates also suggest that foreigners hold considerably less than half of the voting rights.

Novo Nordisk, the Danish pharmaceuticals company, did place about 80 per cent of its "B-class" shares internationally in the 1980s, representing about 35 per cent of voting rights. This was highly successful and allowed Novo to reduce its cost of capital and place it on a more competitive footing. However, during the 1990s, Novo experienced a significant flow of shares back to Denmark, with the result that more than 80 per cent are now once more in Danish hands.

Most foreign listings in New York are held in American depositary receipts. In this arrangement, a package of the shares of a non-US company is placed with a US bank to open a local book in the stock. This concept has been extended to global depositary receipts, whereby such books can be opened on more than one exchange simultaneously. While a useful innovation, the existence of such devices itself demonstrates that markets remain far from integrated.

Some Anglo-Dutch combines have evolved in a different way. Royal Dutch/Shell and Reed Elsevier merged but kept domestic listings in place. Thus, Reed Elsevier is not a listed entity, although it is possible to invest indirectly via Reed International in London or Elsevier in Amsterdam.

Conclusion

The stage is set for a period of value creation in Europe. Tempted by the release of latent value, European companies are likely to take the lead in changing their governance arrangements and increasing transparency. Second, market forces will chip away at takeover protection. The hostile takeover of the German Mannesmann by the UK's Vodafone illustrates the point. Mannesmann's managers joined battle in Anglo-American style, eschewing the protection of many of the usual Rhenish devices.

In January 2001, two changes of significance occurred: the final stage of the euro and the abolition of capital gains taxes for German companies. These events reflect the wider changes taking place in Europe. Both will have a considerable impact and will accelerate the deconstruction and reinvention of Rhenish governance.

Copyright © Rory Knight and Deborah Pretty 2002

Further reading

Bertoneche, M. and Knight, R. (2000) *Financial Performance*, London: Butterworth-Heinemann.

Knight, R. (1991) "Optimal currency hedging and international asset allocation: an integration", *Finanzmarkt und Portfolio Management*, 5, 2, 130–63.

Disclosure:
inside information for all

The relationship between large investors and the companies in which they invest is changing. **Ewen Cameron Watt** describes the new landscape.

Ewen Cameron Watt is global head of investment strategy and research at Merrill Lynch Investment Managers.

Twenty years ago some young stockbrokers were greeted with the instruction: "There's no substitute for inside information." Although offered in jest, this statement held more than a grain of truth. Stock analysis was based on "informed" briefings to sell- and buy-side professionals. The term "investor relations" in many markets meant just that – relation (by blood) of investors to the controlling shareholder. Minority shareholders were, in every respect, a minority. One of the most profound changes for institutional investors has been in their relationships with portfolio investments. A culture where the few sought benefit from privileged information has been replaced with one based on even-handed disclosure.

Introduction in 2000 of a regulation on corporate disclosure by the Securities and Exchange Commission in the US profoundly altered the landscape of investor relations. Forcing a statutory code for disclosure of material information onto companies has significantly increased the number of trading statements. Equally, it has increased the proportion of such announcements that are "neutral" and merely confirm what the market already assumed. The SEC has changed the relationship between company and shareholder. In effect, Regulation FD immediately translates short-term performance to share prices. Little or no first-mover advantage exists. Institutional investors' behaviour has begun to respond, paying more attention to fundamental valuation, medium-term strategy and corporate governance, and less to immediate news.

In the UK, although regulation is less explicit, similar patterns have evolved. Companies no longer give privileged information to favoured analysts or shareholders. Information flows straight from company to share price, leaving little opportunity (other than criminal behaviour) for over-informed speculation. Increasingly, investors focus more on business plans and corporate governance than on the immediate outlook for profits.

Outside developed economies, the game may be played by different rules. Knowledge is still power, more so if vested interests are able to profit from it. It is a fallacy, by the way, to imagine there is any relationship between frequency of disclosure and a level playing field. Taiwanese companies, for example, disclose sales and profit figures monthly. Yet few would claim the Taiwan Stock Exchange is less prone to manipulation than, say, the US or UK markets. If companies feel directed towards regulated disclosure, investors are equally bound. Investor relations becomes the field where these regulatory patterns unfold.

Plural relations

Fund managers' relations with companies differ by type of investor. A strategic industrial shareholder has different priorities from a pension fund. Hedge fund investors may well have their own agenda and offshore investors will reflect their home market practices when investing abroad. This melange is often confusing for listed companies seeking to align operational policies with the objectives of capital providers.

Even within apparently homogenous investor groups, significant differences arise. Take, for example, hedge funds. A long-short market-neutral manager may well focus on an incidental consequence of corporate policy such as share price volatility. By contrast, a directional manager may buy and sell companies where profit announcements exceed or disappoint market expectations and thus engages from a different perspective. More traditional investors may also differ, with some using active management, others passive management.

Active and passive managers' investment processes differ so much that they must have differing, albeit adjacent, approaches to their investment holdings. In essence, passive managers have limited discretion in raising capital. Their first consideration is the degree of tracking error involved in an investment. They are not asked to make an explicit judgement on the success or otherwise of fund-raising, acquisition or divestment, but to base their decisions on market reaction. In many cases, passive funds cannot accept takeover offers because this involves an implicit judgement of market response, that is, active management. This dilemma has led passive managers into a halfway house where there may be active behind-the-scenes engagement with senior managers and passive public acceptance and support.

Active managers, by contrast, are not obliged to support corporate capital-raising. They can and do accept takeover bids, reject rights issues and generally make discretionary decisions about supporting companies or otherwise. Hedge funds, often the most active of active managers, are even more unconstrained, being able to short-sell. Anecdotal evidence suggests, for example, that hedge funds may have played a role in driving down BT's share price while its rights issue was in progress.

The short term

Share price levels often cause tensions between investors and companies. Chief executives are rarely satisfied with their share price (generally a good sign of over-valuation). Consistent complaints about investor short-termism are a public demonstration of this point. Executive concern about share price level is a real business issue – too low and the company is vulnerable either to a takeover or, more often, to concerns being felt by suppliers of debt capital.

Are fund managers too concerned with short-term considerations? This question lies at the heart of the relationship between investor and company. It usually surfaces when capital markets have delivered an unpleasant message. This can take the form of a falling share price in the wake of a good set of company profits, or fund managers might accept an unsolicited takeover offer for their shares. In the latter case, academic evidence suggests that hostile takeovers destroy value. All the more reason, therefore, for fund managers to accept these offers for the target shares in their portfolio and to discourage outright corporate adventurism. Close behind-the-scenes consultation by potential acquirers seems to have become regular practice in recent years.

Broadly speaking, a low or falling share or bond price increases the weighted cost of capital and reduces the range of available business strategies. Too high a price can lead to unrealistic business plans as managers seek to match inflated expectation. In both cases there is a temptation for managers to engage in cavalier accounting practices to meet or beat market forecasts. This does not lead to healthy investor relations.

Another source of conflict is the trend of linking pay to share price performance by the use of share options. This represents a good deal for companies on the way up, as it involves a non-cash outlay which apparently enhances profits. It is rare for a company to charge the price of granting such options in full to the accounts in the year they are granted. Only Berkshire Hathaway has adopted this policy in full in recent years. Equally, once the price falls, managers may be caught by Morton's Fork: they either lose valued staff or are unable to defray cash payouts through issuing options.

Disclosure

Shareholders have also learnt to use their voting power. In the UK at least, institutional investors used not to vote on issues at general meetings unless strong-armed by company advisers. Pressed in part by legislation and best practice, more institutions now vote on all or most resolutions. The Myners Report on institutional investment in the UK highlighted that only 50 per cent of shareholders vote and concluded this was evidence of fund managers neglecting their duty. Yet this seems reasonable. Overseas holders often find it difficult to vote. Individual investors sometimes find the issues confusing. Hedge fund ownership may be so transient that the issues are irrelevant and passive funds are in some cases forbidden to vote. Adjusted for these issues, voting levels, while capable of improvement, are not disgracefully low.

The Myners Report also criticizes an apparent UK institutional distaste for engaging in dialogue with underperforming managers, while the law clearly encourages such engagement. Pension fund managers have to act in the best interests of other clients. Pension fund trustees are required to exercise judgement "as ordinary men of business" in the interests of the fund. Thus both parties – trustee and manager – have a clear requirement to challenge company managers to act in shareholders' best interests.

The debate is not whether to engage with management but how. Most investor issues fall into two areas. The first involves issues relating to equitable treatment of shareholders, open and transparent disclosure and an honest and clear market. All investors should stand up for these principles in a public and consistent fashion. The second area contains a more diverse range of judgements. Often these include such topics as corporate strategy, at other times socially responsible investment. These judgements challenge fund managers to reflect the views of their diverse and disparate client base. This does not exempt fund managers from action. Rather, it suggests a more subtle and less public approach. Only if managers resist privately expressed pressure does public confrontation become necessary. In such cases it is often easier for a single pension fund to take a stance because it has only one set of trustees. The lead taken by funds such as Calpers in the US and Hermes in the UK arises in part from this.

The Myners Report concludes that legislation is required to make open debate more explicit. In particular, it states that legislation similar to the US Employee Retirement Income Security Act is needed, which forces trustees and fund managers to engage in public with companies on proposed actions and strategies. Critics argue that this may give rise to entrenched positions and unnecessary conflict.

Shareholder activism in reality works only where public shareholders hold most of a company's equity. An effective market for corporate control has shaped the rules of corporate governance in the US and UK. Elsewhere, for example in Asia, Japan and emerging markets, the rules are different. Minority shareholders in these regions have little option other than to sell when a company is not run in their interests. This works well in conveying a message on owners' attitudes through the share price.

The 1997 Asia crisis ended a long and often baffling period where minority shareholders bid share prices up and supplied inexpensive capital in spite of growing evidence of misallocation. Low valuations in regions where bankers are unwilling to lend can cut off capital flows just as effectively as hidden activism in industrial democracies.

IPOs

Initial public offerings can present more difficult ground. In some countries, such as the US, published research by the sponsoring bank is banned for a time before and after the offering. Elsewhere, these restrictions do not apply. In this respect US legislation makes more sense. It forces investors to focus on the prospectus, a legally binding document for company management. Much of the recent dialogue about analysts in the US blindly promoting company offerings misses the point of *caveat emptor*.

Professional investors have to act in their clients' direct interest rather than that of any other intermediary. Blaming a broker or banker for incorrect advice after the event ignores the fact that the buy, sell or subscribe decision lies with the fund manager. In this context the growing use by fund managers of in-house research is wholly understandable.

Socially responsible investing

Rarely seen as little as five years ago, socially responsible investing (SRI) is now an everyday issue in professional investment. However, the principles of responsibility and return in SRI are still confused. It is not the job of a fund manager to set SRI principles. Rather, it is down to the ultimate beneficiary (the pension fund, individual and so on) to determine their ideal policy. In so doing, beneficiaries have to tackle for themselves the proposition that SRI generates better returns.

Screening out certain investment companies reduces the size of the investment universe and thereby alters the parameters of risk and return. The resulting risk-adjusted return may be higher but this will be the result of market preference, not some systematic boost. And market preference is subject to change – witness the strong performance of tobacco shares on Wall Street.

As before, the key lies with the ultimate beneficiary. If savers want to pursue SRI in isolation, a range of options exists. Products such as green funds and alternative energy funds invest in line with their owners' targets. These products are a part of a fund's asset allocation decision. These views do not discredit SRI. Rather they place it in the context of investor choice. Where SRI makes particular sense is in the proposition that companies engaging in unethical work practices, as opposed to unpopular products, are more likely to be antipathetic towards shareholder rights and thereby represent poor investments.

In this respect SRI and corporate governance are aligned. Fund managers should support moves for companies to be run in the interests of their clients. If, as proposed, a statement of ethical principles becomes part of pension funds' statement of investment principles, then trustee and fund manager will apply any resulting tests in selecting investments. In consequence, SRI would become part and parcel of the normal relationship between fund manager and corporation. This process would echo the embargo on South African investment practised during the apartheid era.

Governance

The surge in interest in corporate governance began in the late 1980s and gradually spread over the next decade, affecting the activities of fund managers. In many cases, the impetus was corporate failure and consequential investor loss; examples include the Maxwell fraud in the UK, the Asian crisis, and the aftermath of the late 1980s leveraged buyout crash in the US. As a community, investment managers have a responsibility to encourage change before disaster strikes. In many cases, however – witness the dot-com bubble – fund managers aided and abetted the process of wealth destruction, only to cry foul thereafter. It could be said that subsequent regulation is necessary to protect investors from themselves.

It seems clear that fund managers should support the evolution of corporate governance. In particular, they should be concerned with issues arising from separation of ownership and control. For this to work, fund managers need to ensure that the board of directors is accountable to shareholders and managers in turn are accountable to the board.

Conclusion

At best, the relationship between fund manager and corporate executives should be an alliance. The two parties should, and often do, share the same ambition of boosting long-term shareholder returns so that both groups achieve their goals. Different investors have different goals, but all would sign up for an increase in private sector wealth. Equally, most capital market participants would agree on the principle of equitable disclosure.

Chief executives who grumble about disclosure might reflect on the folly of favouring one supplier of capital against another. Investors looking back to the days of selective disclosure should recall their anger when they were not on the inside track. All should agree that their shared aim is a fair, open and clearly priced market for capital. In such a market, the chance that provider and user will achieve their aims increases.

Copyright © Ewen Cameron Watt 2002

Further reading

Calpers shareowner forum (http://www.calpers-governance.org/forumhome.asp).
Institutional Investment in the United Kingdom (The Myners Report), HM Treasury (http://www.hm-treasury.gov.uk/docs/2001/myners_report0602.html).
OECD principles of corporate governance, OECD (http://www.oecd.org//daf/governance/principles.htm).

The bottom line
to a social conscience

Restrictions on socially responsible investors appear to limit their potential financial success. However, **Geoffrey Heal** finds that ethical funds may in fact perform better than average.

Geoffrey Heal is Paul Garrett Professor of Public Policy and Corporate Responsibility and a professor of economics and finance at Columbia Business School.

Socially responsible investors hope to do well by doing good. They seek to harness their influence in capital markets to social goals that transcend return on investments, so strengthening incentives for ethical fund management. Socially responsible investing is widespread and growing in the US and trends appear to be similar in other markets. According to criteria set out by the Social Investment Forum, in 1999 one dollar in every eight under professional management in the US was invested in an SRI fund, a total of $2,160bn, up more than 80 per cent from $1,185bn only two years earlier. Already large enough to be influential, SRI funds could soon become a major factor in capital markets at anything like recent growth rates.

The growth of these funds raises two major issues. How well are they doing and are they doing good? This article addresses these issues.

Socially responsible investing

Socially responsible investors have diverse goals and correspondingly varied definitions of social responsibility. Although the movement originated in the campaign to divest from South Africa, where the anti-apartheid campaign emerged as the first political movement to enlist investors ideologically, current targets of SRI funds typically go beyond a single issue.

Most SRI funds do not invest in companies that make or sell armaments, alcoholic drinks or tobacco products. Many funds avoid companies with a poor environmental record or those thought to exploit labour in developing countries. Funds with investors of a religious persuasion eschew companies promoting gambling or running casinos. Animal rights also affect the targets to be avoided. Indeed, it is safe to say that each ethical viewpoint championed by an active non-governmental organization has an investment fund to support its aims.

This is a new and growing source of business and of competitive advantage. It has reached the point where a management company without an SRI fund is at a disadvantage in the US pension fund market.

The best employers have traditionally offered staff a choice of methods for investing defined contribution funds and understand that many value the ability to choose an SRI fund. A fund manager whose product line includes growth, income, international and large-cap but no SRI fund is unable to offer the full range, so we see a proliferation of offerings. This is a business move and does not imply that the management companies sympathize with the social aims of the funds. To most of them, social goals are simply constraints placed on their portfolio choices. Indeed, a management company may run funds with contradictory goals.

The growth of SRI is a natural extension of a phenomenon already well established in retail markets to capital markets – the use of consumer buying power to attain social goals. Anita Roddick popularized this trend in the UK with The Body Shop and the US outdoor clothing brand Patagonia has had similar success. McDonald's and Nike have suffered from it and learned to come to terms with it. This movement is particularly influential in the human rights and environmental fields, where major clothing and shoe brands – Nike prominent among them – have been boycotted for their use of sweatshop labour, and oil companies such as Shell have been punished for their alleged environmental transgressions.

Companies selling to highly educated and socially aware customers with a global viewpoint can expect this to continue and indeed become more widespread: it is natural for these customers to link consumption choices to political beliefs and actions.

In 1994, *The Economist* spoke of "the era of the corporate image, in which consumers will increasingly make purchases on the basis of a firm's role in society: how it treats its employees, shareholders, and local neighbourhoods…" In many respects SRI is simply an extension of this process to capital markets: aware investors are looking at all dimensions of their choices. These developments have led to the growth of a closely linked industry providing the data on which socially responsible funds base their choices. Until recently a manager could not look up a company's environmental or human rights record online in the same way as its credit rating or its earnings forecasts. Now this is possible through companies that specialize in providing the data for managers to screen investments and assess their consistency with a fund's goals. Some go beyond this and compile lists of companies rated by financial and environmental performance, for example, the Innovest group.

Dow Jones, the doyen of financial indices, joined this trend several years ago by introducing its Sustainability Index. This ranks companies according to criteria believed to assess the sustainability of their contributions to society. The *Financial Times* announced that the FTSE will introduce a range of indices covering corporate performance on environmental issues, human rights, social issues and relations with stakeholders. Even for managers not running SRI funds, this extra information adds value, providing a broader picture of a company and its relationship to the outside world than is available through conventional financial indices.

The cost of virtue

Economists might think that there would be a cost to the limitations imposed by an SRI approach. After all, they believe there is no free lunch – everything good comes at a cost. So SRI funds should in principle offer lower returns than those without any constraints on their portfolio choices. Surprisingly, this does not seem to be the case.

Several studies claim to show that SRI funds offer returns as good as those on other funds and, indeed, that performance on environmental and human rights criteria is a good predictor of the overall financial performance of companies. The studies supporting the stronger of these claims leave something to be desired in terms of statistical rigour, but the basic data do, to a considerable extent, speak for themselves. For example, the Dow Jones Sustainability Index outperformed the Standard & Poor's 500 over the 1990s by about 15 per cent. Innovest's website reviews performance data and concludes that, "depending upon the sector, companies with above average EcoValue '21 ratings have consistently outperformed lower-rated companies by 300 to 2,500 basis points per year". Data from Morningstar, a company that rates mutual funds, show that SRI funds on average have earned higher returns than others.

Figure 1 shows the Goodmoney Industrial Average and the Dow Jones Industrial Average since 1977. Goodmoney is an index of 30 shares chosen to cover the same industries as the shares in the DJIA but screened according to ethical criteria. The picture here is similar.

Each of these numbers refers to averages. They suggest there is no cost to socially responsible investing. On average, there may even be a gain. But few

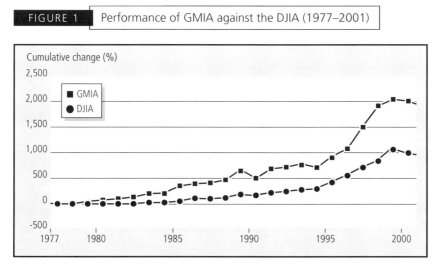

FIGURE 1 Performance of GMIA against the DJIA (1977–2001)

Source: Good Money Inc

investors or managers aim for average performance, whatever they eventually attain. And the very top performers are usually not SRI funds, so there may possibly be some cost in terms of a reduced probability of a very high return. The performance of SRI funds is a puzzle. While they are not among the top performers, they do perform above average. Given the constraints on stock selection posed by ethical guidelines, this is surprising. As noted, several recent studies report that environmental and human rights performance is a good predictor of overall performance. This is an interesting and suggestive point. There are several possible reasons for the performance edge that SRI funds appear to provide.

One is that technology stocks meet their screening criteria – the likes of Intel and Microsoft are free from association with pollution, exploitation, alcohol and tobacco – so SRI managers have inadvertently been steered towards the sector that has performed best in the recent bull market. If this were the entire explanation, it would imply that the superior performance is a coincidence that may not be repeated. However, data indicate that there is more than an accident at work here. Even on a sector-by-sector basis, shares of companies with a superior environmental or human rights record appear to outperform. Clean chemical companies will outperform dirty ones, clean oil companies will outperform dirty oil companies.

This type of finding suggests a deeper and more intrinsic connection between responsible management and superior returns. In the case of the environment, academic Geoffrey Heal (2000) has pointed to evidence that superior performance is indeed linked to higher profits. Pollution is waste, and cutting back on or finding ways to reuse waste feeds back to reduced inputs and higher profits. Dow Chemicals, DuPont and Anheuser-Busch have all found improved environmental performance to be a source of profits.

A similar effect may be at work with human rights: paying workers a living wage and protecting them from harassment may cost a little more in the short run, but if it improves morale and reduces turnover, it may still be good for profits after a few years. So socially responsible management practices may contribute directly to profits. A 2000 statistical study by academics Glen Dowell, Stuart Hart and Bernard Yeung is consistent with this interpretation. They looked at the environmental performance of US companies operating in developing countries, where environmental standards are lower than in the US. They divided the companies into three groups that:

- use US standards in their home operations and lower standards in developing countries;
- use US standards worldwide;
- adopt a standard worldwide higher than that mandated in the US.

If environmental compliance were a cost, other things being equal, one would expect the first group to be the most profitable and the third the least. In fact the authors found the opposite to be true. This and similar findings led them to suggest that capital market valuations incorporate the negative social costs of a company's operations. To Dowell, Hart and Yeung, higher environmental standards are a sign of state-of-the-art equipment and of alert management, all presumably contributing to financial performance.

A rather different argument for superior performance of SRI funds stems from consumer behaviour, suggests academic Peter Singer (2001). The increasing use of consumer buying power to attain social goals has already been mentioned. The obvious implication for profits is that companies boycotted by consumers will lose market share to competitors who enjoy a better image. Socially responsible buying is thus able to lay the foundations for successful socially responsible investing. Companies failing ethical screens will lose sales and at the same time, and for the same reason, SRI funds will stay away from them. Socially responsible investors reaping what they have sown as socially responsible consumers produce a self-reinforcing process.

This makes sense from another perspective. Standard advice to individual investors is to invest in companies whose products you know and like. It is a simple step from this sound and sensible advice to saying: "Don't invest in companies that people like you will shun."

The impact of SRI

Socially responsible investors appear to be attaining their goal of doing well. The performance of SRI funds seems to be at least above average. But are they also doing good? Are they attaining their ethical goals? What may seem like a rhetorical question in fact requires examination. Assume that SRI funds attained their above-average returns simply by investing substantially in technology stocks. In this case their ethical leverage has been minimal. They have run with a successful sector, delivering no specific ethical message to managers.

If we adopt another of the theories, that superior environmental and human rights performance pays off financially, and that ethical investors have benefited from this, it is again not clear that the success of SRI funds has given an ethical message to managers. In this case, managers' incentives to act ethically have been primarily conventional, not linked to the behaviour of SRI funds.

Finally, assume that ethical investors are reaping what they have sown as ethical consumers and that the behaviour of consumers in favouring retail companies with superior ethical records has contributed to the superior financial performance of these companies. In this case, there is an argument that the combined operations of ethical consumers and investors have had an impact on corporate behaviour. The truth probably contains some of each of the last two arguments, so that ethical investors have had an impact, possibly small, on corporate behaviour.

There are in fact two ways in which SRI might influence company behaviour. The most obvious, alluded to above, is through the cost of capital. A company that is out of favour with investors will have to pay more for capital, either by issuing more shares or by paying higher interest rates. Over and above this is the mechanism of shareholder advocacy. Corporate law in the US, and indeed in most countries, allows shareholders with a minimal stake in a company ($2,000 in the US) to place items on the agenda of shareholder meetings and require that a vote be taken on these matters at meetings. This is a powerful mechanism for embarrassing management about alleged ethical failures. The annual meetings of large corporations receive wide press coverage and these critical resolutions produce negative publicity, possibly leading to boycotts and diminished retail sales.

Shareholder advocacy has been used to great effect by large institutional investors, such as the College Retirement Equities Fund in the US, as a route to more open corporate governance. Large investors have influenced corporate policies on such matters as chief executive succession, board membership and poison pills. Ethical investors can use the same route. According to a report by the Interfaith Center on Corporate Responsibility, in 1999 SRI managers filed about 220 resolutions with more than 150 US companies. The largest number covered environmental issues, with equity and corporate responsibility taking the next two places.

A notable success was the decision by Home Depot, a major US DIY outlet, to stop buying mature wood from endangered forests. In this case, shareholder activism was accompanied by a consumer boycott organized by rainforest-related non-governmental organizations. Baxter International, a maker of health care products, also agreed to stop using polyvinyl chloride in some of its products. PVC releases carcinogens when it is burnt. Chevron and Exxon were facing similar actions intended to force them to abandon plans to drill in the Alaskan Arctic wildlife refuge.

Through these and other examples, SRI funds do seem to be influencing corporate policies through shareholder advocacy, although the effect of shareholder advocacy alone is perhaps limited: it appears to be most effective when accompanied by a credible threat of consumer responses. The responsible consumer and the responsible investor form a team that is more than the sum of its parts.

Conclusion

Socially responsible investors are a significant presence in capital markets. The amounts in SRI funds are large and growing. What are SRI funds seeking, over and above a competitive return? What returns are they actually achieving? What impact have they had to date, and how might this change if the practice spreads?

The aims of SRI funds are as diverse as the aims of political pressure groups and non-governmental organizations. There are funds for all persuasions. A company might appeal to some but be anathema to others. There does seem to be general agreement among funds on a set of criteria that are used to define social responsibility. Weapons, pollution and abuse of human rights are all seen as unethical as, often, is gambling. Executives who want to court socially responsible investors should place their corporations strategically on these issues.

On average, socially responsible funds have performed well. There are several possible explanations for this and whether this is likely to continue depends on which are valid. An interesting possibility is that socially responsible behaviour proxies for general managerial competence and several studies seem to confirm this. There is also the fact that socially responsible investing interacts with similar behaviour by consumers, each reinforcing the former. This is part of the process of consumers thinking about all dimensions of their choices.

It is not clear yet what effect SRI is having. Certainly shareholder activism by socially responsible investors, along with consumer activism, has affected the choices of influential corporations. However, socially responsible funds adopting a passive role towards their shareholdings may have little influence beyond a minor reduction in the cost of capital to favoured companies.

Copyright © Geoffrey Heal 2002

Further reading

The Economist (1994) "Brand new day", 19 June, 71–2.
Heal, G. (2000) "Environmental disaster: not all bad news", *Financial Times*, 30 October.
Dowell, G., Hart, S. and Yeung, B. (2000) "Do corporate global environmental standards create or destroy market value?", *Management Science*, August, 46, 8, 1059–74.
Singer, P. (2001) "A buoyant market for ethics", *Financial Times*, 12 March.

Websites

Social Investment Forum (www.socialinvest.org).
Innovest Group (www.innovestgroup.com).
Dow Jones Sustainability Index (www.sustainability-index.com).

Early-stage **investing** 10

Contents

Business as usual after boom and bust 298
Amar Bhidé, Columbia Business School

The 1990s was a tumultuous decade for venture capitalists. What are the enduring principles of venture capital?

Investing in private equity 305
Andrew Metrick, University of Pennsylvania

Public markets allow investors to buy and sell shares easily and provide information on performance and future prospects via the share price. Private equity, however, calls for very different skills on the part of its investors.

Reading the signs from first-day returns 313
Kent Womack, Dartmouth College

In the 1990s, the investors who gained most from first-day underpricing were institutions favoured in the underwriting process. Is it worth others investing in IPOs after the first day?

Introduction to Part 10

The failure of scores of businesses launched in the late 1990s on a wave of dot-com optimism has turned many investors away from the promise of the new enterprise. Many were caught up in the general enthusiasm and lost heavily. Investors should be cautious, however, of disregarding entrepreneurial companies; individuals will continue to strike out on their own in pursuit of opportunities, and some of these will be wildly successful for their originators and financial backers. Here writers discuss the methods by which new businesses obtain finance, such as venture capital and private equity, and take a retrospective look at the value of IPO investment.

Business as usual
after boom and bust

Amar Bhidé is Glaubinger Professor of Business at Columbia Business School.

Following the heady returns of the internet boom years, venture capitalists are going back to their tried and trusted business models. **Amar Bhidé** explores these and looks to the future.

During the internet boom, the venture capital model seemed omnipotent. Now, after scores of dot coms backed by blue-chip venture capitalists have gone bust, it is time for a sober evaluation: in normal times, what are the advantages and limitations of the venture capital model?

Venture capitalists occupy an important niche as investors. Businesses backed by venture capital have profoundly influenced high-technology fields such as semiconductors and genetic engineering. Capital and advice provided by venture capitalists have helped propel companies such as Sun Microsystems and Compaq to global leadership. But such cases are not typical. Contrary to popular belief, only exceptional entrepreneurs can secure start-up venture capital. Of nearly a million businesses formed each year in the US, venture capitalists fund a few hundred. Most companies, exemplified by Hewlett-Packard, Microsoft, Cisco and Dell, start with limited funds provided by founders or by their families and friends.

This article examines the attributes of companies in which venture capitalists tend to invest. As shown in Figure 1, entrepreneurs pursue opportunities with high subjective uncertainty and low resource requirements. When public companies mature they undertake projects that require substantial capital and managerial resources. Failure can lead to substantial losses, but such projects do not involve much subjective uncertainty, because the risks and returns can be assessed.

Venture capitalists use criteria that demand investments with medium resource requirements and uncertainty. Only a few, unusual entrepreneurs meet these criteria. Some businesses, such as Cisco, that cannot raise venture capital at the outset can do so later, after uncertainty has declined and resource requirements

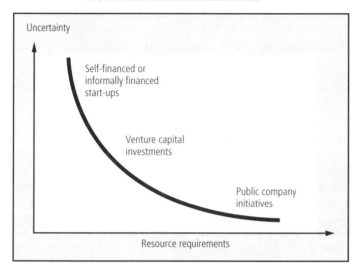

FIGURE 1 Three stages of management

have increased. The venture capital industry typically gives about two-thirds of its funds to companies which are not start-ups. As these businesses prove themselves further, so uncertainty continues to decline and their resource requirements increase. Then they can access public capital markets. Thus venture capital is a source of medium-term, "bridge" financing.

Evaluation

Investors in start-ups have an incentive to conduct more due diligence than investors in public companies. Investors in publicly traded shares are not rewarded for assuming company-specific risk. The risks are diversified by holding a portfolio. The "market" or "systematic" risk of the portfolio, rather than astuteness in choosing securities, determines an investor's long-term return. Efforts to analyze a company's prospects carry little reward because market prices already allow for all available information.

Funding start-ups is different. Discrimination among opportunities is crucial, because investors cannot depend on free research and due diligence reflected in market prices. Prudence demands some diversification, but this is no substitute for choosing each investment carefully. Buying 20 listed stocks at random eliminates most company-specific risk and provides a return that tracks the overall stock market. Historically, this return has been about 10 per cent a year. Providing venture capital to 20 random entrepreneurs will likely provide, given the dubious prospects of most new businesses, a return of close to zero. Moreover, backing randomly selected ventures makes investors vulnerable to opportunistic founders.

Investors in start-ups have to undertake considerable monitoring and oversight. In public markets, the diversified investor's ability to monitor and intervene is low. Companies cannot discuss strategy and performance with dispersed investors, so shareholders lack the confidential information to monitor managers and distinguish between their luck and skill. Also, the shareholder who incurs the costs of inducing a company to change must share the benefits with others who made no effort. Unhappy stockholders therefore sell shares rather than incur these costs. In small, private companies, however, investors can demand access to information they need on performance. And they cannot avoid intervention by selling their holdings in a liquid market.

Partnership terms

Professional venture capitalists, who invest others' funds rather than their own, face additional incentives to develop systems for evaluating and monitoring investments. Wealthy individuals, pension funds and others who have the capital to invest in start-ups often lack the resources (or confidence) to evaluate and monitor such ventures. Instead, they invest in limited partnerships organized by venture capital companies. In such partnerships, venture capitalists have discretion over the funds under management. At or before the end of the life of the partnership, usually within 10 years, they sell the illiquid holdings of the partnership for cash or convert them into marketable securities and return the proceeds to clients. For this service, venture capitalists receive an annual fee (usually 1–2 per cent of assets managed) as well as a "carried interest" or share (about 20 per cent) of profits generated.

The terms of their deals with clients encourage venture capitalists to formalize investment processes. Limited partnership structures allow venture capitalists to avoid delays and the leakage of information that might result from having to raise funds for individual investments. However, they also require clients to cede control over investment decisions for an extended period. The "carried interest", which gives venture capitalists a share of the profits but not of the losses, creates an incentive to invest in excessively risky projects. Venture capitalists therefore have procedures to reassure clients that they will not make reckless investments.

Evidence suggests that venture capitalists devote considerable effort to due diligence, structuring deals and providing advice and oversight. Academic William Sahlman (1990) reports that partners in venture capital companies usually have responsibility for just under nine investments and sit on five boards. They visit each company 19 times a year and spend 100 hours either on site or in contact by phone. They "help recruit and compensate key individuals, work with suppliers and customers, help establish tactics and strategy, play a major role in raising capital, and help structure transactions such as mergers and acquisitions. They often assume more direct control by changing management and are sometimes willing to take over day-to-day operations."

Typical criteria

The limited number of deals venture capitalists can manage sets a high threshold for the returns they require. Instead of dividing their time between many opportunities, they concentrate on a few ventures that have the potential – based on objective data – to make substantial returns. Significant failure rates and limited time horizons reinforce this preference. Even after extensive due diligence and monitoring, many venture capital investments yield disappointing returns.

One study of venture capital portfolios by Venture Economics reported that about 7 per cent of investments accounted for more than 60 per cent of profits, while a third resulted in a partial or total loss. Venture capitalists therefore avoid small opportunities where even substantial returns on a percentage basis will not cover the opportunity costs of their time or compensate for failures. Every venture must hold the promise of returns in millions of pounds, rather than in the tens or even hundreds of thousands.

The attractiveness of a company also depends on how long venture capitalists expect it will take them to sell their investment. Venture capitalists have to cash out before their partnership expires. In a 10-year fund, a venture that does not fold is taken public or sold to another company typically within five years. This consideration leads venture capitalists to favour investments with the potential for large payoffs: small companies cannot afford to go public and conform to regulatory and reporting requirements.

Unusual ventures

In trying to identify big winners, venture capitalists look for companies that serve large markets with a proprietary technology or process. A small company can be profitable as a result of its founders' drive, energy, relationships and so on, but a significant payoff, realized through the sale of the company or a public issue of its stock, generally requires something inherently proprietary in its products or processes. Venture capitalists also favour seasoned founding teams who can significantly increase a venture's chances of becoming large quickly.

Some entrepreneurs who start niche businesses without a proprietary model may discover large markets and build sustainable advantages. Similarly, inexperienced founders may learn how to manage rapidly growing companies. But it is difficult to predict which entrepreneurs will be able to do so. The absence of a specific plan or technology and verifiable credentials puts the subjective uncertainty of the venture above the venture capitalist's acceptable threshold.

My research suggests that most start-ups, including those in *Inc* magazine's list of the 500 fastest-growing private companies in the US, do not meet the criteria used by venture capitalists. Most entrepreneurs do not have a proprietary product or service capable of generating significant revenues. They are often not the first or second entrants in their markets. Often, they copy from other companies or develop an idea independently but at the same time as others.

Usually the revenue potential of an initial concept is limited. Most entrepreneurs start in niches that cannot justify the million-dollar investment thresholds of venture capitalists. For example, Microsoft co-founders Bill Gates and Paul Allen launched the company in 1975 by writing a programming language for a computer sold to a tiny market of hobbyists. Even if such companies can find larger markets, their growth tends to fall short of the size necessary to meet venture capital standards of success. An investment in Microsoft in 1975 would probably not have produced an attractive return over the usual three- to five-year venture capital horizon. Five years after launch, Microsoft had sales of $5m. It took nine years to book the same revenues as the software company Lotus, which was backed by venture, did in its first year and 10 years to go public.

Most entrepreneurs do not have the experience that venture capitalists believe is necessary to build and manage large companies. The founders of Compaq had been senior managers at Texas Instruments. Michael Dell and Bill Gates were students when they started. In exceptional cases, an inexperienced founder may team up with a seasoned manager and venture capitalists can help entrepreneurs create such teams. This requires, however, a high-potential idea or technology. If, as is often the case, entrepreneurs start off with a me-too concept or a differentiated product for a small market, they cannot recruit partners or employees with the experience that venture capitalists consider necessary.

Later-stage finance

Many ventures whose prospects are small or uncertain at the outset qualify for venture capital later, as their business models and management capabilities are proven. And venture capitalists give more to these later-stage businesses than to start-ups. The National Venture Capital Association's annual report shows that in 1996, 77 per cent of companies receiving venture capital were three years or older and 80 per cent had more than 25 employees. Similarly, data collected for the US Federal Reserve by George Fenn, Nellie Liang and Stephen Prowse (1995) show only about a third of investments are "early stage".

Cisco illustrates how the fit with venture capital increases as subjective uncertainty declines. Sandy Lerner and Len Bosak started Cisco in 1984. They raised money by running up bills on their credit cards and persuaded friends and relatives to work for deferred pay. Although the business was consistently profitable, it faced persistent cash shortages and at one point in 1986, Lerner took a job as a data processing manager to provide more cash. In 1987, Cisco received funding from Sequoia Capital – the 77th venture capital company the founders approached. By then the products had proven themselves – Cisco had sales of about $300,000 a month, without a professional sales staff and marketing campaign.

But not only did Cisco lack capital, it also lacked professional management. Sequoia partner Donald Valentine helped provide these in 1989 by hiring an experienced manager, John Morgridge, to run Cisco. Morgridge paved the way for a public offering in 1990. After going public, Cisco became the leading supplier of routers that link computer networks. In 2000, it took revenues of nearly $19bn and profits of $874m.

Symbiotic relationship

Cisco exemplifies the relationship between venture capitalists and public markets. Markets provide exits for venture capitalists and venture capitalists create a "product" for public investors. Public companies can then undertake projects whose resource requirements and time horizons lie outside the scope of venture capitalists. For example, the research and marketing costs of a drug compare with the total capital of many venture capital funds and the time taken just for regulatory approval typically exceeds their investment horizon.

Public companies have an obvious advantage in such projects with their extensive management structures. Investors are also more prepared to entrust funds for an indefinite time to organizations with well-developed management rather than to a few talented individuals. However, management systems make public companies more averse to subjective uncertainty than venture capital companies.

Mania and its aftermath

The IPO mania that started in earnest with the 1996 flotation of Netscape distorted this natural order. Investing in any growth stock turns on the optimism that small profits will turn into large profits. With Netscape and subsequent offerings, investors were betting on a fundamental change in trajectory, believing that companies making significant losses would, one day, make substantial profits.

New economy optimism did wonders for venture capitalists. Before, they had to wait for ventures to establish a record of profits over several years. And they had to write off investments in businesses that, in spite of star-studded founding teams, could not develop profitable business models. As the IPO market became less discriminating, venture capitalists had fewer write-offs, holding periods shrank and exit values multiplied.

Contrast Sun Microsystems, incorporated in 1982, with Chemdex, incorporated in 1997. Both started with concepts that could lead to substantial long-term profits, had exceptionally capable founders and secured financing from Kleiner-Perkins. The difference? It took four years for Sun to go public and only two for Chemdex. In its pre-IPO fiscal year, Sun booked revenues of $115m on which it earned $8.5m in net income. Chemdex booked $29,000 in revenues and lost $8.5m. By design, Sun turned profitable in its first quarter and has remained so ever since. Chemdex (now renamed Ventro) has never made a profit. Its stock, which peaked at $243 in February 2000, now trades for about $1. But as far as its venture capitalists are concerned, what might once have been a write-off counts as a winner.

By my calculations, returns from venture capital funds between 1981 and 1996 were indistinguishable from those of publicly traded stocks. Between 1996 and 1999 many funds sported triple-digit returns each year. These returns enabled venture capitalists to raise huge funds and attracted many new entrants and substitutes. The investment banks which underwrite IPOs moved up the value chain and put billions into their venture capital activities. All of the top consulting and accounting companies set up incubators. As the money poured in, venture capital had neither the time nor the incentive to apply traditional criteria and due diligence procedures.

What happens next? The boom and bust in biotechnology companies provides a good preview. In the early 1990s, markets seemed to think genetic engineering would help cure every disease. These companies could issue stock without any obvious route to profitability. Venture capitalists courted academics and medics with implausible business plans. Then the bottom fell out. According to Josh Lerner and Alexander Tsai (2000), external financing raised by US biotechnology companies halved – from $5bn in 1992 to $2bn in 1994. Biotechnology stocks had a wilder ride. The Amex biotechnology index peaked at 250 and in the next two-and-a-half years lost 80 per cent of its value. It would take almost a decade to regain that peak.

But research into drugs and therapies, and the formation of companies, did not end. It just reverted to more sensible patterns. And although biotechnology did not meet expectations, it will make significant contributions to medicine. So it will be with the new economy. Valuations and expectations will fall, but not for ever. The party is over, but it isn't the end of the world. Once they have recovered from their hangovers, investors will resume their distinctive roles.

Copyright © Amar Bhidé 2002

Further reading

Bhidé, A. (2000) *The Origin and Evolution of New Businesses*, New York: Oxford University Press.

Bhidé, A. (2001) "Taking care: ambiguity, resource pooling and error control", working paper (www.bhide.net).

Fenn, G., Liang, N. and Prowse, S. (1995) "The economics of the private equity market", Washington DC: Board of Governors of the Federal Reserve System (http://www.federalreserve.gov/pubs/staffstudies/168/ss168.pdf).

Gompers, P. and Lerner, J. (1999) *The Venture Capital Cycle*, Cambridge, MA: MIT Press.

Lerner, J. and Tsai, A. (2000) "Do equity financing cycles matter? Evidence from biotechnology alliances", National Bureau of Economic Research, working paper 7464 (http://papers.nber.org).

Sahlman, W. (1990) "The structure and governance of venture capital organizations", *Journal of Financial Economics*, 27, 473–521.

Investing in private equity

Investing in public equity is easy because it is so well supported. Leveraged buyouts and venture capital are a different kettle of fish, says **Andrew Metrick**.

Andrew Metrick is an assistant professor of finance at the Wharton School of the University of Pennsylvania. His research interests are in venture capital, corporate governance and the investment management industry.

Investing in public equity is easy. It is not easy to "beat the market", of course, but it is extremely easy not to lose by much. Take your money, stick it in an index fund from a big mutual fund company, and you will do just fine. Even if you want to pick your own stocks, you won't lose your shirt as long as you follow a "buy-and-hold" strategy on a diversified portfolio and keep your turnover low. Things are easy because there is an army of professional investors and analysts working full time to squeeze all the profits out of stock trading. It is nice to know when you buy a stock that there are probably a few professionals buying alongside you at close to the same price. This is not always true, but it is true often enough to provide a safety net for investors.

Investing in "private equity" is another matter. Here, there is no safety net, no army of analysts, and nobody else buying at the same price. To see why these investments are so dangerous – and so interesting – one must examine the reasons that they are "private" in the first place. The classic examples of private equity are venture capital – investment in young companies before they become traded on public exchanges – and leveraged buyouts – purchases of entire companies that are financed largely by debt. While these investing activities may seem very different, they share the common feature that, after the investment is made, the investor cannot just turn around and sell his stake to the public. This defining characteristic of private equity also applies to investments in a restaurant, a physician's practice or a relative's latest scheme to get rich.

Consider a classic venture capital investment: a scientist needs money to develop a new drug. There are many ways that this venture can fail. The drug might not work. The drug might work but have terrible side effects. A better drug might be discovered soon afterwards. Before an investor gives this scientist any money, he must carefully weigh all of these risks. He must then monitor the scientist to make sure she does the work instead of just going on holiday. These activities – assessing risks and monitoring performance – are costly and require special skills. When companies are large enough, it is worthwhile for intermediaries like brokerage analysts to perform some of these activities as a service to their clients. Then, once the firm is public and possesses a significant market value, other large investors find it worthwhile to purchase stakes and enter into a research and monitoring role. The resulting market prices then convey some (if not all) of what these professionals have learned. The new drug company described above, however, is too small to deserve this costly treatment. Instead, it is up to individual private equity investors to make these judgements, with no market prices to rely on.

While a broad definition of private equity includes everything from investments in local restaurants to multi-billion-dollar leveraged buyouts, the "organized" private equity market is much narrower. In the organized market, private equity firms invest pools of capital supplied mostly by large institutional investors. While these pools of capital are called "funds", they are organized very differently from the mutual funds available to retail investors. In principle, most mutual funds exist in perpetuity, with new investors taking the place of old ones, and a single legal entity representing the fund from its inception.

Partnerships

In contrast, private equity funds are almost always organized as limited partnerships, with the private equity firms serving as the "general partners" and the institutional investors serving as the "limited partners". Each partnership is set up for a fixed length of time – usually 10 years – and all capital is committed right at the beginning. A successful private equity firm will successively raise multiple private equity partnerships, sequentially numbering all of these partnerships and labelling them by the year of inception. As with fine wine, these labels are known as "vintage years". Such terminology facilitates comparisons across funds and is more than just whimsy: just as the success of a vintage year in wine depends on prevailing weather conditions for growing grapes, the success of private equity partnerships depends on the prevailing market conditions for growing companies.

With few exceptions, private equity funds are not open to ordinary investors. In the US, investment in these funds is limited by law to certain institutions and "accredited investors" – those with income above $200,000 or net worth of $1m. In practice, most funds look for investments of at least several million dollars from each limited partner, with large funds expecting investments of $25m or more. Also, since fund-raising is a time-consuming activity, most private equity firms prefer investors that can assure contributions to future partnerships. In practice, these requirements rule out all but the largest and most stable institutions. Smaller institutions and wealthy individuals can often only get access to the most sought-after funds through investments in "funds of funds" – limited partnerships that themselves invest in other limited partnerships.

In the past few years, several innovative financial products have been developed in an attempt to bring private equity investing to the masses. The most famous of this group is the meVC Draper Fischer Jurvetson Fund I, a closed-end mutual fund available to any investor. meVC is organized to make venture investments in private companies, a feat not tried before by a retail fund because of time-consuming and costly regulatory hurdles. The markets have not been kind to meVC – the fund has traded at a substantial discount to its net asset value virtually since its inception on 31 March 2000 – but the final results of the experiment will not be in until meVC attempts to exit its investments.

Changing views

Notwithstanding the innovative products, the vast majority of private equity is still raised by old-style US-based limited partnerships. By any measure, the growth of the asset class has been explosive in the past few years. According to Asset Alternatives, a firm that tracks fund-raising activity in the industry, the total amount raised by US-based private equity partnerships rose steadily from $8bn in 1991 to $97.3bn in 1999 and $153.9bn in 2000. While part of this increase simply reflects an overall rise in US markets, there has also been a fundamental shift in the way this asset class is viewed by institutional investors.

For example, according to a survey by the consulting firm Greenwich Associates, large US pension funds increased their percentage allocations to private equity from 1.8 per cent in 1996 to 2.9 per cent in 2000. While a 1 per cent difference may not seem like much, it adds up quickly when large-pension assets increased from $3.3tn to $6.3tn over the same period. In addition, many smaller pension funds have been entering the asset class for the first time through funds-of-funds vehicles, and percentage allocations to private equity by university endowments are at record levels.

Organized private equity activity in Europe, Asia and the rest of the world lags far behind that of the US. Even with a recent surge of activity in Europe, the total size of the private equity market there is probably less than one-third of the US market, and the fraction is even smaller if one looks only at the venture capital component. At first glance, this seems puzzling: since the US has the most liquid public markets, one might think that this provides relatively little scope for private equity. Paradoxically, however, a liquid public market is much more of a complement than a substitute for private equity. The reason is that private equity investors rely heavily on the availability of "exits" and the most profitable exits are through public offerings. European public markets, while liquid for mature companies, still lack a deep IPO market for young technology companies such as the Nasdaq. None of the secondary national markets has managed to achieve the necessary critical mass, and the pan-European Easdaq has not yet succeeded in filling the void.

Things were not always so busy in the private equity industry. In fact, the modern industry dates back only to 1946 (see Box 1) and total fund-raising in the US was less than $1bn a year as recently as 1978. An important milestone for the recent growth came with the development in the 1960s of the limited

> **Box 1 George Doroit and the birth of venture capital**
>
> Venture capital, in some form, is as old as commerce itself, but the modern organizational forms date back only to 1946. Bank lending rules, then as now, looked for evidence that borrowers had collateral and could make timely payments of interest and principal. Most entrepreneurial firms did not meet these standards and required risk capital in the form of equity. There was, however, no regular source of such capital, and entrepreneurs without wealthy friends or family had little opportunity to fund their ventures.
>
> Then along came George Doriot. "General" Doriot, so named for his rank in the US Army quartermaster's office during the second world war, recognized the need for risk capital and created a firm to supply it. His firm, American Research and Development Corporation (ARD), began operations in 1946 as the first modern venture capital firm.
>
> Unlike modern funds, it was organized as a corporation and was itself publicly traded. In their thorough survey of the private equity industry, the economists George Fenn, Nellie Liang and David Prowse (1997) report that ARD earned returns for its investors of 15.8 per cent over its 25-year existence as a public company. ARD also set a standard for generating these returns that has persisted to the present day. Excluding the $70,000 investment in their biggest success, the Digital Equipment Corporation, ARD's 25-year annualized performance drops to 7.4 per cent.
>
> Many modern venture capitalists spend their days searching for their own private Digital, now with more fanciful names like Yahoo!, Amazon and eBay – all firms which started as venture capital investments and made legendary reputations for their investors.

partnership as the dominant organizational form. In this arrangement, limited partners put up the capital, with 1–2 per cent going every year to pay expenses of the fund. The remaining capital is then invested by the general partner in private companies. Successful investments are excited, either through a private sale or a public offering, before the 10-year life of the partnership expires. The most common profit-sharing arrangement is 80–20: after returning all of the original investment to the limited partners, the general partner keeps 20 per cent of everything else. This profit-sharing, known as "carried interest", is the carrot that makes private equity investing so enticing for investment professionals. In recent years the most successful general partners have demanded – and received – as much as 30 per cent carried interest on new partnerships.

The next big change for the private equity market came in 1979, when the relaxation of investment rules for US pension funds led to historically large inflows from these investors to the asset class. To this day, pension funds continue to supply nearly half of the money for private equity in the US. As of 20 years ago, most private equity was venture capital. Significant growth in the other major category, leveraged buyout, would have to wait until the financial innovation of junk bonds in the mid-1980s allowed large takeovers financed by relatively small amounts of equity. The large buyouts of this period, epitomized by Kohlberg, Kravis and Roberts's (KKR) 1989 buyout of RJR Nabisco for $25bn catapulted leveraged buyout firms into the limelight for the first time. The collapse of the junk bond market and recession of the early 1990s curtailed their activities, but buyout firms still claimed the majority of all flows into private equity until venture capital recaptured the lead in 2000.

Allocation

How should an investor treat private equity in the portfolio? This question has relevance not only for the traditional private equity investors in large institutions but also for wealthy individuals who can gain access to the asset class through funds of funds and for retail investors who can invest in private equity using vehicles such as meVC. The investment question can be broken into two parts. First, what fraction of the portfolio should go to private equity and its sub-classes? Second, how should an investor choose among different managers within the asset class?

To answer the first question, one needs some information about the expected returns to private equity. On logical grounds, private equity represents a part of the overall capital stock of the economy, and investors should try to buy the broadest possible cross-section of this capital stock in order to build a diversified portfolio. Nevertheless, investments in private equity carry some cost, as the general partners will capture at least 20 per cent of the profits. Thus, it is necessary to make some rational forecast of net returns after fees.

Since forecasting the future is a tricky business, a good place to start is usually with the past, and to analyze the past one needs some data. Public equity managers provide mountains of data every day, but private equity managers are not so forthcoming. Since most private equity investors are unregulated limited partnerships, they are not obligated to report their results to anyone except their investors. The only centralized repositories of these results are trade organizations like the National Venture Capital Association in the US, and "gatekeeper" consultants who manage relationships between large institutional investors and private equity funds. One such gatekeeper, Cambridge Associates, publicly provides aggregate quarterly snapshots of portfolio value and dividends, known as "distributions", for a good fraction of both venture capital and leveraged buyout funds. (Available on the web at http://www.cambridgeassociates.com/indexes/index.html.) After-cost returns for these asset sub-classes can then be computed from these snapshots.

As an illustration of these returns, consider the venture capital subclass. Figure 1 plots the cumulative return on $1 invested either in venture capital or in the Nasdaq composite index over the period from 1 January 1981 to 30 September 2000, the latest date for which returns are available. As the figure shows this $1 investment would have grown to $18.15 if invested in the Nasdaq composite and $68.37 if invested in the "average" venture capital fund, implying annualized returns of 15.9 per cent and 24 per cent, respectively. What is also notable about this figure is that the advantage of venture capital over the Nasdaq composite comes almost entirely since mid-1997.

So it appears that a typical venture investor fared better than a typical Nasdaq investor, but returns are only half of the story. Financial economists

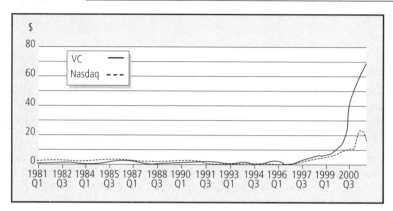

FIGURE 1 Value of $1 invested from 1 January 1981 to 30 September 2000

Source: Cambridge Associates, Wharton Research Data Sevices

view asset allocation as a game of trying to maximize expected portfolio returns for any given level of risk. Viewed from this perspective, the "riskiness" of an asset class depends not on the everyday notion of risk but on how much the asset class tends to reduce or increase the volatility of the whole portfolio. For example, an investment in a new drug venture may at first appear to be a very risky investment. Perhaps there is only a 10 per cent chance that the new drug will work, and a 90 per cent chance that the investors will lose all their money. For a financial economist, however, the risk that the drug won't work is "diversifiable", and by taking small pieces of many such investments, an investor can essentially reduce her risk to zero. Under this view, the only risks that matter are the ones that cannot be diversified. When the whole economy sours, the cost must be borne by somebody. The exposure to this cost is "undiversifiable" risk and the acceptance of such risk trades off with return.

One way that analysts measure undiversifiable risk is by the "beta" of an investment, where beta represents the degree to which that investment moves with the rest of the stock market. Then, an investment with a beta of 1 should earn the same expected return as the whole stock market, and investments with betas higher or lower than 1 should have expected returns higher or lower than the market, respectively.

Unfortunately, it is very tricky to measure the beta risk of a venture capital portfolio. Standard measures are based on historical correlations between an investment and the market – such correlations require that returns be measured carefully at regular intervals. While the data from Cambridge Associates allow a good guess at average returns, inconsistent portfolio updates provided by general partners do not allow for accurate measures of correlation. In a 2000 study distributed by the National Bureau of Economic Research, "The risk and return of venture capital", Professor John Cochrane of the University of Chicago attempted to overcome this difficulty by focusing only on the most timely information: the value of venture-backed companies when they go public, are acquired or go out of business. Even though these observations are just for the known "winners" and "losers", it is possible to use statistical techniques to back out the beta risk for *all* venture investments. Professor Cochrane's results suggest that venture investments have a beta close to 1, although the exact estimate varies depending on assumptions and methodology.

Taken together, this evidence supports inclusion of venture capital as an additional asset class in investors' portfolios, as long as a diversified portfolio of average venture capital funds is available. Particular allocations to venture capital should depend on the risk-reward trade-off of the investor, but 5 per cent – far higher than the share of venture capital in the overall market – should probably be an upper bound for all but the most aggressive and informed.

Fund performance

The second question – how to choose a specific private equity manager – is a particularly difficult one. While investors need only visit the nearest newsstand to find detailed rankings of mutual fund managers, the available data on private equity performance gives only aggregate returns or distributions of returns for each vintage year. Unless you are lucky enough to employ an investment consultant with a large proprietary database, you will have no way of knowing how an individual manager stacks up unless the manager decides to tell you himself. Even then you will probably lack sufficient data to make meaningful comparisons on a risk-adjusted basis.

So what is an investor to do? One option is to follow a strategy that works well for public investing: index. Although broad-based indices do not yet exist for private equity, the next best thing – a managed fund-of-funds partnership – usually takes stakes in many different partnerships. Sophisticated fund-of-funds managers work hard to find experienced private equity managers across a wide variety of investment styles. Even here, though, it is necessary to be careful. Some funds of funds, particularly those marketed to high-net-worth individuals, charge an additional layer of carried interest on top of the 20–30 per cent taken by the private equity funds they invest in. It seems unlikely that such extra charges can be justified by any but the most successful managers. Although funds of funds remain restricted to "accredited investors" in the US, these barriers are falling and it will likely not be long before all investors have some access to these financial products. For investors who want to choose managers themselves, be aware that the choices are very limited unless you are extremely rich and well connected. Furthermore, while there is anecdotal evidence that skilled venture capitalists can consistently outperform their peers, there is not yet any careful statistical studies on this issue or any scientific method for identifying who these skilled managers are.

Private equity investors in 2001 face a rapidly changing environment where fundamentals have taken a terrible turn for the worse. The public market's appetite for IPOs, always a crucial outlet for the best venture-backed companies, has dried up considerably from its record-breaking run in 1999 and early 2000. At the same time, the high-yield debt markets, critical for the activities of leveraged-buyout investors, have been in the doldrums for even longer. While these short-term conditions look grim, the structural changes in the industry mean that even after a recovery, the landscape will look very different than it did just a few years ago.

In the past few years, top-tier private equity firms have sold stakes in themselves to diversified financial services firms, made strategic moves towards globalization, and planned for inter-generational transfers of control. An industry previously dominated by personality has begun to create brands that outlive their founders and, if not yet for the masses, is moving towards democratization. Perhaps soon, the challenge for investors will not be to discover the next Microsoft but to pick a venture capitalist to do it for them.

Further reading

Cochrane, J. (2000) "The risk and return of venture capital", National Bureau of Economic Research, working paper 8066.

Fenn, G. W., Liang, N. and Prowse, S. (1997), "The private equity industry: an overview", *Financial Markets, Institutions, and Instruments*, 6, 4.

Gompers, P. A. and Lerner, J. (2000) *The Venture Capital Cycle*, Cambridge MA: MIT Press.

Gompers, P. A. and Lerner, J. (2001) *The Money of Invention*, Boston, MA: Harvard Business School Press.

Reading the signs
from first-day returns

Access to new share offerings has looked like a licence to print money, but do the companies perform in the long term? **Kent Womack** investigates.

Kent L. Womack is an associate professor of finance at the Tuck School of Business, Dartmouth College.

When markets are booming, there is probably no better annualized return for investors than shares at the offer price in initial public offerings. First-day returns in internet IPOs averaged 65 per cent in the 1990s, so the rule was simple: get as much as you can from the underwriter at the offer price.

Alas, if only investing were so simple. As one digs deeper, investors report that obtaining those shares was about as unlikely as landing on the moon. The average IPO in the US had about 4m shares to sell and for the best deals institutional buyers wanted anything up to 100m shares. With only 4m shares available, investors were disappointed with the number of shares they were allocated. Smaller individual investors had little chance of obtaining any attractive IPO shares.

Such a scenario begs two important questions. First, what are the costs and benefits of these stupendous first-day underpricings? As others have put it, what could explain the amazing amount of "money left on the table" by issuing companies for the initial investors ($27bn in the US in 1990–99)? Second, should institutional and individual investors who do not get privileged allocations from underwriters invest in IPOs after the opening of the stock on the first day? If so, how?

Underpricing

A 40-year perspective on the first-day returns that initial investors receive shows that an average IPO increased 18.4 per cent on the first day. In the internet boom of 1999 and early 2000, however, 176 offerings more than doubled from the offering price on the first day. The average first-day price soared by more than 60 per cent. So a typical IPO that was sold to investors at $15 opened its first day for trading at $24 on average. The same typical IPO, selling about 4m shares to investors, raised $60m for its internal coffers and its pre-IPO investors, before paying underwriting fees.

Yet the first trading price made the same shares worth roughly $96m. The difference? An immediate profit of $36m for the initial investors. What did they do to deserve such incredible returns? Certainly the answer does not include taking on substantial risk as one might expect: it is difficult to find IPOs that do badly on the first day. So, there's the benefit for investors, but where's the cost? The company did not take in part of the $36m left on the table. (It is unlikely that most IPOs could have been offered for sale at the price at which they opened for trading, but certainly some portion of the $36m could have been captured for the company and its early investors.)

It is important to realize that investors who did not receive preferential shares from underwriters could not reap these large first-day gains by subsequent trading in the market. Once an IPO stock opens for trading, the easy money has already been made. Future returns are substantially smaller and much less unpredictable than the huge windfall gained between the offering price and the opening price. Obviously there were, and are, exceptions, with shares trading both higher and lower after the opening price, but the average price change for the first few days after the opening has been about zero.

With the markets down substantially from the highs recorded in Spring 2000, first-day underpricing has been more sanguine (in February and March 2001, first-day underpricing averaged only 5 per cent). Figure 1 shows the level of the Nasdaq and the average level of first-day returns, and hence underpricing, monthly from 1999 to 2001. Not surprisingly, as the market fell from mid-2000, the valuations that issuing companies could expect declined and the number of companies entering the market dropped precipitously. In the first quarter of 2001, only 18 IPOs were made, compared with 117 in the first quarter of 2000, at the peak of the internet boom.

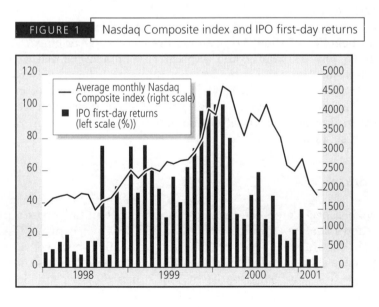

FIGURE 1 — Nasdaq Composite index and IPO first-day returns

What is the cause of such variability in the first-day gains? Several factors are relevant. First, in a bull market, investors appear to have more money to put to work and are more willing to buy newer securities about which less is known. Simply put, investors are more willing to gamble when they have the expectation or, more accurately, the "hope" that the market will keep going up. In falling markets, such as the US recently, institutional investors' appetites for new securities dries up. Second, the lower valuations that issuing companies expect to receive are also a factor in slowing the supply of IPOs, because managers are often unwilling to sell at a price lower than a previous price they thought obtainable (a phenomenon also seen in real estate markets).

Public (or private?)

A second factor affecting the level of IPO first-day underpricing is the system used for choosing the price and allocating shares to investors. In the US, the system used is called "bookbuilding", whereby the lead investment bank tallies up demand after the roadshow in which (usually only institutional) investors can meet the company's managers and hear their sales pitch. After tallying demand, the investment bank sets the issue price, and usually the issue opens for trading immediately or the next day (often at a substantially higher price).

Naturally, the investment bank has incentives to protect its own interests and future business opportunities in this process, unlike in an auction process where competing investors might competitively raise the price to one that "clears the market". As Francois Derrien and this author (2001) have shown in research on French IPOs, in a market where both bookbuilding and auctions occur for IPOs, auctions produce significantly less underpricing than bookbuilding, and virtually never underpricing that is above 20 per cent.

Hence, policymakers would do well to question the fairness of the bookbuilding process that often allows egregious, triple-digit windfall gains to some investors, when clearly other investors would pay more while simultaneously providing less money for the issuing companies. Bookbuilding is by nature preferential and exclusive, giving the underwriter extraordinary powers to allocate windfall returns to its preferred customers, usually those that pay the most in trading and underwriting commissions. While this is not illegal, a convincing argument could be made against this preferential system by regulators and policymakers, since the outcomes are not always competitive or "public".

Legal and regulatory investigations are under way in the US that question the appropriateness of investment banks' policies that are claimed to have allowed "tie-ins" of preferential treatment in IPOs to trading or higher commission rates for other or future business. One might hypothesize that such problems are directly a result of the bookbuilding system. In rising markets, the system does not issue shares at a competitive price but at a substantial discount, providing a direct transfer of the funds that issuing companies should have obtained to the investment bank's buy-side clients. This first-day windfall certainly appears to be anti-competitive. The alternative, a more competitive auction market where investors that bid higher prices get the most shares, still produces positive first-day returns to investors, but these returns tend to be lower (in France, about 10 per cent versus 17 per cent, on average, for bookbuilt offerings in the 1990s). In the view of many, a 5–10 per cent initial return is more appropriate as compensation for taking on the risk of a new issue.

Larger first-day returns appear to be something other than compensation for taking risk. Academics Raj Aggarwal, Laurie Krigman and this author (2001) support an explanation that company managers encourage underpricing because they are usually "locked up" from selling their shares for at least six months by covenants with the underwriter. Thus managers underprice initially to maximize their personal wealth and their ability to sell at a high price at the end of the lock-up period.

First-day underpricing generates more interest among security analysts, who may recommend the stock, maximizing the price at six months, the end of the lock-up period. In essence, managers of IPO companies may have a conflict that pits their personal aggrandisement against raising more money for their company at the initial IPO price.

After the windfall

Most investors, without the connections or levels of commission business at the underwriters' brokerage houses to obtain shares of IPOs at the offering price, are left to decide whether to invest in IPO shares once trading has opened. Investors have few sources from which to form opinions in the first months. In the US, a "quiet period" is required by the Securities and Exchange Commission, in which those companies in the underwriting syndicate must refrain from giving an opinion on the issuer and its prospects. Therefore, in the first month after the IPO, price changes and trading volumes are almost the only signals an investor gets.

Perhaps not surprisingly, empirical evidence shows that trading volume is quite high for the first two or three days after an IPO and then settles down for the next few weeks, as investors wait for earnings reports, investment advice from brokerage analysts and other information. The size of the early spike in trading volume is correlated with the amount of the underwriter's underpricing.

Figure 2 shows trading turnover for IPOs in their first five days. (Turnover for a day is trading volume divided by the number of shares issued by the IPO company, hence it is a scaled measure of trading volume.) One notices that extremely underpriced IPOs (that is, the most popular ones) have substantial turnover on the first day. In some cases, IPOs trade more shares on the first day than were offered, implying that some of the shares are bought and sold more than once during the first day.

The intense trading pressure in popular IPO shares is known as "flipping" and is regularly demonized by investment bankers who view it as a destabilizing force. One of the services an investment banker provides issuers with is stabilization, or propping up of weaker offerings. The investment banks' traders stand ready to buy shares at or below the offering price for a few days after the offering. This support can be costly if too many shares that

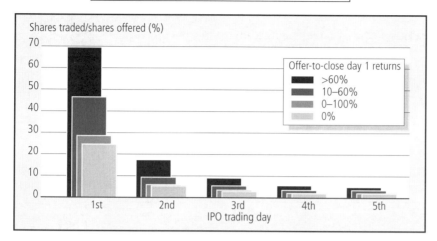

FIGURE 2 Trading turnover for IPOs in their first-five days

are originally sold to investors are resold in the marketplace too quickly and the investment banker is forced to take a risky long position in the IPO stock or face a falling price for the offering. When an investment bank's recent issues fall in price, the market takes it as a very negative signal of the bank's ability to place offerings successfully. Hence, investment banks have attempted with some success to persuade institutional investors not to flip but to hold if they want future offerings by the same banker.

The phenomenon of flipping by larger investors has an interesting twist. If the larger institutions are the smartest "informed" investors, then perhaps their collective buying or selling activity in the early trading is an important omen of future returns (see Box 1). Academics Laurie Krigman, Wayne Shaw and this author (1999) have demonstrated that IPOs in which there is the highest level of block selling on the first day are on average the poorest performers over the next year.

Conversely, when institutions were not flipping but holding their shares tightly on the first day, those target companies did relatively and significantly better. In a recent update and extension of that study, Boulat Minnigoulov (2001) found not only that first-day flipping was important but that high levels of flipping throughout the 25-day quiet period were a very significant predictor of poor future performance of the IPO stock. In addition, he found that higher levels of average trading volume in the quiet period was usually associated with higher returns for one year after the quiet period.

Since earnings reports and brokerage reports are rare during the quiet period, volume information and price changes are virtually the only information an investor has for making an assessment of a share purchase. Stock prices and returns on the first day and during the quiet period appear to be useful, but not as useful as flipping and volume indicators in predicting future performance. Using data from 1993–99, the above research by Krigman, Shaw and this author, as well as that by Minnigoulov, concludes that poor performance on an IPO's first day (where the price is at or below the offer price at the end of the first trading day) is a pessimistic indicator of future share price health.

Box 1 Flipping out on Martha Stewart

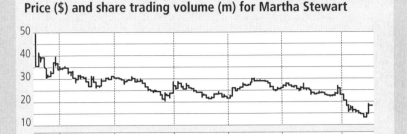

Martha Stewart Living Omnimedia, which opened trading on 18 October 1999, provides a classic case of first-day performance. The stock was priced to investors at $18 a share and opened for trading at $37, an increase of 107 per cent.

On the first trading day, sellers of blocks (10,000 shares or more per trade) accounted for 47 per cent of the 11m first-day trading volume, a disproportionately high amount relative to other stocks. In the next six months, the share price declined 48 per cent.

The trading rule of avoiding stocks with a high flipping percentage of total volume was valuable in the 1990s for predicting relatively poor performance for 6- and 12-month periods after the IPO quiet period.

The bottom line

For investors with a one-year investment horizon, three signals from the early trading environment are valuable in picking the IPO wheat from the chaff. First, company shares that do not close above the offer price on the first day are, on average, poor performers over the next year. Second, when institutional investors aggressively sell blocks of shares on the first day and during the quiet period, these shares tend to underperform over the next year. Third, IPOs with the highest levels of turnover during the first 25-day quiet period tend to be better investments than those with low turnover ratios.

These indicators tell an interesting story about investors in IPOs. It would appear that, collectively, early institutional investors have a good sense of high-quality and low-quality IPOs in that they flip on day one and throughout the quiet period the ones that perform poorly in the future. Similarly, they are more likely to retain the ones that ultimately do well. But at the same time, the more successful offerings have higher trading volume (turnover) during this 25-day quiet period, presumably signalling greater interest in the shares.

If one takes a longer view of investing in IPOs as a portfolio over a three- to five-year time horizon, the results are not as encouraging. Academic Jay Ritter (1991) has shown that IPOs tend to underperform appropriate benchmarks over this longer period, and this is particularly true of the smallest offerings (usually underwritten by underwriters of lesser reputation). While some researchers have questioned the significance of IPO long-term underperformance, academic research has not shown that a portfolio specializing in IPOs is an attractive investment vehicle in the long run.

Copyright © Kent Womack 2002

Further reading

Aggarwal, R., Krigman, L. and Womack, K. (2001) "Strategic IPO underpricing, information momentum and lockup expiration selling", working paper, Dartmouth College (http://www.mba.tuck.dartmouth.edu/pages/faculty/kent.womack).

Derrien, F. and Womack, K. (2001) "Auctions vs. bookbuilding and the control of underpricing in hot IPO markets", working paper, Dartmouth College (http://www.mba.tuck.dartmouth.edu/pages/faculty/kent.womack).

Ibbotson, R., Sindelar, J. and Ritter, J. (1994) "The market's problems with the pricing of initial public offerings", *Journal of Applied Corporate Finance*, 7, 66–74.

Krigman, L., Shaw, W. and Womack, K. (1999), "The persistence of IPO mispricing and the predictive power of flipping", *Journal of Finance*, 54, 1015–44.

Loughran, T. and Ritter, J. (2001), "Why don't issuers get upset about leaving money on the table in IPOs?", *Review of Financial Studies*, (http://bear.cba.ufl.edu/ritter/parnov.htm).

Minnigoulov, B. (2001) "Post-IPO flipping and turnover", working paper, Dartmouth College (http://www.mba.tuck.dartmouth.edu/pages/faculty/kent.womack).

Ritter, J. (1991) "The long-run performance of initial public offerings", *Journal of Finance*, 46, 3–27.

Regulation 11

Contents

Regulation and asset management 324

Julian Franks, London Business School, **Colin Mayer**, University of Oxford and **Luis Correia da Silva**, Oxford Economic Research Associates

This article argues that the variety of institutional arrangements in Europe makes different regulatory systems essential.

Why managers hold on to risk 331

Charles Himmelberg, Columbia Business School and **Glenn Hubbard**, Columbia University

Knowing the benefits of diversification, how can managers and entrepreneurs risk most of their investments in the company they work for?

Ways of taking care of tax 337

Terry Shevlin, University of Washington

This article describes the broad conventions of investments taxation in the US and UK, and explores the ramifications of annual and deferred taxation at ordinary income and capital gains tax rates.

The coming of the single financial regulator 344

Howard Davies, FSA

This article describes the role of the new single financial regulator, the FSA, and outlines its risk-based approach to the task.

Introduction to Part 11

Relations between government and financial markets can greatly affect investment performance, not simply in respect of taxation. Governments set the framework of rules within which markets operate, and while recent years have seen many rules converge in national markets, there remain significant discrepancies in such areas as procedures, financial disclosure, shareholder rights and freedom from corruption. Elsewhere in this part we look at the rise of socially responsible investing, a form of investment that incorporates environmental and ethical considerations in the portfolio decision.

Regulation and asset management

Julian Franks is Corporation of London Professor of Finance at London Business School.

Colin Mayer is Peter Moores Professor of Management Studies at Saïd Business School, University of Oxford.

Dr Luis Correia da Silva is director of Oxford Economic Research Associates.

Controlling risks and protecting investors is not straightforward, especially when regulation methods vary so much. **Julian Franks**, **Colin Mayer** and **Luis Correia da Silva** report on their survey of seven European countries.

The goal of regulation for banks is clear: it is to provide stability to the financial system and to limit the risks of systemic failures. Analysis of the risks of the asset management industry reveals that systemic risks are much less significant. Unlike commercial and investment banks, and brokers and dealers, asset management companies do not often take large positions on their own account. They invest on behalf of others.

This article assesses the response of regulators to the risks of asset management and how regulation should be framed at the European level, based on a survey of seven countries. Proposals by the Basle committee on banking supervision to extend capital requirements to operational risk of financial institutions have lent greater importance to this issue.

Different forms of investor protection give rise to different costs and benefits, including an impact on entry and competition. In the absence of systemic risks, the regulation of asset managers is closer to that of professional partnerships than that of banks. For example, in the legal profession, some of the principal risks are fraud against client funds and professional negligence. These are similar to the risks in asset management. Literature on regulating the professions points to a trade-off, enhancing quality by restricting entry and competition. In the same way, an important issue arises as to how regulating asset managers can improve investor protection without limiting competition.

Inadequate investor protection can incur costs. Uninformed investors, fearing that they might be exploited, will be reluctant to invest, or will invest in other financial centres. "Good" companies will be tainted with the failure of "bad" companies and will withdraw from the market or migrate to other centres. Conversely, over-regulation can entail higher costs for companies and investors, may alter the costs of entry and competition and cause loss of competitiveness. Regulation is therefore crucial in determining the success of financial institutions and financial centres.

Institutional setting

The most striking feature of asset management is its diversity. For example, the size of the business varies markedly across France, Germany, Ireland, Italy, the Netherlands, Spain and the UK. Assets under management by pension funds in the UK comprise more than half of all pension fund assets and assets managed by insurance companies comprise just under half of all insurance companies' assets. However, US pension fund business is more than five times that of the UK and insurance company business is twice as large.

One reason for these disparities is that continental Europe has had less-developed stock markets and therefore less need for a substantial asset management business. That may well be changing as stock markets expand, but asset management remains a more substantial part of Anglo-American systems than of Continental ones. A second aspect of this diversity is the differing nature of the business. While the UK dominates European pension fund and insurance asset management, it is a smaller player in mutual funds. Differences in the size of pension-managed funds reflect the UK emphasis on funded schemes. In other European countries, state pensions, pay-as-you-go and corporate schemes predominate. Distinctions also arise within continental Europe. For example, insurance companies are dominant in Germany, while the numbers of mutual funds and insurance company funds are similar in France.

One implication is that both the business being regulated and the type of investor differ greatly. In some countries, clients of asset management companies are mainly large institutional investors and in others, private clients. In some countries, most investments are through pooled funds – our research found this was a feature of France and Italy – and in others, through mandates (in Germany, the Netherlands and the UK).

Third, countries differ in the ownership as well as the activities of asset management companies. In our survey, 87 per cent of respondents said they were part of a larger group. Outside the UK and the US, companies are mainly owned by banks and insurance companies, many of which may be classified as parts of conglomerates. While this is the case in some of the largest companies in the UK, there are many small, independent companies, and there are nearly six times as many in the US as in the UK.

Concentration of ownership is therefore appreciably higher in continental Europe than in the UK and the US. Furthermore, there are differences within the Continent, where France has seen a rapidly increasing number of small, independent companies. The significance of this is that organization and ownership crucially affect investors' exposure to loss. Large groups have larger financial resources than independent companies and may have more incentive to provide protection to investors. If parent companies believe that either the intrinsic value of their asset management companies or the loss of their reputations outweigh the cost of compensating investors, they will protect investors against loss.

Different countries

How have regulators responded? Seven main forms of regulation are employed:

- financial resource requirements;
- conduct-of-business rules;
- separation of clients' assets requirements;
- disclosure rules;
- enforcement;
- auditing;
- investor compensation schemes.

Some differences are illustrated below in relation to France, Germany, the UK and US.

There are expenditure-based capital requirements in the three European countries. The broad rule is a quarter of annual expenditures, but adjustments to take into account exposure to position risk, foreign-exchange risks, separation of clients' monies and so on are also present. Furthermore, there are initial capital requirements. In the US, there are no capital requirements at the federal level, but there may be at the state level.

There are extensive conduct-of-business rules in the UK and self-regulatory (professional ethics) rules of conduct in France. Conduct-of-business rules are far fewer in the US and include "fair execution", which is common in other countries. In France, client assets and those of the company must be kept separate. In Germany, managers must keep securities at a credit institution or be regulated as credit institutions themselves. In the UK, companies that hold clients' monies or assets are subject to more extensive capital requirements and conduct-of-business rules. In the US, investment advisers holding clients' securities can expect more rigorous and random auditing. Also, there are extensive disclosure rules, private and public auditors, and enforcement through the courts.

There have been significant calls on the compensation fund in the UK, amounting to more than £130m in the past five years. However, companies regulated by the Investment Management Regulatory Organization – and, in particular, asset management companies – account for only a small part of this. A limited compensation scheme for investment companies was recently introduced in Germany. There are no (direct) compensation schemes in France or the US.

In summary, France emphasizes conduct-of-business rules and custody requirements for collective investment schemes and mandates; Germany, capital requirements and separation of clients' assets; the UK, capital requirements, conduct-of-business rules and a compensation scheme; and the US, disclosure, auditing and enforcement.

The various forms of regulation complement the structures of asset management business. In Germany, investors are in general institutional and asset management companies are part of large institutions. Investors are therefore for the most part relatively well informed and can be compensated in the event of failure by parent institutions wishing to preserve their reputations. As a result, the cost of a mandatory compensation scheme is likely to be lower than in the UK, which has more small retail investors. Imposing large capital requirements is consistent with the concentration of the German asset management business in large organizations.

In some countries, such as France, asset management has emerged over the past decade outside the banks and insurance companies, in particular in the form of mutual funds. Investor protection has therefore focused mainly on these institutions – for example, the imposition of depository (trustee) requirements in France on collective instruments or mutual fund management business, but not on mandated portfolio management. Separation of clients' assets has, however, been imposed on collective instruments as well as on individual mandates. The UK has a significant independent private client business but a relatively small mutual fund business. Regulation has therefore sought to protect investments made through mandates as well as collective schemes. This is done through capital requirements, conduct-of-business rules, incentives to use separate custodians and a compensation scheme.

The US has the largest independent asset management business both in mandates and collective schemes. However, its approach is very different from that of the UK. It emphasizes disclosure, auditing and enforcement. UK regulation relies on public contracting (monitoring by public agencies, while the US emphasizes private contracting), providing information to investors and the ability to enforce contracts in the courts.

Other protection

The most serious failures reported in the survey were misdealing and breach of client guidelines. In reported complaints, the most significant items were computer systems failure, misdealing and breach of client guidelines. Most losses were below £1m, although there were losses of, for example, £3m for breach of client guidelines and £7m for misdealing. Losses from operational failures could be as much as £20m. Operational risks relate primarily to securities transactions and internal systems, and involve modest losses.

Provided that investors are informed, they will be able to price these risks appropriately and will only be willing to use asset management services at a suitably reduced price. However, if investors are ill informed, services will not be properly priced. In this case, good companies will be unable to charge a premium over poor companies. Information problems are therefore a primary source of market failure. The response in the US has been to require extensive disclosure.

In a 1989 study, Julian Franks and Colin Mayer recorded that fraud was the main threat to investors. The Robert Maxwell pension case later reinforced the potential exposure of investors to this risk. However, risks of fraud now appear to be appreciably lower. While there was some reference to fraud by respondents in the survey, it was by no means regarded as the primary risk. Incidents of losses were small, perceived frequency was low and there were no reported complaints about fraud.

A significant change since the study is the growth of custody. In 1989, use of separate custodians by investment management companies in the UK was rare. Possibly in response to the Maxwell affair, or as a consequence of the development of the custodian industry, custodians outside the group to which the asset manager belongs now hold 80 per cent of UK companies' assets under management. The survey reports that the use of non-group custodians is in general lower on the Continent. This may reflect the greater use of custodians within the same group of companies on the Continent.

As noted above, most operating losses are modest. As a result, companies finance losses from earnings. However, large losses do occur. The case of Morgan Grenfell Asset Management is an example. The firm suffered losses of £210m when protecting investors against a loss in one of its fund management companies. The case also illustrates the limitations of custodianship and trusteeship. While there was no theft of securities or monies, there were irregularities in managing the funds that were not detected by trustees. As a result, the regulator, IMRO, imposed fines of nearly £400,000 on the two trustees.

It is unclear to what extent the trustees or custodians would have compensated investors for losses had Deutsche Bank not injected £180m to rescue the asset management firm. In particular, it is unclear whether investors would have been fully protected from loss by the existence of both a trustee and custodian had Morgan Grenfell Asset Management not been part of a large group. Therefore, while custodianship and trusteeship can help to mitigate failures, they may not provide complete protection.

Further protection can come from insurance markets. In the sample, 19 companies had indemnity insurance, 15 employee fidelity and fraud insurance, and nine other insurance policies (covering civil responsibility, real estate, and directors and officers). Companies regard insurance as particularly relevant to areas where substantial losses can occur, such as fraud and failures in computer systems. However, some companies have doubts about the promptness and reliability with which claims are met. Insurance markets, both private and mutual, are better developed in the US than in Europe.

Instead, there is more emphasis on compensation funds in Europe, in particular in the UK. Over the past five years, the Investors Compensation Scheme in the UK has paid out more than £100m. Since 1988, more than 12,000 people have received compensation and more than 700 companies have been declared in default.

Compensation schemes encourage entry and competition where they are large in relation to the regulatory burdens imposed on companies. In general they subsidize high-risk companies at the expense of low-risk companies or the taxpayer. They therefore, at least in part, make entry easier by mitigating the consequences of other forms of regulation, in particular capital requirements. However, like state aid, they distort competition between countries. The imposition of a common European compensation scheme might be thought to reduce this risk. In fact, differences in industry structures across countries mean that harmonized compensation schemes can be highly distorting. For example, a particular level of compensation will, on average, benefit the UK asset management industry, with its comparatively large number of small companies relative to the more concentrated German industry.

In addition, compensation schemes encourage companies to hold insufficient capital because they do not bear all the costs of failure. While this might be thought to justify the imposition of capital requirements, regulators cannot readily establish the extent to which compensation schemes influence companies' capital structure decisions. The relationship between required levels of capital and the scale of compensation schemes is therefore unknown, and for the reasons mentioned above will be dependent on the structure of a particular country's asset management business.

Instead, distortions to competition from compensation schemes can be avoided by having risk-based fee structures. Since such structures reflect companies' holdings of capital, they automatically induce managers to choose optimal capital structures. Again, the question is, how can regulators determine fee structures? One approach might be to encourage private insurers to offer standard contracts equivalent to those of compensation schemes. Since systemic risks are not a substantial problem in asset management, the market failures that cause insurance contracts to fail in relation to bank deposits should not be present. The option of having privately supplied standard compensation contracts is worth investigating.

Judging systems

Systems of regulation should be judged against the degree to which they provide effective investor protection and their effect on competition. Private contracting in the US emphasizes the operation of markets through information disclosure and auditing. It encourages high levels of entry and competition, but relies on the legal system to enforce contracts through private as well as public litigation. It is therefore essentially a system of *caveat emptor*.

The public contracting system in the UK offers investors greater protection through a compensation scheme, but at the expense of limiting competition through the imposition of capital requirements and rules on conducting business. The scale of protection is therefore determined primarily by the size of the compensation scheme, and the effect on competition by the size of capital requirements and the nature of conduct-of-business rules. The results of the survey confirm that the cost of capital varies greatly across companies, indicating that the costs of extra capital are potentially high for some companies.

The parent firm system of Germany places less reliance on public agencies; to that extent, it is less interventionist than the UK. However, it limits entry to companies that have access to substantial amounts of capital and are in general a part of large organizations. As long as asset management companies have deep pockets from which to draw, and can rely on the reputation of the parent firm to bail them out in the event of failure, they offer investors high degrees of protection.

Where investments occur largely through mutual funds, as in France and Spain, protection comes from "depositaires" or "depositarios" respectively, which act as a custodian.

Where the parent company system is not dominant, there is a greater potential for entry, but also greater possibility of contractual disagreements between asset managers, custodians and trustees, as shown by the UK case study. Investors may therefore be exposed to greater risks than under the parent company system.

Conclusion

Attempts to harmonize regulatory rules across countries are inappropriate. Regulation and institutional arrangements are complementary. So long as pronounced institutional differences persist, then so, too, should different forms of regulation.

There is, in general, a trade-off between investor protection and competition. High levels of investor protection can be achieved through large compensation funds and high capital requirements, but at the expense of competition, product variety and entry. The costs of higher capital requirements are large for some companies and could therefore have significant effects on competition.

Market failures in asset management are different from those that occur in banks. They arise from information asymmetries and fraud, not in general from systemic risks. They should be corrected directly by a combination of disclosure, auditing, enforcement, insurance, custody and trustees, rather than indirectly through capital requirements.

The development of insurance markets, greater clarity of investor protection in custody arrangements, auditing, and enforcement through the courts are important components of a move towards a more market-oriented system. The creation of an integrated financial market in Europe would benefit from such a development, but requires careful consideration of the way in which information, insurance and legal structure can be strengthened.

A move towards raising capital requirements would be counterproductive. It would discourage the necessary development of markets in information and insurance, as well as having a direct impact on competition and entry. Unless capital requirements are set at unrealistically high levels, they could also provide a false sense of security.

This article is based on a study by the authors for the European Asset Management Association. It is published as *Asset Management and Investor Protection* (Oxford University Press, 2001).

Copyright © Julian Franks, Colin Mayer and Luis Correia da Silva 2002

Further reading

Franks, J. and Mayer, C. (1989) *Risk, Regulation and Investor Protection: The Case of Investment Management*, Oxford: Oxford University Press.

Instefjord, N., Jackshon, P. and Perraudin, W. (1998) "Securities fraud", *Economic Policy*, 27, 587–623.

Mayer, C. and Neven, D. (1991) "European financial regulation: a framework for policy analysis", in Giovannini, A. and Mayer, C. (eds), *European Financial Integration*, Cambridge: Cambridge University Press.

Why managers hold on to risk

Why do managers flout the accepted wisdom of diversification and hold such large stakes in the companies they control? **Charles Himmelberg** and **Glenn Hubbard** offer some answers.

Charles P. Himmelberg is an associate professor of finance and economics at Columbia Business School.

R. Glenn Hubbard is chairman of President Bush's Council of Economic Advisers. He is on leave from Columbia University, where he is Russell L. Carson Professor of Economics and Finance and academic director of the Eugene M. Lang Center for Entrepreneurship.

Modern portfolio theory sets out reasons for, among other things, the wisdom of diversification. It shows that when multiple risky assets are pooled into a single portfolio, the variance of the portfolio is less than the variance of any single asset. The practical application of this can be seen in the explosion of mutual funds over the past decade. Investors around the world are more diversified than ever.

Yet the theory presents a problem, which arises when we consider an important aspect of corporate investment behaviour. The difficulty is this: entrepreneurs, sole proprietors and even the managers of large corporations are surprisingly – even shockingly – undiversified by virtue of their large stakes in the companies they manage. Given that these investors are so financially sophisticated, what explains their apparent disregard for the principles of modern investment advice? The key to this is the importance of managerial incentives. The portfolios of the managerial class are for the most part overwhelmingly invested in the assets of the companies entrusted to their oversight.

For sole proprietors and entrepreneurs, the point is self-evident: bearing the idiosyncratic risk of your company is a cost of going into business by yourself. What is more surprising is that bearing idiosyncratic risk appears to be as important (and unavoidable) for managers of publicly traded companies as it is for sole proprietors and entrepreneurs. Among the smallest publicly traded companies in the US (those in the bottom third of the size distribution, with sales of less than $22m), our research has shown that the average fraction of equity held by top managers is over 30 per cent. For the top third of the size distribution (those with sales in excess of $188m), the average ownership stake is closer to 13 per cent.

The accepted view that entrepreneurs in the US can easily

diversify risk by taking their companies public is only half true. Even in the warmest of financial climates for initial public offerings, managers of newly public companies are obliged to keep large equity stakes in their companies. So they continue to bear a large part of the idiosyncratic risk that could have been eliminated if incentive considerations were not so important.

At the top of the size distribution, our more recent research has found the average ownership stake of managers for the largest 150 companies in the US is in the range of 1–2 per cent. Critics of corporate governance have argued that such "small" ownership stakes are insufficient for aligning the interests of managers with owners. However, this complaint overlooks the fact that these companies are enormous. For a company with a market capitalization of $10bn, for example, a 1 per cent stake represents $100m – enough to focus the attention of all but the very wealthiest of top management teams.

Another interesting fact that flies in the face of common wisdom is the finding that the fraction of equity owned by managers of publicly traded corporations in the US is if anything higher today than in the past. Research by academics Clifford Holderness, Randall Kroszner and Dennis Sheehan (1999) has shown that managerial ownership stakes rose from an average of 13 per cent in 1935 to 21 per cent in 1995. In short, the size of inside shareholdings suggests that the financial interests of managers in the US are not (and indeed, never were) so different from those of the company's shareholders.

A third finding that helps to complete empirical knowledge of ownership structures is evidence on the structure of ownership around the world from academic Rafael La Porta and his colleagues (1998). They have shown that in financially sophisticated countries where the level of investor protection is high (that is, where the legal and regulatory environment makes it easier for firms to honour the terms of debt and equity contracts), managerial ownership concentrations tend to be low, whereas in countries with less-developed financial markets, concentrations tend to be high.

Our empirical research has backed up these findings by showing that country-level measures of investor protection are important even after controlling for company characteristics associated with information, risk, and incentive problems that are also known to affect managerial ownership concentrations. Figure 1 makes the same point, revealing wide disparities in inside ownership concentrations in the largest 150 companies across countries. At one end of the scale, countries such as the UK and the US have very low inside ownership concentrations – in the order of 1–2 per cent – while at the other end of the scale, less-developed countries such as Turkey and Peru display extraordinarily high concentrations of 70 per cent and more. Generally speaking, poorly developed financial markets and less developed economies tend to have high concentrations of managerial shareholding.

Managerial entrenchment?

While there is less separation between management and ownership than one might fear, managerial ownership stakes have been growing, not falling, since the 1930s. Evidence shows that concentrated ownership structures are found

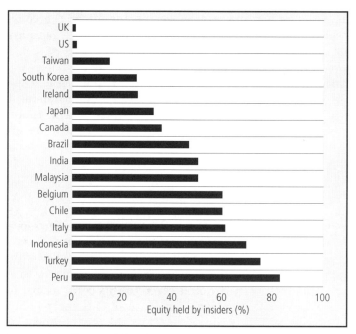

Source: Himmelberg et al. (2001)

in economies that are less rather than more successful. It might be argued that this reflects self-entrenching behaviour by managers. If true, this view would suggest that the beneficial incentive effects of large stakeholdings are offset (at least in part) by the disincentives that arise when managers need to defend themselves against hostile (disciplinary) takeover attempts.

While managerial entrenchment is a realistic concern, we do not think it explains the extent to which managers are forced to hold undiversified portfolios in their own companies, especially given the way shareholdings are concentrated in countries outside the UK and the US. The most important argument for this view is that there are less costly ways for managers to entrench themselves. They can, for example, design a "dual class" share structure whereby they issue and retain for themselves a class of shares with extra voting rights (for example, 10 votes per share) and issue shares with weaker voting rights to outside investors. This structure entrenches managerial control over the company without forcing managers to hold a large part of their financial wealth in the company's stock. But few managers choose this option.

Those who are persuaded by the entrenchment view also commonly note the considerable lengths to which managers go to defend themselves from hostile takeovers. But managers acting on behalf of stockholders (including their own stakes) have good reasons for resisting initial offers because when hostile takeover attempts succeed, as they often do, the target usually sells for a price substantially higher than the initial offer.

Legal environment

Even if it does not reflect managerial entrenchment, is the concentration of managerial shareholding necessarily such a good thing? There are reasons to think it is not.

More likely than self-entrenching behaviour by managers, we think, is the likelihood that managerial ownership concentration is like a "canary in a coal mine". It warns of a weak legal and regulatory environment that obliges entrepreneurs and managers to hold larger equity stakes than they would otherwise prefer. It is useful to think about the concentration of managerial ownership from the perspective of an entrepreneur writing a contract with initial outside investors. If contracts were easy to write and enforce, a risk-averse entrepreneur would say: "I'll manage the company at an agreed level of effort if in return you agree to purchase 100 per cent of the equity and pay me a fixed salary." In addition to paying the manager for her services, this contract would, if executed, successfully transfer the entrepreneur's risk exposure to outside investors, where it could be easily diversified.

The obvious problem with this contract is that the level of effort exerted at the entrepreneur-manager's end of the bargain is difficult to observe and enforce. No reasonable investor would agree to this contract because paying a fixed salary destroys the manager's incentives: no matter how hard the manager works, the reward is the same. Thus the entrepreneur's exposure to diversifiable risk cannot be removed (at least not completely) because to do so destroys company value by destroying incentives.

The moral of the story: incentive considerations make it difficult (that is, costly) for outside investors to provide external funding and risk diversification to the managers of the company. We would add an important corollary to this: to the extent that the legal and regulatory environment makes it difficult to write and enforce contracts, entrepreneurs and managers find it in their best interests to retain a higher fraction of the company's equity.

In difficult contracting environments where incentive problems are extreme and the legal framework for protecting investors is weak, entrepreneurs and managers cannot credibly convince investors that their money will be efficiently used and returned to them as high future returns. The expectation of future conflicts of interest resulting from self-interested behaviour by managers and inside owners is reflected in low prices for the shares at the time of the offer and discourages entrepreneurs and managers from fully diversifying. Perfect risk sharing becomes unfeasible and, in the extreme, companies may choose not to go public. This describes the environment in many if not most developing economies. It may even describe a few highly developed countries like Germany and France where, until recently, the financial climate for entrepreneurship and new business formation was notoriously poor.

Partly because of the success of the US financial system in financing new high-tech companies in the 1990s, and partly because of the grim evidence from privatization schemes in Russia and the former Soviet Union, the role of the legal and regulatory regime has attracted renewed interest among researchers in corporate finance. In the Soviet Union, state-owned companies were privatized and markets introduced into a legal environment lacking the laws, courts or enforcement powers to adjudicate and enforce contracts. In hindsight, it perhaps seems obvious that the newly privatized companies would be subject to massive incentive failures, including many cases of outright theft and looting. It also seems fair to say that even cynical observers were surprised by the degree to which the absence of legal infrastructure mattered. Newly created shares were widely distributed among the population at large, but these soon became nearly worthless as diffuse shareholders came to recognize that managers were expropriating wealth from the company with no legal repercussions.

Limiting growth

Evidence collected by academics Robert King and Ross Levine (1993) (and many others) shows a strong positive relationship between the quality and efficiency of a country's legal system and its level of economic development. Our own research with Inessa Love (2001) suggests that the concentration of managerial ownership provides an important clue about the source and causal direction of the relationship.

We have also found evidence suggesting that companies with high managerial ownership stakes are more reluctant to fund new projects. They apply "hurdle rates" to new projects that are several percentage points higher than companies with lower stakes. For every 10 percentage points of managerial ownership, managers apply an additional 50 basis points to the threshold rate of return that new projects must meet to be accepted (the hurdle rate). For example, our calculations show that a company where 60 per cent of the shares are owned by insiders uses a hurdle rate which is 200 basis points (two percentage points) higher than a company in which managers own only a 20 per cent stake. Increases in the cost of capital of this magnitude substantially reduce the managers' incentive to invest in assets that contribute to the future growth of the company. This includes not only tangible assets such as structures and equipment but intangibles such as the products of research and development expenditure.

Our research with Inessa Love shows that differences in the quality of investor protections are large enough to explain why some countries invest and grow rich, and others do not. For example, Figure 1 indicates that the desired level of productive assets (structures and equipment) is three times higher in the UK, where ownership stakes average just 1 per cent, than in Peru, where they average more than 80 per cent. These estimates suggest the possible extent to which the allocation of capital is discouraged by weak legal and regulatory environment. This results in high concentrations of managerial ownership. The estimates also explain why, despite the dramatic reduction of international barriers on capital movements, capital still does not flow from rich countries to poor ones to the extent that it should given the presumably high returns to capital in poor countries.

Thus there may be gains beyond "financial liberalization" which involve only the reduction of barriers. Most studies of benefits to an economy of opening financial markets emphasize gains from a lower risk-free rate of interest or price of risk. Our results suggest that consequences of financial liberalization depend on the level – or changes in the level – of investor protection, a point sometimes overlooked in liberalization arguments offered by international financial institutions. In complementary research, for example, academics Geert Bekaert, Campbell Harvey and Christian Lundblad (2001) have shown that the pre-existence of an Anglo-Saxon legal system enhances investment gains following financial liberalization.

The research we have surveyed here merely attempts to put on paper the wisdom that investors have always learnt the hard way: it is unwise to put your money into countries where the quality of investor protection afforded by the legal and regulatory environment does not make it easy to get future returns out.

Copyright © Charles Himmelberg and Glenn Hubbard 2002

Further reading

Bekaert, G., Harvey, C.R. and Lundblad, C. (2001) "Does financial liberalisation spur growth?", NBER (http://papers.nber.org/papers/W8245).

Himmelberg, C.P., Hubbard, R.G. and Palia, D. (1999) "Understanding the determinants of managerial ownership", *Journal of Financial Economics*, 53, 353–84.

Himmelberg, C.P., Hubbard, R.G. and Love, I. (2001) "Investor protection, ownership and capital allocation", working paper, Columbia University (http://www.columbia.edu/~cph15/hhl.pdf).

Holderness, C.G., Kroszner, R.S. and Sheehan, D.P. (1999) "Were the good old days that good?", *Journal of Finance*, 54, 435–69.

King, R.G. and Levine, R. (1993) "Finance and growth: Schumpeter might be right", *Quarterly Journal of Economics*, 108, 717–37.

La Porta, R., Lopez-de-Silanes, F., Shleifer, A. and Vishny, R.W. (1998) "Law and finance", *Journal of Political Economy*, 106, 1113.

Ways of taking care of tax

Taxes should not drive investment decisions, says **Terry Shevlin**, but ought to be considered when evaluating alternative investments.

Terry Shevlin is Deloitte & Touche Professor of Accounting at the University of Washington.

Poor tax planning can dramatically reduce investment returns. In the US, for example, selling appreciated securities a day before a holding period related to capital gains tax can result in a 39.6 per cent tax rate instead of 20 per cent. This article examines the role of taxes in portfolio investment decisions.

One can examine the effect of taxation using a simple example of investing £100. Assume a fixed annual pre-tax rate of return of 10 per cent over five years. The effect of taxes can be looked at along three dimensions:

- When is income taxed – in each period (as with interest on bonds) or is it deferred?
- At what level is income taxed – tax-exempt, favourable capital gains or as ordinary income?
- Is the initial investment tax deductible?

To begin, £100 invested will return £161 before tax. Now compare the accumulations when the income is taxed each year with those when it is deferred and taxed at the end of the holding period. (Assume income is taxed at the same rate whether taxed in each period or when withdrawn at the end of the holding period.) With periodic taxation at 40 per cent (the highest rate on ordinary income in the UK), £100 accumulates to £133 after tax – compared with £161 with no taxes. The after-tax earnings are only 55 per cent of the untaxed earnings. Compare this with income taxed when it is withdrawn, as happens with a lump-sum withdrawal from a retirement account in the US. The £100 now accumulates to £161, less the taxes due on the £61 income, which at 40 per cent leaves £36 – a higher total accumulation of £136 because taxes are deferred on each period's earnings.

In some instances, earnings may be taxed at 20 per cent when withdrawn: in the US when shares taxed as long-term capital gains are sold; and in the UK when shares held for three years are sold. In this case, the £100 investment comes to £100 + £61.05 × (1 − 0.20) = £128.84. It is clear, then, that the differences in tax treatment result in real disparities in investment return.

Finally, consider whether the initial investment is tax deductible. Another way of saying this is whether the investor invests using after-tax money or pre-tax money. Investments in qualified pension plans are tax deductible, such as the UK's personal or stakeholder pension schemes, and in the US, traditional individual retirement accounts (IRAs) and 401(k) plans. If we invest £100 of after-tax salary in a pension it will accumulate thus:

$$£100/(1 - t_0) \times [(1+0.10)^5 \times (1 - t_n)]$$

where t_0 denotes the tax rate at the point of investment or contribution and t_n the tax rate at withdrawal. Earnings are not taxed until withdrawn as a lump sum after five years.

In the US, because the investment is tax deductible, the total withdrawal is taxed (earnings and initial contribution). In the UK, there are generally limits on lump-sum withdrawals, but these are often tax free. If an investor expects the tax rate to stay unchanged over the holding period, the pension simplifies to £100 × (1 + 0.10)^5 = £161, which is equivalent to tax-exemption.

It is useful to convert these after-tax accumulations to annualized after-tax rates of returns to allow comparisons across different investments and their returns as we lengthen the investment horizon. This is done using:

$$(\text{After-tax accumulation}/\text{After-tax investment amount})^{1/n} - 1$$

Table 1 shows accumulations for the four investments considered above as we lengthen the holding period. The top part shows accumulations and the lower part gives annualized after-tax rates of return. These are also plotted in Figure 1.

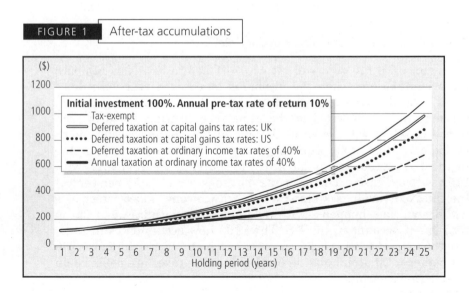

FIGURE 1   After-tax accumulations

TABLE 1 Effects of differential taxation on after-tax accumulations and annualized after-tax rates of return

After-tax accumulations

	Holding period (years)							
	1	2	3	4	5	10	20	50
Tax exempt	£110.00	£121.00	£133.10	£146.41	£161.05	£259.37	£672.75	£11,739.09
Annual taxation	£106.00	£112.36	£119.10	£126.25	£133.82	£179.08	£320.71	£1,842.02
Deferred taxation:								
ordinary	£106.00	£112.60	£119.86	£127.85	£136.63	£195.62	£443.65	£7,083.45
capital gains (US)	£108.00	£116.80	£126.48	£137.13	£148.84	£227.50	£558.20	£9,411.27
capital gains (UK)	£106.50	£114.70	£126.48	£141.77	£154.95	£243.44	£615.47	£10,575.18

Annualized after-tax rates of return (%)

	1	2	3	4	5	10	20	50
Tax exempt	10.00	10.00	10.00	10.00	10.00	10.00	10.00	10.00
Annual taxation	6.00	6.00	6.00	6.00	6.00	6.00	6.00	6.00
Deferred taxation:								
ordinary	6.00	6.11	6.22	6.33	6.44	6.94	7.73	8.89
capital gains (US)	8.00	8.07	8.15	8.21	8.28	8.57	8.98	9.51
capital gains (UK)	6.50	7.10	8.15	9.12	9.15	9.30	9.51	9.77

Assumptions:
Initial investment £100. Annual pre-tax rate of return 10%. Tax rate on ordinary income 40%. Tax rate on capital gains in US is 20%. In UK, declines as function of holding period

The table gives two sets of results for deferred taxation with capital gains treatment. The first line represents the case in the US – assets held longer than a year are subject to 20 per cent capital gains tax. The second line gives the case in the UK where the capital gains tax rate declines as the holding period increases. For business assets (such as shares held by an outside investor in a listed company), the percentage of income is included in taxable income as the holding period increases, as shown in Table 2.

From Table 1, the following points can be made:

- Tax differences are magnified as the holding period increases.
- With annual taxation (and constant tax rates across time), the annualized after-tax rate of return does not increase with the length of the holding period but remains constant.
- With deferral of taxation, the longer the holding period, the greater the annualized after-tax rate of return. Also, taxation at the end of a holding period offers a valuable timing option.
- Investors can choose when to pay the taxes, for example, selling when they incur losses from investments.

| TABLE 2 | Taxable capital gains in the UK and US |

Holding period (in whole years)	UK income included in taxable income (%)	UK income included in taxable income (%) (assuming 40% tax)	US capital gains tax rate (%)
<1	100	40	40
1	87.5	35	20
2	75	30	20
3	50	20	20
4	25	10	20

- Regardless of the holding period, capital gains tax is preferable to taxation at ordinary income tax rates.

Examples of the four types of investments are as follows. First, tax-exempt investments include: National Savings Certificates (municipal bonds in the US exempt from state income taxes); tax-deductible pensions (if tax rates are constant across time); individual savings accounts (ISAs) in the UK and Roth individual retirement accounts in the US. Pensions are better than tax exemption for investors whose tax rate will decline in retirement. Examples of annual taxation include corporate and Treasury bonds, money market funds, traditional savings accounts, preferred stock and companies that pay out 100 per cent of their earnings as dividends (although in some countries shareholders receive tax credits for corporate taxes, so reducing taxes on dividends). Deferred tax at ordinary income tax rates is charged on single premium deferred annuities (the investor buys an annuity contract from an insurance company using after-tax money, earnings in the annuity grow tax-free each year, and are taxed as ordinary income on withdrawal).

Finally, an example of deferred taxation at capital gains tax rates is non-dividend paying corporate stock (such as Microsoft) or growth stocks.

Earlier, the pre-tax rate of return was held constant and the tax treatment was varied to highlight the effects of differential taxation on the accumulations and after-tax rates of return. However, different investors face different tax rates, so it is likely that investors subject to high tax rates bid up the prices of securities that are favourable towards them in tax terms (such as municipal bonds and non-dividend-paying stocks), lowering the expected future pre-tax returns. For example, after controlling for risk differences, US municipal bonds give lower yields than corporate bonds. Suppose municipal bonds are priced to yield 7 per cent while corporate bonds are priced to yield 10 per cent a year. At a marginal tax rate of 30 per cent, both offer a 7 per cent after-tax return (so the investor is indifferent between the two bonds). For an investor facing a tax rate of 40 per cent, the municipal bond offers the higher after-tax return (7 per cent versus 6 per cent). For a taxpayer facing a 20 per cent tax rate, the fully taxable corporate bond offers better after-tax returns (8 per cent versus 7 per cent).

Thus while tax-exemption appears to dominate in our example, this comparison assumed equal pre-tax rates of return. Tax-exempt (or tax-favoured) securities are generally preferred for high-tax rate investors while lower-tax rate investors are attracted to fully-taxed (or less tax-favoured) securities. Efficient tax planning aims to maximize the after-tax rate of return and not to minimize (explicit) taxes. When selling less than 100 per cent of holdings in a particular stock or mutual fund, a simple way to reduce tax is to sell the highest-cost shares first, assuming the stock in the portfolio was bought at different prices. US tax authorities assume a first-in first-out cost basis, which in a rising stock market is generally the lowest cost basis resulting in the largest taxable gain. If the investor designates (in writing to the broker or mutual fund) the highest cost shares as being sold first, this reduces tax. However, this strategy is not available in the UK.

Retirement accounts

In traditional retirement accounts, investment amounts are tax deductible and earnings are tax deferred. Investors should maximize investment in these, especially if an employer matches the contributions. Many investors have a wide choice of assets in which to invest pension funds. At the same time, most investors have savings or investments outside pension funds. Because the fund is "tax-exempt" (earnings are not taxed until withdrawn), it is generally better to place fully taxable investments inside the pension account and buy tax-favoured investments on personal account (for high tax payers).

Further, withdrawals from pension funds are taxed as ordinary income. This means it makes little sense to place stocks that pay no dividends inside a pension account – the price appreciation which could be taxed at favourable capital gains tax rates outside the fund will be taxed at ordinary income tax rates on withdrawal.

ISAs and Roths

For individual savings accounts (ISAs) in the UK, contributions are not tax deductible but withdrawals and earnings are tax exempt. Traditional retirement accounts (personal pension schemes) and ISAs offer identical returns when the investor faces constant tax rates. However, traditional retirement accounts are more attractive if investors expect their tax rate to fall when withdrawals are made.

The US also has an alternative retirement account called the Roth account. This is similar to an ISA in that contributions are not tax-deductible but withdrawals including earnings are tax exempt. However, US investors cannot contribute to both accounts (and note that there are restrictions in both the UK and US on who can contribute and how much, with the UK being more generous). An eligible US taxpayer can put $2,000 after tax into a Roth account, but only $2,000 pre-tax into a traditional IRA. This means a taxpayer facing a tax rate of 40 per cent can put only $1,200 after tax into a traditional IRA. To compare a traditional IRA with a Roth IRA when the investor wishes to place the maximum amount in either account, we need to compare accumulations assuming an equal amount of investment. So $2,000 after tax in a Roth account will earn R per cent a year tax-free. In contrast, for a taxpayer facing 40 per cent tax, a traditional IRA which will earn R per cent tax-free on only $2,000(1 − t). That comes to $1,200, plus after-tax earnings on the remaining $800 invested elsewhere. An investor is unlikely to earn the same interest rate tax free on this remaining $800, so the Roth is generally tax favoured (assuming a constant tax rate over time).

Mutual funds

Instead of buying individual shares, many investors use mutual funds, which offer the advantages of diversification. Mutual funds themselves are generally tax exempt, but mutual fund holders pay taxes each year on their dividends and in the US on any gains realized by the mutual fund through their trading activity. That is, mutual fund investors pay tax each year on these allocations even though they may not have sold any of their mutual fund shares. Whether the gain is taxed as a long-term or short-term capital gain (and thus at higher ordinary income tax rates) depends on the mutual fund's holding period, not the investor's holding period (see below).

Mutual funds that are most likely to be affected by taxes are those classed as income funds (because they receive lots of dividends) and actively traded funds (with high turnover, these are more likely to realize capital gains unless managers also trade loss positions to offset gains). Index funds should not be unduly affected.

The importance of mutual fund taxation in the US was brought home to many in 2001 when investors suffered substantial declines in the value of their holdings. At the same time they owed substantial taxes because of gains arising from many mutual funds liquidating appreciated positions early in tax-year 2000. While some funds claim to be tax efficient, new disclosures required by the Securities and Exchange Commission will enable investors to better assess these claims and to evaluate after-tax returns. The SEC requires after-tax returns to be reported for 1, 5 and 10-year holdings, with returns calculated under two assumptions, which investors need to understand. Under the first method, investors are assumed to hold shares and pay capital gains taxes only on distributions. Under the second method, investors are assumed to sell their shares at the end of each year and pay taxes on their gain (or loss) at top ordinary income tax rates. The latter method is likely to understate after-tax rates of return for most investors expecting to hold shares for longer than a year (because of deferral and taxation at lower capital gains rates).

Derivatives

Different investments give rise to future earnings that vary not only in size but in timing, risk, source (foreign or domestic) and form (active or passive). It is often efficient to repackage ownership rights in these investments to allow some of the risk and return components to be sold to investors who value those components most highly. This repackaging can occur through financial contracts such as futures, forwards, options, swaps and warrants, and securities that promise their holders payoffs that depend upon the value of another asset such as a market index or the price of a commodity. Taxation of these securities differs. For example, in the US, year-end holdings of futures contracts are taxed as though they are sold at year-end (with some of the gain/loss treated as long-term capital gains and some treated as ordinary income). Sophisticated investors and tax planners often use derivatives and financial instruments. Examples of tax planning using financial contracts are provided in Scholes's book in the further reading. However, such strategies are not recommended for the faint-hearted.

Conclusion

Poor tax planning can dramatically reduce investors' wealth. However, taxes should not drive investment decisions. Rather, efficient tax planning focuses on maximizing investors' after-tax rate of return. This is not the same as minimizing taxes. In evaluating the effects of taxes, investors must examine pre-tax rates of return, when and how returns will be taxed, current and expected future taxes, tax rules and holding periods.

Copyright © Terry Shevlin

Further reading

Inland Revenue website (http://www.inlandrevenue.gov.uk).
Scholes, M.S. *et al.* (1992) *Taxes and Business Strategy: A Planning Approach*, Upper Saddle River, NJ: Prentice-Hall.
Seida, J. and Stern, J. (1998) "Extending Scholes/Wolfson for post-1997 pension investments: applications to the Roth IRA contribution and rollover decisions", *Journal of the American Taxation Association*, 20, 100–10.

The coming of the single financial regulator

Howard Davies is chairman of the UK's Financial Services Authority.

In 2001 the Financial Services Authority took on its full powers as the single regulator of financial services in the UK. **Howard Davies** explains its approach and what this will mean for investment businesses.

Economic slowdown may have hit the US, but the financial services industry in the UK remains buoyant. Most sectors have seen an expansion of business since 2000 and in the number of authorized companies, in spite of continued consolidation. In 2001 there were 664 UK-authorized banks, a 6 per cent increase over the previous year, and more than 7,600 investment companies, a 4 per cent increase. London remains the leading international financial centre and continues to attract a growing volume of mobile international business. Most large US and Asian companies have their European headquarters in London.

One of the main reasons companies give for choosing to base their business in the UK is that the regulatory system is seen as strong, rigorous and cost-effective. But there has been general agreement that the sector-based approach needed updating and reform if the UK were to continue to keep its world-leading position in regulation. The confusing mixture of self-regulating organizations and statutory bodies operating on different legal bases no longer reflected what was happening in the financial services industry. Distinctions between investment companies, banks and insurance companies were becoming blurred, with mergers and takeovers creating multi-purpose conglomerates.

Under the old regime, these groups had to apply to several regulators, comply with several sets of standards and grapple with differing regulatory styles. Further, no single regulator could take an overall view of a major financial group and the interactions between the risks it was taking. So the government's decision to form a single regulator in the shape of the Financial Services Authority (FSA) – and a single statutory basis for regulation in the Financial Services and Markets Act 2000 – has been welcomed within the industry. That is particularly true in the investment

> **Box 1 The single regulator**
>
> Following the passage of the Financial Services and Markets Act, the Financial Services Authority in the UK will centralize the roles of the following institutions:
>
> - IMRO (Investment Management Regulatory Organization) is the regulator of companies in the field of investment management.
> - SFA (Securities and Futures Authority) is the regulator of trading and dealing companies operating in organized investment markets in the City of London.
> - PIA (Personal Investment Authority) is the regulator of retail investment and financial advice companies.
> - SIB (Securities and Investments Board) was the designated agency under the Financial Services Act 1986 for regulating investment businesses in the UK. In October 1997 it was renamed the Financial Services Authority.

sector, which had hitherto the most fragmented and complex regulatory structure.

Investors and their representatives were also enthusiastic, sensing an end to the alphabet-soup of SIB, PIA, IMRO and SFA, and the confusion over ultimate responsibility that such fragmentation created (see Box 1).

In anticipation of the act coming into full force in November 2001, the FSA created a *de facto* single regulator, with staff of the former bodies working in a unified management structure in a single building. The FSA has also devoted much thinking to the question of what being a single regulator means in practice. How can it regulate in a more focused, efficient and effective way, to the benefit of companies and consumers?

Risk-based approach

The FSA has devised a risk-based approach to regulation, with a clear statement of the realistic aims and limits of regulation. It recognizes both the proper responsibilities of consumers and of companies' managers, and the impossibility and undesirability of removing all risk and failure from the financial system. The prime aim of the strategy is to identify, prioritize and address risks to the four statutory objectives set out in the act – to maintain market confidence, promote public understanding of the financial system, secure appropriate consumer protection, and reduce financial crime. Risk in this specialized sense should not be confused with the commercial risks undertaken by finance companies and within financial markets as a core component of day-to-day business.

For regulators, there are two basic questions. First, what developments, events or issues pose significant risk to the stated objectives? Second, how should they use resources to focus on the risks that matter most? In tackling these questions, the act requires the FSA to observe certain principles of good regulation, including economy and efficiency in the use of resources, the position of the UK as an international financial centre and the need to be proportionate in regulatory responses. The approach aims to ensure that the

FSA uses its resources to deliver the most effective regulatory action within these parameters.

In developing the framework, the FSA first identified a set of high-level, generic risks to its objectives. For example, risks to the consumer protection objective can usually be classified under failure of companies; crime and market abuse; misconduct or mismanagement by companies; market malfunction; and inadequate understanding of products or services preventing informed decision-making. These stated risks provide a common language that enables us to assess possible sources or instances of risk in the same way. Traditionally, regulators have tended to focus on individual companies, but the framework recognizes that risks to objectives can also arise from, for example, worldwide economic trends, new products, developments in social policy and changes in consumer behaviour.

After identifying and classifying risks to objectives, the next task is assessment and prioritization. First, the FSA assesses how likely a risk to its objectives is to crystallize. But this is not the only relevant measure. Another question arises: how important is the risk? It is this indicator of impact that helps us set priorities when allocating resources. Where we face different risks that are equally likely to occur, it makes sense that we should focus on those risks that are likely to have the most significance in terms of, for example, consumer loss.

New tools

Once risks have been assessed and prioritized, the question is how to deal with them. In the past, regulators have generally focused on the individual company. But past experience of financial regulators, the broad range of the FSA's statutory objectives and the powers given to it in the act suggest that this may not always be the most effective solution. In particular, it can often result in regulators reacting to events in companies only when there are opportunities to be proactive and wide-ranging in managing risks. Hence the FSA must select from the full range of regulatory tools available to it, not just those that act on individual companies. The key point is to decide what is the most effective way of addressing risks.

A good example of such a tool is the provision of comparative information to consumers on a range of financial products. The FSA has asked all investment companies offering retail products to participate voluntarily by providing comparable information on their products, which will then be made available to investors on a website and in print. Market research shows that consumers want clear, up-to-date information, provided by an independent organization, to help them to make investment decisions. Comparative tables have been available since September 2001. The FSA is also introducing a more thematic approach to regulation, where it examines and responds to particular themes or issues that may affect its ability to meet objectives, such as those arising from particular markets, sectors, products or the external environment. Recent themes have been as diverse as the implications of a low-inflation environment, consumer protection beyond the point of sale and e-commerce.

Changing relations

How will this approach affect the way the FSA interacts with regulated companies? Investment companies should not imagine that because the FSA is looking at wider thematic issues it is going to abandon company-focused regulation. One of the most useful regulatory tools remains the power to set rules and requirements for the protection of consumers and to check that companies comply with them. (These are set out in the FSA Handbook of Rules and Guidance.) However, routine compliance visits will be a thing of the past. The FSA will instead focus on companies that pose the greatest risk and on areas of perceived highest risk to the authority's objectives.

The FSA has assessed the 10,000 or so companies it regulates to identify the level of risk they pose to its objectives. That assessment will inform its relationship with each company. Where companies pose substantial risks, through a combination of their impact and the likelihood of problems arising, the regulator will have a strong incentive to anticipate problems by maintaining a close relationship. Where risk is lower, the relationship will be less intimate. All companies, however, must comply with rigorous conduct standards and reporting requirements. Each will be allocated to one of four categories, imaginatively labelled A to D. At one end of the spectrum the FSA will maintain the closest relationships with category A companies (high-risk). At the other end of the risk scale, category D companies will be monitored remotely, supported by sampling of particular lines of business and thematic work.

Many of the 7,600 investment companies regulated at present by the PIA, IMRO and SFA will therefore see a substantial change in their relationship with the regulator. Companies that are part of large conglomerates will be regulated by a division covering major financial groups. Insurance companies monitored by the PIA for compliance with conduct-of-business rules will move to an insurance firms division, which will have responsibility for all aspects of the regulatory relationship. However, most investment companies, ranging from global fund management operations and large UK brokers to solo financial advisers, will be regulated in the investment firms division.

Under the old system, this was organized in a way that reflected the old SRO responsibilities, with staff working in separate departments covering companies regulated by the PIA, IMRO or SFA. In future, however, issues will be handled as a portfolio of thematic projects, such as the Free Standing Additional Voluntary Contributions review or the development of a regulatory regime for energy market participants. These will be taken forward by a themes department, while the relationship management department will focus on the larger or higher-risk companies within the division. There are about 1,050 of these, engaged in a variety of investment businesses and operating in both wholesale and retail markets. The department will carry out risk assessments and design risk mitigation programmes.

Finally, the regulatory events department will mainly be responsible for the lower-impact category D companies, which number about 6,000. In practice, this means that an individual company supervised by the department will not have a relationship with a dedicated supervision team but material regulatory events will be dealt with case by case, using events teams assigned to particular industry sectors.

It is not surprising that the financial community both in the UK and overseas is closely examining how the FSA will operate with its full statutory powers. The FSA believes that its new approach will deliver better and more focused regulation of investment business, going with the grain of the market rather than forcing companies to conform to a standard regulatory model.

Copyright © Howard Davies 2002

Further reading

Financial Services Authority (2000a) "A new regulator for the new millennium", January (http://www.fsa.gov.uk).

Financial Services Authority (2000b) "Building the new regulator. Progress report 1", December (http://www.fsa.gov.uk).

Subject index

accounting standards 89, 91–2
accumulation patterns 269
acquisitions and mergers 87, 283
    merger arbitrage 114–15, 210
active investment strategies 135–40, 282
adjusted residual income (ARI) model 78–80
administrative costs 31
advance-decline lines 270–1
airline companies 94
alliances 86–7
alpha performance 32–3, 240
Alternative Risk Transfer 49, 50
ambiguity aversion 249–50
American depositary receipts 279
American options 47
arbitrage 252–6
    convertible arbitrage 210
    costs of 263
    fixed-income arbitrage 210
    law of one price 252–3, 261–6
    merger arbitrage 114–15, 210
    no-arbitrage principle 252–3
    performance-based arbitrage 255
    professional arbitrageurs 254–5
    risk arbitrage 253–5
Arbitrage Pricing Theory 81
Arch-Garch models 227
Argentina 189
ARI (adjusted residual income) model 78–80
arithmetic averaging 10
asset allocation 128–34, 153–6, 157–62, 219, 237–40
    and active investment strategies 135–40
    and derivatives 50
    and downside semi-variance 220
    for the elderly 153–6, 160
    framework 130–3
    and funding priorities 131–2
    and human capital risk 147–8, 157–60
    of investment managers 129–30
    liability-replicating portfolios 132
    and liquidity 133
    of pension plans 129, 131–2
    risk and return trade-offs 131
    socially responsible portfolios 238
    and taxation 129, 133–4
    for young households 128–9
    see also diversification
asset location 129
asset management companies 324–30
    and fraud 327, 328
    and insurance 328
    losses from operational failures 327–8
asset ownership *see* ownership structures

asset pricing
    capital asset pricing model 40, 61, 63, 71–2, 81, 143
    lifecycle approach 144–5, 151
asset selection 37, 138, 139, 219
assisted living costs 155

back-history returns 14
background risks 147–9
balance sheets 78, 91–2
    off-balance sheet financing 92, 94
Basle committee 324
Bayesian estimators 62
behavioural finance 246–51
Bermuda options 47
best execution 109
beta risk 40, 61–3, 143, 310–11
    industry-adjusted betas 62–3
    shrinkage betas 62
bid-ask spreads 100–1, 102, 107–8
biotechnology companies 303–4
"bird in the bush" theorem 75
Black-Scholes option pricing model 228, 253
Blue Chip Economic Indicators 28
bonds 36–41
    asset selection 37
    corporate bonds 42–5, 340
    correlation of returns 36–8
    and derivatives 44, 45
    diversification of portfolios 36–7
    duration measures 39
    government bonds 37–9
    and inflation 5
    inflation-indexed bonds 134
    junk bonds 308–9
    mortgage-backed bonds 36
    municipal bonds 340
    rate of returns 37
    risk management 39, 44–5
    risk premiums 40–1
    tracking error 39
    volatility 224–5
    yield curves 37, 38–9, 42
    yield spreads 37, 38, 43–4
bookbuilding 315
brand equity 94
Brazil 189
bribery and corruption 190
brokerage *see* trading industry
brokerage commissions 100, 102, 105, 107
business cycle 24–9
    predicting 28–9
    stock returns and timing 26–8
    turning points 25–6, 27

business model analysis 76

capital asset pricing model (CAPM) 40, 61, 63, 71–2, 81, 143
capital gains tax 339–40
carried interest 300, 308
Cash Flow Return on Investment (CFROI) 89, 91
China 191
classification of assets 18
classification of hedge funds 208–9
clearing fees 100, 105
CLOB (consolidated limit order book) 118–23
company lifecycles 76
comparative tables 346
compensation schemes 326–7, 328–9
conduct-of-business rules 326, 329
conservatism 248, 250–1
consumption-based asset pricing 144–5, 151
contrarian investing 18
convertible arbitrage 210
corporate bonds 42–5, 340
    default risk 42–3
    and option pricing 43–4
corporate governance 276–80
    cross-shareholding structures 277–8
    disclosure 205, 211, 281–6, 327
    in Europe 276–80
    investor relations 282–3
    and performance 276–7
    pyramid shareholding structures 277–8
    socially responsible investing 285, 287–93
    voting restrictions 277
correlation coefficient 167, 169
correlation of returns 19, 69, 171
    in bond portfolios 36–8
corruption and bribery 190
cost of capital calculations 60, 64
cost structures and company valuation 86
costs 102, 105, 107–12
    administrative costs 31
    and arbitrage 263
    best execution 109
    bid-ask spreads 100–1, 102, 107–8
    brokerage commissions 100, 102, 105, 107
    clearing fees 100, 105
    of directly held portfolios 31
    of diversification 147, 150
    of index funds 111–12
    of institutional orders 110
    and investment style 109, 111
    and market capitalization 109
    opportunity costs 108
    of overseas diversification 184
    predicting 112
    price impact of trades 108
    and trade difficulty 108–9
    and trading systems 110–11
creditor rights 191
cross-shareholding structures 277–8
currency risk 182, 221, 278

custodian industry 328

data integrity 91–2
data mining 65
data patterns 248
dealer market 101
default risk 42–3
deferred taxation 339, 340
derivatives 44, 45, 46–51
    Alternative Risk Transfer 49, 50
    and asset allocation 50
    exchange traded 48–9
    forwards 46–7
    futures 48–9
    and investment strategy 50
    margin payments 49
    negotiated 48
    offset system 48–9
    options *see* options
    regulation 49
    and risk management 51
    swaps 47
    and taxation 342–3
developing countries 186–92
directional strategies 209, 210
disclosure 205, 211, 281–6, 327
discount rates 81
disposition effect 249
distressed securities 210
diversification 67–9, 147–50, 299
    and bond portfolios 36–7
    costs of 147, 150
    and hedge funds 198–9, 211–12
    and managerial ownership 331–3
    and real estate 53
    see also overseas diversification; portfolio theory
dividends
    and cost of capital calculations 64
    dividend-price ratios 65
    high dividend yield stocks 19
    reinvesting 12–13
    tax credits 116–17
Dow Jones Industrial Average 11, 12
downside risk 220
downside semi-variance 220
dual class share structures 333
duration measures 39

early-stage finance 299–300, 302
earnings-based valuation 78–80
earnings-price ratios 65
ECNs (electronic communication networks) 101, 103, 105
economic cycle *see* business cycle
economic growth 174
Economic Value Added (EVA) 89, 90
Ecu basket convergence trade 199
efficient market theory 7, 115–16, 246, 251, 265
efficient portfolios 68–9, 166–72, 219–20
elderly people, asset allocation 153–6, 160
electronic communication networks (ECNs) 101, 103, 105

electronic open limit order books 101
emerging markets 186–92
    creditor rights 191
    GDP per head 187
    profitability of GDP growth 189–90
    regulation 192
    shareholder rights 191, 192
enhanced indexing 44, 238
equity hedge strategies 210
equity loans 113–17
    beneficial ownership 116
    and efficient markets 115–16
    by index funds 115
    interest on collateral 114
    legal issues 116–17
    market size 116
    pricing 113–14
    rebate rates 114–15
    revenues from 115
    tax credits 116–17
equity risk premium 15–16, 40–1, 63, 64, 81, 141–6, 149–51, 161–2
estate taxes 155–6
ethical fund management 238, 285, 287–93
Europe
    asset management industry 324–30
    corporate governance 276–80
    IPOs (Initial Public Offerings) 315, 316
    real estate 55
    regulatory systems 326–7, 329–30
    single currency 19
European options 47
EVA (Economic Value Added) 89, 90
event-driven strategies 210
excessive trading 247, 258
exchange rate risk 182, 221, 278
exchange traded derivatives 48–9
exchanges 100–1
expected returns 60–5, 167
    and active asset allocation 135, 137, 138–9
    and asset selection 138, 139
    and beta risk 40, 61–3, 143, 310–11
    on bonds 37
    capital asset pricing model 40, 61, 63, 71–2, 81, 143
    components of 136–8
    data mining 65
    dividend-price ratios 65
    earnings-price ratios 65
    equity premium 15–16, 40–1, 63, 64, 81, 141–6, 149–51, 161–2
    market-timing performance 26–8, 33, 53–4, 219
    and overseas diversification 168–9, 174–7
    policy returns 135–6, 138
    from real estate 53
    return histories 19–20
    risk and return trade-offs 131, 167
    risk-free rate 61–2
    sample average returns 60–1
    and taxation 340
    time variation of 65

expenditure-based capital requirements 326
exponential smoothing 227

factor models 241
fat tail effect 228
financial liberalization 335–6
Financial Services Authority (FSA) 344–8
Financial Services and Markets Act (2000) 344–5
fixed-income arbitrage 210
flipping 316–18
forecasting volatility 227–8, 240
foreign exchange risk 182, 221, 278
foreign share listings 279
forwards 46–7
401(k) payments 154
fraud 327, 328
free cash flow valuation 78
free-float weighting 11–12
funding priorities 131–2
funds see mutual funds
funds of funds 213, 311
futures 48–9

Garch model 227
GDP (gross domestic product) 25, 187, 189–90
geometric averaging 10
globalization 189, 279
    see also overseas diversification
Goodmoney Industrial Average 289
goodwill 92
Gordon growth model 64
governance see corporate governance
government bonds 37–9
Greece 189
green funds 238, 285, 287–3
growth investing 18, 19, 20–1

hedge funds 196–200, 201–6, 207–14
    capital preservation 197–8
    classification of 208–9
    consistency of returns 197
    directional strategies 209, 210
    disclosure and compliance 205, 211
    and diversification 198–9, 211–12
    funds of funds 213
    high watermark provisions 211
    history of 207
    hurdle rates 201, 211
    investment styles 201, 207, 209
    leverage 199–200, 209
    long-short equity funds 238–40
    minimum investments 209–10
    non-directional strategies 209, 210
    offshore funds 208–9
    onshore funds 208
    operational risk 196
    performance assessment 196, 201–5, 211–13
    performance fees 197, 201, 211, 213
    qualified investors 208
    regulation 205, 208, 209, 212

returning capital to investors 200
selection bias 212
size of fund 200, 213
size of industry 196, 205, 207–8
survivorship bias 212
withdrawal of funds 210
high watermark provisions 211
home-bias puzzle 183, 249–50
hotel investments 56
human capital risk 147–8, 157–160, 157–60
hurdle rates 201, 211
project hurdle rates 335

implied volatility 228
income statements 91–2
index funds 13–15, 111–12
enhanced indexing 44, 238
equity loans by 115
style funds 19
India 189, 190
indicators 270
indices *see* market indices
Individual Savings Accounts (ISAs) 341–2
industry pairing 238–9
industry-adjusted betas 62–3
inflation 6, 182
and bond markets 5
inflation-indexed bonds 134
information access 7, 182, 231–2
insurance 328
insurance companies 347
intangible assets 92, 93, 95
intellectual property 79, 93
Intermarket Trading System (ITS) 120–1
internal rate of return 89
international diversification *see* overseas diversification
internet trading 232
investment horizons 153–6
investment managers 129–30
investment policy returns 135–6, 138
investment psychology
ambiguity aversion 249–50
behavioural finance 246–51
conservatism 248, 250–1
disposition effect 249
exploiting psychology 250–1
learning process 257
narrow framing 248–9, 250
over-confidence 246–7, 257–60
representativeness 247–8, 250
self-attribution bias 247
investment styles 17–23, 109, 111
of hedge funds 201, 207, 209
style-based performance measurement 18, 19, 22–3
investor protection 324, 332, 335–6
see also regulation
investor relations 282–3
IPOs (Initial Public Offerings) 313–19
allocation of shares 313, 315
bookbuilding 315
and disclosure 284–5
and equity loans 114, 116
first-day returns 313–16, 318
flipping 316–18
in France 315, 316
future performance indicators 317–19
issue prices 315
quiet period 316
short-selling 263
trading volume 316–17, 318
underpricing 313–16
and venture capital funds 303–4
ISAs (Individual Savings Accounts) 341–2
ITS (Intermarket Trading System) 120–1

Japanese real estate 55
junk bonds 308–9

Korea 187–8, 190

labour income risk 147–8, 157
large-cap companies 18
later-stage finance 302
law of one price 252–3, 261–6
learning process 257
leasing 94
legal systems 334–5
leverage 86, 199–200, 209
leveraged buyouts 308–9
liability-replicating portfolios 132
lifecycle approach to asset pricing 144–5, 151
lifecycle of companies 76
limit orders 101, 118–23
limited partnership structures 300, 306–7
liquidity 30–2, 33–4, 133
loan contracts *see* equity loans
long-short equity hedge funds 238–40
loss aversion 233–4

managerial ownership 331–6
and diversification 331–3
and dual class share structures 333
and project hurdle rates 335
manufacturing 94
margin payments 49
marginal utility 143, 158, 219
market capitalization 109
market indices 9–16
averaging 10
back-history returns 14
and dividend reinvestment 12–13
Goodmoney Industrial Average 289
and performance measurement 14–15
rebalancing 13–14
and the risk premium 15–16
style indices 18, 19
Sustainability Index 288, 289
trackability 13–14
types of 10
uses of 9–10

VIX index 229
volatility index 229
weighting 11–12
market orders 119
market timing 26–8, 33, 53–4, 219
marketmakers 101
markets
    efficient market theory 7, 115–16, 246, 251, 265
    foreign share listings 279
    major tops and bottoms 5
    volatility of 224
mean-reversion 228
mergers and acquisitions 87, 283
    merger arbitrage 114–15, 210
Metcalfe's law 85
micro-cap companies 20
mid-cap companies 18
minimum variance frontier 219
minority shareholders 281, 284
modern portfolio theory (MPT) 67–73, 131, 331
momentum investing 18, 19, 21, 256
momentum oscillators 270
mortgage-backed bonds 36
moving averages 270
multiple-based valuation 76–8
municipal bonds 340
mutual funds 30–4
    cost advantages 31
    ethical funds 238, 285, 287–93
    funds of funds 213, 311
    liquidity advantage 30–2
    performance assessment 30, 32–4, 202
    "prudent man rules" 6
    taxation 342
    see also index funds; pension funds; private equity funds
Myners Report 283–4

narrow framing 248–9, 250
National Market System (NMS) 120
negotiated derivatives 48
net present value 89
network effect 85–6, 93
Nikkei 225 index 11
no-arbitrage principle 252–3
non-directional hedge funds strategies 209, 210
nursing home costs 155

off-balance sheet financing 92, 94
offset system 48–9
offshore hedge funds 208–9
onshore hedge funds 208
operating leverage 86
operational risk 196
opportunity costs 108
optimal portfolios 68–9, 166–72, 219–20
options 47–8, 50, 228, 264
    Black-Scholes pricing model 228, 253
    and corporate bond valuation 43–4

implied volatility 228
put-call parity 264
share options and pay 283
value of options 84–5
volatility options 229
outsourcing services 83
over-confidence 246–7, 257–60
overseas diversification 166–72, 173–7, 179–84, 278
    correlation of returns 171
    costs 184
    currency risk 182, 221, 278
    and economic growth 174
    emerging markets 186–92
    expected returns 168–9, 174–7
    home-bias puzzle 183, 249–50
    information access 182
    optimal portfolios 166–72
    Sharpe ratios 180
    standard deviation of returns 170
overtrading 247, 258
ownership structures 94, 100–5, 116
    managerial ownership of companies 331–6

paired trades 238–40
partnership structures 300, 306–7
partnerships and alliances 86–7
patterns in data 248
penny jumping 103
pension funds 153, 231–2, 325
    asset allocation 129, 131–2
    private equity investments 307, 308
    in Switzerland 279
    taxation 338, 340, 341
    trustees 284
performance
    alpha performance 32–3, 240
    benchmarks 14
    and corporate governance 276–7
    of ethical funds 289–91
    of hedge funds 196, 201–5, 211–13
    and liquidity demands 33–4
    market-timing 26–8, 33, 53–4, 219
    of mutual funds 30, 32–4, 202
    of private equity funds 311–12
    risk adjusted measures 14–15
    style-based measures 18, 22–3
    of venture capital funds 309
performance fees 197, 201, 211, 213
performance-based arbitrage 255
personal investing 233–6
Poland 189
policy returns 135–6, 138
portfolio optimization 68–9, 166–72, 219–20
portfolio theory 67–73, 131, 331
Posit 104
post-earnings announcement drift 248
price patterns 269
price-earnings multiple 76–7
price-to-book ratios 93

pricing decisions 85
pricing equity loans 113–14
pricing models *see* asset pricing
private equity funds 305–12
    carried interest 308
    funds of funds 311
    funds raised by 307–8
    organization of 306–7, 308
    performance 311–12
    portfolio allocation 309–11
    profit-sharing arrangements 308
    see also venture capital
privatization 334–5
probability distributions 166, 167, 220
product information 346
productivity 189–90
professional arbitrageurs 254–5
project hurdle rates 335
property investing *see* real estate
"prudent man rules" 6
put-call parity 264
pyramid shareholding structures 277–8

Quantal Pro system 238
quiet period 316

ratio analysis 65, 76–8, 93
real estate 52–6
    diversification benefits 53
    in Europe 55
    hotels 56
    in Japan 55
    offices 56
    pricing model 52
    rents 52, 54
    returns 53
    skills requirements 55–6
    timing 53–4
    in the US 54–5
rebate rates 114–15
recessions 24–6
    see also business cycle
reduced-form models 241
regulation 277–8, 324–30, 344–8
    and asset management companies 324–30
    comparative tables 346
    compensation schemes 326–7, 328–9
    conduct-of-business rules 326, 329
    and derivatives 49
    in different countries 326–7, 329–30
    disclosure 205, 211, 281–6, 327
    of emerging markets 192
    expenditure-based capital requirements 326
    Financial Services Authority (FSA) 344–8
    of hedge funds 205, 208, 209, 212
    of insurance companies 347
    product information 346
    risk-based approach 345–6
rents 52, 54

representativeness 247–8, 250
research and development investment 79–80
retirement *see* pension funds
returns *see* expected returns
revaluation of assets 92
Rhenish business model 276–80
risk arbitrage 253–5
risk budgeting 223
risk management 4–8, 39, 44–5, 218–23, 231–6
    currency risk 182, 221, 278
    defining risk 220
    and derivatives 51
    downside risk 220
    human capital risk 147–8, 157–160
    loss aversion 233–4
    minimum variance frontier 219
    models 240–2
    in personal investing 233–6
    portfolio optimization 68–9, 166–72, 219–20
    portfolio theory 67–73, 131, 331
    process of 221–2
    risk and return trade-offs 131, 167
    stress testing 234
    utility functions 143, 158, 219
    Value-at-Risk (VaR) techniques 198, 222–3, 234–5
    see also asset allocation; diversification; volatility
risk premium 15–16, 40–1, 63, 64, 81, 141–6, 149–51, 161–2
risk tolerance 150, 219
    utility functions 143, 158, 219
risk-based approach to regulation 345–6
risk-free rate 61–2
rotation of styles 21–2
Roth accounts 341–2

sample average returns 60–1
scenario analysis 83
Securities and Exchange Act 120
security selection 37, 138, 139, 219
selection bias 212
self-attribution bias 247
share options and pay 283
shareholder activism 283–4, 291–2
shareholder rights 191, 192
    minority shareholders 281, 284
shareholding structures 277–8
short selling 113, 238–40, 263–4
short-termism 283
shrinkage betas 62
simulation 83–4
single currency 19
small-cap companies 18, 19, 20, 21
small-cap indices 13–14
socially responsible investing 238, 285, 287–93
Soviet Union privatization 334–5
specialization 93
standard deviation of returns 167, 168–9, 170, 220
stock exchanges *see* exchanges
stock market indices *see* market indices

strategic partnerships 86–7
stress testing 234
structural models 241
stub values 262–3
style indices 18, 19
style investing *see* investment styles
style-based performance measurement 18, 19, 22–3
survivorship bias 212
Sustainability Index 288, 289
swaps 47
Switzerland, pension funds 279
systematic risk 68

Taiwanese Stock Exchange 282
takeovers *see* acquisitions and mergers
tangible fixed assets 92
tax credits 116–17
taxation 129, 133–4, 337–43
    capital gains tax 339–40
    deferred taxation 339, 340
    and derivatives 342–3
    estate taxes 155–6
    and expected returns 340
    Individual Savings Accounts (ISAs) 341–2
    and mutual funds 342
    and pension plans 338, 340, 341
    Roth accounts 341–2
technical analysis 267–71
technology and information 231–2, 237–42
technology stocks 254
tick size 102–3, 122
time variation of returns 65
timing 26–8, 33, 53–4, 219
tracking error 39
trade difficulty 108–9
trading floors 101
trading industry 100–5
    bid-ask spreads 100–1, 102, 107–8
    electronic open limit order books 101
    exchanges 100–1
    Intermarket Trading System (ITS) 120–1
    limit orders 101, 118–23
    market fragmentation 103–4
    market orders 119
    marketmakers 101
    National Market System (NMS) 120
    ownership structure 104–5
    penny jumping 103
    Posit 104
    tick size 102–3, 122
    see also costs
trading systems 110–11
transaction costs *see* costs
trends, and technical analysis 268–9
trustees 284, 328

uncertainty 4–8
    see also risk management
United States
    real estate 54–5
    regulation 326–7, 329–30
unsystematic risk 68
utility companies 60
utility functions 143, 158, 219

value investing 18, 19, 20–1
value metrics 89–95
    data integrity 91–2
Value-at-Risk (VaR) techniques 198, 222–3, 234–5
valuing companies 75–88
    adjusted residual income (ARI) model 78–80
    "bird in the bush" theorem 75
    business model analysis 76
    company lifecycles 76
    cost structures 86
    discount rates 81
    earnings-based methods 78–80
    free cash flow method 78
    multiple-based methods 76–8
    network effect 85–6, 93
    operating leverage 86
    price-earnings multiple 76–7
    scenario analysis 83
    simulation 83–4
    strategic partnerships 86–7
    value of options 84–5
variance of returns 167, 168–9, 170, 220
venture capital 298–304
    beta risk 310–11
    carried interest 300
    early-stage finance 299–300, 302
    history of 308
    investment criteria 300–2
    later-stage finance 302
    partnership terms 300
    performance 309
    see also private equity funds
vertical integration 93
VIX index 229
volatility 224–30
    of bonds 224–5
    changes over time 228
    forecasting 227–8, 240
    implied volatility 228
    mean-reversion 228
    and option pricing 228
    of shares 224–7
    variance of returns 167, 168–9, 170, 220
    see also risk management
volatility index 229
volatility options 229
voting power 277, 283–4

weighting market indices 11–12

yield curves 37, 38–9, 42
yield spreads 37, 38, 43–4
young households 128–9

Name index

Agarwal, V. 207–14
Aggarwal, R. 316
Alamouti, K. 196–200
Alexander, G.J. 14
Aliber, R. 173–7
Allen, P. 301
Ang, A. 171

Bailey, J.V. 14
Banz, R. 19
Barber, B. 247, 258
Barberis, N. 246–51
Bayes, T. 62
Beebower, G. 135
Beim, D. 186–92
Bekaert, G. 171, 336
Bellinger, R. 53
Bernstein, P. 4–8
Bhidé, A. 298–304
Black, F. 228, 253
Bollerslev, T. 227
Bosak, L. 302
Brennan, M. 182
Brenner, M. 224–30
Brinson, G. 135
Britten-Jones, M. 179
Buffett, W. 75, 155

Campbell, J. 144
Cao, H. 182
Cavaglia, S. 166
Chen, Nai-fu 63
Claus, J. 170–1
Coase, R. 65
Cochrane, J. 144, 310–11
Collin-Dufresne, P. 43
Constantinides, G. 144, 145, 157
Cooper, I. 179–84
Correia da Silva, L. 324–30
Coy, P. 65
Culp, C. 46–51, 218–23

Das, S. 182
Davies, H. 344–8
Davis, S. 157–62
de Soto, H. 190
De Zoete 14
Dell, M. 95
Derrien, F. 315
Dimson, E. 14, 17–23, 40
Dodd, D. 19
Donaldson, J. 144, 157
Doriot, G. 308
Dow, C. 12

Dowell, G. 290
Duffie, D. 145

Edelen, R. 30–4
Eggert, R.J. 28
Elmiger, G. 231–6
Engle, R. 227

Fama, E. 19, 64, 150, 171
Fenn, G. 302, 308
Franks, J. 324–30
French, K. 19, 64, 150, 171
Fürst, O. 75–82, 83–8

Galai, D. 229
Gates, Bill 301
Geczy, C. 113–17
Georgi, R. 52–6
Gervais, S. 257–60
Gillies, J. 181
Glosten, L. 100–5, 122
Goldstein, M. 122
Gomes, F. 252–6
Gordon, M.J. 64
Gorton 14
Graham, B. 19, 263
Grinold, R. 204

Hagel, J. 93
Hamel, G. 92
Hanachi, S. 202
Hart, S. 290
Harvey, C. 336
Heal, G. 287–93
Heaton, J. 147–51
Henry, P. 60
Heston, S. 180
Higson, C. 89–95
Himmelberg, C. 331–6
Hodrick, R. 166–72
Holderness, C. 332
Hood, R. 135
Huang, Jing-zhi 43–4
Huang, Ming 43–4
Hubbard, G. 331–6

Ilmanen, A. 41
Ineichen, A. 202

Jegadeesh, N. 19
Jones, A.W. 207
Jones, C. 100–5
Jorion, P. 182

Kahn, R. 204
Kamich, B. 267–71

Kao, Duen-Li 43
Kaplanis, E. 182
Kavajecz, K. 118–23
Keim, D. 107–12
Kerrey, J. 156
Keynes, J.M. 67, 173
Kindleberger, C. 153–6
King, R. 335
Knight, R. 276–80
Krigman, L. 316, 317
Kritzman, M. 154
Kroszner, R. 332
Krugman, P. 189–90

La Porta, R. 332
Lamont, O. 261–6
Leeson, N. 50
Leinweber, D. 65
Lemkin, J. 53
Lerner, J. 304
Lerner, Sandy 302
Lev, B. 94
Levine, R. 335
Levis, M. 22
Levitt, A. 118
Liang, N. 302, 308
Lintner, J. 72
Liodakis, M. 22
Lipson, M. 103
Litterman, Bob 38
Lo, A. 271
Longin, F. 171
Love, I. 335
Lucas, D. 147–51
Lundblad, C. 336

MacKinlay, C. 135–40, 271
Madhaven, A. 107–12
Markowitz, H. 67–9, 219
Marsh, P. 9–16, 40
Marsh, T. 237–42
Maxwell, R. 285, 327
Mayer, C. 324–30
Mehra, R. 141–6, 157–62
Melumad, N. 75–82, 83–8
Merton, R. 72, 253
Metrick, A. 305–12
Miller, M. 253
Minnigoulov, B. 317
Modigliani, F. 253
Mohamed, Mahathir 211
Morgan, J.P. 8
Morgridge, J. 302
Mossin, J. 72
Muhtaseb, M. 201–6
Musto, D. 113–17

Nagel, S. 17–23
Naik, N. 207–14
Nelson, T. 227

Odders-White, E. 122–3
Odean, T. 247, 257–60

Pástor, L. 60–5
Pfleiderer, P. 237–42
Prescott, E. 144, 145
Pretty, D. 276–80
Prowse, D. 308
Prowse, S. 302

Reed, A. 113–17
Ritter, J. 318
Robertson, J. 207, 211
Roddick, A. 288
Roll, R. 63
Ross, S. 63
Rouwenhorst, G. 181

Sahlman, W. 300
Sampler, J. 92
Samuelson, P. 24
Schaefer, S. 36–41, 42–5
Scheinkman, J. 38
Schneeweis, T. 203–4
Scholes, M. 62, 228, 253
Sharpe, W.F. 14, 22, 72
Shaw, W. 317
Sheehan, D. 332
Shevlin, T. 337–43
Shiller, R. 227
Shleifer, A. 253
Siegel, J. 24–9, 141
Singer, B. 135
Singer, M. 93
Singer, P. 291
Solnik, B. 171, 183
Soros, G. 155, 211
Spurgin, R. 203–4
Stambaugh, R. 63
Staunton, M. 14, 40
Summers, L. 261
Sundaresan, S. 128–34

Telmer, C. 149
Thomas, J. 170–1
Titman, S. 19
Tobin, J. 70–2
Treynor, Jack 72
Tsai, A. 304

Uppal, R. 67–73, 182

Valentine, D. 302
Valéry, P. 8
Vishny, R. 253
Vissing-Jorgensen, A. 150

Watt, W.C. 281–6
Weinbaum, D. 228
Willen, P. 157
Williams, J. 62
Womack, K. 313–19

Organization index

Allianz 278
Amazon 308
Anheuser-Busch 290
ARD (American Research and Development Corporation) 308
Asset Alternatives 307
At Home 114
Aventis 279

Barclays Capital 14
Barings 50
Baxter International 292
Berkshire Hathaway 283
Body Shop 288
BP 184
British Airways 94
BT 282

California Public Employees' Retirement System 211
Calpers 284
Cambridge Associates 309, 310
Chemdex 303
Chevron 292
Chicago Board Options Exchange 229
Chicago Board of Trade 48
Chicago Mercantile Exchange 48
Chrysler 279
Cisco Systems 298, 302
Citadines 56
Coca-Cola 94
College Retirement Equities Fund 292
Compaq 298, 302

Daimler-Benz 279
Dell Computers 95, 298
Deutsche Bank 328
Deutsche Telekom 278, 279
Digital Equipment Corporation 308
Dimensional Fund Advisors 19
Dow Chemicals 290
Dow Jones 288
DuPont 263, 290

eBay 308
Economist 288
Elsevier 279
Ericsson 239–40
Euronext 105
Excite 114
Exxon 292

Financial Services Authority (FSA) 344–8

Financial Times 288
First Quadrant 65
Ford 94
France Telecom 278
Frank Russell 181

General Motors 61, 62, 263
Global Fund Analysis 205
Goldman Sachs 166, 208
Greenwich Associates 307

Hedge Fund Research 205, 208
Hermes 284
Hewlett-Packard 298
Home Depot 292

IBM 19, 69, 270
Innovest 289
Instinet 101
Intel 290
Investment Management Regulatory Organiza (IMRO) 326, 328, 345, 347
Investors Compensation Scheme 328
Island 101
ITG 104

KKR (Kohlberg, Kravis and Roberts) 308
Kleiner-Perkins 303
Kodak 19
KPMG Peat Marwick 208

LIFFE 48
Long-Term Capital Management 50, 200, 211,
L'Oréal 278
Lotus 302

McDonald's 288
Mapeley 56
MAR Hedge 205
Market Technicians Association 267–71
Martha Stewart Living Omnimedia 318
Merck 69
Merrill Lynch 62, 166, 172
Metallgesellschaft 50
meVC Draper Fischer Jurvetson Fund 307
Microsoft 86, 94, 103–4, 290, 298, 301–2
Monep 229
Moore Capital 200
Morgan Grenfell Asset Management 328
Morgan Stanley 166
Morgan Stanley Capital International (MSCI)
Morningstar 289

Munich Re 278

Nasdaq 101, 103, 104, 254
National Bureau of Economic Research (NBER) 24–5, 28, 310
National Venture Capital Association 302, 309
Nestlé 278, 279
Netscape 303
New York Stock Exchange (NYSE) 101, 103, 105
Nike 86, 288
Nintendo 86
Nokia 239–40
Novartis 279
Novo Nordisk 279

Office Depot 114
Orange County Investment Pool 218

Palm 261–6
Patagonia 288
Personal Investment Authority (PIA) 345, 347
Procter & Gamble 50

Reed Elsevier 279
RiskMetrics 227, 229, 235
RJR Nabisco 308
Robert Morris Associates 116
Royal Dutch 279
RR Capital Management Corporation 208

Securities and Exchange Commission (SEC) 281, 342
Securities and Futures Authority (SFA) 345, 347
Securities and Investment Board (SIB) 345
Sequoia Capital 302

Shell 279, 288
Social Investment Forum 287
Sony 86
Staples 114
Stern Stewart 90
Sun Microsystems 298, 303

Taiwanese Stock Exchange 282
Tass 196, 205
Texas Instruments 302
3Com 261–6
Tokyo Stock Exchange 103
tom.com 265
Toronto Stock Exchange 103
Trillium 56

UBS Brinson 166, 172
UBS Warburg 202

Van Hedge Fund Advisors International 208
Vancouver Stock Exchange 13
Vanguard 115
Ventro 303
Venture Economics 301
Vodafone 184
Volvo 278

Wall Street Journal 7

Xerox 19

Yahoo! 308
Yeung, B. 290

Finance Matters for the [financialmind]

For who to read, what to know and where to go to increase both personal and professional profits, visit us at www.financialminds.com

Here you can connect with the latest thinking from some of the world's leading financial experts, and sharpen your own financial mind with new ideas and solutions.

www.financialminds.com is designed for people who want to develop that edge and succeed in finance. At its core – a selection of books, ideas and services that will support you in bridging the gap between cutting edge models and down to earth practical advice, ensuring you stay ahead of the game.

Receive information on the latest financial ideas and products straight to your desktop by signing up to our monthly e-newsletter, which delivers an infusion of insight, interviews and articles designed to make you, your business and your investments more effective. To subscribe for free, simply go to

▶ www.financialminds.com/register.asp

Read about the most innovative ideas and strategies for financial success by downloading articles by some of the world's finest financial gurus. Written specifically for the financialminds service, these articles come direct from the cutting edge and will keep you up to date with the hottest principles and practices. To link through to the newest insights, log on to

▶ www.financialminds.com/goto/articles

Spreading knowledge is a great way to improve performance and enhance business relationships. If you found this book useful, then so might your colleagues or customers. If you would like to explore corporate purchases or custom editions personalised with your brand or message, then just get in touch at

▶ www.financialminds/corporate.asp

[www.financialminds.com
www.business-minds.com]